THE ROMAN MONETARY SYSTEM

The Roman monetary system was highly complex. It involved official Roman coins in both silver and bronze – which some provinces produced while others imported them from mints in Rome and elsewhere – as well as, in the east, a range of civic coinages. This is a comprehensive study of the workings of the system in the Eastern provinces from the Augustan period to the third century AD, when the Roman empire suffered a monetary and economic crisis. The Eastern provinces exemplify the full complexity of the system, but comparisons are made with evidence from the Western provinces as well as with appropriate case studies from other historical times and places. The book will be essential for all Roman historians and numismatists and of interest to a broader range of historians of economics and finance.

CONSTANTINA KATSARI is Lecturer in Ancient History at the University of Leicester and a Fellow of the Royal Numismatic Society. Her publications include numerous articles and reviews on the Roman economy, comparative slavery and ancient identities, as well as three co-edited books: *Patterns in the Economy of Roman Asia Minor* (2005; co-edited with Stephen Mitchell); *Slave Systems: Ancient and Modern* (2008; co-edited with Enrico Dal Lago); and *From Captivity to Freedom: Themes in Ancient and Modern Slavery* (2008; co-edited with Enrico Dal Lago).

THE ROMAN MONETARY SYSTEM

The Eastern Provinces from the First to the Third Century AD

CONSTANTINA KATSARI

CAMBRIDGE
UNIVERSITY PRESS

CAMBRIDGE
UNIVERSITY PRESS

Shaftesbury Road, Cambridge CB2 8EA, United Kingdom

One Liberty Plaza, 20th Floor, New York, NY 10006, USA

477 Williamstown Road, Port Melbourne, VIC 3207, Australia

314–321, 3rd Floor, Plot 3, Splendor Forum, Jasola District Centre, New Delhi – 110025, India

103 Penang Road, #05–06/07, Visioncrest Commercial, Singapore 238467

Cambridge University Press is part of Cambridge University Press & Assessment, a department of the University of Cambridge.

We share the University's mission to contribute to society through the pursuit of education, learning and research at the highest international levels of excellence.

www.cambridge.org
Information on this title: www.cambridge.org/9780521769464

First published 2011
First paperback edition 2015

A catalogue record for this publication is available from the British Library

Library of Congress Cataloging-in-Publication data
Katsari, Constantina.
The Roman monetary system : the Eastern provinces from the first to the third century AD / Constantina Katsari.
p. cm.
Includes bibliographical references and index.
ISBN 978-0-521-76946-4
1. Money – Rome – History. I. Title.
HG237.K38 2011
332.4′9394 – dc22 2010043682

ISBN 978-0-521-76946-4 Hardback
ISBN 978-1-107-52656-3 Paperback

Contents

List of charts

Acknowledgements

Over the years I have had inspiration and help from many people within and outside academic circles. Some of them I still remember vividly while others faded with the passing of time. Among the ones that I would like to thank are the following. First and foremost, Kostas Buraselis who has remained a constant influence in my life as teacher, mentor, friend and guide. He is responsible for introducing me to the realm of history and supporting me in all endeavours for the past twenty years. From early on he instilled in me the passion we now share for the ancient world and he guided me unfailingly through the intricacies of the modern academic world. This book would never have been started, if I had never met him. Stephen Mitchell is the other force that supported me, since I first met him in 1999. When I was desperate that my career had finished before it even started, he was there to encourage me and to undertake the difficult role of a postdoc supervisor. In this capacity he read my PhD manuscript, commented on it and taught me everything I needed to know on the economy of Roman Asia Minor. My PhD supervisor, Michael Crawford, should also be mentioned as the person who has been patient enough to undertake the task of teaching me the working of the ancient economy. Even though our views differ substantially, I cannot deny that I was intrigued by the depth of his knowledge and the sharpness of his intellect. Andrew Burnett, my second supervisor, has also been exceedingly helpful in the completion of this book. I owe him many helpful comments on several drafts of the PhD manuscript and the facilitation of the use of the library and collections of the British Museum. Indirectly, he trained me in numismatics and he gave me an insight on the complicated methodology I was expected to follow. However, I owe the roots of my numismatic knowledge to Aikaterini Liampi. I attended her seminars in the National Foundation of Research in Athens for the best part of three years, while I was still an undergraduate student. During this time I was prepared for the difficult task that lay ahead. Ian Carradice and Richard Alston were the readers of my thesis. Their comments helped me to draw a new strategy and turn towards a different direction. While I was completing my postdoc in Exeter I relied heavily on the advice of seasoned historians, such as Richard Seaford and David Braund. Both of them commented on my work and taught me how to combine the results of different disciplines. I also profited greatly from the academic environment of Leicester University. My colleagues at the School of Archaeology and Ancient History have supported me over the past five years not only with their helpful comments but also with their infinite patience and indulgence. Among them I would like to especially thank Neil Christie, Graham Shipley, David Mattingly, Colin Haselgrove and Lin Foxhall. Apart from the anonymous readers from Cambridge University Press who read the initial manuscript, I must pay my dues to Kevin Butcher. He read the book in detail and commented on the ideas and the source material. I relied heavily on his advice, although I have not always followed it, for which I hope he will forgive me. Other researchers whose work has influenced me over the years are Walter Scheidel, William Harris, Jean Andreau, David Hollander, Wim Jongman, Peter Temin, Kuroda Akinobu and Peter Ban. The debate has been intense and the disagreements many. Therefore, the results I hope will be equally interesting.

Since I started my PhD thesis I have received several grants from a number of research organisations in different countries. I would like to thank the Greek State Foundation of Scholarships for providing adequate funding for three and a half years that enabled me to finish my thesis. Later, the Foundation of the Hellenic World at Athens provided the funds to complete my first two-year postdoc in Exeter on the economy of Roman Asia Minor. In addition, the Humboldt Fellowship for Experienced Researchers allowed me to work in the DAI in Berlin and Athens for a year and a half. At the same time, I used a six-month Research Leave from the University of Leicester. Lesser grants were the Centenary Bursary for Research from the British School at Athens, the Martin Price Fund from the Royal Numismatic Society and a grant from the UK Numismatic Trust.

List of abbreviations

CIG	*Corpus Inscriptionum Graecarum*
CIL	*Corpus Inscriptionum Latinarum*
CPR	*Corpus Papyrorum Raineri*
IG	*Inscriptiones Graecae*
IGRR	*Inscriptiones Graecae ad Res Romanas pertinentes*
ILS	*Inscriptiones Latinae Selectae*
MAMA	*Monumenta Asiae Minoris Antiqua*
OGIS	*Orientis Graecis Inscriptiones Selectae*
SEG	*Supplementum Epigraphicum Graecum*
Syll.	*Sylloge Inscriptionum Graecarum*
TAM	*Tituli Asiae Minoris*

Framing the Roman monetary system: An introduction

The main goal of this book is to properly frame and analyse the operation of the Roman monetary system from the first to the third century AD in the eastern provinces. The comprehensive study of a system such as the Roman may also give us the opportunity, in the future, to compare it with the medieval and the early modern ones, since they all share a range of similar characteristics. Here I may restrict myself to the use of comparative points with selected case studies (from Europe, North America and China) but I am convinced that fully comparative studies could and should emerge. I also hope that such a volume will enhance our understanding of the nature of ancient money and that, at the same time, it will prove that the Roman monetary economy was based on a sophisticated pre-industrial, pre-capitalist, pre-modern system. By this, I mean a monetary system that regulated the economic agents, controlled the money supply and identified the specific medium of transactions. Behind this system, at least in the case of the Roman empire, hid the central government, which guaranteed the value of money and the exchange of currencies, while it determined its monetary policies according to the needs of the treasury and the demands of the markets.

This study will be restricted to the geographical area of the eastern Mediterranean provinces. These provinces represent a mosaic of different coinages, all of which were unified under Roman political rule. The regions of the southern Balkans, Asia Minor, Palestine and Syria[1] are characterised by the production of local civic coinages, which complemented the 'official' currency. On the other hand, the areas of the northern Balkans (esp. Dacia and Pannonia) resemble the western provinces, since they had not established their own mints but relied exclusively on the distribution

[1] In the text the provinces of Palestine and Syria will be called wider Syria. This term will describe all the area south of Cilicia that includes the regions of (a) Palestine (southern Syria) and (b) Phoenicia, Coele Syria, Commagene and Cyrrhestica (northern Syria).

of coins from the mint at Rome. Despite the self-imposed geographical restriction to the eastern regions, there are regular references to evidence from the western provinces and the closed currency system of Egypt. This way, we may be able to acquire a more rounded understanding of the Roman monetary system across the Roman empire. In addition, although the role of the Mediterranean in the movement of commodities and money is uncontested,[2] I decided to include regions (e.g. Dacia or Dura Europos) that are more distant and without a close connection to the sea. This inclusion paints a more accurate picture of the manifold economic natures of the frontier zones at the fringes of the empire, while it may highlight the impact or not of land routes on the movement of populations and the use of coined money. Furthermore, since large numbers of troops were stationed in these zones, the results from the study of coin distribution could be contrasted with the results from other, non-militarised but highly urbanised areas of the eastern provinces.

Chronologically speaking, this volume refers to the Augustan monetary system from its establishment in the late first century BC until its collapse in the 260s. Although there are references to the entire period in question, the core numismatic material that is statistically analysed here ranges from the end of the first century AD (the reign of Trajan) until the end of the reign of Gallienus in AD 268. This material allowed for the contrast between a stable economic era – the Antonine – and an era characterised by reforms and general instability – the Severan and Military Anarchy periods. It is well known that periods of crisis can highlight the operation of the political, economic, social and other systems. The Roman empire during the third century AD went through a political, military and, eventually, numismatic crisis that revealed the weaknesses of the governance system and led to widespread reforms in the socioeconomic structures. Most scholars agree that plagues and wars caused a demographic decline, the increase of military expenses, stronger state intervention in the provinces, changes in the labour system and possible economic decline.[3] From an environmental point of view, Haas[4] recently emphasised a crisis in climate, combined with a decline in population, soil exhaustion and forest clearances that may have caused the crisis of the third century.

Several scholars, though, have contested the use of the term crisis in describing the otherwise well-known economic decline. For example,

[2] Selectively, see Horden and Purcell 2000.

[3] Selectively, see Alföldy 1989; Potter 1990; Herrmann 1990. For limitations on the archaeological evidence see Millet 1981; De Blois 2002.

[4] Haas 2006.

Strobel shows explicit preference for the terms 'change and transition'.[5] Similarly, Witschel suggests that existing evidence does not prove the occurrence of a *Weltkrise* (world crisis) but, instead, indicates a slow transformation from the second to the fourth centuries, which is characterised by the further enrichment of the elite.[6] Despite the value of these opposing viewpoints, I find myself siding with the recently expressed views of Duncan-Jones[7] and Giardina,[8] who acknowledge the existence of an economic crisis but refuse to believe that it had cataclysmic consequences or that it caused the collapse of the economic system. Instead, they think that the crisis became a powerful force, which led to the transformation of the Roman empire. In this volume, though, I will not engage further in the debate but will restrict myself to the discussion of the numismatic decline during the third century, in an attempt to find concrete evidence with regard to the function of the monetary system throughout the Principate.

In order to achieve my goal, I will further refrain from getting entangled in the primitivist–modernist debate, which in our case may prove to be counterproductive. So far, scholars tend to have opposing views on the nature of ancient money and the workings of the monetary systems in antiquity. I understand that any attempt on my part to describe these opposing views in the short space of an introduction bears the danger of oversimplification. It is necessary, though, to briefly mention the main protagonists of the debate and to evaluate their contribution. First of all, Bolin's work on *State and Currency in the Roman Empire* was the first to analyse seriously the role of the Roman monetary system in connection to the state.[9] His elaborate statistical analysis and theoretical mathematics effectively undermined the value of his writings and placed him in the disreputable modernist group. In all fairness, although his study revolutionised traditional numismatics, he seemed overzealous in trying to apply modern economics to the ancient material without taking seriously into consideration the constraints of pre-industrial economies.

The rise of the star of Polanyi[10] and the continuation of his school of thought by Finley[11] in the 1970s, who studied extensively the ancient economy, gave the final blow to the modernist school and drove almost all monetary historians into substantivism. Most prominent among them, Michael Crawford denied the existence of economically motivated monetary policies, while he claimed that the monetary system underwent no sudden changes during the reign of Augustus.[12] This is because, as he

[5] Strobel 1993. [6] Witschel 1999. [7] Duncan-Jones 2004.
[8] Giardina 2008. [9] Bolin 1958. [10] Polanyi 1968.
[11] Finley 1973. [12] M. Crawford 1970: 46. These views were repeated in his later works.

stated, 'coinage was probably invented in order that a large number of state payments might be made in a convenient form and there is no reason to suppose that it was ever issued by Rome for any other purpose than to enable the state to make payments, that is, for financial reasons'. With the same point in mind Duncan-Jones elaborated on Crawford's perspective and declared that 'the empire of the Principate was not fully monetised', while 'government policy ignored economic rationalism'.[13] This attitude, though, restricted the study of the Roman monetary economy to its state dimension, disregarding almost completely the power of the markets. The acknowledgement of such a deficiency led a number of researchers, among them Rathbone[14] and Howgego,[15] to position themselves between modernism and substantivism, thus avoiding the ensuing polarisation. In this volume, I hope to avoid the trap of the debate altogether, so that I can focus on the continuity and change in the Roman monetary system. Nevertheless, I cannot deny that its direct or indirect comparison with other pre-industrial systems may be considered suspicious by the researchers who insist on placing everyone in one or the other school.

In my attempt to explain the nature of money in the Roman world, I will employ certain theoretical tools, whose careful application to ancient economics highlights different angles of our object. In the first instance, I will analyse the bimetallic laws that defined the Roman system and I will demonstrate how these were applied in practice, even if the Romans did not develop any economic theories with regard to this issue. Bimetallic systems were in force from the Roman period until the nineteenth century, when economic and political analysts abandoned them in favour of the 'modern' monometallic systems.[16] The long duration of bimetallism gives the opportunity to study the subject in comparative perspective and, thus, allows us to form a clear idea of its function in antiquity. The manipulation of the bimetallic laws was profitable for the states during medieval times and the early modern period and up until the end of the nineteenth century. The depreciation of the silver currencies brought quick profits to the minting authorities, which needed additional revenues for the maintenance of the governmental military and bureaucratic mechanisms. However, the unrestricted manipulation of the bimetallic system may have brought about the devaluation of gold coins and their subsequent demonetisation, export outside the area where they were legal tender and/or melting, in accordance with Gresham's Law.[17]

[13] Duncan-Jones 1994: 3–4. [14] Rathbone 1991. [15] Howgego 1992.
[16] Bordo 1992; Redish 2000. [17] Laughlin 1897; Flynn 1982.

In addition, I will explore the practical implementation of the Quantity Theory of Money (its elements being inflation, monetisation, velocity of money, mint production) and, this way, I will show how Roman imperial policies were actually subject to the laws that also define modern economies in the Western world. The employment of the Quantity Theory of Money could help economists of the ancient world identify changes in prices or in the monetisation of a region. According to this model the amount of money inserted in the economy multiplied by the velocity of money is equal to the price level of goods and services multiplied by the transactions of goods and services offered: $M^*V = P^*T$. A rise in the money supply will be met by an exactly proportionate increase in prices, while the velocity of circulation (V) and the quantity of the transactions in goods and services (T) remain largely stable. The effects of changes in this equation will not be felt in the short run on the economy; instead, inflation will rise only in the long run (for modern economies the time was estimated at three to ten years later).[18]

Last but not least, I intend to demonstrate that the theories of chartalism or metallism are most appropriate for the description of the non-modern monetary economies: metallism referring to the use of coins, which are accepted in the markets at their real value, while chartalism refers to coins as tokens of value. Even if we accept that metallism could describe the early monetary economies of the archaic and possibly also the classical period, by the Augustan period the inhabitants of the empire may have used intrinsically inferior coins for their transactions. Even so, the value of money may not have been entirely independent from its medium, as the metal could either have been sold as a commodity or exchanged as coins. If the metal content predetermined up to a point the value of money in circulation, then we should exclude the possibility of the application of pure chartalist theories in ancient monetary economies. Therefore, it would be more accurate if we developed a new theory that bears some (but not all) of the characteristics of both chartalism and metallism.

In the first chapter I intend to clarify the numismatic methods I followed in analysing statistically the coin finds. Since statistical analysis has been employed in the study of ancient coins, a range of scholars positioned themselves either for or against it. My first step will be to evaluate the use of large numbers of finds (coin hoards, stray coins and coins found in the course of excavations) as evidence in the writing of economic history. The next step will be to stress the problems that the study of the different

[18] Fisher 1926; Friedman 1956; Friedman 1969.

categories entails and how it affects economic discourse. It cannot be doubted that the antiquity of the material, the lack of written evidence from the Roman world and modern prejudices in the collection of coins could affect our results. Despite pessimistic approaches regarding the value of the use of statistics in numismatics, some of the results reflect more or less accurately the prevailing conditions in the Roman empire and give us insights into the inflation, monetisation, integration and general use of money.

The scope of the second chapter is to determine the role of the state in the production and circulation of precious-metal coinages across the empire. None could deny that the Roman government was interested in the direct control and the centralisation of the mints, which produced silver and gold coins either in Rome or in the provincial cities. Whether the coins were based on the official denarial standard or on other Hellenistic standards, they were exchanged at a fixed rate that was set by the central administration. The reasons for such strict control over the numismatic issues were predominantly financial. The need to balance the budget and to make certain that the revenues would have covered the expenses commanded the intervention of the state and its dominance over the production of precious-metal currencies. As will be shown in this chapter, the emperor's need for stable revenues to pay for the army, his building projects, handouts to the populace and gifts to his friends prompted him to impose annual taxes paid in cash and to mint his own coins. At the same time, the significance of the military expenses will be assessed by comparing them to other imperial expenses and by estimating the impact of the increasing salaries of soldiers on the monetary economy during the first half of the third century AD. In addition, the state monopoly over the production of currencies, which remained an unchanged imperial policy throughout the centuries, could give us an idea of the flow of taxes and the rate at which coins were recalled to the mint. Even if this process does not provide accurate numbers, the rates could be compared with other pre-industrial societies and give us an idea of the overall level of the taxes.

The third chapter is dedicated to the implementation of the bimetallic system in the Roman Principate – a system that remained in use for centuries after the fall of the empire. The lack of gold coins from the excavation records during the third century AD prompted me to reconsider the monetisation of the economy, the valuation of precious metal coins, the intervention of the state in the production and circulation of currencies and the impact of individual decisions on the future of specific denominations. The numismatic reforms that took place during the economic crisis of the third century also hinted at the multiple functions of the monetary system within the wider economy. On the whole, it will be shown that bimetallic laws determined the function of money in the Roman world. When these laws were not broken, then the state prospered and the transactions of the citizens were facilitated. Yet, if the laws were stretched to their limits, then the currency system came closer to the brink of collapse and the economy was in danger of becoming demonetised.

In the fourth chapter I employ the Quantity Theory of Money in order to explain changes in the level of inflation and monetisation (the extent of the use of money) of the Roman economy. The main indicator for such changes were the abrupt increases (or decreases) in coin production, as the statistical analysis of coins coming from hoards, excavations or museum collections indicates. Additionally, epigraphic material from Asia Minor attests to the level of monetisation in the eastern provinces and how this changed gradually until the end of the third century, when the weight standards became irrevocably altered. Once more, numismatic reforms and the general state of the economy during the third century seem to have been the main forces behind structural changes in the monetary system, which eventually collapsed by the end of the reign of Gallienus. Despite its collapse, though, monetised transactions probably continued to occur in the eastern markets, albeit not with the same density as in previous decades.

In the next chapter, the study of the monetary integration of the empire by comparison to similar pre-modern monetary unions (through the study of differences in the processes of local, interregional or long-distance trade) expands our understanding of the development of ancient monetary economies and the power of the markets. Despite the variations in weight standards, Rome managed to keep all of its silver currencies under a 'denarial umbrella', since traditional Hellenistic coinages were connected to the denarius at a fixed exchange rate. In true imperialistic fashion, they allowed some administrative freedom to the local authorities, while they supervised the effective operation of the entire system. The *pax Romana*, the monetary edicts and the regulation of mint production created the right commercial environment for the development of a monetary system that lasted for centuries. In the process of this creation, there is a possibility that the monetary economy became more integrated, even if trade tended to generate more restricted numismatic circulation pools. Main forces behind this integration were the upper and middle social strata of the Roman Principate, who traded their commodities under the auspices of the central government. Comparative points with other integrated economies, e.g.

the *Zollverein* and China, could highlight similarities and differences in integrating processes and their effect.

In chapter 6 I study the production, circulation and use of small change especially in the Roman provinces of Greece, Asia Minor and Syria. Deeply rooted Hellenistic traditions seemed to have substantial impact on the decisions of Rome, regarding the continuation of civic mints and the legal circulation of their bronze currencies. Once the city undertook the minting of its own small change, its authorities also were expected to react to any local demands for more coins (army movements, debasements etc.), even without central approval; this way, the markets remained functional. Of course, in some cases we notice attempts to regulate the situation at a provincial or at a state level but these did not change the overall diverse picture. Despite the colourful mosaic of civic currencies, which may have caused some uncertainties about their exact value, daily transactions were greatly facilitated. In fact, monetisation remained quite high in this pre-industrial society, even if we cannot assess the exact level. This level could become less ambiguous if we attempt to compare it to the monetisation of the classical and Hellenistic transactions or the markets of the Roman Republic.

In the last chapter the nature of ancient money is explored in more detail. By using the theories of metallism and chartalism I try to assess the impact of the civic authorities and the extent of the intervention of the Roman state in the control of the monetary supply. Consequently, I emphasise the effect of private enterprises (trade, banking or other) on both the production and the distribution of money in the provinces. Economic mechanisms, based either on the direct intervention of the Roman state or the secondary impact of the markets, guaranteed the effective operation of the monetary economy. So, when one of the determinants changed, for whatever reason, the monetary system was endangered and/or reformed. The example of the Roman Principate from Augustus until the end of the third century indicates that aspects of both metallist and chartalist theories may be applicable and that this unique system was strong enough to remain unaltered for centuries.

CHAPTER I

Statistics and numismatics

Over the last few decades a lot of ink has been spent in order to decide what is the most efficient way to study ancient coins. In particular, several articles were dedicated to answering the following question: should we or should we not use statistics in the analysis of ancient material? Since statistical analysis is fundamental in economics, a response to this problem may change basic perceptions with regard to the study of the discipline. However, scholarly views range from the nihilistic approach that denies all value to statistics to the opposite side that promotes the use of advanced mathematical formulas. Such polarisation seems to be counterproductive and it inhibits rather than facilitates the reconstruction of the ancient economy. Instead, a combination of the opposing positions may give us some tangible results and at the same time further our knowledge on the subject. In my study I employ simple statistical practices, which could assist in the economic analysis of Roman coins, while I still believe strongly in the qualification of the available data. In this chapter I intend to reveal in more detail the methodology I followed throughout the entire book: a methodology based on the experience of several numismatists who have studied coins since the beginning of the twentieth century. In addition, I will attempt to explain the problems arising from the study of the ancient monetary economies as well as the possible solutions. I am aware that these solutions are nothing more than simple recommendations, which cannot be applied in all circumstances but should be taken into consideration at all times. To start with, we should categorise our numismatic finds according to the conditions under which they have been found, the circumstances of their loss in antiquity and the reasons for their loss. In order to achieve this goal, numismatic finds should be divided into three main groups: (a) coin hoards, (b) site finds and (c) stray finds.

COIN HOARDS

On the night of 12 June 1667, Samuel Pepys decided to conceal his money. His main concern was to protect his wealth from the Dutch fleet that made its way into the Thames estuary. The next morning he sent his father and his wife off by coach with 1,300 pounds in gold. According to his explicit instructions, they had to conceal the treasure at his country estate in Huntingdonshire. Pepys later sent another 1,000 gold pieces through a special messenger. The money remained concealed for four months, when he became able to recover them. Meanwhile, he wrote in his diary that his wife gave him

> so bad an account of her and my father's method in the burying of our gold, that made me mad; and she herself is not pleased with it, she believing that my sister knows of it. My father and she did it on Sunday, when they were gone to church, in open daylight, in the midst of the garden, where for aught they know, many eys might see them; which put me into trouble, and I presently cast about, how to have it back again to secure it here, the times being a little better now.

In order to safeguard his wealth, he dug at night until he recovered two bags filled with gold. In the meantime, though, the bags had rotted away and the coins were scattered. Pepys eventually recovered most of his gold, with a loss of only twenty pounds.[1] This example is indicative of the nature of hoards and the circumstances of their concealment.

It is essential, though, to distinguish between hoards that came together for economic purposes and 'ritual' deposits that have been used as part of religious ceremonies. Coins as votive offerings can be found in springs, close to the statue of a god or in graves. In the first two instances, the process may have taken several years until the hoard was completed, while in the last case the hoard is formed at the moment of the burial. Strictly speaking, these are hoards, but we should bear in mind that the coins have been immobilised without the intention to recover them. Money offered to gods or to a dead person is not used in the markets, unless the god's devotees bring these coins back into circulation, if the circumstances demand it.[2] Since in most cases they did not function in an economic way, they should form a separate category and, thus, will not be studied here. Nevertheless, burial hoards, which were formed in a specific point in time, will be used sparingly for comparative purposes, if their structure resembles the structure of other hoards from the same area and period.

[1] The story can be found in Kent 1974: 188; Grierson 1975: 124. [2] Guest 1994: 27–8.

For practical purposes the minimum size of a coin hoard consists of only two coins as long as they have been brought together deliberately. The size of hoards varied widely from a handful of coins to hundreds of thousands of pieces, according to the socioeconomic status of the owner. The majority of hoards including gold denominations were of small size in inverse proportion to their value. Silver and copper hoards could either consist only of a couple of coins or, occasionally, they amounted to tens of thousands of coins. Depending on the number of coins and the value of the hoard, we may be able to establish the financial profile of its owner. For this profile, the metal and the denominations of the coins are equally important characteristics.[3] In general, wealthy people owned pieces of higher value,[4] while poorer inhabitants probably acquired lower value denominations. Bronze was commonly hoarded, while silver was rarer and gold is to be found in even lesser quantities. Since the value of a hoard corresponded to the social status of its owner, we should not ignore the study of bronze coins, which normally represent the use of money from lower social strata.

Hoards do not exclusively consist of one denomination or one metal only. Within the same hoard we may encounter two denominations that followed different weight standards, such as tetradrachms and denarii.[5] Such hoards could give us valuable information on the circulation of coins and probably the ability of the exchange system to unify the monetary economy.[6] Also, the existence of gold, copper and silver denominations in the same hoard reveal an exceptional pattern of a highly monetised economy. Examples of this are the coin hoards from the excavations of Pompeii, which represent the money the inhabitants of the city carried for their daily transactions on 24 August AD 79, when Vesuvius erupted.[7]

The life of individual coins and denominations during different periods is equally important. According to an inscription from the city of Palmyra old gold denarii were still in AD 193 a favourite coin.[8] In one case legionary denarii of Mark Anthony were still circulating in the early third century, almost two and a half centuries after they entered the circulation pool.[9] Similarly, copper coinage could circulate within hoards for as long as one century.[10] If we estimate the life of the individual coins within the hoards from a specific geographical zone, we may find intriguing results about

[3] See chapter 5. [4] M. Crawford 1983: 202. [5] Burnett 1987: 86. [6] See chapter 5.

[7] Duncan-Jones 1994: 69–70. Of course, this is a particular type of hoard, purses. Consequently, their characteristics are different from the savings hoards, which we encounter more often in the archaeological record.

[8] *IGRR* 3.1050, ‘παλαιά χρυσά δηνάρια’ (old gold denarii).

[9] Duncan-Jones 1994: 205. [10] Foss 1979.

the turnaround of taxes. It is a well-known fact that the most usual way to recall the coins to the central mint was through the process of taxation. The disappearance of certain coins from hoards indicates how long this process took and how often the entire coin output was replenished.[11] However, in some cases the life of a coin is also determined by its type. Some of these types became 'favourites' in certain areas, and continued to circulate for centuries. When these popular coins were worn down, copies were struck so that they would replace the originals. For example, coins bearing the portrait of Augustus were issued during the reign of Trajan. This situation could cause problems to researchers who study the economy, even if the number of such issues is limited.[12] On the other hand, the lifetime of the coin within a hoard as well as its corrosion depends also on its denomination. R. Duncan-Jones estimated the differences of weight loss between the three metals – gold, silver, bronze. His analysis suggested that low-value coins lose weight earlier than high-value coins, because the speed of circulation of small change is faster. The weight loss for the Roman period was probably for gold around 0.0226 per cent, for silver 0.0598 per cent and for bronze 0.1715 per cent.[13]

Normally, hoards are dated according to the issue of the latest coin in them. In fact, this date should be treated as a *terminus post quem*, since the last coin does not necessarily indicate the exact time of burial. One fairly useful indicator is the wear of this latest issue. If it is much worn, then we can assume that the hoard was buried at a later date;[14] while, if it is in a good condition, we may guess that the coin was buried immediately after its minting. Another important characteristic is the general composition of the hoard. If the coins formed an uninterrupted chronological series ending abruptly with the latest coin, then the hoard was probably closed almost immediately after it was minted.[15] In this study, I attempted the chronological division of coin hoards, according to the date of the last coin in them. The hoards, thus, have been divided according to three periods: (a) the Antonine, from the reign of Trajan until the reign of Commodus, (b) the Severan, from the reign of Septimius Severus until the reign of Maximinus Thrax and (c) the Military Anarchy period, from the reign of Gordian III until the end of the reign of Gallienus.

The coins from a hoard, if arranged in chronological order, reveal interesting patterns and expose the hoard's internal structure. Generally, this

[11] See chapter 2. [12] A. Jones 1974: 77–8. [13] Duncan-Jones 1987: 237–56.
[14] Laing 1969: 61–2. [15] Robertson 1974: 15–16.

structure is divided into three zones: (a) the 'fall out' zone, which is represented by the oldest coins: these are considered to be relatively rare for the period to which the hoard belongs; (b) the 'homogeneous' zone, which includes the coins that have been in circulation for some time until their distribution within the coinage pool became uniform; (c) the 'erratic' zone, which includes the most recent coins, issued just before the burial of the hoard: since these coins have not been in circulation for long, their distribution is not even.[16] The classification of hoards according to the proportion of coins in each zone is divided as follows: (a) 'archaic' hoards, which include mostly older coins or (b) 'modern' hoards, which include mostly modern issues.[17] Somewhere in between lies the 'ideal' hoard, which combines archaic and modern characteristics and forms a peak right in the middle of the chart. In truth, 'ideal' hoards are theoretical constructs that, in practice, do not exist. If a number of hoards from the same area and the same chronological period are either 'archaic' or 'modern', then we may conclude that political, military or financial events may have affected their composition. A 'normal' hoard, as Reece describes it,[18] is defined only in relation to other hoards from the same area and buried roughly at the same time. If a substantial number of coin hoards reveal the same internal structure – the distribution of coins from each reign is roughly similar – then we should expect all the hoards from the same region to demonstrate the same pattern of circulation. If a hoard is not compatible, it should be considered 'abnormal' and may not indicate the existence of wider economic phenomena. Such 'abnormal' hoards may be funerary finds or collectors' hoards.

The reasons that prompted people to withdraw their money from the circulation pool and conceal it are sometimes indicative of exceptional historical phenomena. Hoards were buried for safeguarding with the intention of recovering them later. In antiquity, burial of coins in the ground took place only under special circumstances, *vel lucri causa vel metus vel custodiae*.[19] The usual places to keep money were an *arca* (chest),[20] *armarium* (cupboard),[21] *loculus* (enclosed place)[22] or *olla* (pot)[23] somewhere in the house, so that the money would be available in case of need. Excavations revealed both probable and improbable hiding places, such as the bottom of a river or the crater of an extinct volcano. Their owners placed them in hollow stones, leather bags, cloth purses or other containers or

[16] Guest 1994: 29; Lockyear 1996: 268. [17] Guest 1994: 29–30. [18] Reece 1981.
[19] *Digesta*, 41.1.31.1. Translation: either to win a court case, or out of fear, or for safety.
[20] Cic. *Att.* 1.2. [21] Cic. *Verr.* 4.27. [22] Mart. 14.12.1. [23] Cic. *Fam.* 9.18.4.

they took great care in arranging the coins in boxes. Plautus in *Aulularia* provided evidence of hoarding because of fear.[24] He talked of an old miser, who buried a pot filled with money under the hearthstone because he could not live with the idea that someone might spend it. The same idea is apparent in another play of Plautus, the *Trinummus*, where an Athenian buried his treasure before setting out for a journey.[25] Another kind of fear that may have affected hoarding was related to wars[26] and brigandage. Appian[27] describes a mass concealment of treasures in Rhodes in 42 BC, before Cassius besieged the island. A similar instance is reported by the Roman historian Dio Cassius.[28] He reported that during Trajan's reign, in AD 104, one of the barbarian kings seemed to be afraid for the fate of his treasure after the Romans won the war. So 'with the help of some captives Decebalus had diverted the course of the river, made an excavation in its bed, and into the cavity had thrown a large amount of silver and gold and other objects of great value that could stand a certain amount of moisture; then he had heaped stones over them and piled on earth, afterwards bringing the river back into its course'.

Extensive hoarding sometimes is connected to unstable monetary systems, since circulation of money in the markets is not interrupted when the economy remains balanced. For example, an unsatisfactory reform of the currency prompted people to bury money that would ordinarily have been employed in business. We notice such occurrences when old coinages have been devalued.[29] Sir Thomas Gresham was the first to describe this process with the following sentence: 'In every country where two kinds of legal money are in circulation, the bad money always drives out the good.'[30] Even if Thomas Gresham defined this phenomenon (known also as Gresham's Law in economics), the effect of the debasement of precious-metal coinage on hoarding was recognised as early as the 5th century BC. Aristophanes referred, sarcastically, to the period when gold was removed from the Acropolis and mixed with bronze in order to cover the needs of the Athenian state. Subsequently, the heavily debased coins (τοῖς πονηροῖς χαλκίοις) dominated the circulation pools, while the older coins (τό ἀρχαῖον νόμισμα) of higher fineness (οὐ κεκιβδηλευμένοις) were hoarded.[31]

[24] Plaut. *Aulularia*, 608–9. [25] Plaut. *Trin.* 149–51.
[26] M. Crawford 1969: 76. [27] App. *Historia Romana*, 4.73.
[28] Dio Cassius, 68.14.4. Translation may be found in Loeb. [29] Casey 1980: 53.
[30] Kanellopoulos 1996: 177. Others attribute this law to the Bishop of Paris, Nicolaus Oresmius.
[31] Ar. *Ran.* 718–26.

A classification of the reasons for hoarding has been attempted by P. Grierson in 1975.[32] He divided finds into four groups:

(a) Accidental losses, including coins that have been lost by accident and were found in purses or containers, consisting of uneven sums of money and, therefore, representing the currency used for daily transactions.

(b) Emergency hoards, which were the results of warfare or other life-threatening situations that impelled their future victims to hide their money for safety. Such hoards consisted of different denominations taken directly from the circulation pool during a specific event and, thus, are especially valuable for dating.

(c) Savings hoards, on the other hand, which were used to contain high-value coins, covered a considerable span of years and may have lacked the contrast between worn and unworn coins.

(d) Abandoned hoards were deposited with no intention of retrieving them, e.g. funerary coins or coins buried in the foundations of buildings or coins offered to gods.

Casey in 1986 described three different categories of hoards – emergency, savings and 'purse' hoards – omitting only the 'abandoned'. The classification of hoards in the above categories is problematic, even if they have been found within an archaeological context. Casey realised that, although hoarders tended to collect heavier coins in order to save them, sometimes 'savings' hoards were used as 'emergency' ones. Probably the only visible difference was that emergency hoards included also other precious metals or pieces of valuable jewellery. 'Purses', on the other hand, are easier to identify, because they contain a small number of coins of different denominations, representing the currency used every day for minor purchases.[33] R. Reece in 1987 questioned further the above division, and claimed that it is impossible to detect any distinctions between 'emergency' and 'purse' hoards.[34]

It is obvious that the classification of hoards according to the reasons for their concealment is so problematic that it should not be used for drawing general conclusions. Instead, we should focus on the reasons for the failure of their recovery. The most obvious cause is the death of the hoard's owner, especially in times of war. In such circumstances the normal tendency to hoard money is intensified by fear, particularly in the most exposed regions.[35] A comparatively high number of lost coin hoards have

[32] Grierson 1975: 131–6.

[33] Casey 1986: 56–7. The most characteristic examples are the hoards from Pompeii.

[34] Reece 1987: 61–2. [35] H. Mattingly 1932: 91.

been found in the frontier provinces of Dacia and Pannonia, where troops were stationed. This mass of lost hoards was explained by the existence of the thousands of soldiers in the region and the higher rate of human losses. It seems that during periods of insecurity the non-recovery of buried treasures increased, most likely because of analogous increases in the death toll. Studying the patterns of these 'military' hoards throws light on specific historical events, since the coins are securely dated.[36] It is important, though, to classify the hoards buried during peaceful periods separately from the hoards buried during warlike periods;[37] albeit, only if such a distinction is apparent. Similarly coin hoards from militarised regions should be studied in contrast to hoards from regions where no military actions took place. If we connect the loss of hoards with an increase of the death rate, we could identify changes in the population of the Roman empire.[38] An increase of hoards in a highly militarised area could demonstrate recent military actions. We should not forget, though, that even in the most peaceful provinces banditry was still endemic in antiquity. Travellers faced the danger of being robbed before their journey was completed, in which case some of the money may have been hidden in a hurry at the edge of the road.[39] Furthermore, plagues, intense famines, floods, hurricanes and catastrophic earthquakes were sometimes responsible for the death of thousands of people. In fact, population studies would benefit substantially, if researchers turned their attention to patterns of lost hoards.

It has been suggested that another reason for the non-recovery of hoards could have been the instability of the economic system or significant reforms of currency. Such situations drove individuals to hide money that ordinarily would have been used in transactions – particularly in cases when an old coinage was demonetised and its value was too small to satisfy the owner. Hoards of debased coins were sometimes abandoned, because the older coinage was not worth recovering.[40] This explanation, though, is not satisfactory. No one could deny the decline in the value of silver coins, especially during the Military Anarchy period.[41] Although, according to some researchers, low-value coins are not worth recovering, we should have in mind that the debased coins still contained a portion of silver or even base metal. Why should the owner ignore the fact that he could cover part of the lost value by selling – even half price – the debased or devalued coins to the government or to anyone who was interested in melting them and using the metal again, maybe for the production of jewellery? In some

[36] M. Crawford 1969. [37] Howgego 1992: 3. [38] See chapter 4.
[39] Patterson 1972: 215. [40] H. Mattingly 1932: 91. [41] See chapter 4.

cases he could even exchange them for cheap goods, like bread or lentils. The owners would not normally abandon their money, even if it was of the lowest value, especially if they were not affluent. Instead, we should expect that coins of higher fineness were buried, according to Gresham's Law, while the debased issues remained in circulation.

The study of hoards, in general, should be used cautiously and only by comparison to other pieces of evidence. The methods followed by modern collectors or researchers in the acquisition of hoards sometimes cause significant problems to monetary historians. It is common knowledge that most of the hoards have not been found in the course of excavations. Their accidental discovery probably was followed by their illicit sale to collectors, a procedure that does not always inspire us with confidence about the provenance of the hoard. Furthermore, the contamination of hoards with extraneous material (coins added to them in the twentieth century) or their re-discovery in a different country under conditions of dubious legality cannot be excluded. Especially those coins acquired out of context are open to suspicion because they could have been allegedly found in a place where prices are higher.[42] When I was not certain about the origin of the hoard I preferred not to include it in my thesis in order to avoid possible misinterpretations deriving from erroneous results of the statistical analysis.

Also, publications of hoards tend to list coins according to mints and rulers but they do not date them according to their year of issue. Since these numismatic finds are not dated in more detail, they do not always help us to reach specific conclusions about historical events or monetary changes. For example, specialists may identify coins from the Tetrarchic period but they fail to mention which emperor issued them, let alone the exact time of their minting.[43] This way we cannot possibly know who was responsible for specific numismatic reforms or their precise date. The study of the circulation of coinage in a vast region or the comparative study of hoards of two different areas can prove equally problematic. This happens because for some areas we have a large range of publications that allow us to draw wider conclusions, while for other regions publications are scant and distort our view of the local economy.[44] Especially the publications concerning Greece and Asia Minor are not always satisfactory and they do not give us enough information in order to conduct detailed analysis of the existing material.

[42] Grierson 1962: vi–vii. [43] Bruun 1981: 357. [44] Guest 1994: 44–5.

Selectivity presents us with another problem. As I have already mentioned, Gresham's Law describes the outcome from the preference of people for heavier and better-quality pieces, the better preserved or the ones with metallic purity. Although the difference may not have been visible to the naked eye, the official banks could verify the fineness of the coins. The lack of sophisticated chemical analysis did not seem to prevent the precise evaluation of the fineness of the gold and silver coins in antiquity. In exceptional cases, the process of selection could also be affected by other factors, such as the types on the coins. Some ancient collectors (as modern ones) would have included in hoards only rare and unique coins with certain reverse types.[45] In other cases Roman hoarders used to select them on the basis of political preference for one emperor or another.[46] Alternatively, single-denomination hoards may have been formed when the state paid its soldiers or public servants. However, these instances were rare and they do not seem to distort the overall picture.

There are further implications from the study of hoards, when we attempt to explain wider economic phenomena. Researchers used to treat hoards as economic indicators, claiming that these have been buried with the intent to be recovered later (apart from votive offerings); therefore, we are dealing with temporary immobilisation of coins put together with the intention of returning them to the currency pool. According to the law of probability, the number of hoards lost in time represents pro rata the number of hoards originally buried and subsequently recovered by their owners. Such a representative sample of coinage could correspond to the original pool of circulation, if it has been selected with caution.[47]

Even if we accept that the sample of hoards is representative of the original number of hoards lost in antiquity, I find it very difficult to understand how immobilised currencies represent the mobility of coins in the markets. Precious-metal coinages, gold and silver, as well as bronze coinages are used as a form of wealth and, thus, are regularly stored in the form of hoards. This money may have been immobilised (not used for daily transactions) for years, if not decades. Hoards are not always helpful in the analysis of the monetisation of an area, since they represent the coin populations that have been immobilised, initially, for large chronological periods and, later, forever. In addition, hoards cannot necessarily facilitate the study of the mint output. Every year or more than once a year, the state

45 Robertson 1974: 21. 46 Crawford 1983: 198; Howgego 1994: 12.
47 Crawford 1983: 201.

decided to produce a number of coins in order to cover its financial needs or its desire for political prestige. The size of the minted issues usually corresponded to the amount of bullion the state acquired from mines, from taxes or from military expeditions. However, the fluctuations in the production of these issues are not accurately represented in hoards, since peaks and troughs in the numbers of coins depend also on the internal structure of the hoard ('archaic' or 'modern') and distort the overall profile of the mint output. Despite the shortcomings of coin hoards, we should acknowledge their value in determining the extent of trading activities within a circulation pool. For example, if several coins minted in faraway areas (Syria, Greece etc.) have been found in a city in Asia Minor, this could be a good indication of the existence of long-distance trade.[48] In all cases, though, the analysis of hoards should be compared with the results arising from the study of excavation finds.

COINS FROM EXCAVATIONS

For the purposes of this monograph I have chosen to analyse statistically mostly coins coming from excavations. These represent only single finds.[49] By contrast to hoards, they represent what their possessors could best afford to lose, usually coins of smaller value. They have never been withdrawn from the circulation pool, so that their owners could recover them later, as happened with the hoards. Instead, they were accidentally lost and put out of circulation forever. The loss took place when the coin was not secured in its box or purse, from where it was taken mainly with the purpose of making a monetary transaction.[50] They were usually lost in places which by their nature made recovery difficult, such as muddy, unpaved areas, or floors with gaps between the boards.

Lost bronze (and more rarely silver) coins are recovered not only from towns where regular markets existed but also from rural sites. It has been observed that coins from the countryside have the tendency of spreading outwards instead of upwards on the same spot, or of moving from place to place within a given area when one building becomes run down and another one is needed.[51] Therefore, the concentration of lost coins ought to be low considering the limited time of habitation. Even within cities we can distinguish between zones of intense monetisation and zones where

[48] See chapter 6.

[49] I am aware, though, of the likelihood that many of the 'single finds' from some old excavations (e.g. Dura Europos) came from hoards but went unrecognised as such at the time.

[50] Anonymus, *De rebus bellicis* 1.6, '*emendi et vendendi utilitas*'.

[51] Reece 1987: 18.

only a few coins or no coins at all circulated. It is probable, for example, that we would recover more coins from the agora, from religious sites and from civilian settlements outside military installations. However, the publications of excavation finds from the eastern provinces are not as detailed as one would wish and they do not indicate the exact place of a coin's origin (e.g. market, house etc.). There are, of course, exceptions, such as the bronze coins from the excavations of Beirut, which have been studied in detail and within their context.[52] However, this is one of the few cases I am aware of and as a consequence, in this volume are included mainly coins found in urban centres, within unspecified contexts. Coins from rural sites are very few, mainly because of the lack of excavations in such areas, but they have been incorporated in this study.

The realisation that gold and silver coins are rare, while bronze coins represent the bulk of the finds, should not surprise us. Only 182 of the 16,557 coins that came from Agora excavations in Athens were of silver and 3 of gold, while the rest were bronze.[53] Although these coins were considered beautiful and valuable objects, they were thought to be of minimal archaeological significance, for most of them were found in contexts hundreds of years later than their own dates.[54] Their large numbers facilitate their statistical analysis and the detailed study of the results. With regard to the precious-metal coins from Athens, even though their number seems to be limited, they still give us the opportunity to infer patterns of circulation, which in turn could be compared with the patterns that result from the statistical analysis of other coins coming from different excavations, e.g. Ephesus, Corinth, Rhodes etc. The structure of these silver coins, in turn, indicates the existence of geographically defined circulation pools. These pools were formed as the result of merchants' operations and the expansion of interregional trade and can prove or disprove the monetary integration of the Roman empire.[55] On the other hand, the restricted circulation of bronze coins in the eastern provinces indicates regional trade movements and the impact of the cities on local economies.[56]

There are several factors affecting coin losses:

(a) The original volume of coinage may have a significant effect, given that a period of high coin output will leave more traces.
(b) The intrinsic value of the coins: People can afford to lose those of lower value, but they will not rest, if they lose a silver or gold coin, until they recover it.

[52] Butcher 2001–2. [53] A. Walker 1996: 21, n. 17. [54] Rotroff 1996: 9.
[55] See chapter 5. [56] See chapter 6.

(c) The political situation: Re-coinage has been a well-known procedure in cases of political instability. For example, when *damnatio memoriae* was imposed on Caligula after his death, only a few of his coins survived and even fewer are found in excavations.

(d) Economic phenomena such as inflation which could increase the number of coins in circulation; other phenomena (e.g. deflation) might decrease their number.

(e) The physical size of coins: The truth is that larger coins can be easily detected, if lost. On the other hand, the value of these large coins might be low, so their recovery sometimes is not of major importance to the owner.

(f) A single coin is most likely to be lost, when it is actually in circulation, moving from hand to hand.[57]

(g) One of the most important determinants may be the high or low risk of the coin itself. It seems that small change was far more vulnerable to political and social changes because of its fiduciary nature. When the trust of the people in the government waned, then these coinages may have been rendered worthless; hence they would have been lost at higher rates.[58]

Some, if not all, of these factors are indicative of the economic conditions in the Roman empire. However, in order to study these effectively, we need to be aware of the methodological problems they entail and their possible solutions.

Even if proper excavating procedures have been followed (which is unlikely in the majority of the cases), a large number of coin finds are still illegible, because of corrosion. In the excavations of the Agora of Athens two-thirds of the coins have not been identified, half of those being completely illegible and the other half dated to the time span of one century.[59] Their wear happened for two different reasons. On one hand, a coin that used to be in perfect condition prior to being dropped could have been naturally corroded after a few centuries, if it was buried in soil that was wet, humid or acid or with high salinity.[60] On the other hand, coins could be illegible because they circulated for several decades or even hundreds of years after their issue; so, their relief has disappeared through continuous use. In these cases, we assume that the legible sample of coins is a random one.

[57] Ravetz 1964: 213; Casey 1986: 69–74; Reece 1996: 341. [58] Butcher 2001–2: 31–6.
[59] Rotroff 1996: 10. [60] Casey 1986: 88.

In addition, some publications are incomplete. Coins are attributed to an emperor, while their exact issue date is not attested. For example, the coins that are attributed to the reign of Gallienus may be identified specifically to either his joint reign with Valerian or his sole reign. The same happens with the coins that present the bust of the two Faustinas and can be dated to the reign of either Antoninus Pius or Marcus Aurelius.[61] The reigns of Septimius Severus and Caracalla are also problematic since Caracalla, his brother Geta and their mother Julia Domna appear on coins from both the reign of Septimius Severus and the subsequent reign of Caracalla. In these cases I have chosen to study the reigns of Septimius Severus/Caracalla as one to avoid confusion, apart from the cases that involve hoards which were published in detail. I followed the same method for the reigns of Valerian and Gallienus. Furthermore, I attributed the few coins of Faustina I to the reign of Antoninus Pius and the coins of Faustina II to the reign of Marcus Aurelius. At least, the above disturbances do not affect the date of the closing of hoards,[62] since researchers usually give an accurate date for the last coin.

Another important problem is that a single coin can be found almost anywhere, while we will never be certain about the date the coin circulated in the site. Coins which are found at the top of a stratigraphic layer are particularly suspect, as they could belong to the layer above.[63] For example, Roman coins that have turned up beneath archaic buildings can easily be dismissed as intrusions. In addition, the coins may be a reflection of site formation processes and they may not be linked to the use of the building, where they have been found; thus, deposition and economic factors may be unconnected.[64] We also have to face the fact that a coin could have been lost a long time after its date of issue. Since in some cases the life of a coin stretches into several decades or even centuries, displaying their distribution in the format of a histogram can be misleading, because it fails to show that the coins of each defined period could be present in the currency pool of any later period. Furthermore, different denominations may have longer circulatory lives than others. One example may give us an idea of the lifetime of coins. According to modern estimations for the period 1902 to 1966 the mean lifetime of the penny was 51 years, while for the period 1911 to 1953 it was 109 years.[65] We can obtain information about the longevity of coins, if we study the coins that we found in the context of hoards that have already been dated or if we rely on the written sources. In

[61] Guest 1994: 48–9. [62] M. Crawford 1969: 78. [63] Laing 1969: 71.
[64] Butcher 2001–2: 25. [65] Cole 1976: 207–8.

other instances the coins themselves may give us some indications regarding their lifespan.[66]

The quantitative aspect of coin finds (e.g. how many coins of emperor X have been found on a site) compels us to deal with numbers and statistics.[67] As with all ancient evidence, the published volume of finds is quite low. However, the most serious problem is the exceptionally low number of coins found in excavations by comparison to the coins initially issued by the state. According to Casey we have been able to recover only 0.003 per cent of Roman coinage.[68] Even if we suppose that our sample has been randomly lost, there will always be a strong possibility that our results will change, if new material is revealed. The coins at a numismatist's disposal are no more than a small proportion of those that once existed in antiquity and the validity of any interpretation must depend upon the randomness of the sample. Also, since we compare more than one different coin, we should take into consideration that we recover coins buried or lost in different places, by different people, at different times and under different circumstances. Another problem is the variability of different groups of archaeological material, mainly because archaeologists use a variety of digging methods, which could cause chaos to any numerical study.[69] As for the archaeological finds, we should note that they are usually not of orderly distribution. Furthermore, we face difficulties in the comparison of coins found in sites that had dissimilar functions, such as military forts and rural sites and urban centres. Moreover, if we compare the mint output of one reign with the mint output of another we will realise that this output is proportionate to the length of the reigns. It is obvious that long reigns logically produce more coins.[70]

Despite the problems that the statistical analysis of coin finds entails, its use should not be discarded. Different procedures should be followed in respect to the chronological and regional analysis of our data in order to detect patterns of production, supply and distribution. There are, though, certain similarities in these procedures. First of all, it is important to evaluate the quality and homogeneity of our data and, accordingly, assess their significance. We should start from the cautious exclusion of uncertain or poorly recorded material, having in mind that this process may leave us without ancient material at all, because of the problems I described above. Our second step is to consider denominations and value. We should classify

[66] I would like to thank Kevin Butcher for his comments on these topics and for directing me towards his publication, Butcher 2001–2: 28.

[67] Reece 1982: 497.

[68] M. Crawford 1983: 206; Casey 1986: 84.

[69] Reece 1995: 180.

[70] Casey 1986: 89.

coin finds according to three metals – gold, silver and bronze – because they demonstrate different structures and eventually different patterns of circulation. Subsequently, the coins should be turned into percentages.

If there is an abundance of evidence, different regions should be clustered separately, since their comparative analysis usually demonstrates different circulation patterns. The statistical analysis and the comparison between excavations can help us distinguish between different circulation pools even within the same province. We need to compare evidence from more than one excavation, in view of the fact that individual sites may have issued coinage of different weight standards or the people living there may have been involved in different economic activities, consequently changing the monetary character of the site.

So far, researchers have supposed that different types of sites would produce different results and different circulation pools; so, they try to cluster these sites according to their predominant function. Casey,[71] for example, clustered civil and military sites in two different groups (in the latter he included the scanty rural evidence). Even if the composition of the currency was similar in both cases, only a few military sites were as deeply stratified as the civil ones, since camps were kept clean. The same military unit did not occupy forts for very long periods, while we can also trace variations depending on the military pay of the soldiers and officers and/or the size of units. Casey also noticed differentiations between forts and temples,[72] because the coins found in the latter could have been deposited there as votive offerings and they were not expected to be recovered.

Reece has performed another sophisticated clustering of British sites.[73] On one hand, country sites were divided into forts, temples and villas and, on the other hand, towns and settlements (which included all the sites below the rank of *civitas*) were separated into small and large, and those in the east and west of England. Towns were divided between those which followed a general pattern of coin loss ('good' towns) and those which followed an individual pattern ('bad' towns). We can distinguish 'bad' towns when we compare them with the mean figure from the 'good' (or normal) sites. The different groups showed different patterns of coin loss and changes caused by category (such as town or settlement) and/or geography (east or west). Differences between sites could suggest that also different circumstances of supply, use and loss of coins took place there. Such 'anomalies' existed between sites probably because: (a) different activities went on (e.g. at

[71] Casey 1980: 26–51. [72] Casey 1986: 82.

[73] Reece 1987: 72 and 91–4; 1991: 1–2; 1993: 863–9; 1995: 181 and 183.

forts and temples) or people of different economic status lived in different areas; therefore, they used coinage in a different way; (b) the level of monetisation differed from place to place (for example, in a villa only two or three persons may have used coins, while in the cities more people would find them useful); (c) army movements from one fort to another occurred frequently; or (d) major historical events affected only certain kinds of sites (e.g. forts).[74]

However, the clustering of sites is not always a viable solution for the treatment of the numismatic material. The archaeological finds from Greece, Asia Minor and Syria are not as abundant as in the western or north-eastern provinces. The low number of systematic excavations in the eastern empire is responsible for the few numismatic catalogues of coin finds from the area; consequently, we do not have enough material to conduct valid statistical analysis between different types of sites. Only in a handful of cases can we study the number of coin finds from military sites in comparison with the number of coin finds from other urban centres.

In order to avoid this problem, we should, instead, study the structure of coins coming from neighbouring areas and compare these areas to each other. For example, Reece studied Britain by comparison to northern France, southern France and northern Italy. Although these regions probably carried within them particular clusters of coin groups, they still demonstrated general patterns of circulation, when they were compared and contrasted.[75] For the purposes of this book, it is more effective to cluster provinces or wider regions into two categories: (a) militarised, where large numbers of troops were stationed and (2) less militarised or peaceful, where only few soldiers stayed permanently or passed through. This way, we may detect circulation pools existing within or across the different provinces of the eastern Mediterranean.

Another way of studying the distribution of coins in the empire is by dividing it in two parts, north/south or east/west.[76] However, if we followed this method, we would not have been able to detect provincial or other regional differences caused by individual geographical characteristics (mountains, rivers etc.) or administrative divisions; therefore, our results would have been too vague and even probably misleading. Instead, it is better to divide the provinces into four geographical groups: (1) Northern Balkans (Moesia, Pannonia, Dacia), (2) Greece (Achaea and Macedonia), (3) Asia Minor (all of its provinces from the Aegean Sea to Armenia) and (4) Syria. In the last area are included the provinces of Palestine (southern

[74] Reece 1993: 864–7; 1996: 344. [75] Reece 1974: 64 and 70. [76] Duncan-Jones 1994: 72–3.

Syria), Phoenicia, Coele Syria, Commagene and Cyrrhestica (northern Syria).

At this point I should explain how we are able to detect patterns of circulation across the eastern provinces. It has been demonstrated that the structure of coin finds varies between regions.[77] The first step to establish patterns of geographical distribution is the creation of a detailed catalogue of excavation finds reported in each region or province. Unfortunately, older publications do not always include data such as types and denominations. Therefore I restricted my study to the numerical analysis (with the help of histograms) of groups of coins from various areas during the Antonine, Severan and Military Anarchy periods. Ideally, the data should be arranged and presented with the help of cumulative charts. This procedure could be helpful, because we do not actually know for how long coins circulated. In order to create cumulative charts we should add up the coins belonging to each reign, so that they illustrate, period by period, the total of coins circulating every year.[78] For instance, let us assume that we excavate a site dating from the age of Septimius Severus to the age of Maximinus. Possibly 20 per cent of the coins could have been lost during the reign of Caracalla, another 35 per cent in the reign of Elagabalus, another 40 per cent by the end of the reign of Severus Alexander, and the last 5 per cent during the reign of Maximinus. In these cases we cannot reject the possibility that the coins issued by Septimius Severus could have been lost as late as Maximinus' reign; therefore, at this point we reach 100 per cent of the coins lost on site.

Despite the advantages that such a method has, in this book I decided not to use cumulative charts for the following reason. If I added them cumulatively, they would have reached their highest peak at the time of Gallienus, when my study is concluded. Both the beginning and the ending, though, are artificial. After these dates, coins from earlier periods continued to circulate in the area, even if they would not have been indicated in the charts. Furthermore, we have to take into consideration that we cannot expect the coins from the reign of Trajan to circulate until the reign of Gallienus, as the cumulative charts would indicate. In order to avoid this pitfall, I decided to use plain histograms. My next step was to locate 'peaks' and 'troughs' in the histograms, so that these periods can be examined separately, taking into consideration the historical background of the region. Excavations that produced fewer than twenty coins, though,

[77] Duncan-Jones 1994: 72–3. [78] Collis 1988; Reece 1995: 183.

have not been included here, because they can lead to serious statistical distortion.[79]

The analysis of the geographical distribution of coins is essential for the study of the supply and distribution of money in the provinces. The Roman state seems to have been the main factor in the initial distribution of precious-metal coinages in the Roman empire. The emperor, initially, issued money – especially silver and gold coins but also bronze – in order to pay his soldiers, to sustain an administrative mechanism and, in general, in order to participate actively in the monetary economy.[80] As soon as the money reached the markets, the entire population contributed to its secondary distribution and the subsequent formation of uniform, yet not integrated, circulation pools.[81] In addition, in the eastern provinces hundreds of cities added their own bronze currencies to the existing coin population, with the aim of facilitating transactions in the local markets. Scholars study the coins employed in these transactions with the hope that they will identify their patterns of use.[82] However, the attempt to classify the type of transaction is not always possible; in fact, finding the exact reason for the use of every single coin in antiquity will always be unfeasible. Coins do not indicate securely the reason for their existence in one or another region, even if they have been found in an identifiable environment, e.g. an agora. By studying the distribution of coinages, we can only guess the movements of specific populations within the Roman empire, such as the army, traders, tourists, the emperor's entourage. The more often these movements occurred, the higher were the chances of the creation of distinct circulation pools. These pools will be identified with the help of histograms, which may indicate a similar structure of coins from several excavation sites in the same region.

These patterns could help us prove or disprove the hypothesis of Roman numismatic integration. So far, Duncan-Jones has studied the circulation of individual coin types in more than one province and come to the conclusion that the monetary economy was not integrated,[83] since neither the army nor interregional trade affected extensively the circulation of coinage.[84] Other researchers have reached the opposite results, claiming that taxes and trading activities allowed the circulation of coins in distant provinces and integrated the economy.[85] Lately the prevailing view is that some types of imperial base metal coinage from the mint of Rome were largely confined to one province, while this was not the case with individual types of imperial

[79] Guest 1994: 50. [80] See chapter 2. [81] See chapters 5 and 6.
[82] D. MacDonald 1992: 15–16. [83] Duncan-Jones 1989.
[84] Duncan-Jones 1990: 172–8. [85] Hopkins 1980: 101ff.

gold or silver coins from Rome. Precious-metal coinages were distributed evenly and circulated widely.[86] It seems that a different approach to this evidence could lead to a different interpretation of the Roman monetary economy. First of all, we should set clear objectives: do we aim at proving the integration of the economy as a whole, the integration of the monetary economy or just the numismatic integration of the empire? The patterns of excavation finds from a number of provinces could demonstrate whether the Roman numismatic economy was integrated or not. Especially the distribution of silver coinage could show a variety of circulation pools within the eastern provinces of the Roman empire. The widespread use of credit could also indicate the extent of monetary integration. Nevertheless, a study of economic integration should include the analysis of patterns of trade across provinces, as well as the extent of the imperial intervention in the economy.[87]

On the other hand, the circulation of civic bronze coinage was geographically more restricted and could inform us only about the movements of people within limited areas. Private individuals, who attended local markets and festivals, could have carried bronze as well as silver coins with them. In other cases, the soldiers, as a large and mobile body of people, could have affected the circulation of bronze coins, especially near the frontiers. Unfortunately the circulation patterns of civic and regional coinages do not reveal the entire extent of long-distance movements. Their denominational value confined them mostly, but not exclusively, to the regions where they were minted.[88] In the Roman empire, bronze coinage was distributed only rarely away from the civic mint and tended to circulate within a radius of no more than 100–200 kilometres.[89] However, there are exceptions to this rule. Bronze coins have been found as far as thousands of kilometres away from their provenance, a fact that implies a long-distance movement of people and commodities. The reasons for their employment in trade in neighbouring regions, despite their different weight standards, will also be a focus of this study.[90]

The chronological analysis of numismatic material contributes further to the study of the volume of production of silver, gold and bronze coinage. So far, the analysis of mint output during the Roman period has relied almost exclusively on the study of dies,[91] since no mint records survive from the Roman world and the literary sources do not illustrate the subject. It has

[86] Howgego 1995: 107–9. [87] See chapter 5. [88] Howgego 1995: 102.
[89] T. Jones 1963: 318. [90] See chapter 6.
[91] A recent bibliography on the debate concerning die studies can be found in Savio 1997.

been suggested that, in order to calculate approximately the size of any individual issue, one could count the known dies used to produce the surviving coins and multiply this number by an estimate of the quantity of coins struck per die. Various researchers expressed different approaches concerning the calculation of the number of dies and the number of coins struck by those dies.[92] An alternative method was the extrapolation of die estimates for the majority of issues from die studies of a few selected issues. The next step was then to use the relative frequency of issues in hoards as an index of their original relative size.[93]

Buttrey, on the other hand, insisted that we should avoid all of the above methods as well as the statistical analysis of the coins, because of the poor quality of the ancient material. With his articles he initiated a strong debate concerning the value of statistics in economic history.[94] He suggested that even a tiny variation in the extrapolation of dies could have enormous effects on the output while the rate of attrition is always variable. Furthermore, since we do not know the actual life of a die, we cannot use die studies for the calculation of mint output. Therefore 'there is no way, and never will be any way, to determine the size of the Roman coin stock at any time, in any place'. De Callatay tried to move away from Buttrey's nihilistic approach.[95] Thus, he suggested that the calculation of mint output by extrapolation of hoards is possible, if we do not try to amalgamate them in one master hoard and if we exclude 'abnormal' hoards. He also believes that the estimation of the number of coins struck by one obverse die is possible, although he acknowledges the dangers arising from such a procedure. In conclusion, he dismisses radical views that declare that 'all is wrong' and, instead, he suggests that the results from the study of coins could be used as best guesses for economic evaluations.

Die linking was considered ideal for the study of the mint output, although existing publications are rarely interested in die studies. The reason researchers avoid die linking is that the process is time consuming and, thus, cannot be applied to a large number of coins. Especially for the needs of this book, die linking of more than 400,000 coins would have been unfeasible. At this point we should not consider only the validity of the statistical analysis of dies but also the usefulness of the end product. In an article I published in 2003 about the statistical analysis of stray

[92] On the methodology see Howgego 1992: 2. A general survey on the number of dies used to strike an issue has been written by Esty (1986). The closest possible reckoning of a single issue (23,333–27,250 coins per die) has been estimated by Kinns (1983: 1–22).

[93] M. Crawford 1974: section 7.

[94] Buttrey 1993: 338–9; Buttrey 1994; Buttrey and Buttrey 1997.

[95] De Callatay 1995.

coins,[96] I compared the number of stray coins from the Roman colony of Corinth with the numbers of their dies, according to individual types. Not surprisingly, it soon became obvious that there was no substantial difference between them. The reason for such similarity was the arbitrariness of coin loss in antiquity. If the sample of dies that survived until today has been randomly lost, then we should expect that also the survival of stray coins would have been random. As a result, whether we use dies or stray coins in order to estimate the fluctuations of mint output, the outcome would be almost identical. The same is true for excavation finds, which have been lost arbitrarily. For the purposes of this book I have opted not to estimate the exact size of coin populations, since the results may not be accurate. Instead, I decided to compare the variations between the outputs of different reigns, so that possible fluctuations in the volume of coinage may become apparent. The reasons for these fluctuations have been sought among the political, monetary and military events that took place during a specified period.

The best procedure seemed to be to divide coin finds chronologically by different reigns and according to specific areas of the Roman empire. The coins from every site or every group of sites should be arranged in chronological order and should be divided in clearly defined periods. We should not try to put together two or more reigns, because every emperor may have faced problems in his own distinctive way and defined his own economic policy according to the existing financial situation. Also, it would be advisable to estimate the percentages of lost coins per year, since different emperors reigned for a different length of time. Although the resulting number would normally differ from year to year, in our case it will represent, because of the lack of accurate evidence, only the average number of the coins minted during the reign. The accepted formula is:

(Number of coins per reign/ length of reign)∗(site coin total/100)= annual average coin loss.[97]

The comparative statistical analysis of hoards, excavation finds and stray coins from local museums could demonstrate fluctuations in the annual production of coinage. 'Peaks' of coins would become apparent in histograms that represent the percentages of coin finds per year of reign, assuming that coins found in the course of excavations are probably a random sample of the initial volume of production. Although we do not know when they were lost, we can guess the approximate size of the volume of coinage that the emperors put into circulation during their reigns.

[96] Katsari 2003a. [97] Casey 1986: 89.

The volume of the production of coinage varied during different years or during different reigns according to the needs of the emperor or the needs of the market. For example, the number of precious-metal coins seemed to increase when the emperor increased the payments of the soldiers or when he was getting involved in widespread military activities.[98] On the other hand, the increase of silver and gold coins in circulation could have instigated the process for the extensive minting of bronze coinage.[99] We should always have in mind that the use of precious and base metal coins was interactive and all coins together constituted the Roman monetary system for the first three centuries of the Principate. So, any changes in the volume of one currency probably would have affected the volume of the other in an attempt to cover the needs of the markets for a balanced variety of denominations. The monetary reforms during the third century as well as the changes in the volume of coinages not only were the result of the political and military situation of the era but also caused the reform of the monetary system as a whole. 'Peaks' of coinage from the eastern provinces in histograms could help us locate the dates when significant changes took place as well as their importance.[100]

Even the absence or rarity of coins is considered important in the study of monetary economics. Such a scarcity may be explained either because only a few coins were issued or because of a massive recall of the currencies. Characteristic of this is the research on Alexandrian coinage during the reign of Septimius Severus.[101] Accordingly, the scarcity of one type of coinage, e.g. gold, in the entire Roman empire during the third century (in comparison with the second century) will be studied in this monograph extensively.[102] Another way to evaluate the absence of a certain kind of coinage (e.g. mainstream bronze coinage) in one region is by comparing it with the existence of a substantial number of coins in another during the same period. The differences or similarities of the two areas could lead us to conclusions related to their wider historical, political or economic background.[103]

COINS FROM LOCAL MUSEUMS

Some of the coins kept in local museums are a mixture of hoards and coin finds from rescue excavations (or rarely systematic excavations); nonetheless, the majority of them are stray finds. These coins were probably found

[98] See chapter 2. [99] See chapter 4. [100] See chapters 3 and 4.
[101] Christiansen 1988: 285–7. [102] See chapter 3. [103] See chapter 6.

accidentally in somebody's backyard or traced with metal detectors by amateur archaeologists or were donated to local museums or even constituted part of private collections. It was originally assumed that this category complements the category of hoards, because, supposedly, the structure of both stray coins and hoards reveals similar patterns of circulation. However, the structure of coins from local museums tends to have more similarities with the structure of coins from excavations; therefore, they should be placed in a separate category.

There are several problems connected with the study of much-worn (and even illegible) stray finds. Even if a record of discovery exists, there is a possibility that it is inaccurate and unreliable. The people who found these coins, usually, were not willing to reveal the exact place or the conditions under which they discovered them, especially if their actions could be deemed illegal. Furthermore, the records favour higher denominations, such as silver and gold, while bronze coins are discarded as worthless. Another problem is that the coins have been discovered outside any ancient context; therefore, they give us little basis for any general conclusions relevant to one or another period. Furthermore, the collections from local museums pose more problems for the numismatist:

(a) Most curators, especially in Greece, are unwilling to share 'their' numismatic material with other researchers.
(b) Local museums lack even the basic facilities for the study of coinage, including adequate light.
(c) The catalogues are incomplete, since a large number of the coins remain listed only in the diaries of the archaeologists who excavated the sites. Besides, these catalogues include also hoards that sometimes are not distinguished from stray finds.[104]
(d) Local coins are not always identified by archaeologists, not necessarily because they are not qualified to recognise Roman Provincial coins but also because the coins are very corroded.
(e) The catalogues include also coins that come from private, not localised collections.
(f) Most of the excavation coins or stray finds are bronze.

Despite the difficulties, I managed to catalogue stray coins from eight local museums in Greece (Yiannena, Thessalonica, Kavala, Komotini, Volos, Corfu, Rhodes, Delphi) and four museums in Turkey (Fethiye, Afyon, Yalvac, Sinope). However, I have not managed to secure permission to

[104] Such a problem is encountered also in the case of Dura Europos, where hoards went unrecognised as such during the excavations. I owe this information to Kevin Butcher.

publish any of these results. In this book I will make several references to the material in my PhD dissertation, whenever it is necessary.

On the whole, the validity of stray coins in the study of money should not be underestimated. In more than one case I detected common patterns between the structure of coin finds that come from museums and the structure of coins coming from excavations. The similarities cannot have been created by chance. Although methodological problems still exist, we should reconsider the results from the statistical analysis of stray coin finds from local museums[105] or private collections.

105 Reece 1995: 180; Walker 1996: 23.

CHAPTER 2

Planning the financial policy of the Roman state

The production of coinages in pre-industrial societies has been studied predominantly in conjunction with the financial plans of ancient and medieval states. In the Roman empire, specifically, the emperor – the embodiment of the Roman state – was considered responsible for both the financial imperial policy and the minting of precious-metal coinages during the Principate. It soon became obvious to modern historians that the regulation of the imperial budget depended on the extent of the state payments, especially the ones destined for the Roman troops. Since these payments took the form of minted coins, the direct control of the production of currency became essential. As early as the nineteenth century one of the most pre-eminent historians, Theodor Mommsen, closely linked the fiscal policy of the Roman emperors with the production of coins. He insisted that the minting of precious-metal coinages brought large profits to the Roman treasury, while subsequently he examined in more detail the expenditures of the state and especially the military expenses and soldiers' pay.[1]

The prevalence of capitalism in the Western world and the communist economic model that was promoted after the Russian revolution seem to have altered substantially the views of modern historians with regard to the link between ancient fiscal policies and the production of coinage. Rostovtzeff certainly accepts that money was very important for the payment of salaries. Nevertheless, he approaches the subject from another perspective and goes as far as describing the Roman emperor and his *fiscus* as the greatest owners of coined money. These coins were not just spent on the maintenance of the military machine or the administration of the empire but they were also lent at interest to individuals as the emperor played the role of a state bank.[2] This way Rostovtzeff acknowledges that coins were of both fiscal and economic significance, even though the direct intervention of the emperor continues to remain central in his theory.

[1] Mommsen 1999: 221–39. [2] Rostovtzeff 1957: 182.

A few decades later, in the 1970s, primitivist economic theories, according to which the ancient economies functioned at a subsistence level, became rather popular amidst historians of the Roman world.[3] Michael Crawford was the first to claim that coinage was invented in order to facilitate state payments, that is, for financial reasons;[4] the economic function of coinage was only an accidental consequence. The Roman state designed its financial policy around the needs of the army, which seemed to be the most important element in state expenditure, since most of the revenues of the public treasury were destined to be used for the maintenance of the troops during periods of both war and peace. The payments of the Roman soldiers were made mainly in silver or gold coins that were produced in the imperial mints. Once the coins were in the hands of the soldiers they were used for the exchange of products in the regional and interregional markets and, thus, the army became responsible for the monetisation of the entire economy. This theory not only connected the fiscal imperial policy with the production of precious metal coinages but went a step further and considered the financial decisions of the emperor as the only reason for the existence of a monetary economy within a pre-industrial society. This model became even more popular in the early 1980s when Keith Hopkins, in his article on taxes and trade in the Roman empire,[5] suggested that the economic policy of the Roman emperors was, in fact, restricted to the control of the imperial budget. The state regulated the flow of taxes paid by the wealthy provinces either in money or in kind to the treasury; taxes that, in turn, were spent for the maintenance of the army that was stationed in the areas close to the *limes*.

These two researchers haunted modern monetary economic theories in the 1980s and 1990s. More or less along the same lines Chris Howgego, in an article published in 1996, affirmed that, despite a few exceptions, the primary role of coinage was a financial one, not an economic one.[6] However, in the same article he suggested that the maintenance of closed currency systems and some of the recoinages followed by debasements of silver coins in antiquity brought substantial profit to the state or the city, even if this money was not directly associated with expenditure. In addition, in rare cases coins might have been struck to facilitate private trade.

Researchers who work outside the English-speaking world approached the problem from a different perspective and eventually came to different conclusions. Initially, Elio Lo Cascio suggested as early as the end

[3] Finley 1973. [4] M. Crawford 1970. [5] Hopkins 1980. [6] Howgego 1990.

of the 1970s that the Roman authorities during the Late Republic and the Early Empire had sufficient empirical understanding of some economic notions and that they finally managed to develop a monetary policy, intended among other things to supply the markets with the adequate means of exchange.[7] In fact, according to Lo Cascio, the increase in trading activities and agricultural prosperity may have constituted one of the major objectives of the actions of the Roman state. Almost a decade later Jean Andreau tried to find the middle ground, insisting that the Crawford–Hopkins model may have been of a dubious historical value, since its historical perspective is rather limited.[8] On the other hand, he is equally hesitant to adopt the Lo Cascio model in its entirety. Andreau acknowledges, instead, that Rome needed to spend in order to introduce money into the circulation pools of the Empire. However, these coins were not issued exclusively because of fiscal, budgetary and social preoccupations but because the emperors were conscious of the fact that the Roman financial system depended on the overall cash-flow for its survival.

In this chapter I will demonstrate that the production of precious-metal coinages was affected directly by imperial financial policies, because it was closely connected with imperial expenditure. However, the army may not have been the most important item in the balance of the imperial budget, while the emperor seems to have been actively involved also in the banking system and the trading activities that took place throughout the Mediterranean. It is imperative, therefore, to explore further the significance of the production of silver coins and its effect on the Roman monetary economy beyond the restricted sector of military and administrative expenses.

THE FINANCIAL VALUE OF THE ROMAN ARMY

It is widely acknowledged that the Roman state used the silver and gold coins produced by the imperial mints in order to pay for its administrative and military mechanisms. Since the state was the main force that put precious-metal coins into circulation it would be useful to try to estimate the scale of its payments and their probable effect on the Mediterranean monetary economy. It has already been suggested that the bulk of the Roman state revenues was consumed on an annual basis by the Roman

[7] Lo Cascio 1978a; 1978b; 1981: 82–6 . [8] Andreau 1999: 100–11.

army whether the soldiers were involved in peaceful or in military activities. According to at least one scholar, especially in the Early Empire military costs as a proportion of overall state expenses were held stable at 33 per cent or less, while in cases of intense military activity they may have commanded half of the imperial budget.[9] For approximately the first two centuries AD the role of the army was restricted to the protection of the relatively peaceful borders, the policing of the provinces, the construction of roads and other public works. Even if the preservation of the *pax Romana* around the Mediterranean guaranteed the peaceful life of the inhabitants of the Roman empire, the army remained a central concern in the fiscal planning of the imperial authorities.

The army salaries differed according to the military body to which soldiers belonged (*legiones, auxilia* or *praetorii*) and the rank of the officer.[10] The *stipendium* of an infantryman, which was 225 denarii per year during the reign of Augustus,[11] increased to 300 denarii under Domitian.[12] The next increase, at the beginning of the Severan period, may have been substantial but it is not quantified in the ancient sources.[13] Other increases followed during the reigns of Caracalla and Maximinus Thrax. These increases probably quadrupled the infantryman's salary, since the reign of Septimius Severus.[14] Even though regular payments of coined money was an essential part of the transactions between the emperor and his army, the Roman state complemented the *stipendium* (salary) with the payment of several *donativa* (gifts), distributed to the soldiers in the form of cash at the time of the emperor's accession to the throne or in other instances.[15] So far, it has been impossible to estimate with any accuracy the impact of these donatives on the imperial budget, although it is almost certain that they were eagerly expected by the soldiers at regular intervals. In addition to army salaries and gifts, discharge bonuses (*praemia*) became available after the soldiers completed twenty-five years of service or more. It has been estimated that, because of the mortality rate, only 44–55 per cent of the soldiers would have still been alive by the end of their service and, thus, would have been able to receive their bonuses. If the amount of the *praemia* was fixed at 12,000 sestertii per person,[16] then the State spent more than 1,188 million sestertii a year by the reign of Caracalla.[17] Although it has been suggested that the amount of money spent on the army on an annual basis exceeded 33 per cent or 50 per cent of the

[9] MacMullen 1984. [10] Breeze 1971; Speidel 1992. [11] Tac. *Ann.* 1.17.
[12] Dio Cass. 67.3; Suet. *Dom.* 7.3. [13] Herodian 3.8.4; SHA, *Sev.* 12.2. [14] Herodian 4.4.7.
[15] Harl 1996: 222–3. [16] Dio Cass. 55.23. [17] Duncan-Jones 1994: 34–7.

budget, there is a strong probability that this number should be substantially lowered.[18]

Even though the exact number of active soldiers both in the legions and in the *auxilia* cannot always be accurately established, we may be able to determine the approximate size of the Roman army. It has been suggested that the regular troops and their officers may have reached a maximum of 500,000 men during the second and third centuries AD, although this number was probably smaller during the previous two centuries.[19] If the population of the empire amounted to 50–100 million people, the number of active soldiers surviving upon state payments and dispersed from the one side of the Mediterranean Sea to the other seems to have been rather low.[20] On the positive side, the low number of active soldiers would guarantee that the burden of taxation would not have been overwhelming for the inhabitants of the Roman empire. Depending on the period, the total basic pay of the soldiers who served in the legions, the *auxilia* and the Praetorian Guard ranged from 78,750,000 to 375 million denarii.[21]

Furthermore, it has been suggested that the government's calculations as to the military pay seem to have been made in aurei,[22] although it is possible that the soldiers usually received more easily exchangeable monetary units, such as denarii. However, we should not assume that all of the *stipendium* was actually paid in the form of money. On the contrary, substantial deductions were made, even before the coins reached the military establishment, for food, fodder and clothing.[23] For example, a papyrus from Egypt that records accounts of two legionaries indicates that each soldier received three instalments of 247½ drachms. The deductions made from each instalment for food amounted to 240 drachms for each soldier for a year, while the amount for clothing was equal to 206 and 246 drachms, respectively. These deductions were so uneven and harsh that in the third pay period of the year one soldier lost his entire instalment.[24] Similar deductions have already been noted by Speidel, who suggested that 80 drachms before AD 84 and 100 drachms thereafter were kept back for

[18] The reason for overemphasising the importance of military expenses is probably the fact that we have an abundance of evidence on the subject, while the rest of the expenses are not as precisely described in the ancient sources.

[19] MacMullen 1980.

[20] For population studies in the Roman empire see Beloch 1886; Hopkins 1966; Parkin 1992; Lo Cascio 1994; Scheidel 1996.

[21] MacMullen 1984: 575 and 580.

[22] Alston 1994.

[23] During Tiberius' reign soldiers complained of having to pay for weapons, clothing and tents. The incident is attested in Tacitus, *Ann.* 1.17.

[24] The papyrus has been published in Fink 1971: 243–49, no. 68. The results are analysed in Pollard 2000: 181–2.

food. The deductions of food, combined with similar deductions on fodder and clothes, probably represented 40 per cent of the basic *stipendium* of the foot-soldiers. In addition, occasional contributions were made towards the camp Saturnalia and the standards, while 1 per cent of the salary may have been the service charge for book-keeping. On the whole, the deductions may have amounted to three-quarters of the annual pay of the soldiers and could not be avoided.[25] However, the deductions from the *stipendia* during the first two centuries may have been reduced during the third century, when part of the expenses for food, clothing, fodder and military equipment may have been covered by the Roman state.[26] The rest of the money was paid into the soldier's account and represented his pocket money paid to him in ready cash.[27]

It is clear that the above numbers do not give us the accurate amount of money spent on the army each year, but we can still reach certain general conclusions. First of all, it seems that the imperial treasury covered the needs of only a small percentage of the population, if the number of soldiers did not exceed 500,000. In the unlikely event that half of the imperial revenues was used in order to cover the payment of the soldiers and other military expenses throughout peaceful or war periods, these expenses were not necessarily paid in the form of coins. On the contrary, deductions from the wages of the soldiers imply that only one-third or one-quarter of the payment was received in cash. The occasional donative probably did not change the monetary capacity of the soldiers (especially since part of it was paid in bullion) and the *praemia* were not available to them until the day of their discharge. And yet, we should further question not only the financial capability but also the will of the soldiers to spend in the provincial markets their pocket money. Apart from the occasional visit to the local brothel and the purchase of a few portable commodities (or even luxuries) would a soldier be interested in spending all of his remaining money?

Therefore, we should not be surprised at the results reached by Stephen Mitchell, who in 1993 had good reasons to doubt the thesis that the presence of soldiers with money to spend would be a boon to local markets. According to his views, the civilian communities of Asia Minor were responsible

[25] Speidel 1992. See also Herz 2007: 309–13. Herz, although he acknowledges that this system reduced the state's need for cash, also brings forward the idea that the cash remained with the state, probably the procurator. However, it is unlikely that the mints would have produced coins that would not have been put into circulation one way or another.

[26] Develin 1971: 687–9; van Berchem 1997. Also, specifically about the deductions for food see Pollard 2000: 182.

[27] G. Watson 1959: 376; Boren 1983: 454.

for supplying the troops with provisions, such as food, clothing, housing, armour and equipment. This *munus* was perceived as a distinct economic burden and it certainly did not always involve the exchange of products in the local markets. Mitchell concludes that 'the increased commercial opportunities, which the passage of troops offered to enterprising traders, were outweighed by the oppressive demands that were imposed on the community as a whole'.[28]

Richard Alston also declared in 1995 that the army did not play a crucial role in the monetisation or in the urbanisation of the Egyptian economy. In his book, he refutes the hypothesis that the spending of the army encouraged growth in local economies, while he equally rejects the idea that the army drained the resources of the provinces. Instead, he supports the theory that the expenditure on the army or by the army could only have had a marginal effect on the economy of the province of Egypt.[29] Hugh Elton promotes a similar idea. The author, who has studied the number of bronze coins produced in Cilician civic mints, has reviewed Ziegler's theory and eventually has come to the conclusion that there seems to be no difference in the levels of minting between cities on and off the main military routes.[30] All in all, these studies tend to support the thesis that the impact of the army on the local economies of non-militarised provinces and, consequently, on the monetisation of the markets was not as significant as has been initially assumed. On the other hand, we should not ignore the possibility that the economies of the heavily militarised provinces close to the borders may have been seriously affected by the continuous presence of soldiers.

BALANCING THE BUDGET DURING THE THIRD CENTURY AD

In order to determine whether military expenses dominated Roman imperial finances or not, the obvious chronological period that should be studied in more detail is the third century AD, when the emperors became more military-orientated. As early as the reign of Septimius Severus civil wars and military strife set the political characteristics for the whole of the third century. For eighteen years he spent most of his time and efforts fighting against the Parthians[31] and the British,[32] a policy that forced him to increase

[28] Mitchell 1993: 134. [29] Alston 1995: 112–15.
[30] Elton 2005. [31] Dio Cass. 75.1 and 9–12; ILS 417; SHA, *Sev.* 12.
[32] Dio Cass. 75.5, 76.13; Herodian 3.14; ILS 431, 436.

both the number of his troops and the soldiers' pay.[33] More than once he has been accused by ancient historians of undermining military discipline 'by teaching the men to be greedy for riches and seducing them into a life of luxury'.[34] His son, Caracalla (AD 211–17), raised once more the pay of the army and he bribed the soldiers with donativa,[35] while he fought against the Germans,[36] the Parthians[37] and the Armenians.[38] Caracalla's life was a continuous campaign and an enormous amount of money must have been spent not only on food supplies, military equipment and other expenses but also on subsidies to the Alamanni.[39] The ancient authors once more condemned the moral values of the young emperor and pointed out that the soldiers 'became so exhausted in body and so dejected in mind that they no longer cared at all about the largesses',[40] asking constantly for more on every occasion. The wars continued with the ascension of Macrinus to the throne, who tried to fix the pay of those serving in the Praetorian Guard at the amount established previously by Septimius Severus. This effort, although praised by the ancient historians, was not deemed successful[41] because the soldiers 'were angered by the reduction of their pay and by the withdrawal of the prizes and exemption from military duties which they had gained from Caracalla'.[42] As a consequence, Macrinus did not stay on the throne for more than a year and the Severan dynasty regained its imperial power. Elagabalus' (AD 218–22) financial policy is not adequately described in the sources, although there are references to unlimited spending.[43] Military expenditure probably rose during the reign of his cousin, Severus Alexander (222–35), who had to face the attacks of the Parthians[44] and the Germans.[45] Furthermore, the indication that the praetorian prefects were given senatorial rank[46] allows us to assume that the political (and probably also the economic) power of the army increased substantially.

Information on the post-Severan emperors does not allow us to reconstruct in detail their policies concerning military expenses, although they seem to have followed the same political and financial ideas as their predecessors, since they had neither the time nor the power to promote any

[33] Herodian 3.8.4; SHA, Sev. 12.2. Neither source quantifies the increase. For details on army pay rises see Alston 1994.

[34] Herodian 3.8.4–5.

[35] In 212 Caracalla, according to Herodian (4.4.7), doubled the soldiers' pay. Although Herodian refers explicitly to the praetorians, Dio (78.36.3–4) suggests that the increase was paid to all the troops.

[36] Dio Cass. 77.13; ILS 451. [37] Dio Cass. 77.12, 78.1–3; Herodian 4.10.

[38] Dio Cass. 77.21. [39] Dio Cass. 77.14. [40] Dio Cass. 90.3.4–5.

[41] Dio Cass. 90.12.7. [42] Dio Cass. 90.28.1–2.

[43] Butler 1910. [44] Herodian 6.3–6; SHA, *Alex. Sev.* 55–56.

[45] Herodian 6.8.9; SHA, *Alex. Sev.* 59. [46] SHA, *Alex. Sev.* 21.

lasting innovations. In AD 235 Maximinus (235–8), the first emperor of 'humble' origin to rise completely from the ranks,[47] doubled the pay of the troops as part of his bid for the throne.[48] He spent most of his brief reign conducting wars on the Danube successfully[49] and fighting the usurpers of his throne.[50] After his murder by the soldiers,[51] he was succeeded in 238 by Balbinus and Pupienus,[52] who were eventually also killed by their soldiers. Gordian III (238–44) was finally proclaimed emperor during the same year,[53] and immediately he set about facing the invasions of the Goths, the Carpi[54] and the Persians[55] as well as the rebellion of Sabinianus in Africa.[56] Gordian was murdered in AD 244 and was immediately replaced by Philip the Arab, another political figure who rose from the ranks.[57] Although, initially, he concluded a peaceful treaty with the Persians,[58] he could not avoid the attack of the Carpi and the Germans from the north[59] and eventually also the Goths and the Vandals.[60] The financial situation probably deteriorated further because of the internal conflicts of the emperor against Silbanacus, Pacatianus and Iotapianus. Although they did not manage to displace Philip, they certainly undermined his power with the consequence that Trajan Decius managed to ascend to the throne in AD 249.[61] His main wars were directed against the Goths,[62] who invaded the Balkans, and a civil war in Gaul.[63] After his death the new emperor, Trebonianus Gallus, fought against two fronts: (a) the Persians, who overran Mesopotamia to Antioch and took Armenia,[64] and (b) the Goths, who crossed the Danube and plundered the northern provinces. Trebonianus Gallus made a treaty with the Goths allowing them to keep Roman prisoners and granting them tribute.[65] Aemilius Aemilianus in 253 won a victory over the Goths and was acclaimed emperor while Trebonianus Gallus was alive but his reign lasted only a few months,[66] and he was eventually replaced by Valerian and Gallienus. Although this was the longest reign for the past fifty years the finances of the empire did not regain their former stability. During this period plague[67] and civil strife raged within the provinces,[68] while a large

47 Herodian 7.1. 48 Herodian 7.8.8. 49 Herodian 7.2; SHA, *Max.* 13; ILS 488–490.
50 Herodian 7.1. 51 Herodian 8.5; SHA, *Max.* 23. 52 Herodian 7.10; SHA, *Gord.* 8.
53 Herodian 8.8. 54 *Peter Pat.* fr. 8; SHA, *Gord.* 26, 34; *IGRR* 1.723–4.
55 SHA, *Gord.* 13; Zosimus 1.18. 56 SHA, *Gord.* 23; Zosimus 1.17.
57 York 1972. 58 Zosimus 1.19. 59 Zosimus 1.20; *IGRR* 4.635.
60 Zosimus 1.20; Jordanes, *Gothic History* 89–92. 61 Zosimus 1.21–2.
62 Jordanes 101–2; Zosimus 1.23. 63 Eutropius 9.4. 64 Zosimus 1.26–7; Zonaras 12.21.
65 Zosimus 1.24. 66 Zosimus 1.28–29. 67 SHA, *Gall.* 5.
68 Ingenuus in Pannonia: ILS 539; SHA, *Tyr. trig.* Postumus in Gaul, Spain and Britain: Zosimus 1.38; ILS 560f.; CIL 2.4943, 4919, 7.820. Regalianus on the Danube: SHA, *Tyr. trig.* 10; Eutropius 9.8. Macrianus and Quietus in the East: Zonaras 12.24; *P.Oxy.* 1476. Mussius Aemilianus in Egypt: SHA, *Tyr. trig.* 4.

number of enemy forces attacked the empire from the north and the east.[69] As if the external and internal challenges were not enough, the emperor Valerian himself was captured by the Persians and died in captivity: a defeat that probably was the ultimate moral blow against the Romans.[70]

The quantification of military expenses during the third century AD proved to be an impossible task, because of the irregularity of the data and their uncertain statistical value. The scanty evidence that I already presented could lead us only to the general conclusion that both the number of troops and the soldiers' salaries increased repeatedly from the reign of Septimius Severus until the middle of the third century AD. Furthermore, the cost of other military expenses (e.g. equipment) was also probably on the rise, since the military campaigns against internal and external enemies multiplied over the space of a few years. If the production of coins depended on the expenditure of the Roman state, then the sudden increase in the imperial expenses, and especially the military, should have been reflected in the annual mint output.

The statistical analysis of numismatic finds from excavations in the Balkans, Asia Minor and Syria demonstrate a comparatively small rise in the production of coinage during individual reigns from the second to the third centuries AD and their results will be presented here in detail. First of all, the excavations in Athens, Corinth, Patra and Ephesus indicate that the production and subsequent distribution of silver coinage in the eastern provinces is almost uniform during the Antonine period, while it forms an inconsequential peak during the reigns of Septimius Severus and Caracalla (Chart 1). The volume of coinage increases substantially only during the reign of Gordian III and continues rising until it reaches its highest peak during the reign of Gallienus. The increase during the early Severan period is so small that it should not necessarily be connected with the increasing military expenses. In addition, the later increases of silver coin losses during the period of Military Anarchy deserve different explanations, which will be presented in subsequent chapters.

The study of the structure of numismatic finds from the excavations of the northern, heavily militarised, Balkan provinces indicate different results (Chart 2). The analysis of the coin finds from the cities of Dacia show a substantial increase in the loss of coins belonging to the Severan

[69] Germans: ILS 538. Goths: Zosimus 1.31–5. Persians capture Dura: archaeological evidence. Franks: Aurelius Victor 33.3. Marcomanni: Epitome 33.1. Alamanni: Zosimus 1.37; Zonaras 12.24. Persians: Ammianus 23.5.3; Zonaras 12.23; Zosimus 1.39. Goths: Aurelius Victor 33.3; Eutropius 9.8; Jordanes 107–9; SHA, *Tyr. trig.* 6–7, 11–12; Dexippos, fr. 28.

[70] Zosimus 1.36; Zonaras 12.23.

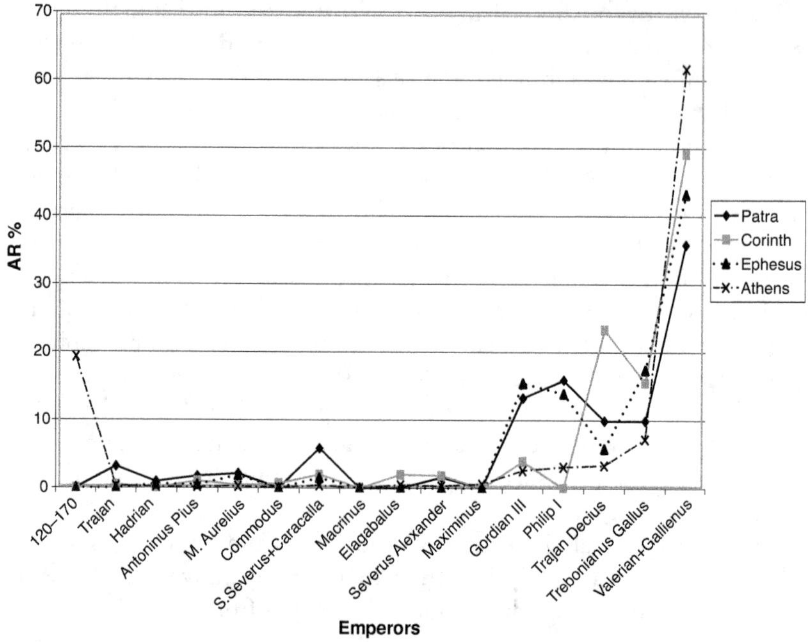

Chart 1 Excavations in Greece and Asia Minor: silver coins, % per annum

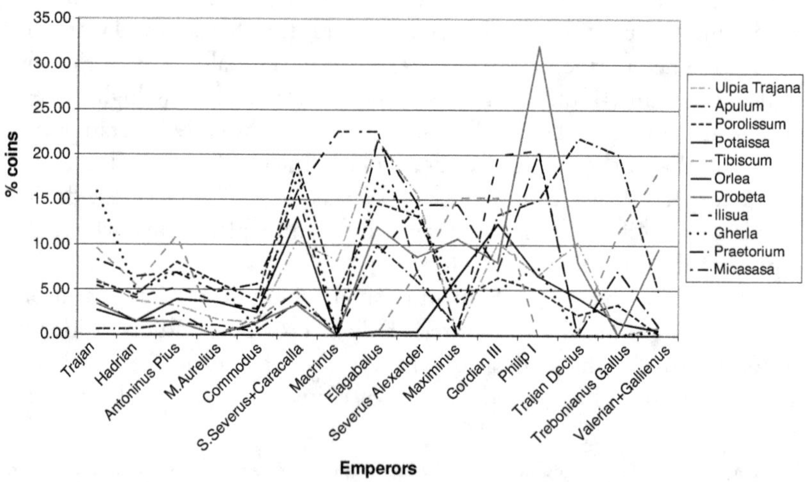

Chart 2 Excavations in Dacia: silver coins, % per annum

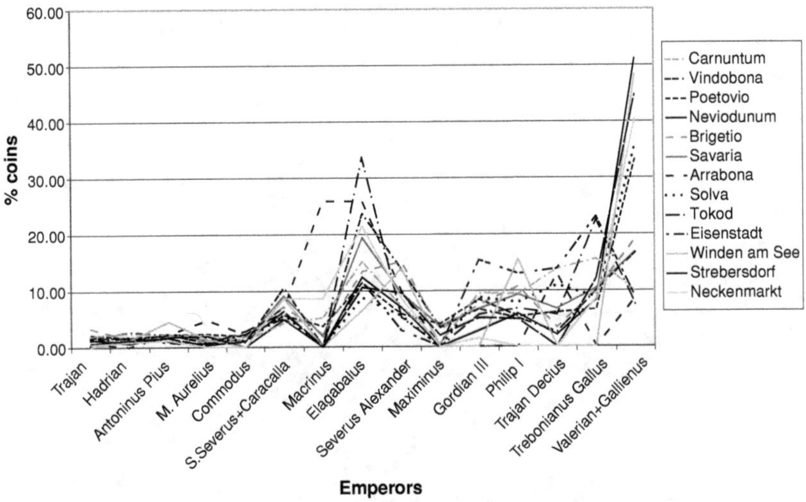

Chart 3 Excavation in Pannonia Superior: silver coins, % per annum

period and especially to the reigns of Septimius Severus and Caracalla. This trend is the same in urban centres (Ulpia Trajana Sarmizegetusa) as well as fortresses (Micasasa, Praetorium, Gherla, Ilisua) or fortress-cities (Apulum, Porolissum, Potaissa, Tibiscum, Orlea, Drobeta).

We observe a similar structure of the coin finds coming from the excavations of Pannonia Superior (Chart 3). In this case also we observe a substantial increase in the loss of coins issued during the reigns of Septimius Severus and Caracalla and, later, during the reign of Elagabalus. The abrupt drop in the number of coins issued during the reign of Macrinus may only prove the attempts of this emperor to moderate military expenses by reducing the salary of the soldiers. Once more, the structure remains the same in urban areas (Savaria), fortresses (Arrabona, Solva, Tokod), fortress-cities (Carnuntum, Vindobona, Poetovio, Neviodonum, Brigetio) and other areas (Eisenstadt, Winden am See, Strebersdorf, Neckenmarkt).

Another highly miltarised area was Pannonia Inferior, which presents us with the same numismatic patterns (Chart 4). The fortress cities of Aquincum, Gorsium and Intercisa are characterised by an increase in the loss of coins which were produced during the early Severan period and later during the reign of Elagabalus.

On the other hand, the coin finds from Moesia Inferior, a province south of the more heavily militarised areas of the Balkans,[71] show different

[71] For the low military presence in the area see Petculescu 2006.

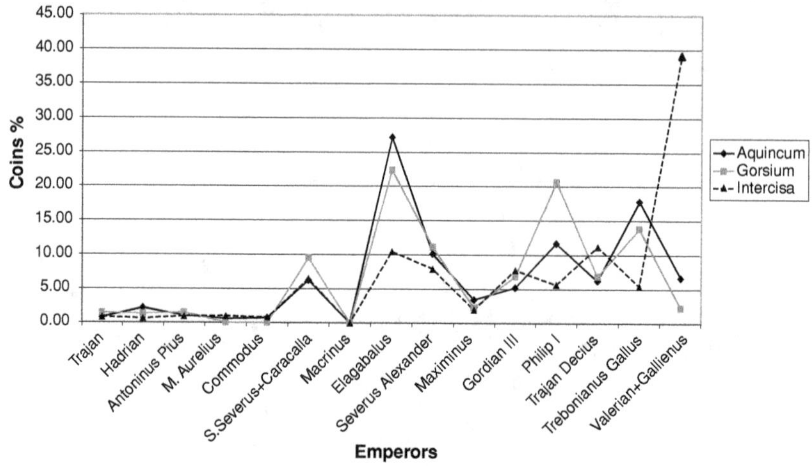

Chart 4 Excavation in Pannonia Inferior: silver coins, % per annum

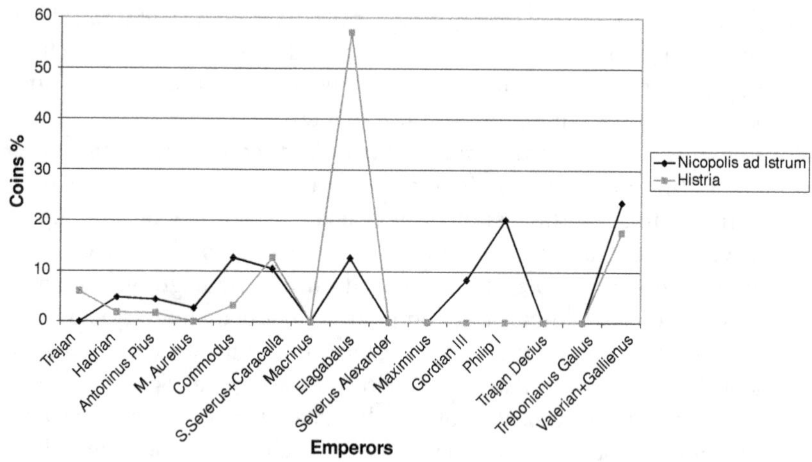

Chart 5 Excavations in Moesia Inferior: silver coins, % per annum

patterns (Chart 5). The silver coins from the city Nicopolis ad Istrum verify the same patterns we encountered in the provinces of Greece and Asia Minor, while the city of Histria resembles the provinces of Dacia and Pannonia in the sense that we observe a large increase in coins produced during the reigns of Septimius Severus, Caracalla and Elagabalus. Since Moesia was not a heavily militarised province, a fact that could explain the

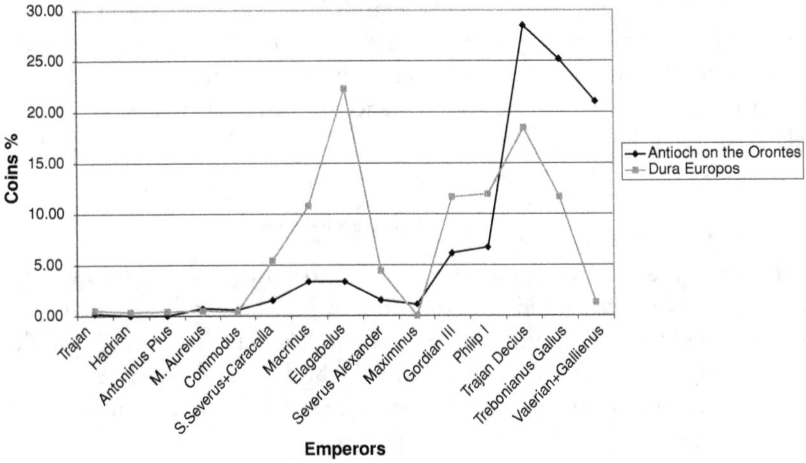

Chart 6 Excavations in Syria: silver coins, % per annum

low or no increase of coins during the early Severan period in Nicopolis ad Istrum, the case of Histria becomes an inexplicable oddity.

On the other hand, the pattern of the volume of coins from the Syrian province, where a substantial number of troops was stationed, resembles the pattern we encounter in the militarised provinces of the Balkans (Chart 6). Specifically, the city of Antioch on the Orontes and especially the fortress-city of Dura Europos indicate a steady increase in the production of silver coins from the reign of Septimius Severus onward. It has been suggested that the army forces in the eastern frontier were almost as significant as the army forces spread along the Danube.[72] The garrisons were stationed close to the existing urban centres and the soldiers took advantage of the facilities of the local markets.[73] Consequently, it is evident that the increase in their salaries during the third century AD would have made a monetary impact on the local economy.

It becomes clear from the study of the above evidence that the increase of the imperial expenditures, which were relevant to the Roman army during the third century, had a direct impact on the circulation of silver currency in the militarised provinces of the northern and eastern frontiers. The increase of the soldiers' payments and other military-related expenses are clearly demonstrated in the structure of coin finds from Dacia, Pannonia and Syria. On the other hand, the areas where only a limited number of

[72] Mitchell 1993: 119–21. [73] Pollard 2000: 38–43.

troops were stationed, such as Greece and Asia Minor, were not directly affected by the new fiscal choices of the central government. In these cases, the pattern of coin finds from the Severan period remains almost the same as it was during the Antonine period; hence the imperial expenses were not related to the military needs.

OTHER IMPERIAL EXPENSES

If the army was not necessarily the largest distributor of coins throughout the empire, then we should look for other imperial expenditures that may have affected the cash liquidity of the imperial treasury. In fact, we should acknowledge that a large part of the imperial budget was basically spent for the maintenance of the bureaucratic structure of the Roman empire both in the provinces and in Rome. We may be certain that the cost of administrative salaries was another significant expense that could have affected the monetisation as well as the circulation of coinage in the Mediterranean. The most conspicuous administrators were the citizen procurators, provincial governors, legionary commanders and lesser procurators. Their salaries, which were determined by rank, ranged from 500 to 10,000 aurei per year during the reign of Augustus, while in the mid second century the majority received 5,000 to 7,500 aurei.[74] We have evidence for a minimum number of 136 procurators by the end of Commodus' reign and 174 at the death of Septimius Severus, as well as 35 governors and 14 legates during the second century AD.[75] Although these numbers fluctuated over the years and might not be accurately illustrated in the sources, they should give us an idea of the proportions of the upper-class salaried posts. All of these posts were complemented by a sizeable infrastructure that consisted mostly of imperial freedmen and slaves, who not only received their usual salaries but also had opportunities to extract fees and bribes from the population, resulting in their buying their way into the upper ranks of provincial society.[76] Although there are inscriptions illustrating the careers of some of them, the written sources are not adequate for the calculation of their exact number throughout the empire; therefore, we are not able to reconstruct their cost to the government in detail.

The connection between planning fiscal policies and producing coins destined for the payment of the army and the administration is well attested also in other pre-industrial societies. For instance, it has been suggested that in the Byzantine empire both the production and the circulation of coinage

[74] Harl 1996: 227. [75] Duncan-Jones 1994: 37–8. [76] MacMullen 1964: 309.

was determined by the military and administrative interests of the state.[77] In fact, the *miliaresion* (a silver coin equal to one-twelfth of a solidus) may have been used as a unit of account for fiscal purposes in the eleventh century, when Alexios Comnenos promulgated his reforms of Byzantine coinage and taxation.[78] The direct link between the political economy and the production of coinage did not cease to exist after the fall of the Byzantine empire. The Ottoman government continued to intervene in fiscal and economic matters, while this intervention extended also to the planning of a monetary policy and its enforcement throughout the empire. In order to achieve its target the government issued a large number of laws to regulate mint activity, the operation of mines that produced gold and silver and the circulation of species in Ottoman lands.[79] In none of the above cases, though, are we able to estimate the exact burden that the army imposed on the imperial budget in comparison to the necessary expenses for the upholding of the administrative infrastructure.

Apart from the imperial expenditure on the annual maintenance of the army and the administration of the Roman empire there must have been other mechanisms that allowed the introduction of money to the markets. A relatively understudied topic is the quantity of money that was minted and subsequently distributed throughout the empire due to the beneficent and the entrepreneurial activities of the emperor. This money was probably not part of the imperial budget that depended on a strict balance of tax revenues and certain expenses (army, administration) in an inflexible way. The emperor was the fortunate recipient of other kinds of revenues, such as inheritances, profits from various imperial estates, gifts and other sources,[80] which, being of an unparalleled magnitude, rightly gave him the reputation of being the wealthiest man in the Roman world. In fact, Marcus Aurelius seems to have been wealthy enough to provide the funds for his military campaigns, even when the Roman treasury could not supply ready money. The event of the selling of the palace's heirlooms and his wife's ornaments[81] may indicate a temporary problem of cash liquidity that in the short term was solved through the auction of precious artefacts. In the long run the emperor, who was also responsible for the minting of coins, probably would have ensured the liquidity of money in the empire by injecting large sums of newly minted coins into the economy through benefactions, the construction of public buildings, commercial activities and loans.

[77] This idea permeates Hendy 1985. [78] Hendy 1969: 26 and 53–5.
[79] Pamuk 2000: 42. [80] Millar 1977: 139–58. [81] Dio Cass. 72 fr.

As the emperor was the charismatic leader of the Roman world and represented the ideal benefactor of his subjects, occasionally he distributed cash gifts to the people of Rome, whenever he resided there, or in the provinces, whenever he travelled. Specifically in Rome, liquidity among the lower classes benefited uniquely from imperial spending on *congiaria*, the emperor's civilian handout offered regularly during specific events (accessions, marriages or the naming of heirs) to privileged recipients who were already receiving regular payments.[82] These were given out every ten, five or three years or even more often, while the amount of money that was distributed, usually a few silver coins per person, increased gradually over the centuries.[83] There has been already an attempt to link the evidence from coin hoards with specific handouts to the *plebs* and donatives to the army,[84] although these results do not necessarily indicate also a correlation between the production of coins and their distribution in the form of gifts. We notice that also in the Byzantine empire, apart from the necessary expenditure for the maintenance of the administration and the army, large quantities of money were further distributed in the form of gifts, such as the large grants of cash (*solemnia*) made out of fiscal revenues by emperors to monasteries and landowners, or in the form of alms for the poor, the sick and the elderly.[85] These types of gifts or charitable handouts certainly boosted the monetised economy of pre-industrial societies and facilitated the participation of the lower classes in daily monetised transactions.

Furthermore, it is likely that the support of public health and the design of pleasing surroundings absorbed part of the imperial budget as well as some of the private funds of the emperors.[86] The evidence found in literary and epigraphic sources in conjunction with the archaeological excavations throughout the empire indicate that imperial building activity (temples, public baths, amphitheatres etc.) was flourishing during the Principate. As far as we know, the emperors undertook the large-scale construction of buildings especially in Rome, thus providing the poor inhabitants of the capital with a fairly steady source of paid work (mostly in coined money).[87] The use of slaves under the supervision of one or more contractors in these constructions cannot be doubted. However, because of the large scale of

[82] Millar 1977: 137.

[83] Of course, we should not forget that not all *congiaria* were offered in cash; some of them may have taken the form of goods.

[84] Duncan-Jones 1994: 39–41, 86–7 and 248–50.

[85] Harvey 2003: 82–4.

[86] Massive buildings were sometimes paid for out of plunder. For example, an inscription on the colonnade of the Forum Trajanum proclaimed that it was built *ex manubiis*, thus indicating that the booty from the Dacian wars covered the expenses of this project. See Mattern 1999: 149–50.

[87] O. Robinson 1992: 23–5.

the projects and the specialised work that may have been essential for their completion, the gangs of slaves would not have sufficed; therefore, Roman poor citizens must have been 'recruited' and paid on a daily basis.[88]

A considerable amount of money was spent every year on public works such as the draining of Lake Fucino, where 30,000 men were employed for eleven years.[89] It has been estimated that, if four men's work was needed to produce the supply of food to the fifth, then we should suppose that at least 150,000 men were directly or indirectly involved in the works of the lake; and this was just part of the Claudian building programme. This multiplier effect in a pre-industrial society puts the work of construction at the time into a colossal perspective. At which point, it must be emphasised that the ratio 1:4 does not take into account the distribution of food, clothing and housing to all of these workers.[90] It has been assumed that the draining of the Fucine Lake probably cost around 400 million sestertii over a period of ten years.

Another example of a major construction project are the Baths of Caracalla in Rome. De Laine[91] calculated that the average minimum number of contracted construction workers during four years could have been 7,200 men, while another 1,800 men and oxen would have been involved in the transportation of these materials. At the other end of the scale, the maximum number of men involved in the project for one year could have reached 13,100. The payment of the workers and the command of the materials may have cost the Roman emperor around 12 million *kastrenses modii*, an amount that is on the same scale as the imperial *congiaria*.

Similar estimates of the public works in and around Rome from 29 BC to AD 69 indicate an annual average expenditure equal to 0.2 per cent of the national product. In addition we should take into account that expenditures throughout the empire might have been substantially higher.[92] It is interesting to note that in all of these cases the multiplier effect of the sustenance of the workers has not been taken into consideration. Similarly, evidence from a later date indicates that around 900 million sestertii were spent during the fifteen years of Domitian's reign, giving an average of 60 million sestertii per annum. Even if Domitian's building programme (the Capitol, the finishing of the Colosseum, a stadium and a palace) is exceptional, the least an emperor would have spent was around 20 million sestertii every year.[93] Although it has been suggested (at least for

[88] Brunt 1980: 86 and 93–4. [89] Suet. *Claud.* 20.2. [90] Shydsgaard 1983.
[91] De Laine 1997: 193 and 224. [92] Goldsmith 1984: 275. [93] Duncan-Jones 1994: 41–2.

the Julio-Claudian period) that any building unless large had little impact on the economy, possibly because imperial civil servants (usually slaves) would have performed routine work,[94] the existing evidence cannot prove such a statement. Even if we exclude minor projects from our calculations of state expenses, we should still acknowledge a large amount of money spent every year. Furthermore, there has been no study on the impact of smaller and yet more numerous projects, which relied on the imperial budget. It is therefore likely that, on the whole, these expensive constructions affected both the mint output and the direct distribution of money from the imperial authorities to the lower classes.

Extensive building activity also took place in the provinces during the imperial period at the expense of the Roman treasury. The foundation of colonies, imperial travelling and the chaotic situation caused by earthquakes usually drew the attention of the emperors and their subsequent involvement in major constructions. The epithets 'Restorer' or 'Saviour' bestowed upon them by the grateful local population indicate the exceptional imperial munificence towards some of the provincial cities. The money used for the payment of these buildings may not have come directly from the mint of Rome, though. No doubt the easiest way to pay for these public works in the provinces was a warrant drawn from the *fiscus* of the province, as it was filled up with taxes or the profits of the imperial estates. Although the ultimate loser might be either the *Aerarium Saturni*, in public provinces, or the imperial *fiscus*, calls must have been made also on the *patrimonium* and on the *res privata*. The form of labour force resembled that of Rome, with the exception that in some cases *coloni* and soldiers may have participated more actively.[95] In any case, the construction of public buildings in the provinces provided work for the poor inhabitants of the region and an abundance of coins, which were immediately put into circulation.

The emperors were also known to lend money to members of the upper classes at a low interest rate or even interest-free,[96] while in other cases imperial gifts in the form of money towards the same group of people were just a compensation for services rendered.[97] In fact, members of the Senate who encountered financial hardships sometimes expected the emperor to pay them a large capital payment, or even a salary for life.[98] The outgoings for these personal gifts were substantial: according to Tacitus' estimates the gifts of Nero to his favourites cost around 2.2 billion sestertii, one

[94] Thornton and Thornton 1989: 24. [95] MacMullen 1959.
[96] Dio Cass. 52.28.3–4; 55.12.3a; Suet. *Aug.* 41.1; Tac. *Ann.* 6.17. [97] W. Harris 1993: 17.
[98] Millar 1977: 135–9, 467–8, 491–500.

of the largest recorded figures from the Roman empire.[99] Accordingly, several emperors abolished the debts of the elite to the imperial treasury; such imperial acts are attested during the reigns of Vespasian[100] and Hadrian.[101]

These loans and monetary gifts solved the cash liquidity problems in the empire, especially when severe crises occurred. The best-known example from the Principate is probably the crisis of AD 33,[102] although similar ones had occurred already in the 80s BC, 63 BC and 49 BC. The study of the financial crisis of AD 33 gave rise to a number of contradictory interpretations. Nevertheless, there seems to be general consensus with regard to the sequence of events.[103] During the reign of Tiberius a magistrate tried to apply Julius Caesar's law (*de modo credendi possidendique intra Italiam*), by which he tried to regulate debts and the lending of money probably by fixing the maximum proportion of a patrimony that could be loaned. Since most of the senators at the time did not abide by this law, Tiberius gave them eighteen months to set their affairs in order. For that reason, a *senatus consultus* was decreed, according to which two-thirds of loaned sums should be invested in land in Italy. With the help of this measure the Senate hoped to avoid the sudden collapse of land prices that normally happens when excessive debts and liquidity crises occur. Nevertheless, the lack of cash in the markets became increasingly more serious until the emperor himself offered interest-free loans amounting to 100 million sestertii (from his personal fortune) for the duration of three years. The senators and knights who borrowed the money offered as security part of their estate, thus 'mortgaging' their patrimony in order to pay their debts. The measures I just described were of a temporary nature and were discontinued after the crisis was over. It is obvious, though, that the emperor was aware of the problems that the lack of cash in the markets might have caused to the economy and consequently also to the finances of the state and, therefore, made certain that more coins would become available through imperial loans.

In an attempt to ensure the liquidity of the markets and the balance between revenues and expenses, the Roman emperors strove to control the sources of precious metals,[104] they systematised the production of gold and

[99] Tac. *Hist.* 1.20. However, some of these gifts may have been in the form of goods/estates.

[100] Dio Cass. 65.10.3. [101] Dio Cass. 69.8.1–2.

[102] Tac. *Ann.* 6.17.1. In this case, Tacitus gives an exaggerated account of how the sale of the properties of the accomplice of Sejanus caused the cash liquidity crisis.

[103] Rodewald 1976; Lo Cascio 1978a; Lo Cascio 1978b; Andreau 1999: 104; Tchernia 2003.

[104] For the monopoly of gold and silver mines see chapter 3.

silver coins and they organised a number of mints under direct imperial administration.

THE ADMINISTRATION OF MINTS

The explicit link between imperial finances and the production of precious-metal coinages becomes evident also through the study of the administration of minting in the Roman empire. In order to maintain a more centralised and controlled production of silver and gold coins, a major mint was situated first in Lugdunum and then in the metropolis of the Roman empire, Rome, from the Early Empire until the middle of the third century AD. The production became firmly centralised despite the wars of Domitian and Trajan on the Rhine and Danube, and the empire-wide wanderings of Hadrian that could have promoted the establishment of local mints.[105] Only occasionally other imperial mints functioned in both the eastern and the western provinces and produced precious-metal coins based on the denarial system. Their output seems to be quite low until the reign of Gallienus, with the brief exceptions of the reign of Augustus, the Civil Wars and the early Severan period.[106]

Until the mid third century, the need for a tight control over the imperial finances probably initiated the process of centralisation of Roman mints and the confinement of most of the coin production to the mint of Rome for more than two hundred years. We know that the city of Rome was the political, administrative and economic centre during the Principate. All the important decisions that enabled the central bureaucratic mechanism to function, even when the emperor himself was not in the city, were allegedly taken within its walls. It seems only natural that most of the precious-metal coinages would have been produced there under the control of the imperial authorities, who also regulated their initial distribution according to the needs and the expenses of the state. Both silver and gold coins issued in imperial mints circulated widely, while the denarius system prevailed in the Mediterranean for more than two centuries and was used in the majority of commercial transactions, as coin hoards from the regions around the Mediterranean indicate.

Apart from the imperial mints that issued precious-metal coins according to the denarial standard we also find in the eastern provinces mints that

[105] H. Mattingly 1960: 111 and 114. For the transfer of the mint from Lugdunum to Rome see Ponting and Butcher 2005: 164.

[106] H. Mattingly 1960: 101–20; 1923: xiii-xxii; 1930: xi-xiii; 1936: xi-xiv; 1940: xi–xiii; 1950: xiii-xvii; Carson 1962: 1–10.

followed Hellenistic standards. One of the most popular and long-lasting coinages issued sporadically in provincial mints was the cistophoric. Its first imperial period of production under Augustus ended *ca.* 19 BC, to be revived only later by Claudius, Titus and Domitian, while the production of issues under Nerva and Trajan did not extend beyond AD 102. The Hadrianic cistophoric coinage was much more abundant than the previous ones, probably approaching in volume the Augustan 'official' issues. The production was discontinued after Hadrian's death until the late second century (AD 198–202), when the production of Severan cistophori was resumed and became the last of these provincial issues.[107] The cistophorus was incorporated in the Roman monetary economy through the official system of exchange, which placed the denarius in the centre of this system. It has been observed that the circulation of the cistophorus was restricted to western Asia Minor, where it was also produced. We should look for reasons for its limited circulation in the special needs of the markets, since there is no direct evidence to suggest that a central authority kept the number of issues low or prohibited its circulation in other regions.

Another provincial weight system of silver denominations had its roots also in the Hellenistic period and was specifically based on the 'attic' standard. Different issuing authorities in Asia Minor and Syria issued selectively some of these denominations. The Lycian League and other cities of Asia Minor (Tarsus, Aegae, Mopsus, Seleucia, Amisus, Cyprus) coined silver drachms, didrachms and tridrachms during the early Roman empire.[108] Prominent among them was the city of Caesarea in Cappadocia, which eventually became the great mint of eastern Asia Minor from the time of Tiberius onwards.[109] Although the decline of this silver coinage became marked under the reign of Septimius Severus, the mint of Caesarea in Cappadocia was reactivated during the reign of Gordian for the last time.[110] Drachms, didrachms, tridrachms and tetradrachms were minted irregularly and in low quantities; consequently the circulation of these coins was limited both geographically and chronologically. The only mint that produced provincial coinages regularly and in large numbers was Antioch. As we will soon see the mint of Antioch provided the bulk of coinage – mainly tetradrachms – that circulated throughout the area of Syria from the first to the third centuries AD, while occasionally other, smaller mints became active in the region.

[107] Sutherland, Olcay and Merrington 1970; Metcalf 1980; Metcalf 1988.
[108] Harl 1996: 100–1. [109] Sydenham 1978: 2–3. [110] Bland 1991a.

With regard to the reason for the production of the tetradrachm coinage of Syria, it has been suggested that this provincial currency was designed primarily to facilitate the payment of the administrative officers and provide for military expenses, while its secondary role was to cover the commercial needs of the Syrian cities.[111] This theory though cannot be extended to the Asia Minor cities, which followed either the cistophoric or the attic standard. In particular, recent studies, although they still acknowledge the idea that the mint of Caesarea in Cappadocia issued silver coins in order to provide local troops with their payments, also recognise the significance of these coins in the local markets.[112] Whether these Asia Minor cities aimed at the boosting of their local commercial activities or at the facilitation of the soldiers' pay, the comparatively low mint output and the restricted circulation of these issues probably did not widely affect the Roman monetary economy. Although there is not always clear evidence about the authorities that controlled the issuing of currencies in provincial mints, there are strong indications that at least the mint of Antioch was under direct or indirect imperial control.[113]

ROMAN MINES

The administration of mints was not the only way the emperors intervened in and eventually controlled the production of precious-metal currency. The protection of their profits required that they also controlled the process of mining, especially since precious-metal bullion no longer came from the undertaking of expansive wars (apart from the Trajanic invasion of Dacia). Current archaeological research has demonstrated that in Spain alone more than 500 mines were in operation during the Republic and the Principate,[114] while archaeological surveys in the Balkans have unearthed more evidence indicating the existence of important mines. On the other hand, the ancient writers give only impressionistic numbers with regard to the annual output of precious metal, while the information on the actual transformation of bullion into coins is even less. Specifically, Polybius mentions that the mines near New Carthage in Spain produced 25,000 silver drachms in or around 140 BC,[115] while Pliny notes that the gold mines in the north of Spain produced 20,000 pounds of gold annually from Asturia, Galicia and Lusitania (from alluvial terraces) during the early Principate.[116] According to one estimate the Duerna valley produced 3,000 kg of gold per annum

[111] Burnett *et al.* 1992: 7–8; Katsari 2003b: 35. [112] Metcalf 1997. [113] Butcher 2004: 239–41.
[114] Domergue 1990. [115] Polyb. 34.9.8. [116] Plin. *HN*, 33.21.78.

for 130 years.[117] Outside Spain there are several indications in the literary sources of the existence of important mines; such an area is Dalmatia, which during Nero's reign produced 1,750 pounds of gold per year.[118] We also find references to the land of the Scordisci close to Aquileia that produced enough gold during the second century BC to cause inflationary tendencies in Rome (the price of gold fell by one-third).[119] The possibility that the extraction of gold and silver could alter its price in the markets would have certainly been realised by the Roman emperors who, for this reason, kept a tight control over the mines. It is natural to assume that the imperial regulation of the extraction of metal would have ensured the stable price of gold and silver as commodities and would not have caused the devaluation of the currency in circulation.

Despite the fact that we cannot fully assess the production of precious-metal bullion in the Roman empire based on the existing evidence, we can, nevertheless, qualify its importance for the emperor, if we take into consideration the effort that was devoted to the organisation of the mines. Although we observe a range of methods that allowed the exploitation of the metal resources, their overall financial control remained in the hands of the central government. One of the ways to exploit these mines was probably through their leasing to *publicani*, especially during the Republican period. In the case of Carthago Nova, for example, the mines during the Republic were owned by the colony, which farmed out mining operations to companies.[120] Part of these profits would have undoubtedly ended up going to the Roman treasury through the imposition of taxes, such as the *stipendium*.[121]

On the other hand, it seems that under the empire both the Asturian and Galician gold mines, which provided the essential material for the issue of precious-metal coinages,[122] were under the direct control of the state for more than two hundred years.[123] Specifically, in some areas of the Asturias the local aristocracies acted as the official representatives of the emperor and had the authority to collect taxes and administer the territory, while other territories that were outside the control of the *civitates* – in particular the gold-bearing *metalla publica* – remained *ager publicus*. Jurisdiction over these geographical areas stayed in the hands of the *procurator metallorum*, who was the representative of the imperial *fiscus* and was directly involved in tax collection, surveillance, regulation of the mines, economic, judicial

117 Domergue and Hérail 1978: 278. 118 Plin. *HN*, 33.21.67.
119 Polyb. 34.10.10–14; Strabo 4.6.12 (208). 120 Orejas and Sánchez-Palencia 2002: 589.
121 Richardson 1976. 122 Corbier 1989; Howgego 1992; Perea and Sánchez-Palencia 1995: 60–3.
123 Domergue 1990: 279–307.

and policing activities. Because of the significance of these regions for the imperial *fiscus*, their autonomy and economic independence became eclipsed. On top of that, the army and a well-developed administrative infrastructure were employed to keep these territories under control, as several inscriptions indicate.[124] The organisation of the precious-metal production under military supervision in the Spanish provinces could only demonstrate the wish of Rome to keep a tight control over its mines.

In the Byzantine empire the system developed in a slightly different direction; so, we encounter the existence of a mixture of state and privately owned mines.[125] The central government continued the appointments of the *procuratores metallorum*, who used to be vital for the administration of mines during the Principate as well.[126] Nevertheless, we observe two major differences between the two periods. During the Byzantine period, (a) the emperor leased out to landowners the right to exploit state-owned gold mines on payment of the *metallicus* canon;[127] and (b) he allowed them to exploit state-owned *metallica loca* on the condition that they maintained certain levels of production.[128] Of course, the existence of privately owned mines did not necessarily reduce the profits of the treasury, since it still levied a special payment/tax (*praestatio auraria*, *aeraria* and *ferraria*) on the metal production, as the legal sources inform us.[129] According to further regulations imposed in AD 424, a landowner, who may also have been responsible for the exploitation of some of the metal resources, could pay his taxes not in coin or kind but in gold, copper or iron bullion.[130] The long-term consequence of such actions may have been a decrease in the role of the central government in the direct administration of precious-metal mines and the increased responsibility of the provincial aristocracy in the organisation of production.[131] Nevertheless, the changes in the administration of the mines did not necessarily have an impact on the imperial revenues that still regulated both the levels of the output and the taxation system.

BRONZE IMPERIAL COINAGES

There is no doubt that the central government paid special attention to the production of precious-metal coinages. In addition, it issued smaller

[124] Orejas and Sánchez-Palencia 2002: 593–4. [125] Vryonis 1962: 3.
[126] *Cod. Theod.* 1.32.5. [127] *Cod. Theod.* 10.19.3, 4, 12.
[128] *Cod. Theod.* 10.19.13. [129] *Cod. Theod.* 11.20.6; Edmondson 1989: 98.
[130] *Cod. Theod.* 11.21.3. [131] Edmondson 1989: 99.

denominations of bronze, whose number increased after the commencement of the reign of Augustus. According to some scholars, these issues facilitated the transactions of either the army or the administration;[132] thus, the mint of Rome remained responsible for the production of bronze coinages. It is possible that some of these coins were used extensively for state payments and served the needs of the imperial administrators. In other cases, though, they may have been shipped to the western provinces, in order to cover the needs of the markets for small change, since the cities did not produce their own bronze coinages.

Other mints under imperial control in the eastern provinces played a secondary, and yet interesting, role. For example, the CA coinages, mostly of sestertii and dupondii, were produced in the provinces on behalf of the central government. Although they were minted in Asia Minor, as the inscription *C(ommune) A(siae)*[133] suggests, these coins have been found in an extensive area from south-eastern Europe to Syria. However, their volume was quite low and, thus, had a limited impact on the markets of the eastern Mediterranean cities. By comparison to the local civic coinages, we observe two differences: (a) their circulation was wider, while (b) their effect was restricted. These differences lead us to believe that the role of these 'official' issues may have been unusual. While civic coinages served the needs of the local markets for small change, CA coinages may have served the needs of the central government in the eastern provinces. Therefore, we cannot exclude the possibility that they were used for army payments or in order to cover for local deficiencies in the circulation of smaller denominations; but only in emergency cases.

Other coins that bear the initials *S(enatus) C(onsulto)*[134] were produced at Antioch and could have served a similar purpose. Unlike the short-term production of the CA series, the SC coinage continued intermittently from the age of Augustus until the reign of Philip.[135] Another difference between the two series is that the circulation of the third-century SC coins was restricted to Syria and never reached European shores or even

[132] Howgego 1985: 20–1.

[133] Burnett 1977: 47. An interpretation of the letters CA as *Caesaris Auctoritate* was suggested by Grant (1969: 108). Another hypothesis that the above letters could be the initials of Caesar Augustus does not seem plausible either (Grant 1969: 108).

[134] For the nominal authority of the Senate over the minting of bronze see H. Mattingly 1960: 191. According to another interpretation by Kraft (1962: 7), SC refers to a senatorial decree conferring honours voted to Augustus from the Senate. This hypothesis was reviewed by Burnett (1977: 45), where he supports Mommsen's theory that bronze had been under senatorial control.

[135] For a comprehensive analysis of SC coinages see Butcher 2004 and Wolters 1999: 115–45. Also, see Rodewald 1976: 65; Howgego 1985: 24; Butcher 1988a: 64–5.

Asia Minor.[136] It has been suggested that they were issued in order to supply the troops of the Levant with small change that would resemble the character of the imperial bronze coinage.[137] This idea seems to be plausible, especially because they were produced in a highly militarised area near the eastern frontier, where the needs of the army were increasing, and also because the countermarks show that these coins were still used by the troops for a century after their issue.[138] Specifically, during the first century AD legionary countermarks on such coins became especially common. They may have been applied during the reigns of Trajan or Hadrian.[139] We also know that the legions III Cyrenaica, VI Ferrata, X Fretensis, XII Fulminata and XV Apollinaris applied countermarks usually on worn coins from the reign of Nero until the reign of Lucius Verus.[140] In additional support of the military character of this coinage, it has been suggested that the SC issues of Trajan, Marcus Aurelius and Verus coincide with eastern wars, even though not all of these issues can be matched with specific campaigns.[141] Another hypothesis, according to which the SC coins were intended for use in the collection of customs duties in Syrian caravan towns,[142] may seem equally possible but is not proven by the evidence. The Italian asses that are mentioned in the text regarding the tax law of Palmyra refer to the assessment and not the payment of taxes.[143] The Italic asses were probably used as a unit of account according to which transactions in coin would be measured.

Even if these coinages were produced in order to facilitate payments to the army or the transactions of the soldiers, we should not forget that eventually they reached the local markets. Once they were used in the agoras, they arrived in the hands of the local merchants who sold their products to the general public. From then onwards these special coinages facilitated small daily transactions in the same way as any other bronze coinage.

[136] Apart from Antioch we encounter such coin finds in Palmyra: Dumant 1975: 103–7; as well as Dura Europos: Bellinger 1949: 73–82, nos. 1599–1699; Apameia: Callu 1979; and Jerash: Bellinger 1938: nos. 50–63.

[137] Rodewald 1976: 65; Howgego 1982; Howgego 1985: 21–4.

[138] Howgego 1985: 23.

[139] Butcher 2004: 241.

[140] Howgego 1982–1983: 49; 1985: 17–20.

[141] Butcher 2004: 250.

[142] Harl 1996: 108.

[143] The inscription, according to which Corbulo re-enacted the older provision that the custom dues at Palmyra should be payable in denarii or Italic asses has been thoroughly translated and interpreted by Matthews (1984). The text can be found in *IGRR* 3.1056 with a Latin translation; also the Greek and Palmyrene text with Latin translation and photographs in Chabot 1926: no. 3913. The text published with English translation and commentary in Cooke 1903: 313–40: no. 147. Standard publication in *OGIS* 2.629.

IMPERIAL REVENUES IN THE FORM OF MONEY

The emperors had a range of resources, which ensured the uninhibited operation of the Roman financial system. The ways they dispensed these funds, in the form of money, to the economy was through military and administrative payments, gifts to the populace, loans to the upper classes and several money-related enterprises (e.g. trade, banking). Imperial expenditure, though, could not have taken place unless the emperor had stable revenues other than the production of currency.

Apart from his imperial position, the emperor was also an individual, who managed his own property. Part of the state's revenues were also the profits the emperor made from his own estates and other enterprises. I suspect that the largest part of the surplus of the vast imperial estates was also turned into money, once the produce was sold in local or interregional markets. The importance of the North African imperial estates in the supply of food across the Mediterranean has been acknowledged by Kehoe, who also noted the increasing control of these estates by the central administration, in an attempt to ensure continuous profits either from the leasing of the land or the direct selling of the agricultural products.[144] In fact, ancient writers testify that the imperial expenditures were directly connected with the administration of imperial lands. Pertinax, for example, tried to create additional revenues for the *fiscus* by giving away unused lands on imperial estates in Italy and the provinces and ten-year immunity from taxation to private owners, hoping that future taxes would compensate for the short-term loss.[145]

The case of the Bagradas valley indicates the direct interest of the imperial administration in the management of the imperial estates, since the profits from the working of the land contributed towards the imperial annual revenues. Usually the *fiscus* took advantage of the competition for land among small-scale cultivators in order to lease its land in exchange for high rents, although this system would not necessarily have yielded very high profits immediately. Instead, the *fiscus* sought to impose a programme that would involve long-term investment in intensive agriculture. Specifically, it dictated a range of crops that the *coloni* could cultivate, offered incentives for the cultivation of more intensive crops, enforced uniform tenant arrangements over a vast area and finally offered favourable terms

[144] Kehoe 1984 1985; 1988a. Similar profits from the leasing of imperial estates have been attested in the province of Arabia (Cotton 1997: 261–2) and provinces in Asia Minor (Abbott and Johnson 1926: no. 142).

[145] Herodian 2.4.6.

of land tenure; this way, it hoped to raise the total production of food in the North African province.[146]

The reliance of the emperor on his landed wealth should not be underestimated and his continuous concern with the agricultural potential of his estates is fully attested in the ancient sources, such as Tacitus[147] and Pliny.[148] However, even if the evidence for the four-hundred-fold increase in the grain yield in African Byzacium during Augustus' and Nero's reigns had not been considered fictitious,[149] and even if we had a more accurate idea of the annual surplus of these estates, it would still be almost impossible to assess the extent of these profits in their entirety and to estimate how much of them was turned into cash. In the private sector, a modest return from farmland in which a minimum amount has been invested should be estimated at 5–6 per cent of the initial investment, according to the financial statements of Pliny the Younger and Columella.[150] Nevertheless, the long-term investment that the emperor opted for would probably have produced a much higher return.

With regard to the imperial revenues, we know that the *coloni* paid to the emperor a share rent of one-third of the produce, as well as the allocated taxes.[151] Although there is little evidence about the taxation system outside Egypt, the taxes of the *coloni* have been estimated at between one-tenth and one-fifth of the farm's produce for the western provinces, including North Africa.[152] We are not certain, though, whether the rents or the taxes were eventually paid to the *fiscus* in the form of cash or goods. If the due amount was paid in kind, then the emperor would have assured a stable provision of foodstuff, despite possible fluctuations of prices in the marketplace.[153] Consequently, the collection of rents in kind would have inhibited the participation of the *coloni* in the local markets; thus, they would have lost control over their surplus. Despite the advantages of such a policy, it seems that the emperor was not interested in imposing a commercial monopoly; so, the *fiscus* restricted its control to monitoring the disposal of produce in the markets.

There is ample evidence indicating that the *coloni* participated in cash transactions in the regional markets, as they paid a cash fee of four asses for each animal they set to grazing on the estate. Furthermore, all fruit

146 Kehoe 1988a: 76, 106, 224–5.

147 Tac. *Ann.*, 14.65. Although in this passage Tacitus delivers moral comments on the greed of the emperors, the text also indicates a conscious imperial policy that aimed at the increase of their landed wealth.

148 Plin. *HN* 18. 94–5.

149 D. Crawford 1976: 54.

150 Duncan-Jones 1974: 33, n. 3.

151 Kehoe 1988a: 107.

152 Neesen 1980: 68–84.

153 Kehoe 1988a: 168.

produced by the *coloni* – except for what was sold in the market – was exempted from the share rent. We may assume that the *coloni* disposed of their surplus in the market regularly. The cash profits from the sale of this surplus as well as borrowings or credit from the *conductores* may have been used for further investments in the land.[154] In order to achieve better profits the *coloni* usually chose cash crops that eventually yielded higher returns for the same plot.[155] Similar examples may be found in Languedoc during the sixteenth century, where peasants replaced cultivation of cereals with the cultivation of vines and olives, since these were in demand at the time.[156] Likewise, in the post-bellum American South the poorest sharecroppers seem to have preferred the exclusive cultivation of cotton.[157] In turn, the collection of rents and taxes in cash would have allowed the emperor to use the profits as capital for other enterprises.

The Roman emperor undoubtedly also invested money in commercial enterprises either directly or indirectly. Even though in some cases this investment probably took the form of loans, the creditor could count on an income from these financial activities to be added to his already substantial income from properties and estates. Jean Andreau informs us that

> the tablets of Murecine indicate that members of the entourage of the emperor and of the entourages of a number of senators were investing money through the financiers of Puteoli . . . Several imperial slave or freedmen are cited as lending money either to the Sulpicii or to traders operating in Puteoli. Such loans of money do not necessarily imply that the emperor or these senators and knights had particular commercial interests. They were simply interest bearing loans, arranged by intermediaries. No particular business venture would be involved, no ownership of ships. Furthermore, the loans agreed in this way were simply investments, involving no specialized activity of money lending for interest. Even if the intermediaries . . . were specialist financiers, the emperor or senator from whom the money came took no interest at all in how the money was managed. They certainly picked up the profits, though, or at least part of the profits.[158]

Vespasian, in particular, has been accused of having continued 'carrying on traffic which would be shameful even for a man in private life'.[159] In most cases, though, the emperor would not have been directly involved in such business. An *actor* or *dispensator* ran most of the imperial business, while making large profits of their own. Suetonius related that Otho received one million sestertii from one of Galba's slaves for having managed to get him taken on as a *dispensator* for the emperor.[160] And a slave of Nero,

[154] Kehoe 1988a: 175–6. [155] Kehoe 1988a: 81. [156] Le Roy Ladurie 1974: 56–66.
[157] Wright 1978: 170. [158] Andreau 1999: 74–5. [159] Suet. *Vesp*. 16.2. [160] Suet. *Otho* 5.2.

who had been his *dispensator*, was able to pay 13 million sestertii at the time of his manumission.[161] If the profits of the slaves were so large, we can only imagine what the profits of the emperors must have been like. As for the form of the profits, we can only guess that a large part of them would have been translated into supplementary capital, cash or credit. In fact, the elaborate credit system that was in place during the Roman Principate cannot be considered a coincidence. It seems that a range of banking activities (loans, transfer of credit etc.) facilitated the participation in long-distance commercial enterprises that involved the use of money either in the form of coins or as credit.

Furthermore, it is widely accepted that until the Early Empire the main source of revenue for the Roman state was the annexation of new territories. During the Republic wars brought in booty (short-term revenues), while in the long run they guaranteed a substantial increase in tax income. Nevertheless, by the time of Augustus the priorities of the Roman state seem to have changed; so, the first emperor of Rome and his successors preferred not to pursue the expansion of the *limes*. Historiographically speaking, the argument that wars were the main causes for the economic growth of states is not new. It also characterises the thought of historians of the medieval and early modern world.[162]

The question that should be asked, though, is did the limited expansion of the Roman state during the Principate reduce the potential of the empire for further economic growth? Analogous examples from early modern Europe seem to have divided historians. According to some researchers the impact of wars on taxation and state revenues was in some cases temporary, especially if these wars were non-global ones, while in other cases they even led the state into debt.[163] However, the majority of scholars acknowledge the fact that the relationship between wars and taxes has long-term and cumulative effects on the economy, also termed the 'ratchet effect'.[164] This suggests that the growth of the state was the result of subsequent wars, whose impact was added to the impact of previous ones. Additionally, in the long run military expeditions not only bring profits from taxation but they also create new forms of political organisation that would sustain the level of these profits.[165]

[161] Plin. *HN* 5.129.

[162] Just a small selection of titles: Peacock and Wiseman 1961; Mann 1986; Rasler and Thompson 1989; C. Tilly 1990; C. Tilly 1993; Hoffman and Rosenthal 1997.

[163] Rasler and Thompson 1989.

[164] Peacock and Wiseman 1961; Ames and Rapp 1977.

[165] Tilly 1990: 90.

As an illustrative example we may use the dramatic growth of the English navy, which occurred between the sixteenth and the eighteenth centuries, when the English naval power increased from 24 ships holding 600 men to 313 ships holding 48,000 men.[166] On a par with the military growth we may observe similar growth in the administration of the state, possibly because more people were needed for the extraction and maintenance of the increasing resources. Again the English state administration grew substantially from 1,211 employees in 1690 to 4,908 in 1783.[167]

Similarly, the cumulative effect of taxes in the early Roman empire may have facilitated its unparalleled growth or, at the least, it did not lead the state into bankruptcy. The tax collection was organised, first, at a local level and taxes, initially, were farmed out to wealthy individuals, while later it was entrusted to the cities.[168] The nature of the taxation system allowed for a greater degree of diversity between provinces, especially since the Romans decided to maintain already established traditions regarding the economic infrastructures in the newly acquired regions. The overall process, however, was overseen by provincial officials, namely the procurators, who collected custom dues, the inheritance tax and other indirect taxes.[169] In a comparable way, tax collection in the early modern states of England and France was a much decentralised process, as taxes were collected by officials elected or appointed and controlled locally.[170] There is no doubt, though, that, despite local differences, the overall system was centrally controlled in order to ensure the ongoing flow of revenues. After all, the most important revenue that filled the state's coffers on an annual basis was none other than taxes.

As I have already mentioned, the organisation of the tax system differed from one province to another, while the emperors did not attempt to impose uniformity, not even after the reforms of Diocletian and Constantine in the fourth century AD.[171] This diversity was not restricted to the administration of the tax collection but it characterised also the form of payments (either in cash or in kind). In some provinces the taxes were assessed in cash depending on the value of land or all the capital. However, there is a strong possibility that part of this amount was paid to the government in kind. For example, Brunt mentions the case of Caesar, who may have assessed the tribute from Gaul in coin but there was very little possibility of retrieving these taxes in cash, since very little money circulated in the region during the early first century AD.[172] On the other hand, the taxes from Asia Minor

[166] Braddick 1994: 31. [167] Brewer 1989. [168] Brunt 1990: 380, 388–9.
[169] Garnsey and Saller 1987: 21, 23. [170] Kiser and Linton 2001: 421–3.
[171] Neesen 1980. [172] Brunt 1981: 161–2.

may have been collected predominantly in cash, even if they were estimated in kind. Specifically, although the land tax was estimated to one-tenth of the harvest (*decuma*), the Roman treasury during the Republic received, in fact, money from the tax farmers.[173] The reason for this preference may have been the fact that the cities of Asia Minor, which were highly monetised in contrast to Gaul, paid their taxes in cash. It is possible that the inhabitants of Asia Minor had to sell their produce or services in order to raise the necessary money.[174] Similar examples are attested in the pre-industrial economies of the Mughal empire and China during the T'ang dynasty.[175]

Although the tax farmers of the eastern regions fixed a sum of money that each city had to pay to the Roman treasury, the majority of this money probably never left the province and was destined to cover the provincial administrative and military expenses. Of course, we cannot exclude the possibility that part of these revenues was physically transferred to Rome.[176] In fact, at least four ancient writers – Appian, Velleius Paterculus, Plutarch and Tacitus – refer to the physical transportation of tribute in the form of money from the provinces to the capital.[177] However, the most important piece of evidence may be found in the *Monumentum Ephesinum* which mentions that the shipment of coin that takes place on behalf of the Roman people should be exempt from custom dues.[178] In addition, some of the taxes from Asia Minor may have been transferred to the Balkan provinces in order to pay the salary of the troops that were stationed along the north-eastern frontier.[179]

In contrast to the eastern habit of collecting the taxes in cash, most of the taxes from Egypt were collected in kind. The Roman government preferred to receive its taxes in fixed quantities of grain that differed from one city to another or from one region to another.[180] Most of these revenues ended up in Rome, where the *annona* was distributed to the population. Nevertheless, a large part of it may have been sold in Alexandria[181] and the cash profits may have been transferred to Italy by Roman officials.[182] All in all, we cannot determine whether most of the overall taxation was paid in kind or in cash. The opinions of researchers seem to be polarised when it comes to the interpretation of the same sources. For example,

173 Caes. *B Civ.*, 3.3.2; 31.1; 32.6; 103.1. 174 Hopkins 1980; Hopkins 1995–6.

175 Bayly 1983: 63–4; Yang 1952: 52–3. For the comparison between Mughal India, T'ang China and the Roman empire see De Ligt 2003: 234–7.

176 De Ligt 2003: 240–4. 177 App. *B Civ.*, 3.11; Vell. Pat. 2.62.3; Plut. *Brut.*, 24.3; Tac. *Hist.*, 3.9.

178 SEG 39.1180, lines 58–61. 179 Gren 1941: 144–5. 180 Brunt 1981: 162.

181 Rathbone 1989: 173–4. 182 De Ligt 2003: 246.

Duncan-Jones,[183] based on a passage of Hyginus,[184] claims that 'taxes were levied to an extent in kind, not in money', while Hopkins based on the same passage suggests that 'at some stage taxes in money widely replaced taxes in kind'.[185] Neither of these scholars, though, has adequate evidence to support either the first or the second theory.

The ownership of large estates across the empire and the participation of the emperor in entrepreneurial activities were certainly sources of substantial revenues. However, the healthy outlook of the imperial budget relied predominantly on the steady inflow of taxes from the provinces. Trade, banking and loans are, by nature, risky enterprises and they do not always return the capital invested in them. On the other hand, taxation presents a regular resource that remains constant for years and allows long-term planning. So far, we have seen that the balance between taxes paid in cash and taxes paid in goods may have differed from one region to another, depending on the regional degree of monetisation. In addition, there may have been differences in the amount of taxes each province paid to the central government. Keith Hopkins supported the view that money taxes were levied in the wealthy regions of the empire and then spent in the highly militarised provinces or in Italy.[186] He describes three economic zones: (a) the frontier provinces where the armies were stationed; (b) the rich tax-exporting provinces of Spain, southern Gaul, northern Africa, Asia Minor, Syria and Egypt; (c) the administrative centre of the empire, Rome and Italy. According to Hopkins, the militarised areas and the administrative centre consumed more taxes than they produced, while the rich provinces exported the surplus of the taxes they gathered. In principle, this economic model is nothing but a commonsensical theory and could be applied in several empires and in different chronological periods. Hopkins, though, did not manage to produce any evidence that would either prove or disprove it, in the case of the Roman empire.

Coins, in this case, should be considered a reliable indicator of the flow of taxes to and from the centre and between the provinces. Specifically, the chronological span of coin hoards (estimated according to the first and last coins) could give us an idea of how long coins circulated before they returned to the mint for recoining. Of course, if we assume that denarii would have been the main denomination in which taxes were paid, then the silver coin hoards would indicate every how often the receipt of taxes replenished the coinage in circulation.[187] Table 1 presents

[183] Duncan-Jones 1990: 45. [184] Hyg. 205 L. [185] Hopkins 1995–6: 55.
[186] Hopkins 1980: 101. [187] For the methodological implications see chapter 1.

Table 1

Provinces	Antonines Average Years	Severans Average Years
Dacia	168.66	211
Pannonia Superior	158.87	112.66
Pannonia Inferior	201.5	185.6
Moesia Superior	161.33	158
Moesia Inferior	153.16	143.16
Greece	79.5	132
Asia Minor	92	46
Syria	103.33	204

the average chronological span of silver-coin hoards in the provinces of Dacia,[188] Pannonia Superior,[189] Pannonia Inferior,[190] Moesia Superior,[191] Moesia Inferior,[192] Greece,[193] Asia Minor[194] and Syria.[195]

The above results show that in all eastern provinces apart from Dacia, Greece and Syria the chronological span of the silver coin hoards during the Severan period was shorter than the chronological span during the Antonine period. This phenomenon should be explained in connection to the increasing need of the Roman state for revenues and the numismatic reforms that took place under the Severans. The repeated debasements

188 The Dacian coin hoards buried during the Antonine period are: Mera, Belcinu, Tibru, Sighişoara, Visea, Salăşuri, Gostavăt, Tibodu, Diviciorii Marj, Drăghiceni, Brad, Barbura, Dumbrăvioara, Butoieşti, Apulum I. The Dacian hoards buried during the Severan period are: Lujerdiu, Frânceşti, Pădrureţu, Dăneşti and Micia.

189 Coin hoards of the Antonine period found in Pannonia Superior are: Wallern, Carnuntum I, Carnuntum II, Neunkirchen, Apetlon, Tokod, Prelasko, Vindobona II. Coin hoards of the Severan period from Pannonia Superior are: Vindobona IV, Poetovio I and Csapon.

190 Pannonia Inferior produced the following Antonine coin hoards: Kurd-Gyulaji, Cornacum, Mursa, Bela Reka.

191 Only few hoards of the Antonine period were recovered in Moesia Superior: Mrcevac, Misaka, Grocka. Only one hoard survived from the Severan period: Ravna.

192 The Antonine silver coin hoards from Moesia Inferior are: Gradeshnitsa, Oescus, Tchervena Voda, Zhinitsa, Medgidia, Oescus IV, Dvrostorum IV, Dvrostorum II, Mokresh, Pavlikeni, Storgosia II, Gruncharovo. The Severan silver hoards from Moesia Inferior are: Tropaeum Traiani, Dimum, Dvrostorum, Katunets, Vicus Tautiomosis, Sanadinovo.

193 Only two hoards from the Antonine period were recovered from Greece, Krani and Cephallenia, while one coin hoard of the Severan period is included in this catalogue, Erestrole.

194 From Asia Minor only one Antonine silver hoard was recovered, Manyas, while two silver hoards of the Severan period were recovered, Yatagan and Sulakyurt.

195 Coin hoards of the Antonine period found in Syria are: Tiberias, Murabba'at and Boston. Silver coin hoards of the Severan period buried in Syria are: Syria 3, Dura 3, Dura 16, Mempsis. Similar patterns are observed also in Nineveh, hence this site is included in the group of Syria.

of the denarius probably involved the recalling of silver currencies to the central mint and the re-issuing of the coins. In this case, we cannot support with certainty the idea that the government imposed more taxes. However, Table 1 indicates a second phenomenon that should be analysed further. The silver coin hoards found in the highly militarised provinces of Dacia, Pannonia Superior, Pannonia Inferior, Moesia Superior, Moesia Inferior and Syria include coins from a wider chronological span than the silver coin hoards found in the provinces of Greece and Asia Minor. There are, of course, regional variations and exceptions but these will not be discussed in the course of this chapter.

The general picture of these hoards demonstrates the faster recalling to the central mint of silver currencies that circulated in Greece and Asia Minor, irrespective of the period. This difference cannot be explained in connection with numismatic reforms, since these would have affected all of the empire in similar ways. In our attempt to look for explanations elsewhere, Hopkins' model is of some use. The soldiers stationed in Greece and Asia Minor were certainly not as many as in the frontier provinces of north-eastern Balkans and eastern Syria. Even though we acknowledge the fact that troops were policing these areas and they were moving regularly from and to Anatolia and the Balkans,[196] their numbers remained comparatively low. The cash payments for these soldiers came from the mint of Rome either in newly minted coin or in coins that were in circulation for years. In any case, if the taxes of the highly militarised provinces were kept at low levels, then the coins that arrived through the imperial mechanism would have circulated in these areas for a long time. On the other hand, the highly taxed, low-militarised provinces of Greece and Asia Minor would have faced a different situation. The central government would have asked for taxes with a regularity that would have been obvious in the structure of coin hoards. The more taxes are imposed in one region, the faster is the return of the coins to the central mint; consequently, the smaller is the chronological span of silver coin hoards. Of course, we should take into account that this model is valid only if we consider that the needs (demand) of the inhabitants in the provinces for traded commodities was similar throughout the empire. Unfortunately, although it is plausible, there is no way to guarantee the validity of such a statement for every province of the Roman empire.

Even if coin hoards allow us to assess the comparative volume of taxes between provinces, coin evidence does not help us estimate the overall

[196] Gren 1941: 135.

volume of taxation. Hopkins assumes that the taxes were very low during the Principate and, in fact, he estimated the tax income of the emperor in the first century AD in the region of 650–900 million sestertii per year,[197] higher than Duncan-Jones, who calculated the imperial income at 670 million sestertii per year.[198] Either way, Hopkins claimed that these tax rates were especially low, especially when he compared them with similar taxes raised in eighteenth-century France or England (although taxes in the same countries admittedly were much lower during the sixteenth century). He, then, interpreted this phenomenon as a direct consequence of the low administrative costs in the Roman empire. Specifically, he estimated the existence of one elite administrator for every 350,000–400,000 persons in the Roman world, in comparison to the one administrator per 15,000 people in southern China of the twelfth century.[199] Nevertheless, the structure of coin hoards from medieval China cannot support Hopkins' thesis that taxes were lower in the Roman empire. While the chronological span of coin hoards in the eastern provinces ranged from a few decades to two centuries, coins in medieval China were in circulation for 700–1,000 years.[200] This indicates that the Chinese coins were not called back to the central mints through taxes as regularly as in the Roman empire. Effectively, the burden of taxation may have been more onerous in the Roman world. This hypothesis could be in accordance with the evidence from early modern France and England, which indicates the imposition of lower taxes. It seems that the phenomenon of higher taxation in Europe could have been a modern habit, connected to the industrialisation and modernisation of the areas.

MONETARY MONOPOLY

It is evident that the emperor was responsible for the maintenance of the standing army that guaranteed peace and defended the inhabitants of the Roman empire from both external and internal enemies. Despite the fact that the payments of the soldiers may not have represented the bulk of the imperial expenditures, the annual amount handed over for the needs of the army remained substantial. On the other hand, the imperial expenditures on the administrative infrastructure of the empire, the construction of public buildings, the generous largesses to the population and the gifts

197 Hopkins 1995–6: 55. 198 Duncan-Jones 1994: 46 and 53. 199 Hopkins 1980: 120–1.

200 I owe this piece of information to Professor Akinobu Kuroda, who is a specialist in the monetary economy of medieval China.

distributed to members of the elite were probably more substantial than researchers initially assumed. The increasing responsibilities of the emperor towards his subjects would have been met only if the influx of revenues continued to arrive at the Roman treasury incessantly. As in other tributary empires, the main revenue of the state came from the imposition of direct and indirect taxes, which were received at regular intervals. In addition, the profits from the imperial estates and other entrepreneurial activities of the emperor complemented this income and allowed the financial flexibility of this system.

Since the use of coins or credit was imperative for most market transactions, imperial payments and the payment of rents and taxes, the emperors opted for the imposition of a monetary monopoly, especially on precious-metal coinages. By this term, we mean that the emperor was a sole 'seller' of a product (money) with no close substitutes. Of course, the imposition of a monopoly over money is not the same as the imposition of a monopoly over other types of products. However, there are certain similarities that cannot be ignored. For example, there is a central control over the value of the goods, the state also controls the quantity of the product in circulation and, most importantly, there is a profit from these actions. In the case of the Roman Principate, the emperor supervised closely the mining of precious metals; subsequently, he was the sole authority issuing gold and silver coins and was eventually responsible for their distribution throughout the empire. This monetary monopoly eventually became another source of revenue and gave the emperor the means to increase public spending whenever he considered that necessary. But there were two advantages from the monopolistic attitude of the emperor. One was the ability to balance the budget and to have the flexibility to increase revenues and expenses at will. The second advantage came in periods of economic crisis, such as the credit crisis of the first century AD, when liquidity became a problem especially for the upper classes. Similarly, the emperor had an advantage over other entrepreneurs, in the sense that he could command substantial monetary resources when this became necessary, e.g. in periods of famine. The intervention of the state in all of these cases did not become an impediment in economic growth. On the contrary, it was essential for the healthy development of the monetary economy and the continuous operation of the markets.

CHAPTER 3

Trimetallism and bimetallic laws

MONETARY STANDARDS

When Augustus established himself as the absolute ruler over the Roman Empire, he quickly realised the need for a stable monetary system across the Mediterranean. However, instead of fashioning an entirely new system, he reinstated the bimetallic standard that his uncle, Julius Caesar, put in place a few years earlier (47–46 BC). The Augustan monetary system was the following:

4 bronze asses = 1 brass sestertius, 15 grains
4 sestertii = 1 silver denarius, about 60 grains
25 denarii = 1 gold aureus, 125 grains

Hence, the ratio between silver and gold was 12:1.[1] The coins were of fine metal; in fact, aurei were struck at forty to the Roman pound, while denarii were struck at eighty-four to the Roman pound.[2] The silver denarius was restored to 97.7–98 per cent fineness until the reign of Nero, while at least until the reign of Galba the aureus remained 98.33 per cent fine.[3] Apart from the main denominations as they are described above, the Roman mints also issued half-aureus and half-denarius pieces, called gold and silver *quinarius* respectively. Apart from the stabilisation of the monetary system, Augustus was also responsible for the increasing production of lower-denomination coins.[4] Orichalcum was used for the striking of sestertii (25 g) and dupondii (12.5 g) and copper was used for the as (11 g) and its quarter, *quadrans* (3 g).[5] Despite the use of two different metals, all of these four denominations covered the need for small change in daily transactions.

In the previous chapter I have already hinted at the fact that the imperial silver coinages minted in Rome were supplemented by a number of provincial coinages. The standards of these provincial currencies, though,

[1] Sutherland 1978: 164; Mundell 2001: 14–16.
[2] Morrisson *et al.* 1985: 82; Walker 1976–8: vol. I, 18 and 108–9. [3] Harl 1996: 74–5.
[4] Belloni 1993: 115. [5] Harl 1996: 76.

were different from the official Roman standards; instead, they followed the older Hellenistic standards. Following the annexation of the eastern provinces the Romans were not interested in imposing a uniform monetary system based on only one set of standards but allowed the production of regional currencies, as these were established after the conquests of Alexander the Great. So, although the gold aureus dominated the numismatic circulation pools, a few gold coins were also produced in the client kingdoms of Bosporus and Mauretania; there are no adequate studies on the standards of these coins. However, the process of the production of silver coins is a lot more complicated, since the mint of Rome issued only a percentage of them. For instance, within the eastern part of the Roman empire we encounter the following currencies: (a) tetradrachms, tridrachms and drachms based on the Asian cistophoric standard (and later on the Attic standard) were issued in Crete, (b) the league of Cyprus minted tetradrachms and didrachms, (c) tetradrachms, didrachms and drachms on the cistophoric standard were produced in Byzantium, (d) silver on the cistophoric standard was issued in Bithynia, while the city of Amisus struck Attic-standard tridrachms, (e) silver either on the cistophoric or the Attic standard was produced in the province of Asia, (f) drachms, hemidrachms and quarter-drachms are found in Lycia, (g) tetradrachms and tridrachms on the Attic standard were coined in Tarsus and other Cilician cities, (h) drachms, didrachms, one-and-a-half-drachms, three-quarter-drachms and hemidrachms on the Attic standard were produced in Caesarea in Cappadocia, (i) mainly tetradrachms were produced in the Syrian cities of Antioch and Tyre (although tridrachms, didrachms, drachms and hemidrachms were also issued) and (j) tetradrachms on the Ptolemaic standard were issued in Egypt.[6] Especially the silver cistophori from Asia Minor, the drachms and didrachms from Caesarea and the tetradrachms from Antioch, Tyre and Egypt circulated in their respective regions in abundance.

All of these coins remained tied to the official monetary system and became an inherent part of it, since they were exchanged at a set rate against the Roman denarius.[7] According to the editors of the *Roman Provincial Coinage*,[8] the weights of the cistophori in Asia and the Salutaris inscription indicate that these coins were tariffed at three denarii during the early Principate; thus they were employed as tridrachms. Under this system the drachm would have been estimated at three-quarters of the denarius. On

[6] Burnett *et al.* 1992: 26–30. [7] Walker 1976–8: vol. I; Howgego 1985: 52–3.
[8] Burnett, Amandry and Ripolles 1992: 26–30.

the other hand, the silver drachms of Caesarea Cappadociae were tariffed at one denarius, while the didrachms and their fractions were equivalent to two-denarii or a *quinarius*. There is also a strong possibility that the Antiochene tetradrachms until AD 60 were exchanged for three denarii, but from that date until the end of the Julio Claudian period the Neronian 'eagle' tetradrachms were exchanged for four denarii. This discrepancy could further indicate the existence of two different monetary standards even within Syria.[9] On the other hand, in the province of Egypt from the reign of Claudius or Nero the Alexandrian tetradrachm was equivalent to the denarius. During the Flavian period the picture changed only slightly. According to Carradice,[10] one Lycian drachm or one Alexandrian tetradrachm was equivalent to one denarius, one Caesarean didrachm was equivalent to two denarii, one Asian cistophorus or one Syrian tetradrachm was equivalent to three denarii and, finally, one Tarsian tetradrachm was equivalent to four denarii.

In any case, since the silver coins based on non-Roman standards were exchanged at a fixed rate against the official denarius, we may assume that debasements, devaluations or overvaluations of the denarius would have affected also the rest of the currencies. For example, the drachm had to adjust in fineness and weight in the third century AD, so that it would be exchanged for the debased denarius at the same rate as before. In the same way, the cistophori were reduced both in weight and fineness during the Severan period in order to adjust to the debasement of Septimius Severus' denarii.[11] The reason for such a reaction was so that the denarial debasements would not cause the overvaluation of the other silver coins in circulation. Since there were set exchange rates between the coins of different standards, they could co-exist within the same circulation pool; there are no attested instances of these currencies being in any competition against each other.

With regard to the lower denominations, it is evident that bronze coins were not minted entirely in Rome. Instead, the majority of small change in circulation was produced by numerous civic mints in the eastern provinces of the Roman empire. The number of mints that were intermittently active, more than 530,[12] created a mosaic of different circulation pools. The coins that emanated from the local mints of the Balkans, Asia Minor

[9] Butcher 2004: 199–200. [10] Carradice 1983: 3.

[11] Burnett 1987: 30; Harl 1996: 99–100. However, this is not always the case. For example, the Severan tetradrachms of Syria remained the same while the denarius was debased. I own this information to Kevin Butcher.

[12] For a list of civic mints in different provinces see T. Jones 1965.

and Syria were referred as 'Greek Imperials'; recently, though, another general term has become customary, a term that I intend to use in this book, 'Roman provincial coinage'. Such abundance of local mints could be explained if we take into consideration the tradition of coinages that were in circulation long before the establishment of the Roman imperial power in the provinces; until then, city-states, former Hellenistic kingdoms and local tribes issued coins intermittently and supplied them to local populations.[13] Following Roman annexation the issue of many of these coinages continued, as if nothing had happened, although the provinces were now under the administration of Rome.[14] Despite the abundance of civic mints in the eastern parts of the empire, it seems that local and Roman monetary standards may have been integrated. It has been observed that there are regional patterns of diameters and weights that may suggest the widespread adoption of the 'official' system. The extent or accuracy of these regional patterns may be far from certain but they clearly demonstrate that the denominational structure of the provincial coins is not chaotic.[15]

All in all, the metals used for commercial transactions within the Roman empire should be divided in three categories: gold, silver and bronze. The gold and silver currencies included denominations used for imperial payments or major commercial transactions, while the bronze denominations represented the small change used in daily transactions. For practical purposes the Roman emperors built a trimetallic monetary system that remained intact for almost two and a half centuries. This system could otherwise be called 'multiple commodity money',[16] according to which the monetary standard provides multiple denominations in a variety of metals. Despite the existence of coins issued in three different metals, the relationship between silver and gold currencies was ruled by the bimetallic laws that also characterise other economies. In this respect I would like to show how the monetary system of the Roman empire was similar to the later bimetallic systems of medieval and early modern Europe that also included silver, gold and bronze denominations.

BIMETALLISM AND PROFITS

As we have seen in the previous chapter, the production of coins and the imperial annual expenses were linked in an inextricable way. Therefore, it

[13] A general account of city-state coinages is given by Kraay 1976; for a general introduction on Hellenistic coinages see Mørkholm 1991.

[14] Butcher 1988b: 15. [15] Burnett *et al.* 1992: 36. [16] Redish 2000.

may be useful to take into consideration the abrupt increase in state spending during the third century (due to the political and military turmoil) and the solutions the Roman emperors came up with in order to solve the problem. The ancient sources inform us that during the first century AD the *stipendium* of an infantryman was 225 denarii per year,[17] but it was increased to 300 denarii by Domitian and remained stable until the end of the second century.[18] The next substantial increase, which is not quantified in the ancient sources, came under Septimius Severus,[19] while another increase took place during the reign of Caracalla. Although Caracalla doubled the pay of the soldiers,[20] this did not satisfy the troops and was followed by a third rise in 234 when Maximinus Thrax once again doubled their pay. Up to that time the salaries of the soldiers and their officers increased substantially, while the irregular bestowal of lavish gifts gave them an additional opportunity to augment their annual income. Dio Cassius and Herodian witnessed a series of instances, which could give an indication of the magnitude of the donatives.

For example, Septimius Severus on the tenth anniversary of his reign distributed a large sum of money that amounted to 10 aurei for each member of the Praetorian Guard.[21] Also, in AD 215 Caracalla distributed money to the soldiers – 25,000 sestertii to the praetorians and 20,000 sestertii to the rest.[22] Although, initially, Macrinus attempted to decrease the *stipendium* to the amount given previously by Septimius Severus, later, he lavished precious gifts on the troops in order to retain his political and military predominance. In AD 217 he promised a donative of 3,000 sestertii (although we do not know if he finally honoured his promise)[23] and in AD 218 he distributed 4,000 sestertii to the soldiers on the spot, while he promised a further gift of 16,000 sestertii.[24] Elagabalus upon his accession to the throne gave the usual donative to the army (although we do not know how much that was).[25] There are a few more instances of similar distributions, such as the 2,000 sestertii he gave to the soldiers in the form of a bribe, so that they would not sack the Roman city of Antioch,[26] or

17 Tac., *Ann.* 1.17.

18 Dio Cass. 67.3; Suet. *Dom.* 7.3.

19 Herodian 3.8.4; SHA, *Sev.* 12.2.

20 Herodian 4.4.7.

21 Dio Cass. 77.1.1–2. Septimius also gave another donative to the soldiers in the beginning of his career as an emperor but it is not quantified in Herodian (2.14.5). On the other hand Dio Cassius mentions the payment of only 250 denarii (46.46.7).

22 Dio Cass. 78.24.1. Referring to the same episode Herodian (4.4.7) mentions the promise of 2,500 Attic drachms. At another time Caracalla gives money to the soldiers upon his visit to Troy but the amount is not quantified (Dio Cass. 78.16.7).

23 Dio Cass. 79.19.2

24 Dio Cass. 79.34.2–3.

25 Herodian 5.5.8.

26 Dio Cass. 80.1.1–2.

during the preparation of an elaborate dinner at the cost of 400 sestertii a piece on his wedding day.[27]

It is worth noting that not only emperors but also other members of the imperial family could abuse the treasury and distribute donatives to the soldiers, an example of which is the clandestine handout by Mamaea.[28] During the war against Artabanus Alexander Severus found it useful to promise similar gifts to the fighting units,[29] while another distribution of money probably took place when they returned to Antioch.[30] The same policy suited emperor Maximinus, who promised the soldiers generous donatives both in cash and in kind upon his accession to the throne.[31] The uncertainty of the times required that he would continue the practice of similar money distributions throughout his reign.[32] In addition, we should take into account the ancient authors, who repeatedly testify to an increase in imperial largesses made to the general population. For example, Dio Cass. 77. 1, 1–2:

> On the occasion of the tenth anniversary of his coming to power (202 AD) Severus presented to the entire populace that received the grain dole and to the soldiers of the praetorian guard gold pieces equal in number to the years of his reign. He prided himself especially of this largess and, in fact, no emperor had ever before given so much to the whole population at once; the total amount spent for the purpose was 200 million sesterces.

These largesses probably burdened the imperial treasury as much as the donatives that were distributed to the soldiers.

The increase in military expenses during the third century was not accompanied by an increase in annual revenues from imperialistic wars. As early as the reign of Augustus, the Roman emperors ceased pursuing the easy profit that came with the annexation of new provinces. Instead, they focused on the maintenance of the existing borders and they sought revenues from other, mainly domestic, resources. The total increase in the necessary volume of precious-metal coins in the Roman Treasury normally burdened the inhabitants of the empire with the imposition of taxes. According to our sources, though, new taxes were not raised during the third century, probably because such an act could have caused social disturbances. In fact, when the emperor Caracalla increased indirect taxes up to 10 per cent (instead of the traditionally imposed 5 per cent) on the value

[27] Dio Cass. 80.9.1–2. [28] Herodian 5.8.3. [29] Herodian 6.4.1. [30] Herodian 6.6.4.

[31] Herodian 7.3.5. This is the first time that Herodian and Dio mention the distribution of money as well as goods to the army.

[32] Herodian in 7.8.9 mentions a generous handout of money to the soldiers before the battle occurred.

of inheritances and the purchase of slaves, he received the negative comments of contemporary ancient historians.[33] Since the emperors needed to find alternative sources of revenue as soon as possible, they reverted to the long-established fiscal practice of re-coining and manipulating the coinage in circulation. The imperial authorities continuously withdrew from circulation the older silver coins of higher fineness, through the use of the taxation system. Subsequently, the imperial mints melted down the precious-metal coins and added more base metals to the new issues; this way the silver coinage of the era became debased. Effectively these mints managed to produce more pieces of silver coin intended for the payments of the soldiers, even though the available amount of precious bullion within the empire remained the same.[34]

Debasement practices have been attested as early as the Republican period, when we notice changes in the fineness and weight standards of the silver coins. In these cases, it is important to note that the exchange rates were not adjusted; at least, not immediately. The reason for the minting of these new heavily debased issues was the production of more pieces of silver coin used for state payments. During the Roman Principate the emperors acknowledged the financial potential of the manipulation of the monetary standards and continued the debasement of their currencies. The manipulation of the silver coinage became an acceptable procedure that allowed emperors to pay for their expenditures, especially when they faced financial difficulties. In fact, Nero partly reformed the Augustan coinage by decreasing the fineness of the imperial denarii from 98 per cent to 93.5 per cent, thus reducing the weight standard from 1/84 to 1/96 of a pound. Slight debasements of the denarius continued throughout the next century, during which time the fineness of the coin was reduced to around 90 per cent. The next more substantial debasement took place during the reign of Marcus Aurelius, who reduced the fineness of the denarius further to less than 80 per cent.[35] It is important to note that none of the above debasements became the reason for changing the face value of the silver currencies or affected the structure of the monetary system in any significant way.

Septimius Severus was the first emperor who attempted more radical reforms and alloyed the denarius to a greater extent than his predecessors.

[33] Dio Cass. 78.9.1–6 and others were against this measure.

[34] For mean weight of silver in silver coins from the reign of Septimius Severus until the reign of Aemilian see: Walker 1976–8: vol. I, 49–50. Walker's results have been corrected by Butcher and Ponting 1997. The extent of the silver debasements is also described in Bland 1996a: 78–9.

[35] Harl 1996: 91–6.

With these actions he aimed at a substantial increase in the annual silver output that, in turn, would have given him the financial capacity to pay for his wars, his elaborate buildings and his lavish largesses. Specifically, the denarius' fineness was gradually reduced from 65 per cent in AD 194 to about 50 per cent three years later, although the weight may have been improved slightly.[36] His successor, Caracalla, followed similar policies in an attempt to increase the revenues of the imperial treasury. However, instead of reducing the fineness of the denarius, he introduced a new overvalued silver denomination, termed for the first time in the *Historia Augusta* as antoninianus.[37] The commercial value remained higher than its real one. Although according to its weight the antoninianus should have been exchanged for one-and-a-half denarii,[38] in reality it was accepted as an overvalued double piece,[39] as the portrait with the radiate crown on the obverse indicates. Furthermore the exchange rate of antoniniani to aurei must have been expressed in a single round-numbered equation, as the rest of the denominations; hence, one antoninianus was probably exchanged for two denarii or twelve antoniniani for one aureus.[40]

Even after the introduction of the antoninianus by Caracalla, the denarius continued to be the basic silver denomination in circulation until AD 238. The small number of antoniniani in the markets ensured that the economic impact of this highly overvalued new silver piece was limited; in fact, it does not seem to have affected major transactions, where denarii continued to be employed.The Roman emperors discontinued the production of antoniniani in AD 219 and these coins did not reappear until their reintroduction by Balbinus and Pupienus in 238 at a reduced weight of 4.75 g, as an attempt to ameliorate the finances of the state even at the expense of stable coinage.[41] Finally, during the reign of Gordian III, the production of the antoniniani increased in an extraordinary way and the new coin almost replaced the older denarius in major transactions, as the evidence from coin hoards shows.[42]

Further debasements of the silver currency followed during the period of the Military Anarchy. Each emperor, in an attempt to acquire the money that would allow the continuation of his wars, lowered the purity of the

[36] For mean weight of silver in silver coins from the reign of Septimius Severus until the reign of Aemilian see: Walker 1976–8: vol. III, 49–50. Walker's results have been corrected by Butcher and Ponting 1997. Bland 1996a and Lo Cascio 1984 believe that the face value of the antoniniani was also rated at $1\frac{1}{2}$ denarii. However, in this case there would have been no financial gain from its introduction.

[37] SHA *M. Ant.* 28.15.8 *argentei Antoniniani.* [38] Callu 1969: 164 ff.

[39] Bastien 1992: 107–8. [40] For a detailed presentation of this hypothesis see Sperber 1974: 38–46.

[41] Carson 1990: 232 and 234. [42] See chapter 4.

antoninianus, while at the same time he withdrew the coins of his predecessors and melted them into new debased issues. This period was characterised by monetary changes both in weight standards and particularly in fineness standards, although the coins' face value probably did not alter with the same speed. The fineness of the antoninianus of the latest coinage of Trajan Decius was about 40 per cent, but from this period onwards the debasement became more rapid until the fineness dropped to 5 per cent in the issues of about AD 266. By the end of the reign of Gallienus the fineness of the antoniniani had dropped to about 2.5 per cent, thus turning silver coins into billon coins of small value. The situation did not improve until the reign of Constantine the Great, although two monetary reforms had already taken place during the reigns of Aurelian and Diocletian.[43]

These consecutive debasements would have brought substantial profits to the imperial treasury only if the financial authorities were aware of the existence of basic bimetallic laws and aimed at their implementation. So far, we have evidence that pre-industrial as well as modern societies manipulated their bimetallic monetary systems in order to increase their revenues. The process of this manipulation is well known to contemporary historians who are trying to reconstruct the mechanism of ancient economies. The term 'bimetallism' was initially used in 1869 by Enrico Cernuschi (1821–96), an Italian-French economist and an advocate of the system. A bimetallic monetary standard can be defined as one in which coins of two different metals (usually precious ones) are legal tender. The central authorities who are responsible for the production of these currencies give them an exchange value that to some extent reflects their intrinsic value. In fact, the prices of gold and silver were determined by their relative supply and demand (both monetary and non-monetary) and this determined both the stock of money and the general price level. The small difference of the value of the metal from the value of the coin (the second was slightly higher) represented the seignorage that covered the cost of minting.[44] In some cases, though, the authorities paid no attention to the rule that the intrinsic value of the coins should almost coincide with their face value and this disregard ensured higher profits. The monetary reforms that took place in the Roman empire during the third century AD reflect exactly this manipulation of the existing bimetallic system.

The first question we should answer is whether the emperors were aware of bimetallic laws or whether they were willing to implement them. As we have already seen, substantial debasement of the silver coinages took place

[43] Carson 1990: 234. [44] Friedman 1990; Bordo 1992; Redish 2000.

during the Principate, and especially after the end of the Antonine dynasty. If the system was not a bimetallic one, then we should have noticed the matching debasement of the gold coinage. Such a debasement would have ensured that the exchange rate between the silver and gold coins remained constant both in terms of their face and their intrinsic value. However, we do not observe analogous reductions in the weight or the fineness of the aureus. The aureus, the gold denomination that weighed the same for about the first twenty years of the third century (except for the later coinage of Macrinus and the early issues of Elagabalus), remained almost intact until the reign of Gordian III. In fact, Septimius Severus not only did not debase the coin but he also restored the aureus, which had been reduced in weight by his predecessor, to its full weight and he maintained it at 7.2 g until AD 215. However, it should be noted that the mean weight of the aurei in circulation in the western provinces was reduced from 6.3–6.7 g during the reign of Severus Alexander to 4.5–4.8 g during the reign of Gordian III; this reduction may be a further indication of substantial changes in the monetary system during this time.

The gold coins underwent sharper declines in weight also later, from AD 238 until AD 268; nevertheless, their fineness did not diminish until the reign of Gallienus. Specifically, Philip's aurei weighed on average 4.62 g, while most aurei issued during the reign of Trebonianus Gallus weighed less than 4 g. Valerian gave the final blow to the gold currency when he reduced its fineness by 65 per cent. However, even then, when silver coins contained almost no silver at all, gold coins retained comparatively higher fineness.[45] The high fineness of the gold coinage along with the comparatively insignificant fluctuations of its weight until the reign of Gordian III intended to give the impression of monetary stability. The illusion of stability was crucial for the prosperity of the empire, since it ensured the uninhibited circulation of the official currency in market transactions. The imperial protection of the enforced monetary system (despite the reforms) provided the Romans with an imperial guarantee for the safety of their accumulated wealth. Whether this wealth was in the form of silver or gold or other denominations the owner felt that he still had the ability to exchange it for the same number of gold coins as before. The trust of the population in the imperial power and the apparent stability of the monetary system allowed for the continuous circulation of the debased

[45] Bland 1996a: 67–73; Morrisson *et al.* 1985: 82–84. For the comparative analysis of gold and silver fineness see Duncan-Jones 1994: 217, table 15.3.

silver coins, as long as they could be exchanged for the unadulterated gold aurei.

The fact that the fineness and weight of the gold coins did not follow the debasement of the silver coins could also indicate the wish of the emperors to maintain the existing exchange rates for as long as possible. Although denarii had undergone significant reduction in weight and fineness, we should not automatically assume that the central authorities aimed at the alteration of the ratio of the denarius to the aureus. So far, we know that the denarius had been tariffed at twenty-five to the aureus in the time of Augustus and this ratio remained the same probably until the end of the Severan dynasty. In fact, the last piece of written evidence we have on the exchange rates comes from the reign of Severus Alexander. A familiar passage from Dio Cassius informs us that a gold coin (*chrysous*) was still worth twenty-five denarii when he wrote his History.[46] So far, we have seen that the numerous and in some cases substantial silver debasements were not followed by similar debasements of the gold coins during this time. The fact that the exchange rates remained the same, despite the reduction in fineness of the silver currency, indicates the power of the central authorities to reform the monetary system without radically changing it. Changes, though, were inevitable and they eventually took place later, sometime between the reign of Maximinus and the mid third century AD.[47] In fact, I would like to suggest that the turning point was probably the reign of Gordian III for two reasons.

Firstly, at that time, the highly undervalued antoniniani replaced the denarii in both regional and interregional markets.[48] Until then, no other emperor attempted to replace a coin that had enjoyed the trust of the population for two-and-a-half centuries. Although we are not certain how the population reacted to the new and undervalued silver coin, we may assume that part of the trust they showed in the monetary system would have been lost. Secondly, for the first time, the weight of the gold coins was reduced.

If we take into consideration also the simultaneous radical change of the silver in circulation, we may assume that the imperial authorities were trying to adjust the exchange rates in a way that would have been acceptable

[46] Dio Cass. 55.12.5; Buttrey 1961. Other researchers prefer a later date for the alteration of the exchange rates (Lo Cascio 1997). Lo Cascio argues that prices remained comparatively stable until the mid third century and he attributes the fact to the stable exchange rates that were imposed by the state. Only when the rates altered during the reigns of Claudius and Tacitus did the prices in gold suddenly increase.

[47] Bland 1997: 34.

[48] See chapter 4.

to the receivers of the new coins. Despite the significance of Gordian's reforms, it is not sensible to assume that the emperor would have adjusted the exchange rates as fast as the coinage was debased, mainly because this undertaking would have reduced his profits. The process of changing the exchange rates may have taken more time; in fact, they may have changed de facto in the course of commercial transactions, before an imperial decree acknowledged this change. Some scholars have suggested that, if rates were not fixed and they followed naturally the debasement of silver coinage, the denarius would have been tariffed at fifty to the aureus as early as the reign of Septimius Severus. In the beginning of the third century, though, the imperial government was still powerful and it could guarantee the face value of the coins; hence the exchange rates were not altered. This power decreased over time and by the reign of Trajan Decius we have for the first time evidence of a definite change of the rates between gold and silver coins, since we find antoniniani overstruck on older denarii.[49] If the Decian antoninianus had the same value as the denarii of the previous reigns, then by this time one aureus would be exchanged with 50 debased denarii or twenty-five antoniniani. However, this evidence is not adequate to help us determine the exact ratio between gold and silver, while it does not give us specific information on the exact point in time of this alteration. The only certainty is that by the reign of Gallienus the monetary system collapsed and at that time the exchange rates were entirely different from the ones set by Augustus.

The financial behaviour of the state was a rational one and can easily be explained if we take into consideration the situation that triggered the monetary reforms. It is important to note that the debasement of silver coinage was intended to cover the expenses of the army, such as the continuous increase of payments[50] (but also equipment and the funding of an increasing number of military campaigns). Recently, it has been suggested that the annual payment of the soldiers and their officers was calculated in aurei during the Principate.[51] If we accept this view, we should also acknowledge that the gold aureus (and not the denarius or the sestertius, as commonly assumed) behaved as a unit of account, at least in connection with military payments. It seems possible, though, that the soldiers usually received more easily exchangeable monetary units, such as silver denarii and in some cases a range of imperial and civic bronze coins. If this is true, then the debasement of the denarii and the issue of

[49] H. Mattingly 1939; Carson 1965: 230.
[50] Herodian 3.8.4 and 4.4.7.; SHA, *Sev.*, 12.2.
[51] Alston 1994.

antoniniani in the third century probably had two consequences: (a) it allowed for the production of more silver coins destined for the payment of the soldiers, without the need to resort to new sources of bullion; (b) it did not provoke the resentment of the soldiers, whose salary was still calculated in aurei of higher fineness and weight, even though they usually got paid in debased denarii. The soldiers would continue to trust the new silver coins, which contained less precious metal, mainly because they could exchange them with the same number of gold coins as before. The emperors probably anticipated that the stable weight of the gold coinage would guarantee the value of debased denarii and eventually would stabilise the monetary system. It seems, though, that the local populations who controlled regional markets were not ready to accept innovations, such as the continuous debasements of silver coinages, indefinitely, even if it was supported by the gold currency; this attitude resulted in the limited alteration of the exchange rates a few decades after the reforms of Septimius Severus.

The above numismatic evidence shows that the uninterrupted use of the two precious-metal coinages within the empire and the stability of their exchange rate facilitated the repeated manipulation of the monetary system. During the first two centuries the emperors reduced the fineness of the silver coins to some extent (as long as this reduction would not seriously interfere with commercial transactions), while they maintained the fine quality of the aureus. Their purpose was to keep one part of the dual relation stable (gold), whilst the second (silver) could fluctuate freely, so that the higher fineness of the aureus would eventually guarantee the value of the denarius. The success of this practice until the third century AD confirms that the cautious debasement of one of the two metals could bring additional profits to the imperial treasury. Thus the imposition of a bimetallic system in the economy was advantageous when the emperors needed to increase their financial capacity at the expense of the existing currency. Similar instances of the use of bimetallic laws for increasing governmental revenues in periods of financial pressures are evident also in other pre-modern and modern societies.

In fact, it would have been surprising if numismatic debasements were not taking place as often as they did. As a prominent example we could offer the case of France between the Carolingian reforms and 1360, during which time a large number of mints competed against each other in order to attract more customers. The possibility of a debasement gave them the opportunity to increase both the seignorage rate and the quantity of the silver returning to the mint. The attraction of more silver was achieved by issuing silver deniers of lower fineness and, thus, offering a slightly higher mint price. Such slight debasements were profitable for both the minting authorities and the citizens, since payments were made in deniers or sealed bags of undifferentiated deniers. The increasing production of coinage, initially, financed the wars with England and Flanders (1295–1313). Later, between 1337 and 1360, eighty-seven numismatic reforms took place, which provided the money for the Hundred Years War. As long as the minting authorities managed to 'fool' the people about the fineness of the intrinsic metal, the revenues will have remained high.[52] Similar profits were achieved in the Roman empire before the period of the Military Anarchy, when the debasements were not considerable and, thus, did not affect the basic structure of the enforced bimetallic system.

ABUSES OF THE BIMETALLIC SYSTEM

The use of multiple-commodity money presents the government with a problem. It has been observed that there is 'a difficulty maintaining a constant relationship between coins in two or more different metals when their relative market prices could, and did, vary'.[53] Accordingly, Roman imperial laws may have determined the official ratio between gold and silver coins but this exchange rate was independent of the commercial value of the metals, which fluctuated constantly at a different exchange rate. Consequently, it is possible that the excessive debasements from the reign of Gordian III onwards caused additional problems that were not initially predicted by the central authorities; hence, the exchange rates between silver and gold coinages were eventually altered.

The first problem arising from the fluctuation of the commercial price of the two metals is understandable, if we apply Gresham's Law, according to which 'bad money drives out good'. In our case, 'bad money' is overvalued coins of lower fineness (silver) and 'good' money is undervalued coins of higher fineness (gold). Within the bimetallic system the minted coins that were commercially valued at less than their face value tended to be used as money, while the coins commercially valued at more than their face value tended to be used as commodity. Consequently, the undervalued coins were withdrawn from circulation as money, thereby turning bimetallism into an unstable monetary system that could not be sustained. There are two main ways to drive 'good' money from circulation: (a) hoarding or (b) exporting to an area where legal tender laws cannot be enforced. It

[52] Redish 2000: 35, 45–8. [53] Redish 2000: 26.

has been observed that the treatment of only one precious-metal coin as money, while the second is driven out of circulation, undermines the nature of bimetallism, which is a system that functions effectively only when it is based on the monetary use of both metals.[54] The Romans probably were aware of Gresham's Law and took advantage of its effects, when they took part in monetary transactions. In fact, the disappearance of 'good' coins from circulation and their replacement with 'bad' coins after the debasement of precious metal coinages was common knowledge as early as the fifth century BC.[55]

We know that such a decline in the circulation of gold coins in the markets took place also during later historical periods as a result of the flaws of the bimetallic system. However, what was the exact mechanism that drove 'good' money out of the circulation pools? During the medieval period we notice that

> wherever or whenever both gold and silver were in use as currency there was always the possibility that the ratios between the two metals would move sufficiently far apart in two countries to make it worth while to export silver from one country to another in return for gold . . . From time to time the relative values of the two metals were sufficiently far apart not only to dictate which metal was to be carried in ordinary commercial dealings, but to make the coinages themselves objects of commerce.[56]

Such bimetallic flows existed between France and Italy in the latter part of the reign of Philip IV, when he raised the value of gold in terms of silver even higher than in Italy. As a consequence, silver flowed out of France in exchange for gold florins that arrived from Italy. The same situation occurred in England, when it adopted a higher value for its gold than on the Continent around 1307. Also, Venice had to face similar problems between the 1320s and 1330s, when it replaced silver with gold as the principal means of payment. The great influx of gold and the diminution of silver supplies caused the ratio between gold and silver to be fixed without taking into consideration the realities of the market. So, silver flowed out of Venice, whilst gold was imported in vast quantities.[57] Two centuries later, in 1544, King Henry VIII of England introduced a dramatic debasement of silver coins coupled with a more modest debasement of gold coins, thus distorting the bimetallic ratio. The merchants who realised that gold was undervalued in England would acquire gold coins at their face value and

[54] Laughlin 1897; Flynn 1982. The value of Gresham's Law has been questioned by Rolnick and Weber 1986. For a revision of these views see Selginc 1996.

[55] Ar. *Ran.* 718–26. See chapter 1.

[56] Spufford 1988: 274.

[57] Spufford 1988: 277 and 283.

would then export them to Flanders in exchange for silver. Subsequently, they imported this silver back to England in order for it to be coined, so that they would profit from the difference in value. In the meantime, gold continued to be struck until 1549 when a real outflow of these coins took place.[58]

Undoubtedly, Gresham's Law was in force also in the Roman Principate. The repeated debasements of silver coinage and the higher fineness of aurei affected the circulation of gold coins within the empire as well as beyond the Roman frontiers. During the third century and for the first time in the Roman empire the circulation patterns of gold coinage changed radically, probably in every province. Especially in the eastern provinces of Syria and Asia Minor we encounter no known gold coin hoards from the Severan and the Military Anarchy period, unlike the previous era.[59] The structure of the coin finds from the Balkans presents us with the same picture. Specifically, only one aureus was found in a Valerian silver coin hoard coming from Pannonia.[60] Another aureus issued during the reign of Caracalla comes from a silver hoard from Nicolaevo (Moesia), whose burial took place after the reign of Philip.[61]

Although I admit that the number of gold hoards from the first and the second centuries AD is not large, the fact that gold coins have altogether disappeared from our third-century records from such a vast area cannot be ignored. The results from the study of the eastern provinces, however, cannot validate any wider conclusions concerning the economic policies of the Roman emperors, unless they are compared with the numismatic evidence coming from other areas of the empire. An analysis of the finds from the western provinces of the Roman empire indicates the same patterns in the circulation of gold coinage during the third century, although sometimes the results present slight variations. Specifically, fifty-five gold coin hoards and seventeen mixed (gold and silver) hoards were buried and were never recovered in Britain, western Europe, Italy and the Danube during the first two centuries of the Principate, while only an insignificant number of small gold coin hoards were lost in the same regions during the third century.[62] Furthermore, after AD 215 hoards of gold coins become

58 Gould 1970; Chown 1994: 49–50.

59 According to publication records, only four gold hoards were buried in the eastern provinces (excluding Egypt) during the first and second centuries AD: the Patra Hoard, the Caesarea Hoard, the Turkey 2 Hoard and the Kusakkaya Hoard.

60 Mirnik 1981: 73, no. 246.

61 Seure 1923: 111–53.

62 The number of gold coin hoards lost in the western provinces during the first two centuries of the Roman empire is substantially higher than the number of gold coin hoards lost in the eastern

smaller.[63] In these areas, the few stray gold coins that have been published also indicate the decline of the circulation of gold coinage within the empire[64] (except in Noricum and in the two Pannonias).

The disappearance of gold coins from circulation continued well beyond the third century and up until the first half of the fourth century AD, although occasionally we encounter some hoards that include gold pieces. Several studies and a survey of the numismatic finds have brought to our attention the absence of gold coins from the Roman provinces in the Balkans during most of the fourth century. The unearthing of a few gold coins has been considered an exception and has been attributed to enemy raids or subsidies paid to the barbarians by the Roman government. This pattern changed only during the late fourth century, from which period come several solidi; thus, these clearly reflect the presence of increasing quantities of gold coins in circulation.[65] The findings from the Balkans could be compared with the findings from another part of the Roman empire, Roman Britain. Also in this case the number of gold coin hoards lost during the first half of the fourth century was lower in comparison to the number of gold coin hoards lost during the first two centuries AD.[66] Similarly, the number of solidius finds from Gaul from the first half of the fourth century confirms that their impact in the interregional markets was probably negligible.[67] Finally, the study of the numismatic evidence from the provinces of Asia Minor and Syria indicates that the circulation of gold coins in the Roman empire was anything but widespread during the fourth century.

Other epigraphic and numismatic evidence from the middle of the third century also demonstrates changes in the attitude of the population regarding the use of gold currency. These changes are probably related

provinces during the same period, according to extensive excavations and subsequent publications. A list of these hoards has been published in Duncan-Jones 1994: 262–263. Bland (1997: 35) estimates that during the third century only eleven out of sixty-one hoards in the western Roman empire contain only gold coins. Furthermore, of those eleven hoards, only four contain significant quantities of aurei, while the rest either include gold multiples, or consist of only two specimens, or are only known from incomplete records.

63 Bland 1997: 35.

64 King 1993: 443, table no. 2. King based these results on the following publications: Callu and Loriot 1992: 26–7; Bost, Campo and Gurt 1983: 140–1; Bost, Campo and Gurt 1992; Loriot 1988: 64–6. More detailed analysis in Bland 1996a: 81, table 1, where the number of stray finds from the western provinces has been estimated per year. He uses the numismatic data from the following publications: Callu and Loriot 1990; Brenot and Loriot 1992.

65 Duncan 1993.

66 Carson and Burnett 1979; Burnett 1981; Bland 1982; Burnett 1984a; Burnett 1984b; Burnett and Bland 1986; Burnett and Bland 1987; Bland and Orna-Ornstein 1984; Robertson 2000.

67 Depeyrot 1982.

to the disappearance of the aurei from the circulation pools and the new attitude of the Roman population towards these scarce issues. According to one inscription it was an honour and a privilege for someone to be paid by the emperor in gold coins; so, aurei seem to have been used as gifts of incalculable value.[68] Naturally, the practice of giving gold coins as gifts pre-existed the monetary reforms of Military Anarchy emperors, as other inscriptions indicate. For example, an account from AD 220 informs us that Sennius Solemnis received his salary from the governor of his province in gold.[69] Despite the high moral (and economic) value of gold throughout the Roman Principate, even before the end of the Severan period, by the mid third century its mention on inscriptions or literary sources became rare and should be considered exceptional. By that time, the bestowal of gold coins or bullion became the standard way for the emperor to reward his subjects for their outstanding loyalty and their special services. However, the act of paying citizens or soldiers in aurei would have been considered such an honour only if the state avoided similar payments on a regular basis.

If we take into consideration Gresham's Law, it seems that the abuse of the bimetallic standard could have caused problems not only to the medieval and early modern economies but also to the Roman economy. As we have already seen, during the medieval period the undervalued gold coins flowed outside the area where they were produced and were sold there for profit. For similar reasons gold coins produced during the third century AD have not been found in hoards or as stray finds (at least not in substantial numbers). In the following paragraphs I would like to present the hypothesis that the scarcity of gold bullion in the Roman empire during the third century AD may have brought about an increase in the value of gold as a commodity and the overvaluation of silver coins may have caused the further devaluation of aurei and their subsequent disappearance from the markets, as we are about to see.

We may safely assume that in the Roman empire the government intervened in order to establish a relative price between gold and silver coins, since any other options would have been unprofitable and even risky. Specifically, the ratio between silver and gold issues was 12:1; hence, twenty-five denarii could be sold for one aureus. Despite the direct imperial intervention in the case of precious-metal currencies, there is no evidence (at least not before the reign of Diocletian) indicating any imperial intervention in

[68] *CIL* 13. 3162; Mrozek 1973. [69] Devijver 1977: 729–30; Devijver 1987: 1718.

the exchange of metals as commodities in regional and interregional markets. Therefore, since imperial restrictions and regulations in that sector were limited, it seems possible that the prices of gold and silver bullion were regulated not by the government but by the laws of the market, such as the law of supply and demand. These prices would have fluctuated according to (a) the demands of both the population and the central authorities for more metal and (b) the amount (supply) of silver and gold bullion available in the markets.

We have seen in the previous chapter how the demand for more precious metals (destined for coined money) may have increased during the third century due to an increase in aggregate military costs. However, this demand was not necessarily met by the existing supplies for two reasons. First of all, the imperial treasury did not receive adequate quantities of silver or gold metals from the 'barbarians', since the Roman state no longer got involved in imperialistic wars. As I have already mentioned, the purpose of warfare changed during the early Principate, since emperors concentrated their efforts on defending the existing frontiers instead of expanding them. In fact, the Roman empire did not seem to experience any major inflows of precious metals after the reign of Trajan, who annexed Dacia, a province rich in gold. By the third century defensive wars did not bring enough profit or raw bullion to allow an increase of revenues and subsequent extensive mint activity.

Secondly, we have no information indicating an increase in the supply of precious metals from the provincial mines of Spain, the Balkans or elsewhere. In fact, if we take into account the silence of the ancient sources in conjunction with the absence of mines in the archaeological record, we may assume that the number of gold mines was probably reduced by the beginning of the third century. Modern researchers have already suggested that Spanish gold mines, which until then provided the central mint with the essential metals, became inactive;[70] therefore, the availability of gold bullion in the markets in the long run could have been reduced. However, there is no indication that there was a complete dearth of available bullion, despite the fact that the literary sources do not note the existence of gold mines from the reign of Septimius Severus onwards. We should not exclude the possibility that already established mines, which are not mentioned by ancient authors, continued to supply the Roman state with precious metals. For example, it is probable that the gold mines in the Balkan province of

[70] Davies 1935: 198–206; Domergue 1990: 215–24.

Dacia, which was not lost until AD 270, continued to be used throughout the third century and thus generated large quantities of gold bullion.

The escalation of the defensive or civil wars, the closure of the Spanish mines and the lack of literary evidence regarding the influx of gold bullion indicates that the amount of gold metal in the markets was definitely not increasing, if not reducing. The stock of available coins would have shrunk even further because of the natural loss and wear of coins. However, the corrosion of the gold coins in circulation or within a hoard may have been substantially lower than the corrosion of the silver and bronze coins. R. Duncan-Jones, who estimated the differences in weight loss between the three metals – gold, silver, bronze – suggested that the weight loss for the Roman period was probably for gold around 0.0226 per cent, for silver 0.0598 per cent and for bronze 0.1715 per cent.[71] Since the weight loss of the gold currency was so small, we should emphasise more the evidence for the draining of the circulation pools through the regular export of coins to the *barbaricum*[72] or through their natural loss during transactions. Although the daily loss of coins was inevitable, the ruling elite was fully aware of the disadvantages attached to the unregulated export of gold coins (outside the Roman empire the debased silver coins were not accepted as medium of exchange) and advised against it.[73] However, it is not certain whether this advice took the form of law or was completed disregarded. In any case, the inability of the Roman state during the third century to replenish the markets with 'fresh' gold metal and the gradual 'loss' of the gold coinage could have caused the rise of its commercial price, according to the Law of supply and demand. At the same time, while the value of the metal sold in the markets was probably raised, the value of the gold coins would have remained the same in order to assure the profits of the central government through the maintenance of the gold:silver exchange rates. Nevertheless, such a situation could only cause the slight devaluation of the aurei in circulation in relation to the price of gold as a commodity.

Undoubtedly, the overvaluation of silver coins through their continuous debasements caused the deterioration of the above situation. During the reign of Septimius Severus, a serious problem possibly originated from an alteration of the weight standards, which was not followed by the natural adjustment of exchange rates. The debasement and consequent overvaluation of denarii probably would have caused the eventual devaluation of

71 Duncan-Jones 1987; Duncan-Jones 1994: 181. 72 Harl 1996: 290 ff.

73 Plin. *HN* 12.41.84. The author, who lived during the first century AD, informs us that the Romans spent more than 25 million denarii (equivalent to one million aurei) per annum on spices that were imported into the empire.

gold coins if the state insisted on sustaining the existing rates.[74] If we take into consideration Gresham's Law, which states that 'bad money drives away good', then we may anticipate a series of hypothetical reactions. For instance, if gold coins were undervalued, then gold bullion would have been valued at a higher price. If the inhabitants of the empire were aware that uncoined metal was sold in the markets for a higher price (and there is no reason to suppose that they were ignorant of this fact), they would have been inclined to melt down the coins and use them as bullion. Actually, we cannot exclude the possibility that the Romans would have tried to 'buy' from the mint gold coins at a lower price, then they would have melted them down and, finally, they would have sold them as bullion in order to get a better price. The immediate effect of this attitude would have been the draining of gold from the monetary metal stock.

Changes in the economic behaviour of the population due to the devaluation of aurei are not attested in the literary sources but they are evident in the archaeological record. For example, gold coins from coin hoards that were buried during the third century have been found pierced, which implies that they were used as jewellery. Although this practice was avoided during the Antonine period, it became widespread from the reign of Septimius Severus onwards. In particular, it has been estimated that by the reign of Trajan Decius pierced gold coins amounted to as many as 27.4 per cent of the total gold coins found in hoards, while this proportion rose even higher after AD 253.[75] Other aurei were mounted in jewellery. This procedure also indicates that the gold coins became demonetised, even though they were still considered a form of wealth. Most of these gold coins were found in the western provinces, specifically in Lugdunensis. However, a number of them were located outside the borders of the Roman empire, in the *barbaricum*, where they may have been sold at higher prices. The phenomenon ceased in the west with the fall of the Gallic empire, although it continued in the *barbaricum*.[76] So, it is obvious that both Romans and barbarians tended to treat gold coins as a valuable commodity as well as a sign of wealth for almost a century. At this point we should note that, despite the fact that the practice of mounting started after the middle of the third century, the coins themselves were issued between AD 96 and AD 235; hence, they were comparatively heavy aurei of higher fineness. Another example from the western Roman Empire demonstrates the demonetisation of gold currency. The rare gold coin hoards that were buried during the third century included also jewellery,[77] in contrast with

74 The phenomenon is initially mentioned in Duncan-Jones 1994: 218.

75 Bland 1997: 34–5. 76 Brenot and Metzger 1992. 77 Huvelin and Loriot 1992.

previous periods when the majority of hoards contained only coins. This phenomenon also indicates that gold coins during the third century were probably handled as artistic artefacts of certain value or even raw bullion rather than money.

The demonetisation of gold coins is a phenomenon that recurs in economic history, specifically when the price of gold as a commodity increases considerably. An example is presented in a study of the currency of the Mughal empire during the seventeenth century, in which it has been suggested that the price of gold rose by 71 per cent in the 1670s and by 47 per cent in the 1690s. The immediate outcome of this change was its demonetisation, since rich people preferred to hoard it both in bullion and in coin form, instead of using it as money. Furthermore, as in the Roman empire during the third century, researchers noticed a widespread tendency to convert gold coins into jewellery and other craft objects. The issuing of gold coins (*muhr*) in the Mughal empire suffered a continuous decline, while at the same time the import of gold as a commodity rose by 10 to 15 per cent during the seventeenth century. Also in this case, researchers assumed that the imported metal was not converted into money but was absorbed into the non-monetary sector of the Mughal economy. The reason for the demonetisation of gold lies once more in the abuse of the trimetallic monetary system, which included gold, silver and copper denominations at fixed rates. This Islamic society seems to have followed the bimetallic rules that defined the relationship of the pre-existing Byzantine and Sassanian coins. Specifically, laws fixed the bimetallic rates in an attempt to 'ensure rightful exchange (*sarf*) and to uphold the Quranic prohibition against usury'. However, between 1615 and 1705 the quantity of silver rose, while it suffered depreciation against both gold and copper. As in the Roman empire, the fixed exchange rates became unstable because of the overvaluation of one metal (silver) and the devaluation of the other (gold) and, hence, the second gradually disappeared from the markets and became demonetised.[78]

During the medieval period the export of gold and silver coins in different countries became a regular practice, when the value of one of these precious metals was maintained at a higher level in only one of the countries. The difference in the price had to be sufficiently wide in order to cover the costs of transportation and the potential risks of such long trips. Entrepreneurs may have followed the same course of action in the Roman empire, although at a significantly smaller scale, if we take into account the number of coins that have been found outside the Roman

[78] Haider 1999; quotation from p. 313.

borders. It is true that, particularly in the third century, the export of gold coins to the *barbaricum* increased substantially. For example, recent publications of stray finds from Central Europe indicate a substantial rise in the volume of aurei in regions beyond the borders of the Roman Empire,[79] at a time when gold coins almost disappear from the regional markets. It is also interesting to note that the overall number of gold coins exported during the third century increased fourfold in comparison to the numbers found in the *barbaricum* during the first and second centuries AD. The volume of stray finds from areas beyond the *limes* may have decreased again during the fourth century, but the number of these coins remained higher than the number of aurei lost during the first two centuries.[80]

Modern researchers usually try to explain the absence of gold coins from the Roman empire as the direct result of subsidies and gifts paid to the barbaric tribes from the reign of Diocletian onwards.[81] There are two problems, though, regarding the hypothesis that the state exported most of the gold coins to the *barbaricum* during this period. First of all, the coin finds from the third century exceed in number the finds from the fourth century. Secondly, there is a possibility that the emperors would have preferred to avoid minting costs by paying gold in the form of bullion to the barbarians instead of gold coins. Researchers have suggested that the imperial treasury preferred to send tribute in the form of golden bars, since this did not involve any additional minting costs.[82]

Consequently, the bulk of third- and fourth-century gold coinage found in the *barbaricum* could have been the result of commercial transactions not necessarily related to imperial payments. If this assumption is correct, then at some point the coins must have been in the hands of Roman merchants who were engaged in trade both within and outside the empire. Therefore, I would like to suggest that the inhabitants of the empire would have preferred to conduct commercial transactions with neighbouring regions that accepted their gold coins at their full intrinsic value. The increasing quantities of aurei found in sites beyond the Roman frontiers allow for the

79 Laser and Voss 1994; Laser and Schultze 1995; Voß 1998. Specifically, five gold coins were issued during the first century AD, none during the second century, eleven coins come from the third century and four from the fourth century.

80 In Germany eleven gold stray finds were issued during the third century, while four were issued during the fourth century. According to the catalogue compiled by Bursche (1996), fifty-four coins that were issued during the third century were lost in the Central *barbaricum*, while twenty-seven gold coins from the fourth century were lost in the same area. According to Duncan 1993: 109, a few sizeable gold hoards were also lost during the fourth century in Romania, far from Roman territory.

81 Bursche 1996: 101 ff. 82 Iluk 1985.

possibility that the purchasing power of gold coins may have been higher outside the empire. If this is the case, then the merchants residing near the frontier line would rather buy products from the barbarians instead of the Roman citizens, a possibility that would have triggered unforeseen consequences in the commercial development of those areas.

IMPERIAL DECISIONS

The central authorities undoubtedly would have noticed the devaluation of aurei, since the imperial revenues relied on the manipulation of coinage, and, thus, would have taken strict measures in order to avoid the melting or export of the coins. It is true that in Tudor England the king stopped the minting of gold coinage altogether when he realised the extent of the problem. However, the end of the gold coinage would not have been an equally acceptable measure in the Roman empire, especially since the aureus was necessary in order to guarantee the value of the heavily debased silver coins. Although we rarely encounter third-century gold coins as stray finds or in hoards or from excavation sites, the continuation of their minting should not be doubted. The abundance of Severan aurei in museums, private collections and auctions indicates that the production of gold coinage did not cease during the third century or even later. Specifically, the gold coins published in the series of *The Roman Imperial Coinage*[83] and in *The Coins of the Roman Empire in the British Museum*[84] show that the production of aurei was never discontinued, although we cannot possibly estimate the exact volume of these issues because of the lack of die studies. Since some of the previously active mines were no longer in operation, we should assume that the emperors of the third century reminted older aurei, thus using effectively the available stock of gold already in circulation.

Nevertheless, one of the immediate dangers that the emperor would have faced, if he continued the production of devalued gold coins, would have been the potential loss of revenue that came from the exchange of gold for silver coins. Since the main financial policy of the state was the balance between revenues and expenses, a loss of profit due to the devaluation of the aurei would have been unacceptable. One rational solution to the problem was probably the removal of the bulk of gold coins already in circulation; the obvious way of removal being through the process of taxation. This

[83] H. Mattingly, Sydenham and Sutherland; H. Mattingly and Sydenham 1936.
[84] H. Mattingly 1940; 1950; Carson 1962.

way, the emperor probably would have kept the aurei in the treasury as a guarantee of the existing monetary system, while he would have had the privilege of using them only in exceptional circumstances as gifts or parts of payments. Once the majority of gold coins were withdrawn from the circulation pools, in all likelihood he would have reduced the number of issues annually produced. Actually, modern numismatists not only noticed a reduction in the number of annual issues during the third century but they also assumed that the absence of gold coins during the third century should be linked to the low mine output.[85] On the other hand, the rich inhabitants of the empire may have been aware of the withdrawal of the aurei but the decrease of the new issues may not have been immediately noticed; so, in the short run the system would have continued to function uninhibited.

If we accept the possibility that the Romans were capable of rational economic thinking and, accordingly, that the emperor would have withdrawn the gold coins from the markets or that the citizens would have melted or exported them, then we should seek the results of this situation. First of all, the disappearance of the aureus from the markets during the third century may indicate that at least during the Severan period it was used as a unit of account rather than coin. By the term 'unit of account' (otherwise called 'imaginary money' or 'ghost money')[86] we mean that the aureus had no longer a physical embodiment and would normally not be used in commercial transactions but, instead, it would have been used in pricing the commodities and would have had an exchange rate with the physical money in circulation (silver and bronze coins). Similar examples of imaginary money come from the Carolingian period, when we find no coins representing the larger denominations, and from the thirteenth to sixteenth centuries, when units of accounts were used as links between coins.[87] Likewise, some economic historians believe that during the medieval period the pound was an imaginary unit of account and its value was determined by the opinion of the people.[88] The higher fineness of the aureus during the first, second and early third centuries probably gave it the necessary quality to function as a unit of account against which prices were set. However, by the middle of the third century, when both its fineness and its weight were reduced, there is a strong possibility that its use as a unit of account would have been deemed inappropriate.

[85] An attempt to prove this view was made by King (1993: 449–50).

[86] Bloch 1954. [87] Redish 2000: 7.

[88] Einaudi 1953: 236. This view, though, was questioned by White 1984; Spufford 1988: Appendix 2; and more recently Weber 1996.

However, did the Roman state have the economic and/ or political power during times of upheaval to sustain a bimetallic monetary system based only on the debased silver coins remaining in circulation and the imaginary aurei? The Roman imperial and provincial precious-metal coinages were based on a purely metallic weight standard, according to which the value of the coin theoretically coincided with the value of the precious bullion in it. The emperors probably realised that the exchange rates had to be adjusted sooner or later in order to meet the new proportions of precious metal in coins. As we have already seen, changes in the fineness and weight of the aureus probably occurred some time after the reign of Severus, although we cannot be certain of the exact date. Accordingly, the exchange rates between silver and gold may have been adjusted during or after the reign of Gordian III either by imperial degree or de facto in the course of commercial transactions. These numismatic reforms, though, did not produce the hoped-for results and by the reign of Gallienus the exchange rates between gold and silver coins possibly reached the rates between gold and bronze coins of a previous era.

If the emperors had endeavoured a radical modification of these rates, they might have solved the problem of the devaluation of the aurei. However, their attempts to restore the bimetallic standard proved to be inconsequential and by the end of the reign of Gallienus gold appears to have been no longer related to the lower denominations as part of a fixed monetary system.[89] Aurelian was probably the first emperor who attempted large-scale, albeit short-lived, monetary reforms after the end of August AD 274. Specifically, he recalled the old debased coinage and exchanged it for newly minted silver coinage. The new issues were heavier, their weight standard was more tightly controlled and their fineness was higher. The weight of the aureus was also improved to the weight standard employed previously by Caracalla.[90] Diocletian was the next emperor to attempt a far more comprehensive reform that aimed at solving the numismatic problem of the empire once and for all. Specifically, he improved the weight and fineness of the gold and he renewed the minting of a pure silver coin, *argenteus nummus*, keeping at 1:12 the gold to silver ratio.[91]

Nonetheless, the attempts of Aurelian and Diocletian did not bring the long-wished-for outcome and the new monetary system did not regain the trust of the population. The reasons for such a failure may be detected

[89] Carson 1990: 233.
[90] King and Hedges 1974; Cubelli 1992: 57 ff.; Estiot 1995; Watson 1999: 127–32.
[91] Bruun 1979; Morrisson *et al.* 1985: 85.

in the Price Edict, a significant inscription from the reign of Diocletian, regarding the revaluation of metals as commodities. Roger S. Bagnal recently tried to prove that the state attempted to devalue gold that was sold as a commodity in the Roman markets, since, until then, its market price probably exceeded by far its official price.[92] Although we cannot be certain about the exact difference between the two prices, modern researchers suggest that the official price of gold bullion may have been comparatively lower than the price the population would normally accept. It is possible that the decision of the Roman State to undervalue gold as raw metal was designed to ease the negative effects arising from the ongoing devaluation of gold coins in the market. The emperor probably came to the conclusion that if he created an artificial exchange rate for gold, silver or bronze bullion, then this rate would probably match the already artificial exchange rate of gold, silver and bronze coins that was maintained even after his reforms.

Regrettably, no economic edicts from the third century survived; hence, we are obliged to look for indications of the imperial economic thinking and the resulting monetary policies in the documents that come from the fourth century. The Diocletianic reforms were followed by the reforms of Constantine the Great, who attempted once more to stabilise the monetary system. His attempts, though, were not crowned with success, since he also gradually reduced the weight of the *nummus*, a billon coin that had already lost a large proportion of its silver content. Despite the changes in its weight and fineness, we notice that this coin was tariffed at the same price as the *nummus* issued by Diocletian. The disparity between its face value and its intrinsic value led to the loss of its credibility and, as a consequence, it eventually ceased to be minted altogether.

It has been suggested that the depreciation of the billon coinage may have resulted in an increase in the price of gold as a commodity in the market. Although the price of silver bullion also increased, it did not match the rises in the prices of gold and, as a result, during the fourth century the traditional commercial 1:12 gold:silver ratio moved downwards and stabilised at 1:14.4. At the death of Constantine in 337 we encounter the following coins: the gold solidus, the two silver denominations (*siliqua* and *miliaresion*), and the debased Diocletianic *nummus*. It has been observed that the gold coin of very high fineness, solidus, remained unaltered throughout the fourth century, while the silver coinage became increasingly more complex. The billon coins underwent subsequent debasements until the end

[92] Bagnall 1989: 71–2.

of the fourth century, resulting in the further instability of the operative monetary system.[93]

The continuous depreciation of silver coins seems to have triggered problems with regard to the relatively stable gold:silver coin exchange rate. Specifically, in 384/5 Symmachus, the Prefect of Rome, in his letter to the emperor Valentinian II mentioned that the co-emperor Gratian had decided that the exchange rate was no longer viable. According to Symmachus, although the moneychangers were obliged to sell solidi at the established price, they refused to do so and, thus, faced the penalties imposed by the state. The reason for such a refusal was the increasing price of gold in the markets. It seems that since the gold coins were reckoned at a higher tariff in the free market, the moneychangers received lower prices when they sold the solidi to the state.[94] Despite the occasional need for reform, the preservation of the official currency exchange rate is a recurring theme throughout late antiquity. In 367 the emperors Valentinian and Valens commanded that 'solidi shaped in the venerability of former emperors to be given and received by buyers and sellers in such a way as to provoke absolutely no dissension, as long as they are of the required weight and honest material'.[95] In 379 the emperors Gratian, Valentinian II and Theodosius I made it known that 'the price demanded for all solidi of refined gold should be uniform and that capital punishment will be inflicted upon anyone who should treat the commands of our majesty with contumely through the blindness of greed, or who should reckon as cheaper the eternal faces in the pursuit of fraud'.[96] Later, during the reigns of Theodosius II and Valentinian III an imperial edict reads as follows:

> Therefore, let it be universally known through the edict that capital punishment awaits him who believes a gold solidus of full weight in the names either of my father the lord Theodosius [II] or of our sacred female relations or of former emperors to be refused or valued at a lower price . . . That a solidus should never be sold for less than seven thousand nummi when bought from a money changer for seven thousand two hundred. For the uniformity of price shall protect both the favourable position of the seller and the established prices of all saleable goods.[97]

The monetary situation during the fourth century certainly reminds us of the analogous monetary reforms of the third century and their unavoidable consequences. Once more the price of gold as a commodity rises and

[93] Hendy 1985: 462–7. [94] Symmachus, *Relat.* 29.
[95] *Cod. Iust.* 12.2.1; translation in Hendy 1985: 365.
[96] *Cod. Iust.*, 10.19.4; XII.6.13; translation in Hendy 1985: 366.
[97] Valentinian III, Edict XVI; translation in Hendy 1985: 365.

probably causes the devaluation of the gold coin that disappeared from circulation. The attempts of the Roman emperors to control the commercial price of gold coins at the beginning of the fourth century seem to have met with little success. Although the Price Edict listed 'gold, refined, in bars or in coins' at 50,000 denarii per pound and 12,000, if drawn out,[98] its enforcement was impossible; eventually, the Edict was abandoned after a few years.[99] The absence of gold coin hoards and stray finds from the provincial circulation pools indicates that the population did not comply with the imperial regulations and continued to melt down gold coins. Modern researchers agree that the gold coins did not circulate for long because they were either recoined or hoarded.[100] The melting of the coins probably took place within a few years after their issue, since fourth-century hoards do not include solidi older than thirty years.[101] It is evident that the devaluation of gold coins continued because of the higher value of gold bullion at least until the reign of Valentinian, when Symmachus mentions the possibility of an adjustment in the exchange rates. The central authorities, however, were aware of the situation long before 384/5. In fact, as early as AD 356 the emperor Constantius II issued an edict according to which

> Whoever is found either melting down or transporting coins to different regions in order to sell them let him come under the sentence of sacrilege and suffer capital punishment . . . No one amongst the traders is to carry on his animals more than a thousand folles in coins established in public use (*pecuniae in usu publico constitutae*) for the purpose of expenses . . . For we order that merchants should not carry every kind of coin in their ships, and in fact we permit only such coins as are established in public use to be so carried, and similarly only such goods as are customarily carried to different regions by merchants to be bought. But it shall be entirely unlawful for anybody to buy or handle forbidden coins, because it is proper for the price of a thing to be in coins established in public use and not in merchandise.[102]

Although the word used for folles is *pecunia*, referring to all coins irrespectively of their denominational value, this harsh measure could have aimed at striking mainly those individuals who would profit from the melting of the devalued gold coins. If the Roman state no longer attempted to control the price of gold metal, it is possible that the commercial value of the gold bullion fluctuated from one province to another.[103] Therefore, the transportation of gold coins, their melting and their selling as bullion

[98] *DPE* 30.1a–2. [99] Williams 1985: 132. [100] Kent 1956.
[101] Depeyrot 1988; Banaji 1996: 45. [102] *Cod. Theod.* 9.23.1; translation in Hendy 1985: 291.
[103] Although it has been suggested that the price of gold coins also fluctuated (Lo Cascio 1997), there is not enough evidence to prove conclusively such a thesis.

would have been more profitable in regions where the value of gold as metal was higher.

CONCLUSION

For almost two-and-a-half centuries from the reign of Augustus until the end of the Severan dynasty the fine gold coin, the aureus, was the stabilising factor of the multiple commodities system, since it guaranteed the set values of the silver and bronze issues. Although debasements of silver coinage took place during the first as well as the second century, they were never sufficient to destabilise the monetary economy. One of the reasons for this constancy was the fact that the aureus was not debased to the same extent as the denarius, while its weight was not significantly reduced. Such monetary decisions allowed the exchange rate to remain unaltered at least until the end of the Severan period, thus keeping the existing monetary system in force. However, the continuous depreciation of the silver currency and the subsequent reduction of the weight and fineness of the gold coins after the reign of Maximinus obviously jeopardised the durability of the bimetallic laws that were fundamental for the continuation of this system.

It seems that the extensive and hasty monetary reforms of that period had long-term consequences for the use and circulation of all currencies, and especially of the gold coins. The inevitable overvaluation of denarii probably caused the devaluation of the aurei, which means that the price of gold coins in the markets was probably lower than their weight in raw metal. If this was the case, then speculators would have preferred to melt the gold coins they possessed in order to sell them as bullion, thus receiving more silver coins in return. This behaviour, though, condemned the aurei to become a rare commodity; so, the citizens considered it a privilege to own some of them not only for their economic value but also as tokens of the favour of the emperor.

The economic attitude of the Roman population would not have escaped the notice of the central authorities, who wished to secure their own profits from the production and circulation of coinage. Since there is no reason to believe that the government was not capable of rational economic thinking, we may assume that the emperor, once he became aware of the situation, took certain steps towards the solution of the problem. First of all, the mints reduced the volume of aurei in circulation, so the gold became inaccessible to the masses and the inhabitants could not easily turn them into metal and use them as bullion. Secondly, the devaluation of the aureus forced the Military Anarchy emperors to change their policy and adjust the exchange rates to some extent, so that the intrinsic value of the gold coins would not be too far from their face value. However, this reaction may not have been adequate, since the monetary system eventually collapsed by the time of Gallienus. Thirdly, as late as the end of the third century, Diocletian tried to adjust the price of gold as a commodity in local and interregional markets, so that it would coincide with the value of gold in the form of coin. It seems, though, that this measure also was short-lived.

By the beginning of the fourth century it became clear that the monetary system needed to be radically reformed in order to survive. Therefore, Roman emperors devised a new system based on the solidus, a gold coin of higher fineness, that remained unaltered in centuries to come and, in fact, became the medium of exchange in medieval markets throughout the Mediterranean and beyond. Despite the stability of the new coin, the continuous depreciation of silver coinages during the fourth century caused similar problems to the ones we encounter in the third. However, in this case the emperors decided to intervene directly and control the numismatic circulation more closely by issuing a series of decrees that regulated the exchange rates and banned the illegal melting of precious metal coins.

The manipulation of the bimetallic laws was deemed to be a quick way to make profit and therefore continued to take place throughout medieval times, during the early modern period and up until the end of the nineteenth century. Until the eighteenth century the depreciation of the silver currencies brought quick profits to the minting authorities, which needed additional revenues for the maintenance of the governmental military and bureaucratic mechanisms. At the same time the thoughtless manipulation of the bimetallic system brought about the devaluation of gold and its subsequent demonetisation, export outside the area where it was legal tender and/or melting. During the nineteenth century, however, the modern governments of Europe and the United States of America moved towards the methodical imposition of a monometallic system based either on the silver or on the gold standard,[104] a move that we do not encounter in the Roman empire. It is clear that the main factors that facilitated the transition from bimetallism to monometallism in the modern world were a combination of technological advancement, the reduction in transportation costs, globalisation and the integration of the national economies. The final choice of the gold coin instead of silver in a monometallic economy reflected the

[104] Flandreau 1996; Frieden 1997; Redish 2000; Laughlin 1897; Girton and Roper 1978; Friedman 1990.

government's desire to acquire a prestigious monetary currency that would be more stable in a global setting. On the other hand, the Roman empire may have been one of the most advanced ancient states but it was neither industrialised nor globalised. Since these favourable factors did not exist in the ancient world, the instigation of a monometallic system was highly unlikely and, in fact, the results of the abuse of the bimetallic laws were fundamentally different.

CHAPTER 4

The application of the Quantity Theory of Money to third-century economics

SILVER AND BRONZE MINT OUTPUT

In the previous chapters I suggested that the repeated debasements of the silver coinages and the simultaneous stability of the gold aurei guaranteed the stability of the Augustan monetary system for more than two-and-a-half centuries. However, this stability was risked in the middle of the third century, when the uncertain political situation in the Roman empire undermined the power of the central authorities and eventually destabilised the monetary economy. The emperors in their attempt to increase their revenues resorted to the manipulation of precious-metal coinage through the debasement of the denarius and its eventual replacement with the highly overvalued antoninianus. The lowering of the fineness of the silver coins gave the emperor the means to increase the silver and possibly also the bronze mint output. As we have already seen, military expenditure probably increased during the Severan dynasty and later during the Military Anarchy period, a fact that seems to have affected the silver and bronze mint output during the third century. The production of denarii minted in Rome was intensified during the reigns of Septimius Severus and Caracalla in order to cover the increased needs of the army for coined metal, while the increasing production of silver coins destined to cover military needs became more apparent during and after the reign of Gordian III. It is worth noting, though, that during this Military Anarchy period we detect the extensive use of antoniniani, instead of their silver predecessors, the denarii.

We have already demonstrated in chapter 2 the changes in the production of silver coinages in the eastern provinces during the third century AD. Specifically, the excavation finds from Greece and Asia Minor (Athens, Patra, Corinth and Ephesus; Chart 1) indicate that a small increase in silver coins occurred during the reigns of Septimius Severus and Caracalla. Other more substantial increases followed during the Military Anarchy period (reaching a peak during the reigns of Valerian and Gallienus).

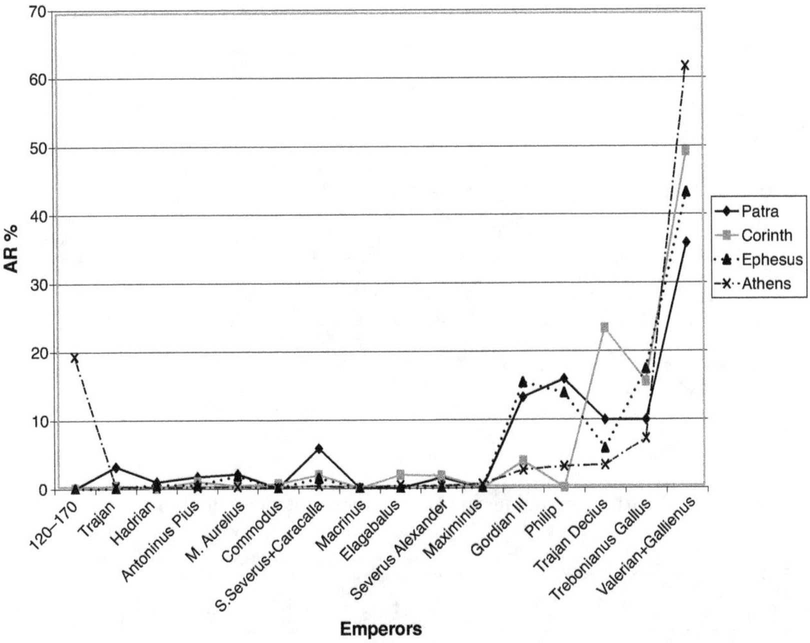

Chart 1 Excavations in Greece and Asia Minor: silver coins, % per annum

These increases only partly reflect the increasing expenses of the central government, while they may also be affected substantially by trade activities.

The excavation finds from Dacia are slightly different, since they indicate increases in the production of silver coinages during and after the Severan period (Chart 2: the highest peaks of coins are concentrated for most areas in the reigns of Septimius Severus/Caracalla and Elagabalus). Nevertheless, all of these peaks are considerably higher than the peaks of coins we encounter during the Antonine period. In this case, we should bear in mind that Dacia is a highly militarised province that relied a lot more than Greece and Asia Minor on the money coming from Rome. It is therefore possible that Chart 2 reflects more accurately payments by the state and increases of the mint output in order to cover the soldiers' salaries.

The peaks and troughs of silver coins coming from the excavations from Pannonia Superior indicate that most of the silver coins seem to have been produced during the reigns of Septimius Severus and Elagabalus (Chart 3). In the case of this province, the height of the peaks remains substantial during and after the reign of Gordian III until the reign of Gallienus, when the production of antoniniani reached its highest peak. Pannonia Superior

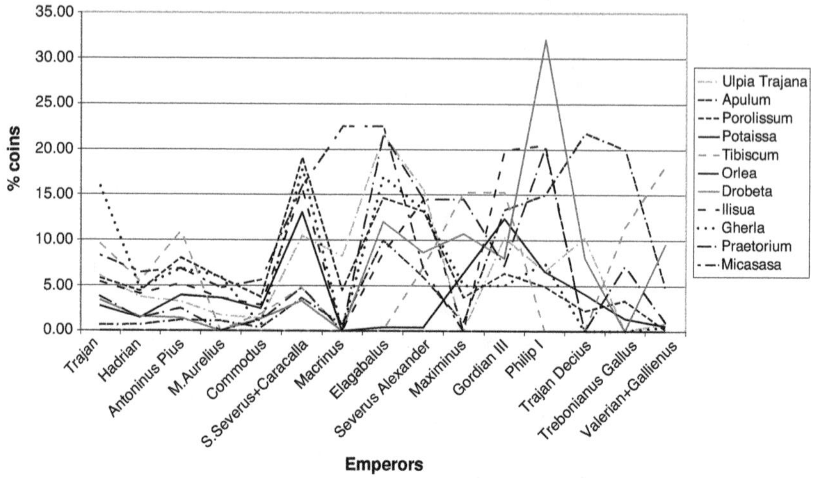

Chart 2 Excavations in Dacia: silver coins, % per annum

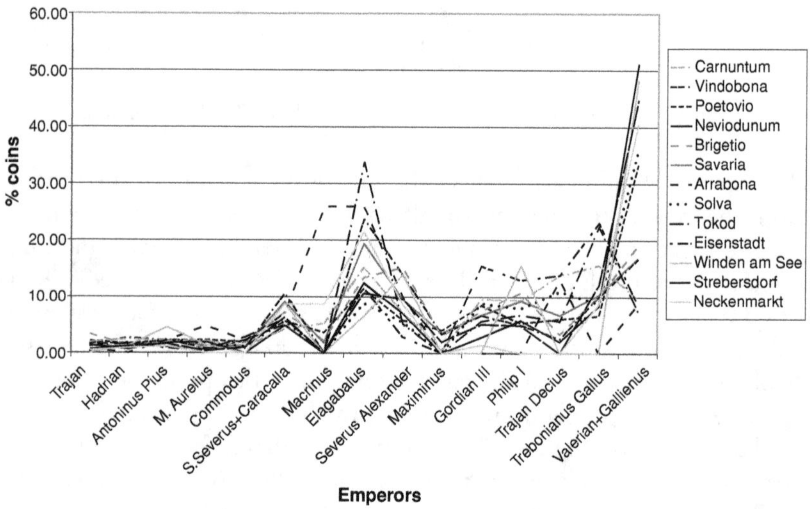

Chart 3 Excavation in Pannonia Superior: silver coins, % per annum

was also a highly militarised province. Therefore, it is not a coincidence that the peaks and troughs in this chart are similar to the peaks and troughs in the Dacian chart.

The structure of excavation finds coming from sites in Pannonia Inferior is similar to the structure of the finds from the neighbouring Pannonia

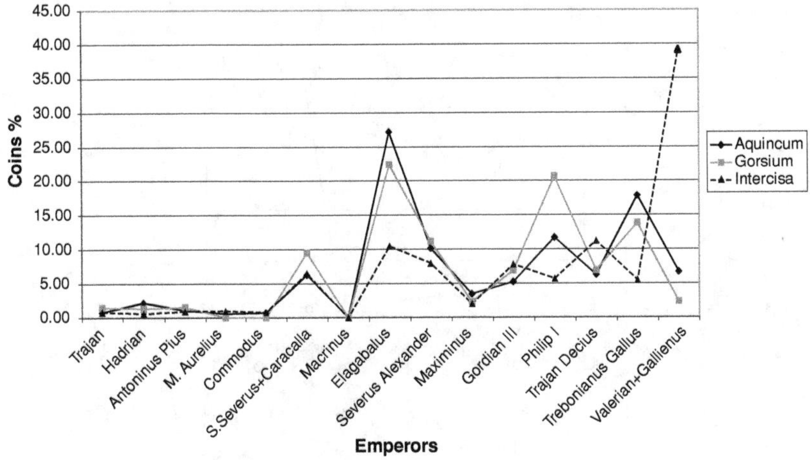

Chart 4 Excavation in Pannonia Inferior: silver coins, % per annum

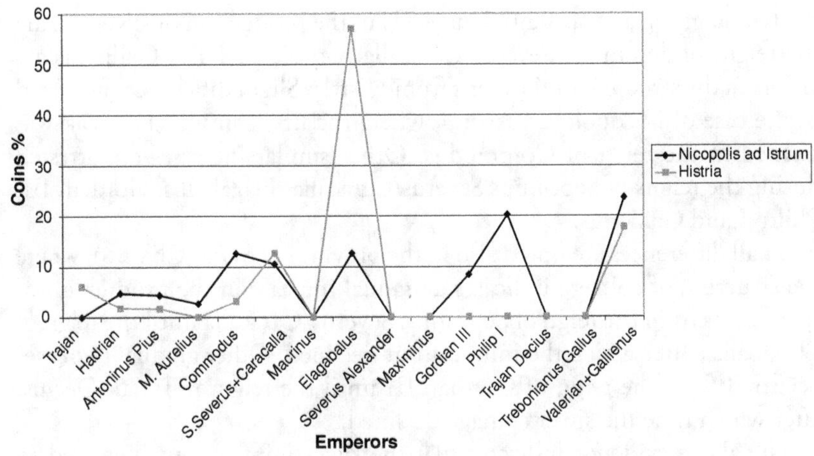

Chart 5 Excavations in Moesia Inferior: silver coins, % per annum

Superior (Chart 4). However, in this province the highest peak of silver production is seen only in the city of Intercisa. There is a possibility, though, that the excavation of more sites may alter these results slightly.

The finds from two excavation sites in Moesia Inferior, Nicopolis ad Istrum and Histria, demonstrate similarities with the other Balkan provinces (Chart 5). Although the number of sites is very small, we may compare the structure of their coins with the structure found in Dacia and

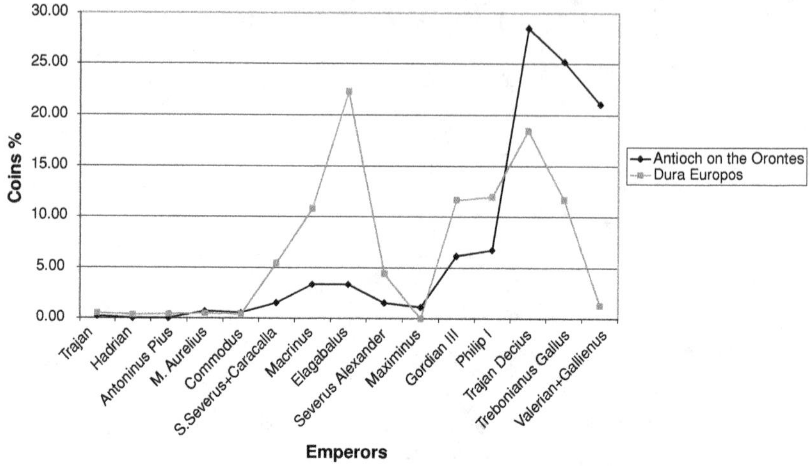

Chart 6 Excavations in Syria: silver coins, % per annum

the two Pannonias. Substantial increases in the production of silver during the reigns of Septimius Severus/Caracalla, Gordian III and Gallienus are visible in the structure of the coins from Histria. Slight differences occurred in the case of Nicopolis ad Istrum, where the first considerable peak was formed in the reign of Commodus. Other similar increases are attested during the reigns of Septimius Severus/Caracalla, Elagabalus, Gordian III, Philip I and Gallienus.

Small differences are noted also in the province of Syria (Chart 6), where the structure of coinage indicates a gradual increase in the production of silver coins from the reign of Septimius Severus/Caracalla until the reign of Elagabalus, after which the mint output declined. Other gradual increases occurred from the reign of Gordian III until the reign of Trajan Decius, after which time the silver coinage declined.

The above evidence indicates that the silver mint output increased to some extent at the beginning of the third century AD, while a continuously higher number of silver coins were produced especially after the reign of Gordian III. No matter how small the overall rise of denarii in circulation in the early Severan period, there was always a possibility that the monetisation of the eastern provinces was affected. As we have already seen, the soldiers received more money from the beginning of the Severan period onwards, since the *stipendium* and the donatives increased substantially. The increasing monetary capacity of the soldiers created new opportunities for new transactions in the local markets, especially near military stations, forts and fortresses.[1] With more money at hand they could demand more products or services to be available; in this case the population involved in trade or services aiming at the purses of the soldiers could theoretically have enjoyed a more active economic life. In this chapter we will explore the effect of the continuous increases in mint production on the economies of the eastern provinces during the third century AD.

Apart from a rise in the excavation finds, we also notice a higher number of third-century coin hoards recently published in numismatic journals and auction catalogues. A preliminary look gives the impression that both silver and bronze hoards lost during the third century in the eastern provinces show a substantial rise after the reign of Gordian III. Specifically, in Greece two silver hoards were buried during the Antonine period,[2] one during the Severan period[3] and six hoards from the Military Anarchy period.[4] In addition five hoards from the Military Anarchy period contain both silver and bronze coins.[5] In Asia Minor one hoard was buried during the Antonine period,[6] another two hoards were buried during the Severan period[7] and ten hoards were buried during the Military Anarchy period.[8] The silver coin hoards from Syria that were buried during the Antonine period are four.[9] The coin hoards that were lost in Syria during the Severan period are six,[10] while eighteen silver coin hoards containing tetradrachms and/or denarii belong to the Military Anarchy period.[11] In Moesia Superior the silver coin hoards lost during the Antonine period were only three.[12] No silver coin hoards were recovered from the Severan period, while during the Military Anarchy period the lost hoards were twelve.[13] (See Chart 7.)

The abrupt increases of bronze coin hoards during the Military Anarchy period in the eastern provinces resemble the increases in silver hoards (Chart 8). Specifically, no bronze coin hoards buried during the Antonine

1 Katsari 2008. 2 Cephalenia and Krani hoards. 3 Erestrole hoard.

4 Roufou B, Karpenisi, Greek 1, Greek 2, Greek 3, Corinth 1 hoards.

5 Porto Rafti, Corinth 2, Athens 2, Lesbos, Kavala hoards. For an explanation of these hoards see below, where I emphasise the exceptional overvaluation of silver coins and their effective use as small change.

6 Manyas hoard. 7 Sulakyurt and Turkey 1 hoards.

8 Eastern, Yatagan, Haydere, Western Turkey 1, Western Turkey 2, Caesarea Cappadociae, Smyrna, Göktepe, Iasos, Pergamos hoards.

9 Syria 1, Tiberias, Murabba'at and Boston hoards.

10 Syria 3, Dura Europos 3, Dura Europos 16, Nineveh, Mempsis and Tell Kalak hoards.

11 Turkey 3, Turkey 4, Antioch 1, Antioch 2, Syria 6, Syria 7, Dura Europos 1, Dura Europos 2, Dura Europos 4, Dura Europos 5, Dura Europos 6, Dura Europos 8, Dura Europos 14, Dura Europos 15, Hama, Rafah, Jordan, Gush Halav hoards.

12 Misaca, Mrcevac, Grocka hoards.

13 Ravna, Sikirica, Dobri Do, Vidinsko, Horreum Margi 1, Glibovac, Granicak, Belo Pole, Jagodina, Singidunum, Jablanica, Smederevo hoards.

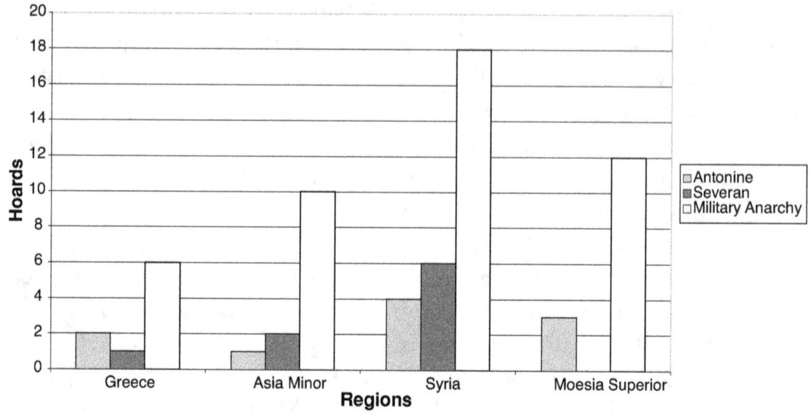

Chart 7 Number of silver coin hoards in eastern provinces

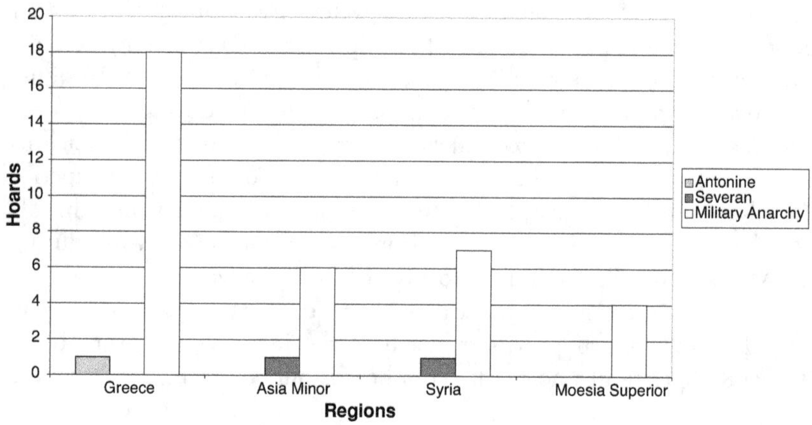

Chart 8 Bronze coin hoards in eastern provinces

period in either Asia Minor or Syria were found. A small bronze hoard (twenty bronze coins and three denarii), that comes from Sebaste Pierias in Greece, probably survived because it was buried in a tomb.[14] The fact that no bronze hoards have been recovered does not necessarily mean that no bronze coins were produced. Only one bronze hoard that was lost during the Severan period has been found in Asia Minor,[15] while no Severan hoards come from Greece. In Syria we notice one bronze hoard during the Severan

[14] Sebaste Pierias hoard. [15] Asia Minor hoard.

period.[16] The period of Military Anarchy produced far more hoards than previous periods (Antonine and Severan). In Greece we notice the record number of eighteen bronze coin hoards.[17] Also, five bronze hoards come from different areas of Asia Minor.[18] During the Military Anarchy period (Gordian III until Gallienus) seven hoards which included mainly bronze coins were buried in Syria.[19] Similarly, from Moesia Superior we have four bronze coin hoards buried during the period of Military Anarchy.[20]

Charts 7 and 8 indicate a clear increase in the loss of silver and bronze coin hoards during the period of Military Anarchy in Greece, Asia Minor, Syria, Moesia Superior and elsewhere. However, the failure of the owner to recover his property does not always imply an increasing number of coins that were removed from the circulation pool ending up in hoards. The most plausible explanation of this phenomenon would be the untimely death of the owner under circumstances that did not allow him to recover the treasure or indicate to someone else the place of concealment. It has been attested that regions suffering from wars or plagues, such as the highly militarised provinces of Dacia and Pannonia, were the most likely places to find hidden hoards.[21] This is the reason for focusing on other regions that are less dangerous. By the third century AD, though, it is possible that the civil wars and barbarian incursions may also have affected Asia Minor and Greece. A series of invasions taking place at that moment caused widespread death and destruction to the unprepared inhabitants of the Greco-Roman cities,[22] who were probably violently killed before they were able to recover their property.

Furthermore, excessive hoarding would have been expected only if the face value of denarii, antoniniani and bronzes in circulation was lower than their intrinsic value, according to Gresham's Law.[23] The repeated reforms of the monetary system in the third century, though, indicate the opposite phenomenon. Several numismatic studies suggest that the military emperors debased the silver currency even further, thus causing the overvaluation of denarii and antoniniani. The weight standards and particularly the fineness standards of these silver coins decreased substantially, especially by the end of the reign of Gallienus, when fineness had fallen to about

[16] Migdal hoard.

[17] Athens 1, Eleusis, Plakanida, Roufou A, Koufalia, Kilkis, Palaio, Leuko, Serrai, Macedonia 1, Macedonia 2, Scarminga, Sparta, Siderokastro, Serrai 2, Strymon, Macedonia 3, Nicopolis hoards.

[18] Gülek Bogazi, Troy 3, Troy 4, Ayvagedigi and Cilicia hoards.

[19] Dura Europos 7, Dura Europos 9, Dura Europos 10, Dura Europos 11, Dura Europos 12, Dura Europos 13 and Silat hoards.

[20] Bošnjane, Vranje, Brezane, Horreum Margi 2 hoards.

[21] M. Crawford 1969: 76–8.

[22] Mitchell 1993: 237.

[23] Gresham's Law: 'The bad money always drives out the good.'

2.5 per cent.[24] In addition to the overvaluation of silver coinages, we could suggest that the civic and imperial requirement for higher minting profits enforced the production of less precious but highly overvalued provincial and imperial bronze issues. Since all of these denominations were so overvalued, it is only sensible that their owners would not have chosen to keep them hidden for long periods of time; instead they would probably prefer to employ the debased coinages in trade. Effectively the reason for the recent recovery of so many silver and bronze hoards[25] should be connected with the increase of the death rate in the eastern provinces and not with any kind of financial speculation.

Even if coin hoards cannot always be a reliable indicator for increases in mint output, we may use other sources. T. B. Jones was the first scholar to attempt a detailed analysis of the excavation finds and the coins found in numismatic catalogues.[26] Initially, he calculated the numbers of mints in every province of Greece, Asia Minor and Syria according to individual reigns. Then, he came to the conclusion that the actual number of civic mints reached its highest peak under the reign of Septimius Severus (232 mints) and then declined to about the level of the Augustan age by the beginning of the reign of Valerian. Although numismatists received Jones' results well, the truth is that proliferation of mints does not necessarily indicate proliferation of coins. Since the production of these coinages was sporadic and in some cases the intervals lasted a few decades, it is probable that some mints may have issued only a few series, while others issued a lot more. A more accurate way to demonstrate that the mint output increased during the reigns of Septimius Severus and Caracalla is the statistical analysis of the coins that are listed in numismatic catalogues.[27] Although I acknowledge the problems with his research,[28] it is likely that worn bronze coins in private and public collections reflect the actual mint output more accurately than the highly selected gold and silver coins we find in museums.[29] The total of 20,000 coins analysed by Leschhorn indicates a substantial peak in the volume of local coinage during the reigns

[24] This figure could suggest a ratio of 800 antoniniani to the aureus (Carson 1990: 234).

[25] See Charts 7 and 8. [26] T. Jones 1963. For a list of mints in each province see T. Jones 1965.

[27] Leschhorn 1981. Leschhorn claims that he used the following numismatic catalogues: *Sylloge Nummorum Graecorum*, Deutchland, Sammlung von Aulock, 18 fasc. (Berlin, 1957–68); *Sylloge Nummorum Graecorum*, Danish National Museum (Copenhagen, 1942); Poole *et al.* 1873–1927; G. MacDonald 1901; Grose 1929; *Sylloge Nummorum Graecorum*, vol. IV: Fitzwilliam Museum, Leake and General Collections, Part VI–VII (London, 1965–7); Babelon 1897. All of the above are major collections that include coins coming through auctions or illegal trade to western Europe. Today, with the publication of the *Roman Provincial Coinage* volumes the renewed undertaking of Leschhorn's task would be infinitely easier.

[28] Review by Johnston 1984. [29] See chapter 1.

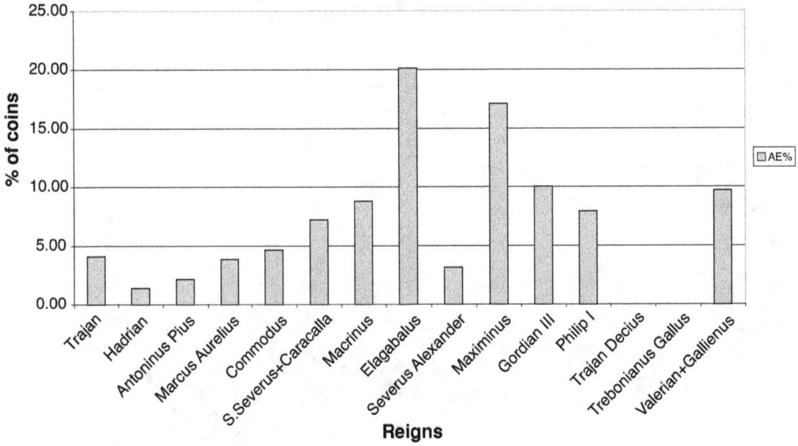

Chart 9 Mint of Dion: bronze coins, % per annum

of Septimius Severus and Caracalla and smaller peaks during the reigns of Commodus, Severus Alexander, Gordian III, Philip the Arab and finally Trebonianus Gallus. These issues faded away by the reign of Tacitus, when the last mints were closed.[30]

The study of several mints could produce an impressionistic picture of rises and falls in the production of small change throughout the eastern provinces, although we should expect the existence of regional differences. Almost the same results as the ones presented by Leschhorn emerge from the study of individual mints such as Dion[31] or Smyrna[32] or Mylasa.[33] The first is a colony in Macedonia, while the other two are cities in the western part of Asia Minor. To begin with, the production of the mint of Dion indicates a gradual increase in bronze coins from the reign of Antoninus Pius until the reign of Elagabalus when the volume forms its highest peak (Chart 9). Another high peak is formed during the reign of Maximinus, after whose reign a gradual decline starts until the reign of Gallienus, when a smaller peak is formed.

Secondly, the coin output of Smyrna shows an increase in production during the reign of Septimius Severus, although it reaches its highest peak during the reign of Gordian III (Chart 10).

[30] Leschhorn 1981: 262, chart no. 5. [31] Kremmydi-Sisilianou 1996a: 35. [32] Klose 1987: 100–2.

[33] Akarca 1959: 66 ff. Even if the publication is old and should probably be completed with the new finds, I suspect that it may still be representative of what the original volume of production may have been.

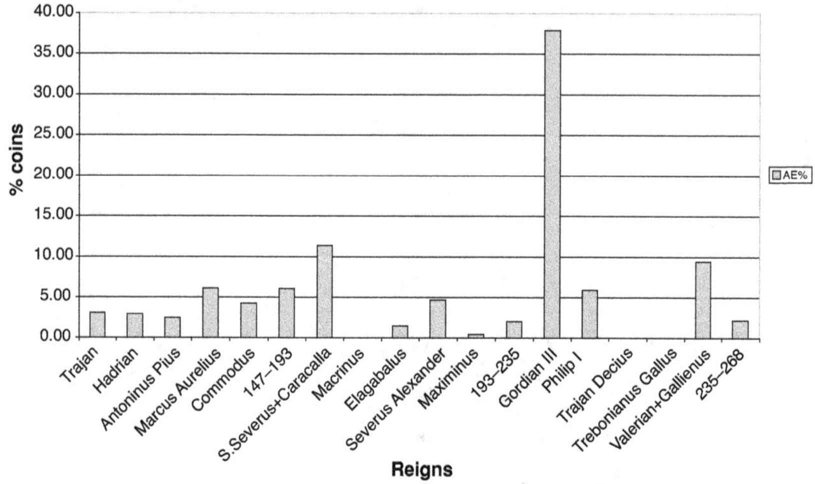

Chart 10 Mint of Smyrna: bronze coins, % per annum

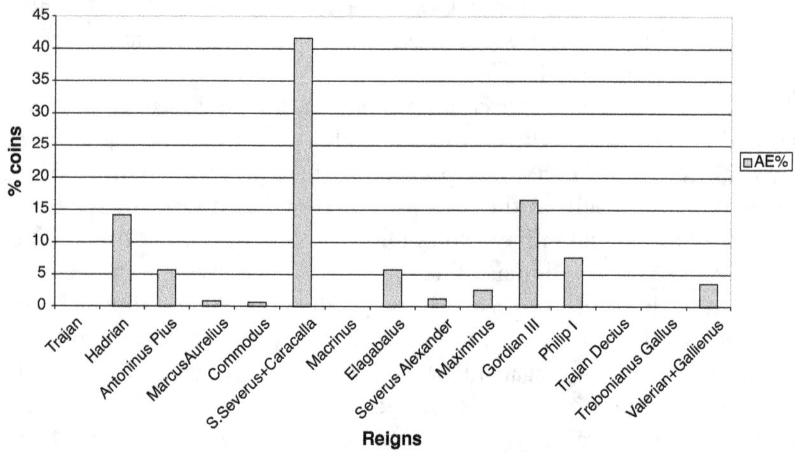

Chart 11 Mylasa Mint: bronze coins, % per annum

Also, the coins issued from the city of Mylasa imply an increase in mint output during the period in question, since they form important peaks during the reigns of Septimius Severus/Caracalla and Gordian III (Chart 11).

Both the study of numismatic catalogues and the publications of individual mints indicate a rise in the overall production of bronze coins in the

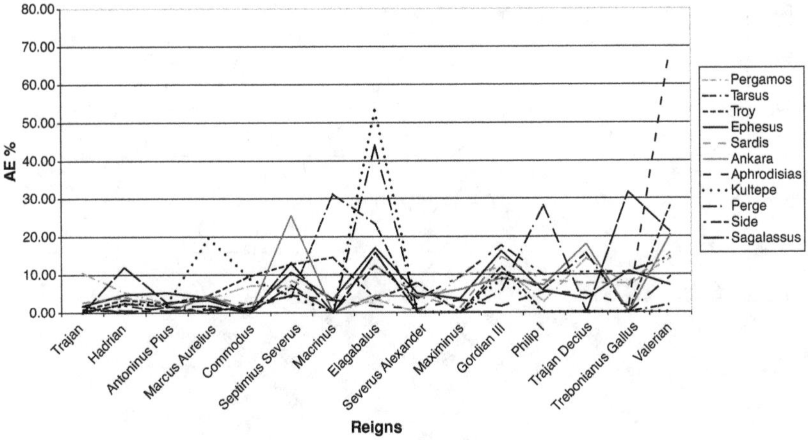

Chart 12 Asia Minor excavations: bronze coins, % per annum

first half of the third century AD, although this increase did not take place in a uniform manner throughout the eastern provinces. In any case, if we take into consideration the widely accepted methodological procedures, we should compare the evidence coming from private or public collections with a different type of numismatic evidence; it may be helpful to analyse statistically individual numismatics finds in excavation sites or coin hoards.

The comparative analysis of the site finds from Asia Minor (Chart 12) indicates that there are no obvious patterns and that every site has more or less its own individual characteristics. However, there are some general similarities. For the construction of this chart I used only the bronze coins found in the course of eleven different excavations:[34] Pergamos, Tarsus, Troy, Ephesus, Sardis, Aphrodisias, Side, Sagalassus, Ankara, Kultepe and Perge. The analysis of the resulting chart indicates that most bronzes from the Antonine era were distributed evenly but the mint production was kept at very low levels. The distribution becomes uneven for the first time during the reigns of Septimius Severus/Caracalla, when a substantial peak in the volume of coinage is formed. However, the majority of the excavation finds show high peaks also during the reigns of military emperors, such as Elagabalus, Gordian III, Trajan Decius and Valerian/Gallienus.[35]

[34] All of these excavations were systematic, although the number of coins that were recovered from Aphrodisias and Tarsus may have been low. Also, the last three rescue excavations yielded only very few coins.

[35] The exceptions of Kultepe and Perge, which form exceptionally high peaks during the reign of Elagabalus, could be easily explained, if we take into consideration the low number of coins that

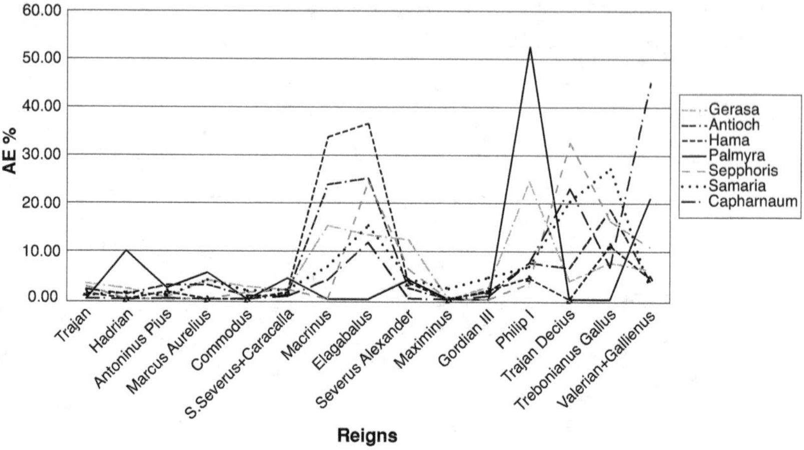

Chart 13 Syrian excavations: bronze coins, % per annum

Excavations in Syria (Gerasa, Antioch, Hama, Palmyra, Sepphoris, Samaria, Capphaernaum) demonstrate that the low output and the even distribution of coinage during the Antonine dynasty changed completely under the Severans (Chart 13). The volume of coinage rises during the reigns of Septimius Severus/Caracalla and the excavation finds form high peaks throughout the Severan period until the reign of Severus Alexander. Most excavations demonstrate increased production of coinage during the reign of Elagabalus. Subsequently the number of coin finds declines, only to increase again during the reign of Philip and until the reign of Gallienus. The coinage from Palmyra and Gerasa forms its highest peak during the reign of Philip. Sepphoris shows an increased concentration of coins during the reign of Trajan Decius. Coins from Samaria, Antioch and Hama increase during the reign of Trebonianus Gallus. Finally, Capphaernaum and Palmyra form their high peaks during the reign of Gallienus.

Dura Europos is one of the sites that not only was excavated with extreme care but also gives us an accurate idea of the circulation of coinage in the area in the middle of the third century, since the city was abandoned in haste after it fell under Sassanid rule. (See Chart 14.) The individuality of the site and the richness of the material prompted the decision to treat it

were found in the excavations. It is probable that new finds will change the results. The high peaks in the volume of coinage from Aphrodisias and Tarsus during the reigns of Gallienus and Macrinus respectively could also easily be explained, since the excavations covered only a small part of the city. The number of coins that was recovered may not be representative of the magnitude of the above cities.

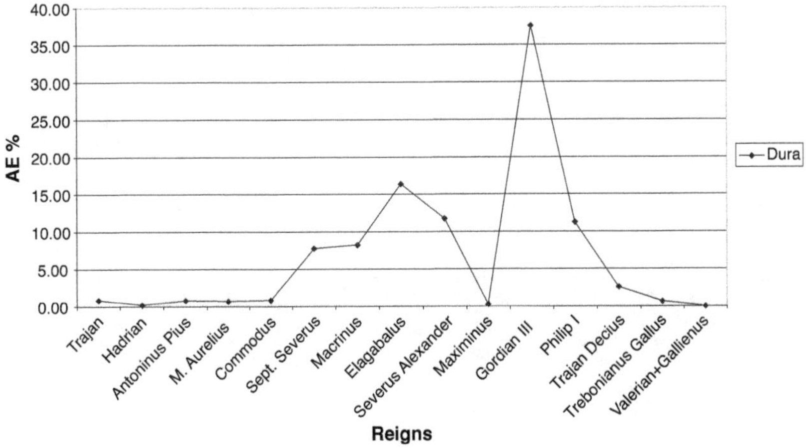

Chart 14 Dura Europos excavations: bronze coins, % per annum

separately from the rest of the Syrian excavations. And yet, we still observe distinct similarities. Few coins come from the period of the Antonine emperors, while the distribution of coinage is even. We can see clearly, though, a peak during the reigns of Septimius Severus/Caracalla that rises to reach a higher peak during the reign of Elagabalus. The production remains comparatively high during the reign of Severus Alexander until it declines during the reign of Maximinus. The highest peak of the coins that were found in Dura Europos is formed during the reign of Gordian III. Subsequently, it declines gradually until the reign of Valerian.

The excavations in Greece (Patra, Argos/Lechaion, Thessaly, Cenchreai, Corinth[36]) demonstrate regional differences, although we observe also common patterns (Chart 15). Unlike the coins from the excavations of Asia Minor and Syria, where the output seems to have been low, the volume of coins from Greek excavations rises from the reign of Trajan onwards to form a peak during the reigns of Septimius Severus/Caracalla. The coinage declines during the reign of Macrinus but it increases gradually once more from the reign of Elagabalus. Different peaks characterise different regions during the period of Military Anarchy. The coins from Thessaly demonstrate an uneven distribution and form peaks during the reigns of Elagabalus, Severus Alexander, Maximinus (highest), Gordian III, Philip and Trebonianus Gallus. Cenchreai reaches its highest peak during the reign of Gordian III, with lower peaks during the reigns of Severus Alexander and

[36] Only Corinth and Cenchreai were excavated systematically.

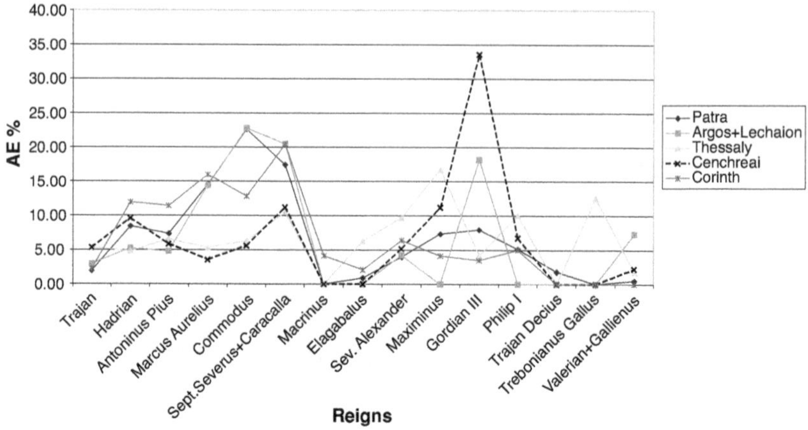

Chart 15 Greek excavations: bronze coins, % per annum

Valerian/Gallienus. Almost the same pattern is attested in the coins from Argos, although the line declines abruptly after the reign of Gordian III. A common pattern is evident in the coinage that comes from the harbours of Corinth and Patra. The distribution of coins between the reigns of Severus Alexander and Philip is both even and quite low in comparison with other areas.

The coins found while excavating the agora of Athens demonstrate an unusual pattern by comparison to the rest of the Greek sites (Chart 16). The volume of coins remains low and it is distributed evenly throughout the second and third centuries AD apart from two periods: (a) reigns of Trajan, Hadrian and Antoninus Pius and (b) reigns of Valerian/Gallienus. The individuality of Athens could be explained if we consider the fact that the mint of Athens was active only during these two periods and that it produced a large number of bronze drachms, hemiobols and obols. Alternatively, the similarities of the structure of the Athenian excavation finds with the excavation finds from Asia Minor may indicate the commercial ties of the port of Athens with the ports of western Asia Minor.

The coinage from the excavations at Curium, in Cyprus, presents a different pattern (Chart 17). The even distribution of coins during the Antonine period is disturbed during the reign of Macrinus when the volume starts rising. The number of coins remains high from the reign of Elagabalus until the reign of Trebonianus Gallus, forming very high peaks during the reigns of Elagabalus, Gordian III and Trebonianus Gallus.

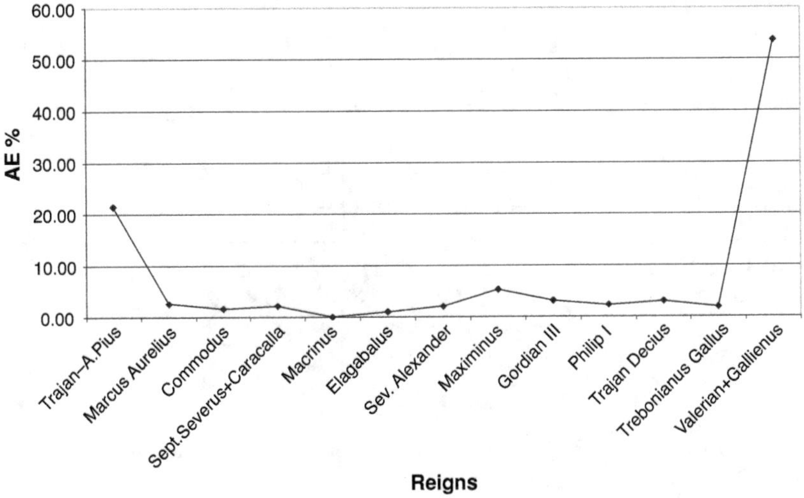

Chart 16 Athens excavations: bronze coins, % per annum

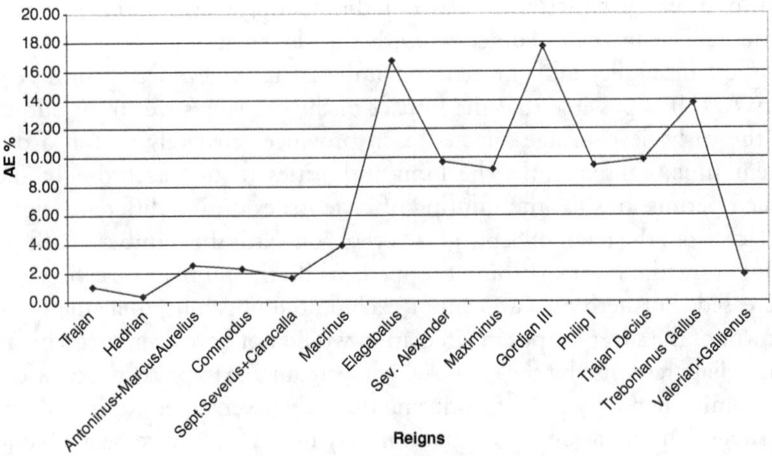

Chart 17 Cyprus excavations: bronze coins, % per annum

To the north of Greece, in the province of Moesia Inferior, the cities of Nicopolis ad Istrum and Histria present patterns similar to each other (Chart 18). The linear structure of bronze coin finds during the Antonine period is replaced by high peaks especially during the Severan dynasty but also in the beginning of the Military Anarchy period.

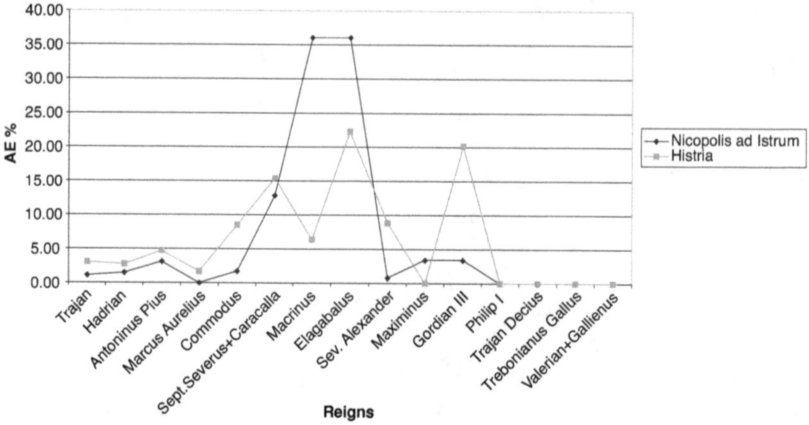

Chart 18 Moesia Inferior excavations: bronze coins, % per annum

The above evidence leads us to the inevitable conclusion that the volume of bronze production increased in different provinces during different periods. The increases coincided with the rise in military expenses, the political instability and the reduced imperial revenues of the third century AD. It is possible that the impact of the growing silver mint output of the early Severan age affected each province separately and at a different time; consequently, the local authorities reacted accordingly and issued permissions for the minting of civic issues during different reigns. In fact, from the reign of Septimius Severus onwards the number of official coins from the mint of Rome dropped, while the number of civic coins increased. Furthermore, we cannot exclude the possibility that the rapid growth of the silver output in circulation would not have been met with an immediate response by the cities, which were unable to predict such wider economic phenomena. At least during the early Severan period the volume of small denominations in circulation may or may not have been able to cover the needs of local markets. Regrettably, it is impossible to estimate the overall rise in the number of civic or 'official' bronze coins because of the lack of adequate data. But the impossibility of an accurate estimate should not hinder us from assessing the relative value of the existing data.

Although the provinces in Syria, Asia Minor and the southern Balkans confirm increases in the production of silver and bronze coins during

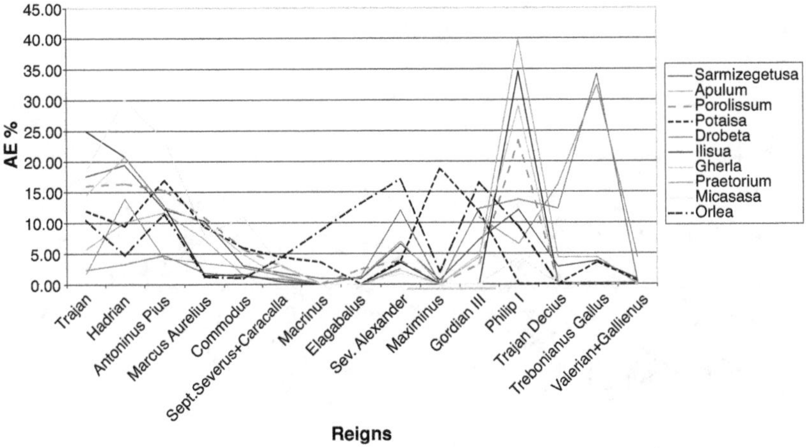

Chart 19 Dacia excavations: bronze coins, % per annum

the Severan period, the provinces in the Northern Balkans demonstrate a different structure. In Dacia, Pannonia Superior and Pannonia Inferior (all of which were highly militarised) the silver finds increase substantially during the Severan and Military Anarchy periods but the bronze finds decline abruptly as early as the reign of Septimius Severus. This is one of the rare instances when we observe more silver than bronze coins lost in the cities. Specifically, in Dacian sites we observe a consistent decline in the number of bronze coins, which reached its nadir during the reigns of Septimius Severus/Caracalla, Macrinus and Elagabalus (Chart 19). From the reign of Severus Alexander onwards the circulation of small change increases once more and reaches very high peaks in several sites during the reign of Philip II.

The same pattern is evident in Pannonia Superior and Pannonia Inferior. For statistical purposes I divided the sites of Pannonia Superior in two groups: (a) Chart 20 includes sites in which more than 100 coins were found and (b) Chart 21 includes the sites in which fewer than 100 coins were found. The structure of coins found in excavations in Pannonia Superior is similar to the structure we observe in Dacian finds. Specifically, Chart 20 demonstrates an abrupt drop in the circulation of bronze coinage during the reign of Commodus. The amount of small change in the markets started rising again during the reign of Severus Alexander and reached its peak during and after the reign of Gordian III.

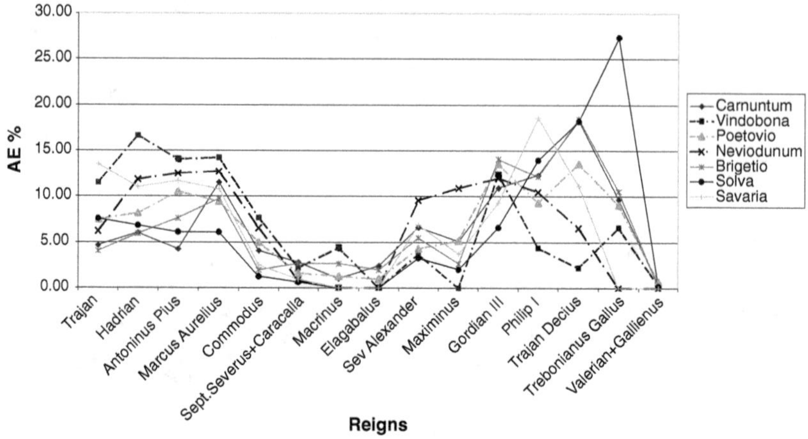

Chart 20 Pannonia Superior excavations (over 100 coins): bronze coins, % per annum

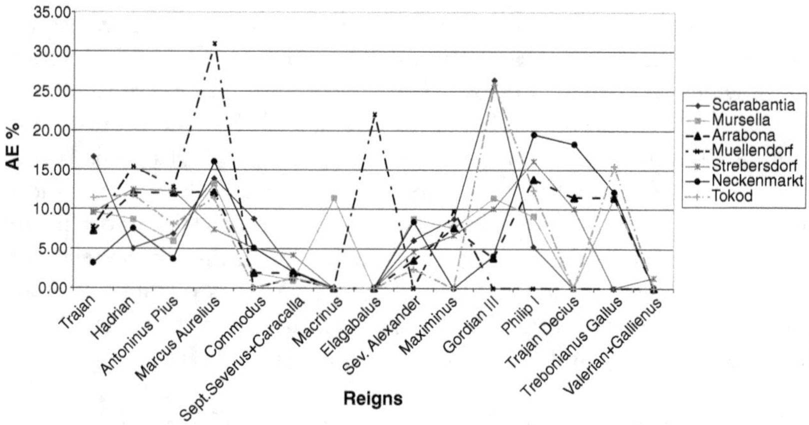

Chart 21 Pannonia Superior excavations (fewer than 100 coins each): bronze coins, % per annum

The rest of the Pannonian sites in Chart 21 present the same picture, with the exception of Mursella and Müllendorf, which form high peaks during the reigns of Macrinus and Elagabalus respectively. Especially in Müllendorf, the bronze coins disappear completely after the reign of Maximinus Thrax. Since this site is so different from the rest we should seek a localised reason for the anomaly.

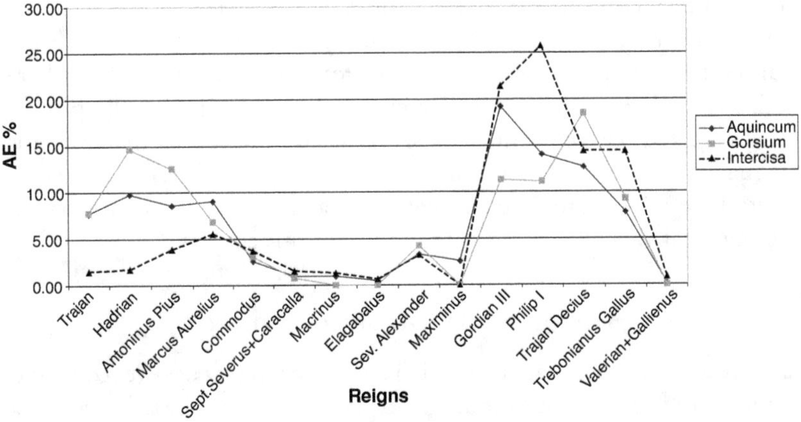

Chart 22 Pannonia Inferior excavations: bronze coins, % per annum

Finally, the coins from the Pannonia Inferior excavation sites confirm the above results (Chart 22). As in Pannonia Superior, the decline in bronze coins starts during the reign of Commodus and continues until the reign of Macrinus. From the reign of Gordian III onwards the circulation of bronze coins increases abruptly.

In all of the above cases it seems that the nadir in the circulation of smaller denominations in the markets was reached during the reign of Elagabalus. The reduction in the quantity of small change in the militarised frontier provinces of Pannonia and Dacia can be explained only if we take into consideration the possible decline in the production of small bronze coins in the mint of Rome. Rome provided almost exclusively the coins that circulated in the area until the third century AD. Only a handful of bronzes issued by the Greco-Roman cities were found in the excavations. If the mint of Rome was burdened with the production of more silver coins from the reign of Septimius Severus onwards, then it is possible that the central authorities decided to curtail the production of small denominations. After all, the focus on the production of precious-metal coinages was essential for the survival of the state and the continuation of the Severan dynasty.[37] We observe the same attitude in other mints

[37] The idea that the central government reduced the quantity of bronze coins during the reign of Septimius Severus has been advanced by several authors. D. Walker 1988: 299; Clay 1989; Duncan-Jones 1994: 108.

under imperial control. For example, no bronze coinage was produced at Antioch under Commodus and Septimius Severus. In addition, there were no imperial attempts to produce small bronze denominations anywhere else in Syria. However, in this case civic coinages – such as the prolific bronzes of Laodicea – continued to be produced.[38] Of course, the problems that may have occurred in the markets following the decision to reduce the production of smaller denominations may not have been anticipated; problems that we will explore in the course of this chapter.

THE QUANTITY THEORY OF MONEY

Various economic historians claimed that the debasement of silver coins and the increasing silver mint output can explain either the alleged increasing monetisation in the empire or the alleged hyperinflation in prices. Both of these economic phenomena are, in fact, directly linked with the Quantity Theory of Money as it was initially presented by the philosopher David Hume in the nineteenth century; since then, the Quantity Theory and its developments influenced the thought of modern economists. According to this model the amount of money inserted in the economy multiplied by the velocity of money is equal to the price level of goods and services multiplied by the transactions of goods and services offered: $M^*V=P^*T$. The economist who actually developed the mathematical formula for this equation was Irving Fischer (1867–1947) in his book *The Purchasing Power of Money*.[39] In the same book he claims that a rise in the money supply will be met by an exactly proportionate increase in prices, while the velocity of circulation (V) and the quantity of the transactions in goods and services (T) remain largely stable. The effects of changes in this equation will not be felt in the short run on the economy; instead, inflation will rise only in the long run (for the modern economies the time was estimated to be between three and ten years later).

This formula fell into disrepute in the 1930s because of certain unresolved problems it presented and because of the restrictions it imposed, although a few economists remained faithful to the initial idea and continued to advocate it. The first problem that the Quantity Theorist had to address was the assumption that changes in the money supply were considered only the cause and not the effect of a sequence of economic phenomena. Secondly, until then this theory could be applied only if the money supply changed abruptly because of exogenous factors (e.g. vast amounts of money

[38] Butcher 2004: 41–2. [39] Fisher 1926.

thrown from a helicopter or other ancient devices, if any). And in the third instance, Fischer wrongly supported the idea that both the V (Velocity) and T (the quantity of monetised Transactions) remained unchanged; so, any changes in the mint output would undoubtedly cause price inflation. All of these problems were addressed mainly in the 1960s and early 1970s by a number of economists, among which Milton Friedman (*b.* 1912),[40] a monetarist of the Chicago School, is the most prominent. A resurgence of the Quantity Theory of Money is attested within economic circles during the 1980s, although controversies about its validity are still expressed.[41]

At a more practical level the obvious question haunting modern economic history is whether the Quantity Theory of Money could be applied successfully to the study of the economy of the ancient world or not. Chris Howgego recently attempted to present us with a positive answer, while at the same time he recognised the above-mentioned problems of the existing formula. He rightly suggested that a greater supply of coinage not only could cause an increase in prices but, in some cases, it could instigate hoarding, thus decreasing the velocity (V) of coins in circulation. In other instances the growth of the money supply could meet the rising demand for money (probably due to a rising income) that would eventually lead to the increasing monetisation of the market (T).[42] The reason for such variations is the acknowledged fact that commodity money was not just a medium of exchange but it was also used as a means for storing value and as a standard for measuring market value. If the Quantity Theory could be applied to the Roman economy, once we have established an increase in the production of coins, we should investigate corresponding changes in the velocity of money, the quantity of transactions or the occurrence of hyperinflation.

If the velocity of money remained stable, then the increasing production of mint output could have affected the general index of prices. In fact, a number of researchers used to favour the hypothesis that inflation rose abruptly at some point between the reign of Septimius Severus and the reign of Diocletian because of the third-century debasements of the silver coinages.[43] The initial evidence for the formation of such a hypothesis was the Price Edict, an inscription from the Diocletianic period regulating prices, which seemingly had increased substantially during the previous

[40] Friedman 1956; Friedman and Schwartz 1963; Friedman 1968; Friedman 1969. This series of articles is only a small sample of the publications dedicated to the subject.
[41] Laidler 1978; 1991. [42] Howgego 1995: 122–5.
[43] M. Crawford 1975; Walker 1976–8: vol. III, 140.

century.[44] The study of inflation was pursued further in the publication of Drexhage's monumental book on prices from the Roman province of Egypt.[45] The large amount of evidence from this province encouraged modern scholars to analyse carefully this material in order to detect inflationary tendencies in the whole of the empire, including the region of Asia Minor. The fact that the Roman central authorities imposed a closed currency system on Egypt rightly did not seem to hinder wider conclusions about the economy of the Roman empire.

If the repeated debasements of silver coinage and the increasing production of coinage could affect the price index, then hyperinflation would have risen substantially already during the early Severan period. The ancient papyri and inscriptions, though, do not verify the existence of such a development. M. Corbier was the first to suggest that the evidence demonstrating high inflation at the end of the third century is not entirely trustworthy, since we cannot verify whether hyperinflation took place in stages or in a single movement. Therefore, it is possible that prices may not have increased substantially until the beginning of the fourth century, as the Edict indicates.[46] Duncan-Jones accepted an inflation of only 0.61–0.83 per cent per year both in Egypt and Ephesus from the beginning of the second century until AD 246.[47] This continuous rise in prices shows clearly that inflation always existed in the Roman empire but was sustained in low, almost insignificant levels. On the other hand, the same author tries to give an answer to the question whether the increase in the production of coinages from the beginning until the middle of the third century had a direct effect on the wider monetary economy or not, but he reaches mixed results. Later, D. Rathbone in two well-acknowledged articles established beyond doubt that inflation was either non-existent or negligible until the reign of Aurelian in AD 274.[48] In these studies he emphasised the significance of determining a general price index based on the unbroken evidence of wheat, wine and donkey prices that would confirm the existence or absence of hyperinflation in the ancient world.[49] At least in the case of Egypt it seems that hyperinflation could be detected only in the last third of the third century AD, a fact that forces us to reconsider

44 For publications on the Price Edict see Erim and Reynolds 1970; Erim, Reynolds and Crawford 1971; M. Crawford and Reynolds 1975; Doyle 1976; Reynolds 1979; Wassink 1991.

45 Drexhage 1991.

46 Corbier 1985.

47 Duncan-Jones 1994: 25–8.

48 Rathbone 1996; 1997.

49 For example, from the mid first century AD to the mid second century most prices for wheat fall within a range of 3 to 8 dr. per *keramion*, while from around 190 to 270 most fall within 8 to 20 dr. Although such an increase reached a 100 per cent over a century, it was still small in scale compared to the increase that took place after 270 (Rathbone 1997: 200).

the connection of inflationary tendencies with systematic numismatic reforms or with the increase of mint output.

Elio Lo Cascio in an article published in 1997 attempted to analyse and explain the stability of prices at the time of external monetary and fiscal pressures.[50] Lo Cascio argued that prices remained comparatively stable until the reign of Aurelian and he attributed the phenomenon to an increase in the monetisation caused by a rise in the population and a growth in the production of the Roman empire. He clearly mentions that the increasing production of coinages in circulation or the repeated debasements could not have caused inflationary tendencies, because the exchange rates between the gold, silver and bronze coinages remained intact until the middle decades of the third century. As long as the empire remained strong and the emperor continued to be the recognised authority to guarantee the monetary system, the Romans would have accepted the face value of silver coins despite the debasements; consequently the value of commodities would still be estimated in refined gold coins and there would have been no need for radical changes. Also, D. Rathbone chose to illuminate the reasons for the maintenance of low prices until the reign of Aurelian under a similar light. He asserted that inflation did not rise because the increase of the mint output was absorbed by an ensuing increase in the monetisation of the economy,[51] hence assuming that the Quantity Theory of Money could still be applied, although he claims otherwise.

It is true that an increasing monetisation of daily transactions could explain both the increase in coin output and the lack of hyperinflation at least until the reign of Aurelian, as has been already suggested. The assumption of growing monetisation in the Roman empire would have been valid, if we took into consideration only the increasing financial capacity of the soldiers from the Severan era onwards, due to the increase of their salaries. Since the payments of the soldiers remained the main state mechanism for the distribution of new imperial coinage, it is believed that the army eventually would have been responsible for an increase in the total amount of money in circulation. A substantial increase in monetary liquidity could effectively mean that more goods and services would become available and a boom in trade would have been observed. However, is it possible that the army alone could monetise or increase the monetisation of the provinces given the limited number of soldiers in active service? We should not ignore the fact that only part of the *stipendium* was given to the soldiers in the form of money, since it was common practice

50 Lo Cascio 1997. 51 Rathbone 1996; 1997.

to make deductions from the salary before the coins reached the camp. Existing evidence of Roman bookkeeping and the widespread use of credit in the army could also indicate the flexibility of a system that was designed to prevent any potential cash problems in the ranks.[52] Another question that springs to mind is: how extensive was the impact of the commercial activities on the maintenance of existing levels of monetisation? Even if the army was the main imperial mechanism for the dispensation of newly minted coins to the markets, how much money was already in circulation at the time? Could the soldiers alone alter substantially the monetised economy of the Roman empire and would monetary transactions have continued at the same rate as before the Severan period?

In theory, the lack of inflation combined with the increasing monetary capacity of the soldiers should have caused an increase in the monetisation and growth of regional and interregional commerce. However, there is evidence for decreasing trading activities during the third century, although we cannot be certain that this problem occurred as early as the Severan period. K. Hopkins in two articles claims that there had been substantial long-distance trade during the period 200 BC–AD 200, a fact indicated by numerous shipwrecks, mostly in the western parts of the Mediterranean. On the other hand, the lack of shipwrecks during the third and the fourth centuries AD could only demonstrate the general trend that commerce was not as important by that time.[53] Despite the fact that Hopkins' assertions may be somewhat exaggerated (especially for the eastern provinces during late antiquity, if we take into consideration the Riviera effect[54]), we cannot wholly ignore them. Especially since, according to more recent studies, a decline in the volume of traffic is attested also in the Egyptian Red Sea and possibly India in the third century.[55] Similarly, there is only one type of wine amphoras from the second half of the third century circulating in Italy, unlike previous periods when more types were available, so more transactions may have taken place.[56] It is interesting that Hopkins also asserts that a growth in the money supply could be connected with the financing of long-distance trade; however, he does not mention any significant expansion in commercial activities during the third century, when the silver and bronze mint output multiplied.[57] As we are about to see, he rightly does not connect increases in the volume of coinages with simultaneous increases in the volume of trade during that period, because both of them were just another illusion.

[52] See chapter 2. [53] Hopkins 1980: 105–6; Hopkins 1995–6: 53. [54] D. Mattingly 2006: 294.
[55] Young 2001: 82–6. [56] Panella and Tchernia 2001: 185. [57] Hopkins 1980: 106.

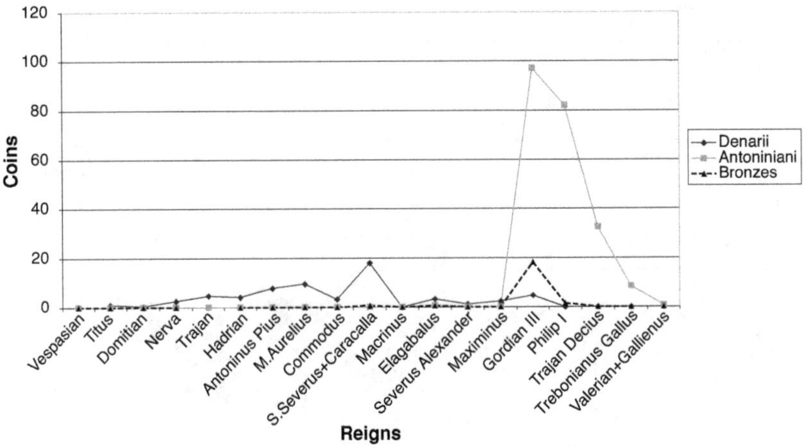

Chart 23 Haydere hoard: comparison of denarii, antoniniani and bronzes

DEMONETISATION AND LOW INFLATION

If the growth of the mint output did not cause hyperinflation or decreases in the velocity of money or increases in the monetisation of the markets, then either the Quantity Theory of Money should not be applied or we should look at our evidence more closely. In our case, I would suggest the second. The solution could come from the detailed study of changes in the circulation pools with regard to specific denominations. It is clear that the new highly debased antoninianus irreversibly replaced the denarius as the standard silver coin in circulation during the reign of Gordian III, as the structures of both the coin hoards and the excavation finds show.

Seven hoards were lost in Asia Minor during the period of Military Anarchy, four of which – Smyrna, Western Turkey 1, Western Turkey 2 and Caesarea Cappadociae hoards – contain mostly antoniniani (only very few denarii are included and all of them were issued during the Severan period), while two – Haydere and Pergamos hoards – contain both denarii and antoniniani.[58] The statistical analysis of the Haydere and Pergamos hoards helps us to detect changes in the use and circulation of different silver denominations during the third century. First, the Haydere hoard includes coins minted during the second and third centuries, and was lost possibly during the reign of Gallienus: (Chart 23). We observe that there is

[58] The denomination of a number of coins in the Goktepe hoard has not been identified, which is the reason for not including it here. It seems, though, that there are no antoniniani from the period before the reign of Gordian III.

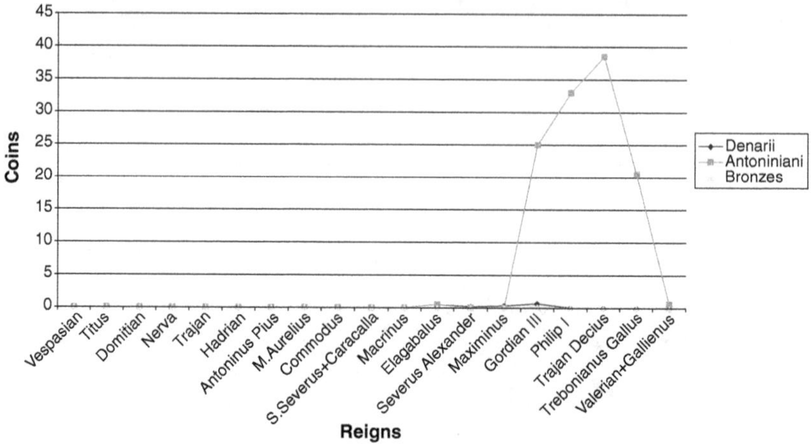

Chart 24 Pergamos hoard: comparison of denarii, antoniniani and bronzes

an even distribution of denarii until the reign of Gordian III, after which denarii disappear. An especially high peak of antoniniani from the reign of Gordian III until the reign of Trajan Decius indicates an equally high volume in the production and supply of this denomination. The number of antoniniani decreases only during the reigns of Trebonianus Gallus, Valerian and Gallienus.

The Pergamos hoard demonstrates a pointed increase in the number of antoniniani from the reign of Gordian III until the reign of Trajan Decius and a gradual decline from Trebonianus Gallus onward (Chart 24). Similarly with the Haydere hoard the number of denarii in this treasure is rather small.

Asia Minor was not the only province where we can attest the terminal decline of denarii and the rise of antoniniani in circulation. The following silver coin hoards from Greece were buried predominantly during the reign of Gallienus: Roufou B, Karpenisi, Porto Rafti, Greek 1, Greek 3, Corinth 1, Corinth 2, Athens 2. Five of these hoards contain only silver coins (Roufou B, Karpenisi, Greek 1, Greek 3, Corinth), while the rest are mixed with bronzes. In all cases, the silver coins are antoniniani with the exception of the Karpenisi hoard, which contains mostly antoniniani with the addition of three denarii (Caracalla, Maximinus, Pupienus).

Coin finds from local museums from the eastern provinces of Greece and Asia Minor indicate the same picture. Stray finds from the museums of Yiannena, Volos, Eireniko (Kilkis), Fethiye, Sinope and Afyon demonstrate a sharp decrease in the volume of denarii in circulation and the simultaneous increase of the antoniniani from the reign of Gordian III until the reign of Trajan Decius.[59] It seems that in all of the above regions the first increase in the number of antoniniani in circulation took place during the reign of Gordian (apart from Sinope). However, the peaks and troughs of antoniniani from these museums vary from one area to another.

Syrian silver coin hoards lost during the period of Military Anarchy demonstrate a somewhat different picture. The basis of their individuality lies mainly in the substantial production of tetradrachms from local mints. Therefore we should divide them into three different groups according to the denominations that they contain. On one hand, we find the tetradrachm hoards (Syria 6, Syria 7, Dura Europos 5, Dura Europos 8, Rafah, Jordan, Turkey 3, Turkey 4), which demonstrate a common structure. None of them contains coins from the Antonine period, as they all begin during the Severan period. Hoards consisting of both imperial and provincial coinage (Dura Europos 1, Dura Europos 6, Dura Europos 2, Dura Europos 4, Dura Europos 15, Gush Halav, Antioch 2) are slightly different, mainly because three of them (Gush Halav, Dura Europos 4, Dura Europos 15) contain coins not only from the Antonine but also from the Flavian period. Because of this unusual stretch in time, we notice the inclusion of more denarii. However, the imperial coins included in these hoards and issued after the reign of Gordian III seem to be exclusively antoniniani, thus resembling the hoards we encountered in Greece and Asia Minor. In addition, there seems to be a substantial number of silver hoards that contain only antoniniani (Antioch 1, Dura Europos 14, Hama, Syria 2, Syria 4, Syria 5, Ihsa), which include coins only issued during the reigns of Trebonianus Gallus, Valerian and Gallienus.

The eastern Roman provinces are not the only ones where we see the disappearance of denarii from circulation and its replacement with the highly debased coin of the antoninianus. Silver coin hoards that came from the western and northern provinces of the Roman empire show similar results: denarii disappeared from circulation during the period between 240 and 274, although the rate of disappearance is uneven between different provinces.[60] Overall, we can observe an empire-wide phenomenon of the replacement of one silver coin by another of lesser fineness in the markets.

At this point we should attempt an explanation of the predominance of denarii until the end of the Severan era and the subsequent prevalence of antoniniani in the circulation pools. A possible reason for the replacement of one denomination by another could have been the simultaneous reform

[59] Katsari 2001: charts 28–33. [60] Bland 1996a: 78–9.

of the exchange system: a reform that might have occurred sometime during the third century. As we have already seen[61] a gold coin (*chrysous*) was worth twenty-five denarii until the reign of Alexander Severus; therefore, the same exchange rates that were established during the reign of Augustus probably remained intact for all the denominations until the end of the Severan period. Since the Roman state continued to guarantee the value of the silver coins, even if they were highly debased, there was no apparent reason for changes in the patterns of circulation. On one hand, if the government continued to employ the same exchange rates as before, the difference between the intrinsic and the face value of the coins would have been too far apart. As a result, the established bimetallic system would have collapsed. On the other hand, if the rates followed naturally the debasement of silver coinage, by the time of Trajan Decius, the denarius should have been tariffed at 100 to the aureus. Instead, we find antoniniani overstruck on older denarii.[62] One of the following scenarios could have been part of the impact of these changes: (a) One aureus could have been tarrifed at twenty-five antoniniani, thus eliminating the denarius and overvaluing the silver currency even further. (b) The government may have kept the exchange rate of fifty antoniniani per aureus, in an attempt to devalue the highly debased silver coinage. Either way, none of these developments would have brought the desirable profits to the Roman state or stability to the system: a system that, even if it did not collapse with the introduction and widespread distribution of the antoninianus, certainly changed irreversibly during the reign of Gordian III, as we are about to see.

According to the above scenarios, the government could have played an essential role in altering or not the exchange rates. However, these hypotheses do not take into consideration the impact of the population on monetary policies. In fact, there is a strong possibility that the increase in the number of highly debased antoniniani in the circulation pools of the eastern provinces during the reign of Gordian III and the simultaneous disappearance of the denarii from circulation should be interpreted in another way. It seems that the merchants preferred the antoninianus for their daily transactions. This happened because its intrinsic value was estimated at one- and-a-half denarii, while it was exchanged in the market at the price of a double denarius. According to Gresham's Law, the debasement and effective overvaluation of the antoniniani would have instigated its increasing use in the Roman markets. On the other hand, the government became progressively more interested in the production of this highly

[61] See chapter 3. [62] H. Mattingly 1939; Carson 1965: 230.

overvalued coin that brought more minting profits to the Roman treasury. Generally speaking, even if the exchange rates remained intact, the radical debasements of the era and the changes in the production of precious-metal coinages would have altered the preferences of the population with regard to the different silver denominations. Subsequently, the situation in the markets would have affected imperial policies with regard to the future of the monetary system.

Despite the rigid central control of currencies, the regular manipulations of currencies could have triggered a growing suspicion towards the imperial coinages. The population probably observed that the content of the silver coins in circulation changed as fast as the emperors in power; so the merchants came to prefer to dispose of their debased coins as soon as possible through the markets or the banking system. A sign of the distrust of the people towards the official currency and the reaction of the State is attested in a papyrus from AD 260, according to which the bankers refused to exchange coins (probably debased silver coins for aurei of higher fineness) and they closed the banks in Egypt. The Roman state had to enforce the acceptance of the official money, so that they could silence the developing distrust of the debased currency.[63] This does not seem to be an isolated incident, as some researchers suggested,[64] but an aspect of the economic conditions that arose from the extreme debasement of silver coinages. Even if the alteration of the exchange rates became inevitable, we should not assume that the Roman state instigated such reforms willingly. Once the fineness of the silver coins was reduced to 2.5 per cent precious metal, by the time of Gallienus' reign, it is possible that some of the merchants may have exchanged the antoniniani at a lower rate, disregarding the instructions issued by the state: a situation that could signify a shift towards a demonetised economy in the markets and/or a de facto alteration of the official exchange system.

This economic behaviour has been recently studied in more detail. Selgin, in his article on 'Salvaging Gresham's Law' says that 'a legal-tender law might punish sellers who attempt to place a discount on "bad" money or refuse it altogether while rewarding would be buyers who report such discrimination'.[65] He continues explaining the effects of the enforcement of such laws. Specifically, he claims that in such cases 'good' money will be hoarded or exported. Alternatively, 'good' money may be exchanged at a

[63] *P. Oxy.* XII, 1411; West and Johnson 1967: 183.

[64] In MacLennan 1968: 31, the author claims that this papyrus reflects a lack of confidence not in the currency but in the rule of Macrianus and Quietus.

[65] Selgin 1996: 641–2.

premium in the mint. His assertions describe perfectly the situation that arose in the middle of the third century AD. On one hand, as we have seen in the previous chapter, the gold coins were either melted or exported. On the other hand, since denarii disappeared from excavations and hoards alike, we may assume that they were exchanged at the mainstream Roman mints for the new antoniniani. However, this exchange may not have taken place willingly. According to the above-mentioned law, merchants were forced to accept highly debased coins for their transactions. On top of that, the regular reminting of the existing coinages compelled the population to abandon the denarius altogether and turn to the exclusive use of antoniniani.

The increased volume of silver coinages in circulation in the form of the higher-valued antoniniani in combination with the apparent stability of the exchange rates and the seemingly unaffected prices of commodities until the reign of Gallienus could give the false impression of an increasing monetisation. The increasing numbers of overvalued silver coins in circulation already as early as the Severan period were indeed used in more major transactions. However, in this case they were just replacing the gold coins that gradually disappeared from the markets. As we have already seen, the aurei, which until the early Severan period represented two-thirds of the total face value of the coins in circulation,[66] became unavailable and, thus, the denarii and antoniniani took their place as the basic means of exchange in major transactions. If aurei were no longer used in the markets and the value of the gold coins in circulation was triple that of the silver coins, then the production of denarii should have been multiplied by three times. And in fact, this is exactly what happened during the Severan period. The increase of denarii would have initially covered for the lack of gold coins and it would have kept a high level of monetisation in large transactions. However, the situation changed during the reign of Gordian III, when the silver coins were further debased and the antoninianus became the most popular coin in the markets. The rapid debasement of the silver coinage, which eventually led to changes in their actual value, caused billon antoniniani to be used as small change. This development, in turn, had an impact on the monetisation of the larger transactions by the middle of the third century.

Despite the increase of antoniniani in circulation, neither inscriptions nor literary evidence seems to indicate a higher degree of monetisation of major transactions, where the use of silver and gold coins would have been

[66] Howgego 1992: 11; Duncan-Jones 1994: 111.

essential. Epigraphic evidence from the middle of the third century also demonstrates changes in the monetary behaviour of the population, as a consequence of the disappearance of the aurei from the circulation pools. According to one inscription it was considered an unparalleled honour and a privilege for someone to be paid in imperial gold coins.[67] In fact, the rare cases of the appearance of gold coins in inscriptions or literary sources should be considered exceptional. The emperors during the third century rarely chose to use aurei in order to reward their subjects for manifestations of outstanding loyalty and the accomplishment of special services.

A number of funerary inscriptions from Asia Minor also indicate a turn towards the use of precious-metal bullion instead of coins. A study of the tombstones from the area shows that the nature of the hitherto standardised fines changed during the third century AD. While in previous centuries the tomb raiders were supposed to pay a certain amount of money in the form of precious-metal coins to the family or the city or the imperial treasury, in some instances during the third century the fine would instead be paid in talents or '*litras argyrou*' or '*chrysou*'.[68] This habit is attested for the first time after the middle of the third century but it becomes more regular throughout the fourth and the fifth centuries in Greece as well as in Asia Minor.[69] In other funerary inscriptions the type of metal and the adjoining number is mentioned without specifying the denomination, if a denomination was indeed expected.[70] The above examples could indicate a change in the attitude of the population towards the function of coins around the time of Gallienus' reign. Although the traditional formulas of 1,000, 1,500, 2,000 etc. denarii were still in use, evaluations in weights made their appearance probably because of the gradual replacement of gold and silver coins with raw metal when a substantial amount of money was in need. If anything, these inscriptions indicate a decrease in the use of precious-metal coins in large transactions; hence, a partial demonetisation

67 *CIL* 13.3162.

68 Thyateira, *IGRR* 4.1977; *IG* 14.2331 (*litras argyrou*); *IG* 14.2336 (*argyrou litras*); Sahin 1994: no. 122 (*gold uncia*); Corsten 1985: no. 39 (*litras argyrou*).

69 Termessus, *SEG* XLI (1991) 1277 (the amount is estimated in unciae); *CIG* 3.4259 (one talent); *IG* 4.410 (one talent); *TAM* II.1 122 (one talent); *TAM* III.1 499 (one talent); *SEG* 6. 635=*TAM* III.1 798 (two talents); *IGRR* 4.1277 (*litra chrysou*) Coupry and Feyel 1936: 53, no. 4 (*litra chrysou*); *IG* 14.2324–2328, 2330, 2332–2333 (*litra chrysou*); *MAMA* VIII (1962) 580 (*litrai chrysou*); *IG* 14.2334 (*litrai chrysou*); *IG* 2.2.13224 (*unciae chrysou*); IG 14.2329 (*unciae chrysou*); *IG* 2.2. 13219 (*litrai argyrou*); *SEG* 16. 417 (*litrai argyrou*); Lechat and Radet 1888: 200, no. 11 (*litrai argyrou*); *IG* 10.2.1.556 (*litrai argyrou*); *IG* 12.2.647 (*litrai argyrou*); *IG* 14.2336 (*litrai argyrou*); *IG* 14.2331 (*litrai argyrou*); Hasluck 1905: 63. Most of the above references can be found in Robert 1946: 106, n. 3.

70 Olympos (Lycia), *SEG* XLI (1991) 1387 '*argyriou myriadas dyo*'.

of the economy occurred at some point during the middle of the third century.

The Quantity Theory of Money could explain not only the decreasing monetisation but also the stability of prices until the 270s, as Dominic Rathbone suggested.[71] According to the Quantity Theory of Money, if the number of gold coins in circulation increases, then the value of gold falls, the prices rise and inflation becomes a possibility. Similarly, according to the Classical Theory, prices rise after the discovery of more gold resources because gold becomes cheaper.[72] This situation could, in turn, cause an increase in commodity prices. Specifically in the third century AD, gold coins, which comprised 70 per cent of the coin economy, seem to have been demonetised. In addition, the amount of gold bullion within the Roman state remained unaltered or (more likely) was reduced though the inactivity of major mints and the usual attrition rate.[73] This situation probably helped the state to avoid the inflation of prices, since only a restricted number of gold coins (aurei) circulated in the markets.

THE DEARTH OF CIVIC BRONZE COINAGES AND THE MYLASA INSCRIPTION

So far, we have studied extensively the fluctuations of silver and gold currencies and their impact on the monetary economy. At this point, it is essential to study another aspect of monetary economics: small change. T. J. Sargent and F. R. Velde already noted that when applying the Quantity Theory of Money, we should separate gold and silver coinages from the smaller bronze denominations.[74] This division is essential because the first are used in major transactions, while the second are used in minor transactions. As they cannot be substituted for each other, they should be studied separately.

In the Roman empire bronze currencies were issued by a number of mints controlled by different authorities. Specifically, we can divide these mints into (a) mainstream or state or 'official' mints, e.g. Rome, Antioch, Milan etc. and (b) civic mints, e.g. Smyrna, Ephesus, Athens etc. The state or mainstream or 'official' mints produced coins intended to cover the needs of the emperor as well as his military and administrative mechanism for payments in coined money. Civic mints, on the other hand, were probably administered by local authorities and were destined to cover local monetary needs. As we have already seen, the production of these mints changed from

[71] Rathbone 1996. [72] Glasner 1989: 86. [73] See chapter 3. [74] Sargent and Velde 2002.

the beginning of the third century onwards. The mint of Rome reduced its production of small change as early as the reign of Septimius Severus in order to focus on the production of precious-metal coinages. At the same time the civic mints in Greece, Asia Minor and Syria increased their production according to local needs. The inability of Rome to provide several of its provinces with small change would have caused problems of liquidity. Such problems are described vividly in an inscription from Asia Minor that has not been adequately studied in economic terms.

In 1885 an inscription was found in the city of Mylasa in Asia Minor; less than a decade later it was partially restored and published in the *Bulletin de Correspondance Hellénique* (1896) by T. Homolle.[75] Due to the historical significance of the inscription a series of publications followed in order to complete the restoration of the fragments. So far, the most widely accepted version is the one published by Dittenberger in 1905 in *Orientis Graeci Inscriptiones Selectae*.[76] Although the 1905 restoration should be taken seriously into consideration, it is imperative to acknowledge the reproduction of the inscription by W. Blümel in the *Inschriften griechischer Städte am Kleinasien: Die Inschriften von Mylasa*.[77]

According to older as well as recent historical interpretations the inscription is in fact a decree issued by the council and the assembly of the city aiming at the punishment of people who exchanged coins illegally in the market.[78] Since the city of Mylasa derived revenue from the exchange of currency, the magistrates attempted to regulate the banking process. In fact, they sought to restrict the right to exchange coins to a small number of bankers who could be controlled. In this inscription, the authorities declared that, if anyone was caught exchanging or purchasing currency, apart from the person who has leased the bank, he should be brought before the banker in order to be punished. If the person in question made no profit from the transaction, then he should forfeit to the bank the amount of the transaction. If he did make a profit, in addition to the forfeiture, he should pay the amount of 850 denarii, to be divided among the imperial treasury, the city council and the accuser. If he was a slave, the penalty was a beating and six months in prison. The secretary was not only empowered but also obliged to summon the court within three days after he was informed of the case. The chief magistrates and the secretary

[75] Homolle 1896. [76] *OGIS* 2.160–5, no. 515. See Appendix 1 for full text of inscription.

[77] Blümel 1987: 220–3, no. 605.

[78] For the text and its interpretation see Abbott and Johnson 1926: 461–3, no. 133; Broughton 1938: 906–7. Further discussion of the inscription can be found in Magie 1950: 682; Pekáry 1959: 464–6; Bogaert 1968: 265 ff.

responsible for the trial of these cases and the punishment of the offenders would also pay a fine to the imperial *fiscus* if they failed to act immediately.

The existing publications of the Mylasa decree took into consideration the political, military and economic changes that affected the whole of the Roman empire during the third century AD. Several researchers attempted to establish a convincing hypothesis with regard to the financial predicament that gave rise to the decree; nonetheless the incomplete restoration of the inscription left a number of questions unanswered. The text finishes with an account of the problems that fell upon the city and the consequences for the daily lives of the citizens. According to the existing restorations and the subsequent translations of the lines 47–52 we may read: 'For in truth the security of our city is shaken by the evildoing and villainy of some few who take advantage of her and embezzle public property. By their agency an exchange crisis has invaded the market place, preventing the city from obtaining necessities, so that the people are without resources and the public is in want.'[79] Although no more information regarding the nature of these coins or the exact financial problems is mentioned in the edict, from the above text the scholars initially concluded that the illegal exchange of coins disrupted the transactions in the local markets and destroyed the regular civic revenues, causing the distress of the civic authorities.

As we have seen in chapter 2, the military upheaval following the death of Commodus led to the financial instability of the Roman state, which reacted immediately to the situation by instigating the reform of the silver weight standards. According to a widely held theory, the debasement of the imperial silver currency was the main reason for the illegal exchange of higher denominations for small change. The accepted hypothesis was that the Mylasa inscription might indicate that, due to the debasements, the commercial ratio between silver and bronze was altered, although the legal ratio might have remained the same. The population showed signs of panic, since gold and silver coins went into hiding or were used for payments outside the empire, whilst bronze began to be in demand as something of real value. This way, both bronze and silver coinages disappeared from the market, since they were probably kept out of the circulation pools and moved into hoards; so the dearth of coins inhibited commercial transactions and eventually triggered the illegal exchange of coins. The *boule* of Mylasa,

[79] The translation of this passage can be found in Lewis 1974: 47–8. The author follows previous translations and interpretations of the passage. According to other translations the word κόλλυβος refers to small change (abundant in the market).

disdaining or ignorant of economic laws, believed that they could find a remedy to this intolerable situation by reinforcing the monopoly of the official moneychangers and by redoubling the penalties.[80]

The above hypothesis remained unquestioned for more than 100 years, thus influencing modern numismatic research and the theoretical trends in Roman economic history. However, in the course of the past century archaeology has revealed a quantity of new evidence that could alter our initial perceptions regarding the monetary reforms, the financial situation of the Greek cities, the circulation of coins in the provinces and the function of the local markets.

In the first instance, it is essential to place the inscription within the particular historical context that gave rise to the illegal exchange of coins in the eastern provinces. It has rightly been suggested that the text was written sometime between AD 209 and 211,[81] but it is not known whether the edict was voted for the first time during the early Severan period or whether it repeated the content of an earlier edict that was renewed in the third century in order to validate an already established law. In either case, the location of the inscription in a public place in AD 209–11 reflects the escalation of the black market in the exchange of currency. This escalation probably forced the city authorities to renew the edict and place it in public view. It seems that the unexpected spread of the illegal exchange of coins created problems not only for the bankers who lost their profits but also for the city itself, thus causing the interference of the imperial authorities, which held the local magistrates liable for the swift punishment of the offenders. Until now, historians have considered the monetary reforms taking place in the early third century as the main reason for the instigation of the black market, though this theory presents us with certain problems that should not be ignored.

First of all, the debasement of silver coins may be an unquestionable fact but it did not necessarily affect significantly the operation of the existing monetary structures, since during the Severan period the gold and bronze coinages remained unaltered, guaranteeing the stability of the system. On one hand, the gold coins retained their fineness long after the death of Caracalla, so that the legal exchange ratio of one aureus to twenty-five denarii would remain unaltered despite the reforms at least until the reign of Severus Alexander.[82] On the other hand, the value of both civic and

80 Reinach 1896: 545 ff.; Broughton 1938: 906–7.

81 *OGIS* 2.515; Abbott and Johnson 1926: no. 133. A slightly different date (AD 209–10) is given by Reinach 1896: 530.

82 See chapter 3.

imperial bronze coinages does not seem to have been adjusted towards the new overvalued denarii or antoniniani. It has been suggested that since the reign of Augustus the legal value of the *as* in Asia Minor had been fixed at one-sixteenth to one-eighteenth of the denarius.[83] The regional variations of the exchange rate could be explained, if we take into consideration that both bankers and civic authorities profited from the exchange of coins by imposing a fee (*agio*). For example, in an inscription from Pergamos we notice that money-changers sold denarii for 18 asses while they bought them for 17 asses.[84] If the official exchange rate was 1:16, then one *as* ended up in the treasury of the city and another *as* went into the pockets of the money-changers. It is possible that this fee differed from one region to another depending on the demands of the bankers or the needs of the city itself. Aside from these variations, bronzes were exchanged with silver coins essentially at the same ratio until the late 250s, when, at last, various cities started to countermark their civic coinages in order to change the face value of bronze issues.[85] It is unlikely that the legal exchange rate would have been adjusted to the commercial rate more than fifty years after the first monetary changes. The alleged difference between the commercial and the legal value, if it continued for the first half of the third century, would not have just triggered the illegal exchange of coins but it would have disrupted seriously private transactions, which were based on the use of money as common trading means, thus resulting in total anarchy in the local markets. However, neither monetary anarchy in the marketplace during the Severan period nor official ignorance of economic laws is historically proven. On the contrary, it is reasonable to assume that the civic authorities would have reacted to the situation almost immediately, if they were aware of the problem and they considered their profits to be at stake. Consequently, the exchange rate was adjusted only when there was a definite commercial need for such a change during the middle of the third century and not before.

[83] Gara 1976: 122–31. Although the official ratio of exchange of the denarius was 1:16, in Asia Minor another ratio (1:18) has been established. The difference in value was probably paid as profit to the treasury of the city or the imperial *fiscus* or even the banker. See also the inscription from Pergamos (note 84 and text).

[84] Standard edition by Dittenberger (*OGIS* 2: 105–12 and 552, no. 484; reproduced by Abbot and Johnson 1926: 401–3, no. 81; also Broughton 1938: 892–5. Discussion regarding the banking system can be found in: West 1941: 93–4; Magie 1950: 624–5 and 1486, n. 51; Bolin 1958: 238–43; Johnson, Coleman-Norton and Bourne 1961: 205–6, no. 246; Bogaert 1968: 231–4; Macro 1976; Oliver 1989: 208–15, no. 84.

[85] Regional differences as well as similarities in countermarking have been noticed by Howgego 1985: 62ff.

Furthermore, recently revealed numismatic evidence indicates that extensive hoarding of high quality silver coins did not take place in the early third century, as researchers used to presume. If we compare the number of published hoards buried during the Severan period with the number of hoards lost during the Antonine period in Asia Minor in relation to the total span of years of the two dynasties, we notice that the rate of the (two) Antonine and the (two) Severan hoards from Asia Minor is in fact 2: 6. However, the increasing number of hoards lost during the Severan period does not necessarily indicate extensive hoarding due to the debasement. Instead it should probably be taken as an indication of either an increase in the death rate in the Roman empire[86] or an increase in the mint output of silver. It is also significant to note that the silver hoards from Asia Minor (the Sulakyurt hoard and the Turkey 1 hoard) demonstrate a similar structure. They contain a relatively low number of coins belonging to the Antonine period, characterised by higher silver fineness, while the bulk of the coins (64 per cent and 91 per cent respectively) was issued during the reigns of Septimius Severus/Caracalla and is of lower intrinsic value. It seems that both hoards were accumulated after the monetary changes of the early third century, when the circulation of numerous debased silver issues probably supplanted the previous coinages. This evidence could suggest that the local populations were not seriously affected by Severan debasement and panic never seemed to trigger the extensive hoarding of higher-fineness silver coins. In reality, hoarding continued more or less at the same pace as before and the population tended to save the new debased denarii with the same care that they demonstrated towards the fine denarii of the Antonine emperors just a few years previously.

The increase in coin production during the early third century AD, as demonstrated in the hoards, is also attested by the excavation finds and verifies the fact that there was a rise in the volume of silver coins produced by the mint of Rome. In the course of the Ephesus excavations (Charts 12, 15) a substantial quantity of denarii was revealed that could be used for statistical purposes. The analysis shows that the distribution of coinage is uniformly low during the Antonine and Severan periods, apart from the reign of Marcus Aurelius (1.83%) and the reigns of Septimius Severus and Caracalla (1.45%), during which we observe the formation of two small peaks in the number of coins. The volume of silver coinage increases abruptly later, during the reign of Gordian III (15.43%) and continues rising until it reaches its highest peak during the reign of Gallienus (43.21%). The

86 M. Crawford 1969: 76–81; Howgego 1992: 3.

peak formed in the early Severan period could be explained only if soldiers, administrative officials or traders used more silver coins in the markets of the eastern provinces on a daily basis.

Such an increase should be expected if we take into consideration the political and military developments of the time. We know that the death of Commodus was followed by civil strife and economic uncertainty, which lasted for a few years until Septimius Severus became the uncontested founder of the next dynasty. The outcome of the wars was mainly determined by the financial capacity of the bidder to the throne, since the army demanded more money in order to bestow its loyalty on one or the other party. Eventually, the heavy funding of the continuous military campaigns drained the imperial treasury and Septimius Severus sought to increase his revenues through manipulation of silver coinages, as we have already seen. The debasement of the denarius aimed at minting more silver coins using the same amount of silver bullion as before.

If the silver mint output was greater than before, then we should expect a comparable increase in the number of bronze coins in order to cover the need for the monetary exchange of higher for smaller denominations indispensable for the conduct of retail transactions in the provincial markets. It has already been suggested that, especially during unexpected events – such as imperial visits, festivals or sudden movements of the army – the city authorities would have been driven to despair, if there was a lack of bronze coins.[87] Similarly, the need for small change in the markets became critical once silver coins multiplied in the circulation pools at the beginning of the third century, a situation that could explain the justified anxiety of the magistrates. The previous suggestions that there was a dearth of silver coins in the markets seem to be unfounded, while the lack of bronze is probably the commonsensical effect of the increasing volume of precious-metal coins in circulation. Consequently, the inscription of Mylasa should be interpreted according to the new evidence, which attests the shortage of bronzes in circulation, and the restored text should be adjusted.

If the need for bronze denominations was not fulfilled in time, then serious disruption would have been noted in the market, while traders would have taken individual measures in order to solve the problem. One possibility is that the citizens would have been forced to address smaller traders dealing mostly in bronze. The inscription from Pergamos that we have already discussed refers to three different classes of merchants involved in retail transactions and using bronze coins in the course of their

[87] Ziegler 1993: 142–3; 1996: 119–227.

trade: shopkeepers (ἐργαστοί), retailers (κάπηλοι) and salt fish traders (ὀψαριοπῶλαι). According to this Hadrianic decree, retail transactions had to be conducted in local bronze, so that the bankers could extract their payment from the exchange of coins and the city would receive the *agio*. Although it has been suggested that fish traders and other such merchants were not obliged by the force of law to receive only bronze coins in the course of their transactions,[88] it is possible according to the Pergamos inscription that the use of silver coins in retail trade was discouraged.[89] To all intents and purposes, if there was a lack of bronze coinage in the official treasury of the city at the beginning of the third century, the merchants who gathered vast numbers of bronze coins every day would have had the capacity to exchange the money with a small profit for them, thus distressing the bankers and depriving the city of its rightful revenue, in the same way as it is described in the inscription of Mylasa (lines 47ff.).

The soldiers who participated in small-scale daily transactions would soon require the exchange of their silver coins for bronze ones through the local banking system. This need was felt in particular when the law demanded that only lower denominations should be used for certain dealings in the market, e.g. in order to buy fish, as at least one inscription indicates.[90] The demand for more bronze coins because of the current *caritas nummorum* soon became an unavoidable necessity throughout the eastern provinces, including Asia Minor. It is possible that in response to this need Septimius Severus gave permission to the cities to undertake the minting of new civic issues destined for local circulation. The dearth of coinage is not a new phenomenon in pre-industrial societies. Carlo Cipolla has already described the efforts of medieval sovereigns to supply the markets with smaller denominations in a chapter entitled 'The big

[88] Buttrey 1991.

[89] *῞Οσα μέντοι τῶν λεπτῶν ὀψαρίων σταθμῶι πιπρασκόμενα τιμᾶται ὑπό τῶν ἀγορανόμων, τούτων, κἀν πλείονας μνᾶς ὠνήσονταί τινες, ἤρεσεν ἡμεῖν τήν τιμήν αὐτούς διδόναι πρός κέρμα, ὥστε ἀπ' αὐτῶν σώσζεσθαι τῆι πόλει τήν ἐκ τοῦ κολλύβου πρόσοδον. ὁμοίως καί ἐάν πλείονες συνθέμενοι ἀργυρῶν δηναρίων δόξωσιν ἠγορακέναι εἶτα διαιρῶνται, καί τούτους λεπτόν διδόναι χαλκόν τῶι ψαριοπώλῃι, ἵνα ἀναφέρηται ἐπί τήν τράπεζαν·*

Translation according to Oliver 1989:

It met with our approval that on these sales (the purchasers), even if some buy amounts weighing several minas, pay the price in bronze, so that the revenue from the exchange be preserved for the city; likewise, even if several who had banded together are seen to have bought for silver denarii and then divide it up among themselves, they too pay in small bronze to the salt fish dealer in order that (the bronze) be taken to the bank.

[90] In AD 121 Hadrian writes a letter to the citizens of Piraeus in order to regulate the sale of fish. The inscription and the relevant discussion can be found in IG 2.2.1103; Abbott and Johnson 1926: 91; Day 1942: 192ff; Pleket 1964: no. 16; Smallwood 1967: 444.

problem of petty coins'. He also noted their relative inability to feed the markets with adequate supplies of small denominations in certain cases. Specifically, he claimed that 'Mediterranean Europe failed to discover a good and automatic device to control the quantity of petty coins to be left in circulation' until the nineteenth century. As a consequence, shortages became a recurring phenomenon.[91]

The condemnation of the black market in the exchange of coins was only a temporary solution that did not resolve the real problem. Eventually, an attempt to increase the production of bronze issues either by the Roman state or by the cities became imperative for the efficient operation of the markets. Nevertheless, it has been claimed that the central mint of Rome did not intensify the production of imperial bronzes, probably because the mint magistrates were preoccupied at the time with the production of debased denarii and antoniniani. Unavoidably the burden fell on the numerous civic mints of the eastern provinces that took upon themselves the production of new issues, even if such task had never before been undertaken by some of the cities. It has already been noted that the actual number of the provincial mints reached its peak under the reign of Septimius Severus and then declined to about the level of the Augustan age by the beginning of the reign of Valerian.[92] Even if the proliferation of mints does not always equal the proliferation of coins, we should at least accept the hypothesis that a rise in production was the initial aim of the local governments.

Although the number of civic mints seemed to increase in order to meet the demands of the local markets during the Severan period, there are certain questions that remain unanswered. The first question is whether the new mints had the capacity to cover the commercial needs of the cities or not. As we have already seen, the exchange rate between silver and bronze was 1 : 16/18. In this case, we should have expected a substantial rise in the volume of bronze that would have been sufficient for at least part of the exchange. Even if we do not calculate the rise to be of sixteen to eighteen bronze coins for every denarius issued by the mint of Rome (after all a number of silver coins probably went out of circulation through loss, hoarding and exports to the *barbaricum*), we should still anticipate a significant increase. A chart comparing the percentage of bronze with silver coins from the excavation of Ephesus indicates that the number of bronze issues was almost nine times more than the silver coins in circulation, unlike in the previous period (Chart 25). In this case it is possible that the

[91] Cipolla 1956: chapter 3.
[92] T. Jones 1963. For a list of mints in each province see: T. Jones 1965: 295–301 and 308.

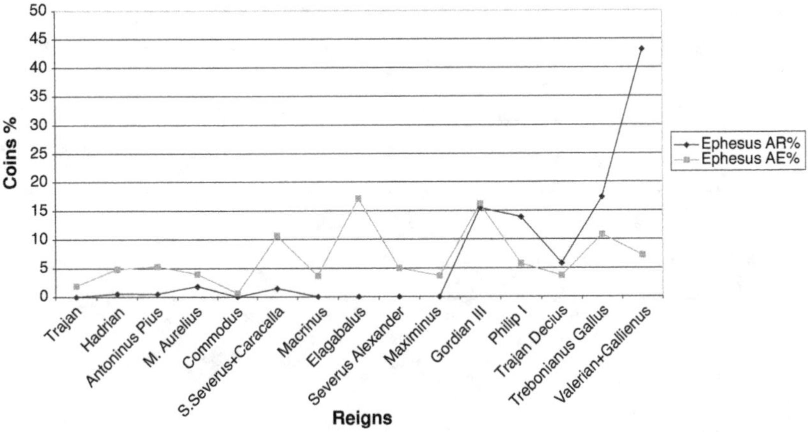

Chart 25 Ephesus excavations: silver and bronze coins, % per annum

authorities realised the problem on time and increased the issues of bronze coins in the city and the surrounding areas.

The results from the excavations of Ephesus alone do not prove the homogeneous and simultaneous increase in bronze coins throughout the Roman empire. Coin evidence from the excavations of Patra and Corinth in Greece show a completely different picture. First of all, a comparison between silver and bronze issues in circulation in the city of Patra and its surroundings indicates that a substantial rise in bronze minting took place during the Antonine period, while the number of bronze issues actually dropped during the reigns of Septimius Severus and Caracalla (Chart 26). In this case, it is possible that the previously minted small denominations were adequate for the needs of the market, even after the rise in the number of denarii in circulation; therefore an increase in the civic production of coins was not necessary.

On the other hand, the numismatic evidence from the colony of Corinth shows that a 7 per cent increase in production of bronze followed the 1 per cent increase in production of silver, thus covering for the exchange of coins in the local markets. Subsequently, the volume of bronze coins in circulation was reduced until minting stopped altogether before the middle of the third century AD (Chart 27).

The numismatic finds from the museums of Greece and Asia Minor that are not included in this section also demonstrate an uneven picture.[93]

[93] Katsari 2001: charts 72 and 73. The first chart includes finds from the following Greek museums: Yiannena, Corfu, Volos, Komotene and Thessalonica. The second chart includes finds from the Turkish Museums of Afyon, Sinope and Fethiye.

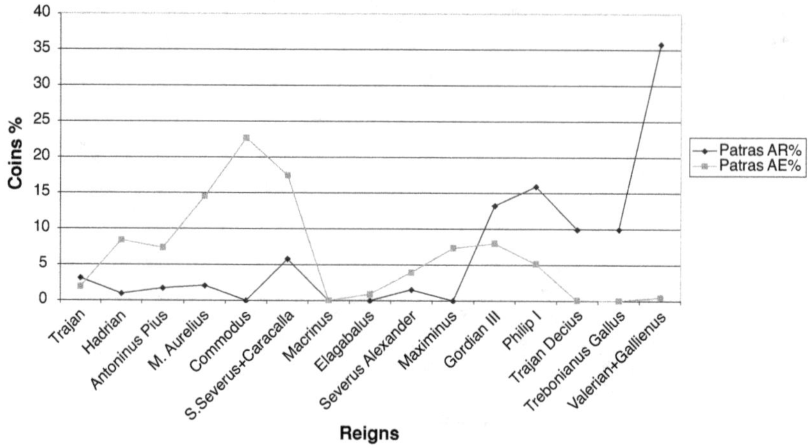

Chart 26 Patra excavations: silver and bronze coins, % per annum

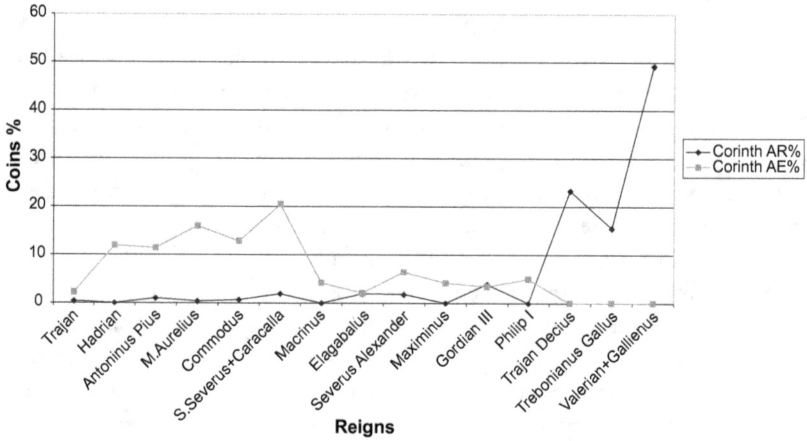

Chart 27 Corinth excavations: silver and bronze coins, % per annum

It is clear that more bronze than silver coins circulated in Greece during the Antonine period, while the number of bronze issues did not rise substantially in the early third century as we would have expected. The study of stray finds from the museums of southern and central Turkey does not confirm the results from excavations in the city of Ephesus, since it shows that the volume of bronze production in Roman Asia Minor did not alter significantly during the reigns of Septimius Severus and Caracalla, thus indicating that the case of Ephesus may have been an exception.

We encounter the same problem in the northern militarised provinces of Dacia and Pannonia (Charts 20, 21, 22). As we have already seen, in these provinces there is a clear decline in the circulation of smaller denominations during the Severan period, while at the same time the silver coins increased abruptly. It is evident that the reduced output of bronze coins from the mint of Rome must have affected not only the north-eastern Balkan provinces but the entire western Mediterranean. In the eastern Mediterranean, Greece, Asia Minor and Syria benefited from the flexible production of the individual civic mints. The authorities of the cities could arrange the striking of new issues, whenever they perceived that a lack of smaller denominations affected the local markets. On the other hand, the western provinces had to rely on the central mint of Rome for the provision of small change in their markets. If the mint of Rome stopped or decreased production, as happened during the Severan period, then the cities would have faced severe liquidity problems.

The differences in the above results illustrate that the problem was either not realised on time everywhere or that the cities (including Rome) did not manage to organise the intensified production of local mints as soon as troubles in the exchange of coinage started. The case of Mylasa could be used as a case study that would help us understand the situation in the rest of the empire, although certain regional differences should be taken into account. Once the black market in the exchange of coins intensified the authorities decided to react by asking the emperor to intervene and impose heavy punishments on the offenders. When they realised that these measures were inadequate, they increased the volume of civic bronzes. Chart 11, based on the published corpus of the Mylasa mint, indicates a high peak in the production of coinage during the reigns of Septimius Severus and Caracalla. It seems that most of these coins bear the portrait of the son and not the father, although we cannot always know if they belong to the period of Caracalla's sole reign or before. Therefore, it is possible that the volume of bronze coins did not cover the needs of the market before the reign of Caracalla, when the mint of Mylasa accelerated the rhythms of production. This hypothesis could explain the flourishing of the black market in the area and the placement of the inscription in public view. The decline in production immediately after Caracalla's death could indicate that the problem was finally resolved in this city and its immediate area, although we cannot be certain about the course of events in other regions.

Taking into consideration the probable dearth of bronze coinage in the city of Mylasa during and possibly after the reign of Septimius Severus, we should go back to the original text and try to restore the inscription.

In line 52 instead of *τοῦ κοινοῦ* we can use the word *τοῦ χαλκοῦ*,[94] thus translating the phrase *ἀπορούντων [τῶν πολλῶν | καί τοῦ χαλκοῦ σ]πανίζοντος* as '. . . while many are in need and the bronze coins are rare'. Another question arises also from line 50 in which the abundance of κόλλυβος in the market is mentioned. So far the accepted translation of κόλλυβος in this sentence has been 'small change', disregarding the fact that in previous lines it is consistently connected with the *agio*. If we accept the previous *agio* interpretation of κόλλυβος, then we should probably reconstruct the whole phrase *ὧν ὑπό || τῆς δυνάμ]εως κόλλυβός τις ἐνπεφοίτηκεν εἰς [τήν ἀγοράν, | κωλύων τήν πό]λιν τά ἐπιτήδ(ε)ια ἔχειν*. First of all, a word that should probably be translated differently is the verb ἔνπεφοίτηκεν, which until now was thought to mean 'invade' in a metaphorical sense. Such an interpretation is suggested also in the Liddell–Scott lexicon but it is based only on the older translations of the inscription of Mylasa, since there are no further examples of the word εμφοιτῶ. Yet, the verb φοιτῶ could also be translated as 'come in' referring to tribute or taxes, an interpretation that is closer to the meaning of *κόλλυβος* as *agio*. The example available in Liddell–Scott (*τάλαντον ἀργυρίου Αλεξάνδρωι ἡμέρης ἑκάστης ἀφοίτα*) should be translated as 'one *talanton* of silver each day came into Alexander's treasury' or 'one *talanton* of silver each day was exacted/received by Alexander'. Consequently, the phrase *κόλλυβός τις ἐνπεφοίτηκεν εἰς [τήν ἀγοράν* could mean that the *agio* was exacted in the market (by the traders instead of the bankers).

Secondly, the phrase *ὧν ὑπό || τῆς δυνάμ]εως κόλλυβός τις* seems to be an awkward expression that makes no sense in the above context. Instead of *ὑπό || τῆς δυνάμ]εως*, we could use *τῆς πόλεως* as the possessive genitive of the noun *κόλλυβος*, while *ὧν* could be replaced by the explanatory ἐπεί, which would connect the first sentence (lines 47–9: *σαλεύει γάρ ὡς ἀλη[θῶς ἡ σωτηρία | τῆς πόλε]ως ἐκ κακουργίας καί πανουργίας ὀλί[γων τινῶν | αὐτῇ ἐπεμβα]ινόντων καί ἀπονοσφιζομένων τ[ά κοινά*) with the second (*ἐπεί τῆς πόλ]εως κόλλυβός τις ἐνπεφοίτηκεν εἰς [τήν ἀγοράν, | κωλύων τήν πό]λιν τά ἐπιτήδ(ε)ια ἔχειν, ἀπορούντων [τῶν πολλῶν | καί τοῦ χαλκοῦ σ]πανίζοντος*). Then, the translation of this passage could be:

The safety of the city is endangered through the evil doing and wickedness of a certain few, who interfere and embezzle the public interest, since the *agio* of the

[94] I took the decision not to use the word κόλλυβος because in this inscription the author gave it previously the meaning of *agio*. On the meaning of *κόλλυβος* in Greek inscriptions see Gara 1976: Appendix III, 173–83.

city was exacted in the market keeping the city from possessing the necessities of life, while many are in need and the bronze coins are rare.

It seems that the lack of bronze in the markets of Mylasa prepared the ground for the exchange of coins in the black market by small traders or others. The small change available to them included either older issues of Mylasa or coins imported from the neighbouring cities, which had already increased their mint production during the reign of Septimius Severus or before. The adopted practice of illegal exchange of coins had further implications for the prosperity of the city of Mylasa. The inscription specifically mentions that the security (σωτηρία) or prosperity (εὐημερία) of the town was threatened by the actions of the few who were involved in the exchange of the coins (lines 47–8). The language of the text at this point becomes quite elaborate in order to paint with dark colours the situation in the market and the grim effects on the lives of the citizens. Specifically, it is mentioned more than once that the city as well as the citizens did not have what was necessary for their survival and the payment of taxes to Rome had to be delayed.

However, the desperate tone of the citizens when they describe the bad luck that has befallen them and their inability to pay taxes to the Roman treasury could be explained only as a rhetorical attempt to impress the imperial authorities. In the first instance, there is no evidence in the literary sources or in the inscriptions that indicate radical changes in the tax system took place in the early third century AD which could explain the failure of the citizens to fulfil their obligations towards the Roman state. In addition, only a small part of the profits of the provincial cities was covered by the *agio* imposed during the exchange of coins, while the most important income was still based on other financial resources, such as the *portoria*, loans and rents. All these sources of revenue seem to have remained unaffected throughout the third century AD; so the desperation of the civic authorities due to the lack of substantial income cannot possibly be justified.

Furthermore, neither the debasement of silver coinages nor the lack of bronze coins in the market could have affected directly the property of the landowners who were the most important taxpayers in the eastern provinces. Apparently part of the taxes was paid in goods, while money taxation did not exceed 20 per cent in most of Anatolia. Money-based taxes included probably the taxes on inheritances of Roman citizens (*vicesima hereditatum*), the manumission of slaves and customs dues (*portoria*), whilst the poll tax (*tributum capitis*) and the taxation on property (*tributum soli*) could have been paid in goods, especially since peasants had little or no cash reserves. The community responsible for the collection and the subsequent payment of taxes to the Roman officials probably accepted goods from the citizens and then transformed most of these into silver or gold coins.[95] As we have already seen, silver coins were minted in abundance throughout the Severan period; therefore it is unlikely that the payment of taxes would have been inhibited in any way or that the city did not have the ability to meet its financial obligations. There is a possibility that the civic authorities decided to exaggerate their misfortunes, blaming the illegal exchange of coins in order to justify their failure to pay the taxes due to the imperial treasury. The reasons for such failure should not be sought in the loss of the *agio* or κόλλυβος but elsewhere, probably in financial mismanagement or in the increasing military demands of the Roman emperors.

The inscription of Mylasa is a text that should be read in the light of the military, political and economic events of the beginning of the third century AD. The increasing numbers of debased silver coins in circulation caused certain imbalances in the exchange system due to the low volume of smaller denominations in the local markets. The cities probably did not succeed in increasing their bronze mint output on time, the banks did not rise to the occasion and the population was left with no option but to approach the traders who could provide them with small change, even if this action was illegal. The initial reaction of the civic magistrates was the prohibition of the black market in the exchange of the abundant silver for bronze coins, as is described in the inscription of Mylasa. Nevertheless, this measure was only temporary and in the medium term had to be combined with a matching increase in the volume of bronze coinages minted in the eastern provinces. The provincial mints undertook at different times the burden of producing small change for the markets but such an action may not have had an immediate effect.

Even though the flexibility of the civic mints may have resolved the medium-term problem of the eastern provinces, they did not solve the problems of the western provinces. The mint of Rome concentrated on the production of precious-metal coinages throughout the Severan period and neglected the needs of the local markets for small change. The lack of liquidity in these areas probably continued for at least three decades and should have created a series of problems in daily transactions. Apart from

[95] Mitchell 1993: 256. For general information on the types of taxes see Neesen 1980; review of Neesen's work by Brunt 1981. For the payment of taxes in gold (Egypt) or silver (Palmyra) see Gara 1976: 14, 64 and 105.

the rise in the black market, I would assume that one of the immediate effects would have been an increase in credit. Once the small change became unavailable, the buyers may have opened an account with specific traders, thus eventually paying them in silver coins. The same devices are employed in modern societies, as similar examples from early Argentina indicate.[96] Regrettably, we do not have adequate evidence from the ancient world that could describe the entirety of the phenomenon. Nevertheless, we have some evidence from Egyptian papyri that demonstrate the use of credit within large estates, albeit not its extent. Credit facilitated daily transactions, especially when there was a shortage of coins. For example, salaries were accredited to the account of the workers and, subsequently, taxes were paid on their behalf by the estate. For dealings outside the estate with, for example, independent craftsmen, the estate could transfer credit between accounts in private banks. Furthermore, the income of the estate, such as payments received from lessees and from larger-scale buyers, also came in a mixture of cash and credit. The transactions, which were based on credit, still represented a large part of the monetary economy, since they did not symbolise fictitious values but they were founded on the values established by the Roman monetary system.[97]

THE TERMINAL DECLINE OF BRONZE COINS IN THE MID THIRD CENTURY

The following period of the Military Anarchy presents the economist with different challenges that demand a different explanation. The production of both civic and 'official' bronze coinages was in irreversible decline after the reign of Gordian III, despite their short resurrection in the eastern provinces during the Severan period.[98] A study by W. Leschhorn demonstrates regional differences regarding the time of the final closure of different mints in Asia Minor.[99] However, the majority of the cities definitely ceased production of their coinages by the end of the reign of Gallienus with only

96 Ennis 2006 (http://findarticles.com/p/articles/mi_qa5407/is_200604/ai_n21394501).

97 The analysis of the Heronimos archive can be found in Rathbone 1991: 318–30. Regarding the phenomenon of shortage of coins in antiquity see Verboven 1997. The use of credit was a common banking process even before the third century AD, as demonstrated by Andreau 1999: 15–18. For more recent studies on Roman credit see W. Harris 2006 and 2008.

98 Salamon (1970) claims that the invasions of Persians and Goths prevented the production of coinage. It seems that the areas invaded by the enemy correspond with the places where minting stopped. I suspect, though, that these invasions did not cause but only accelerated the termination of civic issues in certain regions.

99 Leschhorn 1981: 261.

very few continuing until the reign of Tacitus. It is possible that the state, which undoubtedly realised that such processes would deprive the local markets of the most essential means of exchange, centralised the production of bronze coinages by mid third century in imperial mints, such as Rome, Antioch, Siscia, Milan etc.[100] Despite the initial efforts of the central authorities to control the minting of smaller denominations, by the reign of Aurelian the production of bronze coinage was considered unnecessary. From then onwards, the mint of Rome discontinued the minting of bronze issues.[101] There is a danger of interpreting this situation as the simultaneous decline of smaller-scale daily transactions in coin and the overall demonetisation of the economy; however, there are certain indications pointing in the opposite direction.

First of all, numismatists observed that various cities started to countermark older civic issues with Greek letters. These letters represented the new value of every piece of bronze coin in circulation. Initially and until the middle of the third century, the use of value countermarks was widespread only in western Asia Minor and Bithynia. In addition, we encounter them rarely in northern and southern Asia Minor. Aside from a few exceptions (there are instances of countermarked values even before AD 200), numismatists agree that there was no widespread change in values until *ca.* AD 255. Only then do we see the extensive countermarking of the majority of civic issues.[102] Once the monetary system started collapsing and the exchange rates became uncertain (probably in the 250s), if the value of the coin was not clearly indicated, there would have been no way of knowing if the face value was raised and by how much. The practice of countermarking allowed for the new values to be recognised fairly easily, so that misunderstandings and/or deliberate fraud could be avoided.[103] Furthermore, the fact that the minting authorities went to the trouble of recalling bronze

[100] On imperial mints during the third century see Harl 1996: 138–44.

[101] A. Watson 1999: 127–32.

[102] Howgego (1985: 62ff) notes regional differences as well as similarities in countermarking. The decline in weight standards in Lakedaimon and Argos began under Commodus, continued after 253 and accelerated after 260. The Koinon of Thessaly faced a decline between 235 and 260. In western Euxine, the standards of Tomis declined between Marcus Aurelius and Commodus, while most cities showed consistency between the reigns of Commodus and Philip. In Sarmatia, Tyra kept the same standards from Commodus until Severus Alexander while Olbia weight standards declined in the 170s. The weight standards in Bosporus showed a decline from Claudius to Nero, further reductions from 161 to 186, halving of the value between 196 and 210 and accelerated decline after 239 AD. In southern Euxine, weight standards declined under Gordian and Gallienus. Smyrna demonstrates a gradual decline in weight standards from the Severan period until after AD 260. Finally the weight standards of Pamphylia declined from the reign of Valerian onwards.

[103] Johnston 1997: 205–6.

coinages and countermarking them shows that the smaller denominations were still in use in the local markets by the reign of Gallienus.

The evidence from the countermarking also suggests that an adjustment of the exchange rates between bronze and silver took place during the middle of the third century, probably as part of a wider reform of the exchange rates in the Roman empire. These changes were necessary because the gap in the intrinsic value between bronze and silver coins became negligible after the repeated debasements; consequently the real value of the bronze coins became equal to or only slightly lower than the real value of the silver coins. The excessive reduction in the fineness of the silver currency caused an unsolved problem to the civic authorities. Since the real value of bronze currencies had increased in comparison to the real value of the silver ones, then the bronzes were no longer as highly overvalued as before and the cities probably could not even cover the minting costs. The magistrates who used to buy bronze bullion for a lower price and then distribute ('sell') it in the form of coins with a substantial profit possibly lost this revenue, since the legal value of bronze assaria was now closer to their intrinsic value. As a result, they closed the local mints altogether by the end of the reign of Gallienus and the task of distributing bronze coinage in the Roman empire was undertaken by the emperor and the imperial mints. Despite the end of minting in the east it is possible that the bronze denominations issued in previous reigns would still circulate in the area for several decades as a complement to the official Roman issues.

The terminal decline of civic coinages, though, should not be attributed exclusively to economic reasoning. Undoubtedly the cities saw a loss in their profits when the silver currencies were debased and the bronze denominations became undervalued. However, there was another important cultural shift that took place at the same time and seems to have contributed to the problem. A decrease in the number of honorary inscriptions, especially in third-century Asia Minor, is evident in the epigraphic catalogues. Simultaneously, we notice a decline in the amount of monumental building in the Greco-Roman cities. The assumption that the wealth of the empire was reduced cannot be founded, since we observe the building of new large villas and other privately owned constructions. Instead, we should assume that we are encountering a decline in civic benefactions. The citizens, as early as the Severan period, seem to have altered their perception of their role in their cities and accordingly they changed the level of their contributions. Although the bronze coinages continued to advertise the importance of the *polis* whenever they were issued, the citizens felt that they no longer needed this element in order to promote their fading civic patriotism. The establishment of a novel ideological and cultural orientation effectively led to the decline of the cities and their civic institutions in Late Antiquity.[104]

BILLON ANTONINIANI AS SMALL CHANGE

It is evident that by the reign of Gallienus the fineness of the antoninianus was reduced to 2.5 per cent silver. This amount does not justify fully the description of antoniniani as silver coins and this is the reason for calling them 'billon'.[105] Despite the drastic decrease in the fineness of the billon antoniniani, the authorities probably did not revalue them according to their face value. If such a decision had been taken, then the new silver coins would have resembled the bronze ones and the state would have lost substantial profits. Although an adjustment of the exchange rates did occur in the middle of the third century, this adjustment would not have equalised the face value of the silver with the face value of the bronze coins. The reforms of the monetary system probably would have asserted the higher legal value of silver/billon coins in comparison to the lower legal value of the bronze denominations, in a way that the suspicious population would not have found unacceptable. There is no evidence, though, that these efforts succeeded in stabilising the deteriorating situation or that the silver coinages were finally accepted at substantially higher values than the bronzes; hence the Aurelianic reforms followed. Also, the fact that commodity prices expressed in silver coins rose tenfold by AD 274[106] could in turn indicate that the face value of antoniniani, which were exchanged in the markets for the purchase of low-cost commodities, decreased naturally at a similar rate.

At this point I would like to present a new hypothesis. It is likely that the billon coins were probably used in smaller transactions alongside the existing bronze denominations. If the central authorities realised that billon currency served the economy in the same ways as bronzes, then they also realised that there was no longer a need for the production of bronze coinages; and that is the reason for the termination of bronze production in the imperial mints (as well as the civic mints) by the reign of Aurelian. The combined use of the existing bronze coins already in circulation with the newly minted antoniniani would have been adequate for the effective operation of local markets.

Accordingly, the analysis of the numismatic evidence from Asia Minor shows that the local markets were still monetised. Even though the patterns

[104] Liebeschuetz 2001. [105] Carson 1990: 234. [106] Rathbone 1997.

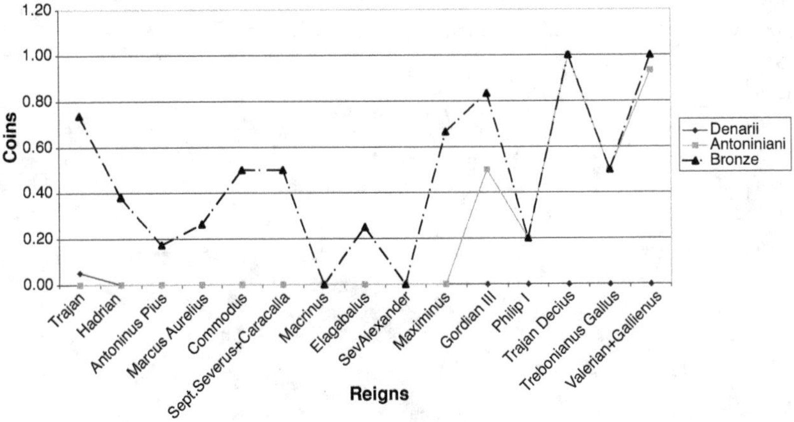

Chart 28 Pergamos excavations: comparison of denarii, antoniniani and bronzes per annum

of circulation changed, as comparisons with the patterns of circulation from earlier periods demonstrate, coins were used widely in smaller transactions. Silver coins dating from before the reign of Gordian III are not usually discovered in the course of excavations. The reason for such a deficiency is that people tend to lose and fail to recover mostly low-denomination coins, since their value is negligible. The pattern changed, though, during the third century when silver coinage started losing most of its intrinsic value. A substantial increase in the number of antoniniani recovered from excavation sites could imply the widespread daily use of billon currency and shows that everyday business was still conducted in coined money. It seems that in the local markets the population used both civic coins minted during previous periods as well as billon antoniniani in order to purchase low-cost commodities. It is apparent that whoever was involved in minor commercial activities would normally use his billon coins in the *agora* on a daily basis.

Excavation finds from Asia Minor show a substantial increase of antoniniani in comparison with bronze coins by the middle of the third century. In Pergamos, antoniniani form a small peak during the reign of Gordian III and subsequently they continue rising until they shape peaks similar to the peak of bronze coinage by the reign of Trebonianus Gallus, while denarii remain at minimal levels throughout the two centuries. (Chart 28).

Coin finds from Sardis show also that the number of antoniniani, which started increasing during the reign of Gordian III, reaches the same height

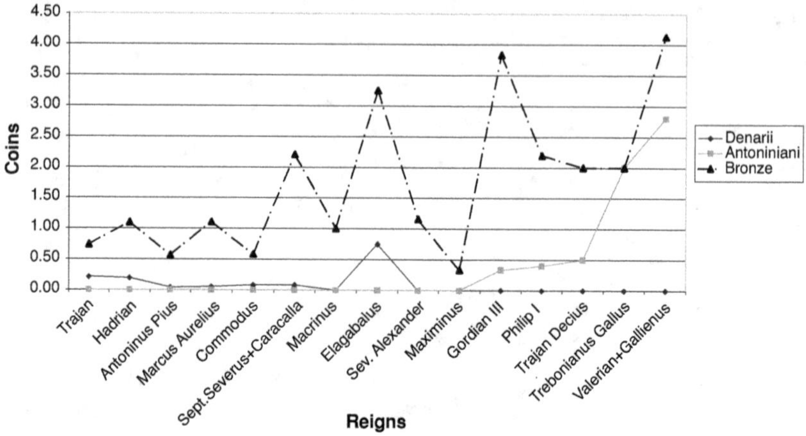

Chart 29 Sardis excavation: comparison of denarii, antoniniani and bronzes per annum

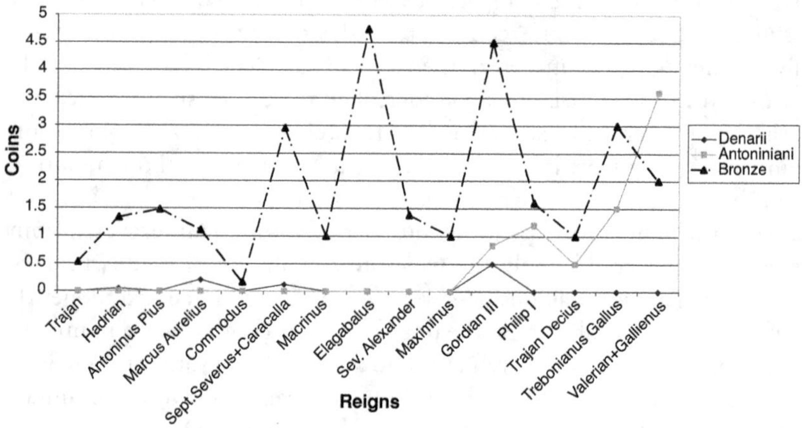

Chart 30 Ephesus excavations: comparison of denarii, antoniniani and bronzes per annum

as the bronze coinage by the reign of Trebonianus Gallus (Chart 29). Subsequently, the number of both antoniniani and bronzes rise during the reigns of Valerian/Gallienus. In the meantime, the high increase in the loss of denarii during the reign of Elagabalus is not repeated.

A small peak of antoniniani is also attested in Ephesus during the reign of Gordian III (Chart 30). During the reign of Philip the number of bronze coins declines while antoniniani remain stable. Both bronzes and

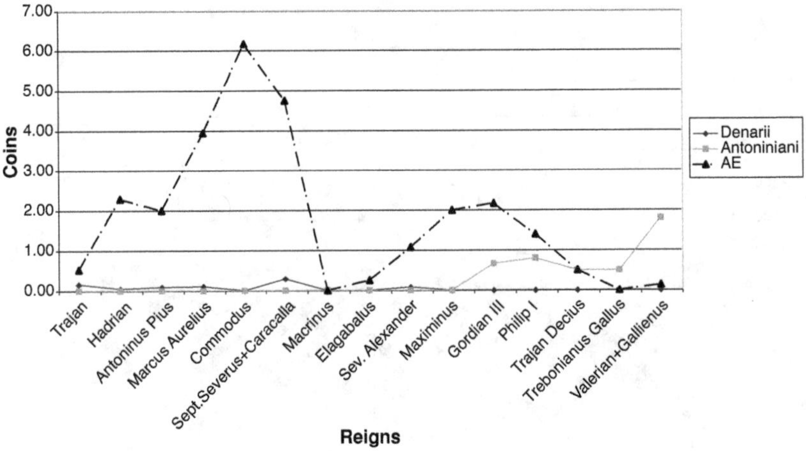

Chart 31 Patra excavations: comparison of denarii, antoniniani and bronzes per annum

antoniniani form high peaks during the reigns of Trebonianus Gallus and Gallienus. Especially antoniniani remain higher until the end of the reign of Gallienus. It is interesting to note that the numbers of both denarii and antoniniani are at the same level during the reign of Gordian III.

Similarly, excavation finds from Greece show a substantial increase of antoniniani in comparison with bronze coins during or after the reign of Gordian III. The bronze coins from the Patra excavations that decline during the reign of Philip are partly substituted by the antoniniani, whose number starts rising during Gordian III in order to form the highest peak by the reign of Gallienus (Chart 31).

In Athens both bronzes and antoniniani rise during the reigns of Maximinus and Gordian III respectively and they both form high peaks during Valerian/Gallienus (Chart 32).

The bronze coins from the excavations in Corinth decline during the reign of Trajan Decius while at the same time the number of antoniniani rises beyond the number of bronze coins (Chart 33).

The excavations in Antioch (Syria) indicate comparable results (Chart 34). The bronze coins found in this area are abundant throughout the third century. During the reign of Gordian III, though, the number of antoniniani rises until it meets the number of bronzes during the reign of Gallienus. The plated tetradrachms that circulated during the reign of Trajan Decius do not seem to distort the overall picture.

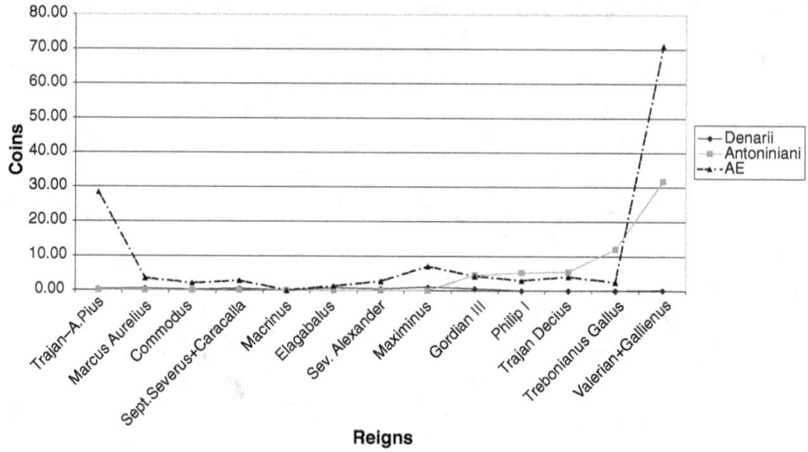

Chart 32 Athens excavations: comparison of denarii, antoniniani and bronzes per annum

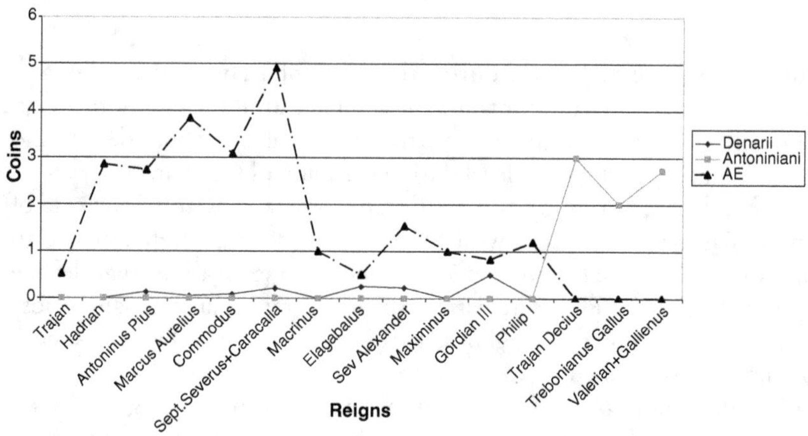

Chart 33 Corinth excavations: comparison of denarii, antoniniani and bronzes per annum

Dura Europos is one of the best excavated sites in Syria (Chart 35). The problem is that we do not have a proper picture of the coins circulating in the area during the reigns of Valerian and Gallienus, because the fortress was destroyed during this period. It is, thus, probable that the antoniniani that were issued in mainstream mints under Valerian or Gallienus did not have the time to arrive at Dura before it was destroyed. Although there is a decline in the circulation of bronze during the reign of Philip, antoniniani do not form high peaks.

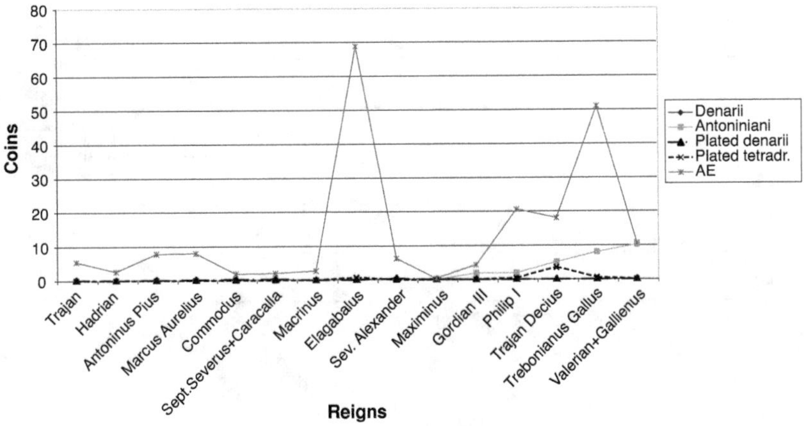

Chart 34 Antioch excavations: comparison of denarii, antoniniani and bronzes per annum

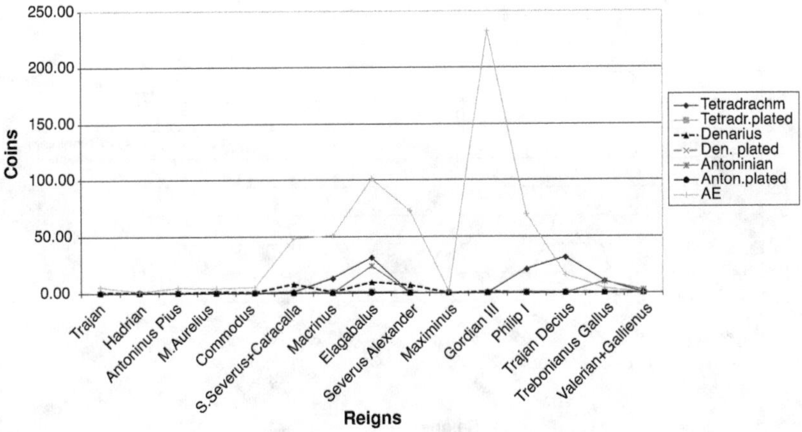

Chart 35 Dura Europos excavations: comparison of denarii, antoniniani and per annum

In addition, there is a tendency for mixed-metal coin hoards to appear during the mid third century, as we have already seen. I would like to bring here a few examples that demonstrate the structure of these hoards. The Iafa hoard from Syria (Chart 36) contains both bronze coins and antoniniani and was lost during the Tetrarchic period. A rise in the number of both antoniniani and bronzes which were issued during the Military Anarchy period is evident. This hoard shows that by the second half of the third

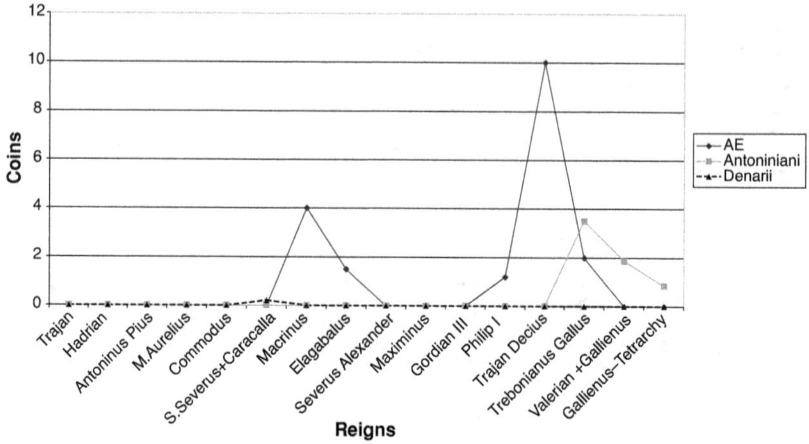

Chart 36 Iafa hoard: comparison of denarii, antoniniani and bronzes per annum

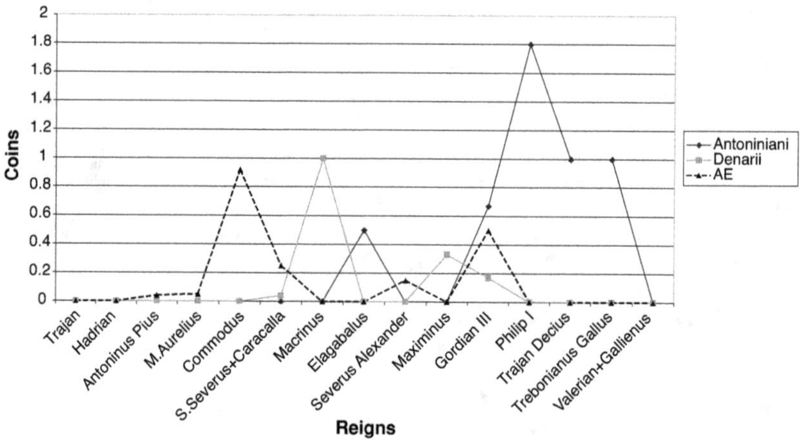

Chart 37 Lesbos hoard: comparison of denarii, antoniniani and bronzes per annum

century there was no choice but the use of antoniniani in the Syrian markets.

A Greek hoard from the Aegean island of Lesbos (Chart 37) shows a similar structure. Once more we observe a rise in the antoniniani from the reign of Gordian III onwards, while bronzes were eclipsed during the same period.

These histograms demonstrate the sizeable increase in the number of antoniniani in circulation especially after the reign of Trebonianus Gallus.

At the same time the production of bronze coinages seems to decrease, although earlier issues may still have been in circulation for several decades. The combined numbers of billon antoniniani and bronze issues probably guaranteed the satisfactory liquidity of local markets by the middle of the third century and even afterwards. In fact, the inhabitants of the eastern provinces did not seem to be concerned about the monetised purchase of goods for daily consumption, once the production of smaller denominations was guaranteed by the state. The situation in the north-eastern provinces during the Military Anarchy period is somewhat different from the situation we encounter in Greece, Asia Minor and Syria, because of the demonetisation of daily transactions in the northern Balkans during the Severan period. Charts 38–41 demonstrate the changes in the distribution of denarii, antoniniani and bronze coins found in excavation sites in the provinces of Dacia, Pannonia Inferior, Pannonia Superior and Moesia Inferior.[107] Instead of presenting each site separately, I decided to aggregate all of the coins found in each province, because of the exceptionally large number of excavations in the region.

In Dacia we observe that the rise in the number of denarii during the Severan period was not followed by a similar rise in the number of bronzes in circulation (Chart 38).[108] The consequent liquidity problems that may have occurred in the markets would not have been resolved before the reign of Gordian III, when an unprecedented increase in small change occurred. This increase was combined with similar rises in the numbers of antoniniani, which reach their peak from the reign of Gordian III until the reign of Gallienus. Interestingly, it is worth noting a substantial increase in plated coins during the reigns of Septimius Severus, Elagabalus and Severus Alexander. This phenomenon should not be connected with the lack of bronzes in the markets but with the debasement of silver coins at the time. It is possible that the newly debased denarii were not easily distinguishable from the plated ones; hence, illegal monetary practices found fertile ground.

[107] Gazdac, in his PhD thesis on monetary circulation in Dacia (2002b), studied extensively the coin finds from excavations in Dacia, Moesia and Pannonia. For the charts shown here I used the material he included in his general tables D1, D2, D3 and D5. The unidentified denominations Gazdac mentions are incorporated here in the bronze coins category.

[108] Coins from the following sites have been included here: Ulpia, Apulum, Porolissum, Napoca, Potaissa, Tibiscum, Drobeta, Dierna, Sucidava, Ampelum, Bucium, Resculum, Certiae, Tihău, Ilişua, Orhei, Gherla, Gilău, Micia, Hoghiz, Războveni, Sighişoara, Cumidava, Angustia, Ramidava, Rupea, Olteni, Praetorium, Arutela, Slăveni, Răcari, Ad Pannonios, Acidava, Odorhei, Micăsasa, Cristeşti, Orlea, Romula, Buciumi, Brăncoveneşti, Inlăceni, Sinpaul, Bumbeşti, Pojejena, Mediaş, Reghin, Gornea, Villae, Călugăreni, Comalău, Săpata de Jos, Castra Traiana, Comalşu, Urluieni, Jidava, Cătunele.

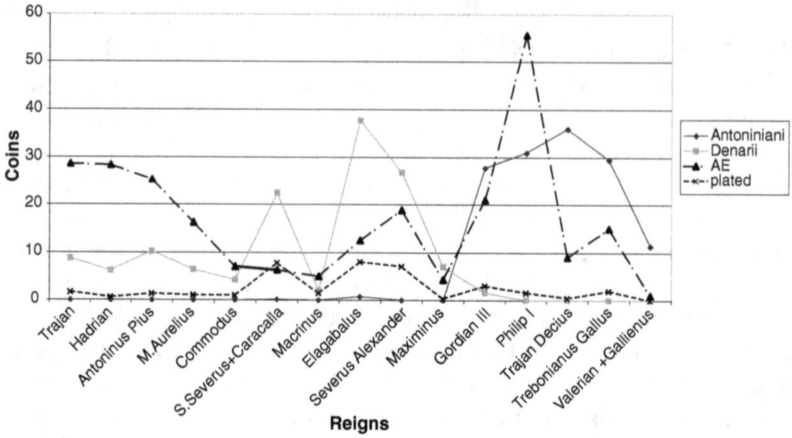

Chart 38 Dacia excavations: comparison of antoniniani, denarii and bronzes per annum

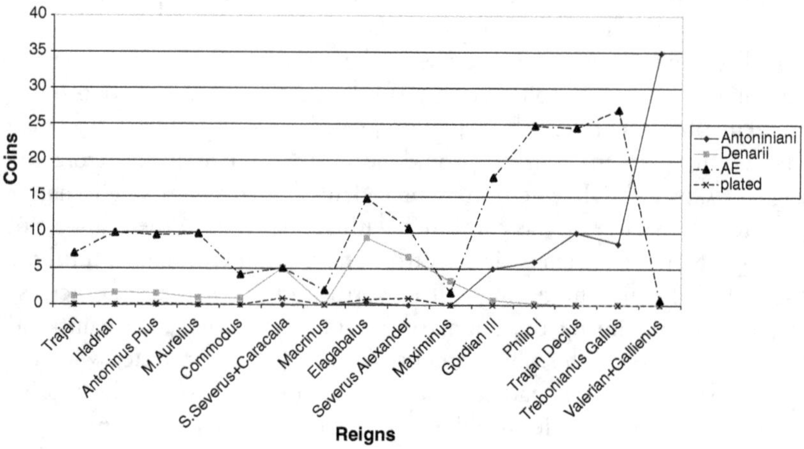

Chart 39 Pannonia Inferior excavations: comparison of antoniniani, denarii and bronzes per annum

The coin finds from Pannonia Inferior may not be as many as the ones found in Dacia but they still present a similar structure (Chart 39).[109] We observe an uneventful continuity in the number of bronze coins and silver denarii during the Antonine period. This continuity changes with a decrease in the number of bronze coins and an abrupt rise of denarii

[109] The coins have been found in the following sites: Aquincum, Gorsicum, Sopianae, Vetus Salina, Annamatia, Intercisa, Doboj, Alba Regia, Gomolava, Rumenka, Banostor.

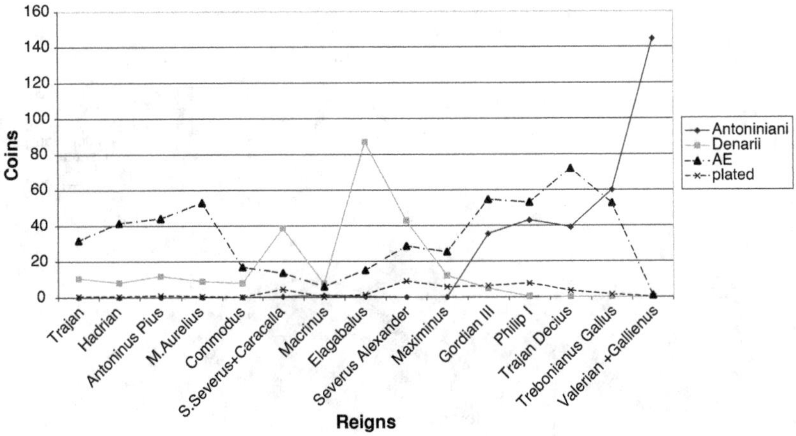

Chart 40 Pannonia Superior excavations: comparison of antoniniani, denarii and bronzes per annum

as early as the reigns of Septimius Severus and Caracalla. The production and circulation of small change started increasing again during the reign of Elagabalus, possibly in an attempt to tackle problems of liquidity. By that time a decline in the number of denarii became a trend that continued until their disappearance during the reign of Trajan Decius. Once more, the antoniniani became the main silver coin in circulation from the time of Gordian III, while they reached a very high peak by the middle of the third century.

Pannonia Superior confirms the observations we have made, so far, about the north-eastern frontier (Chart 40).[110] The decline of the bronze coins during the Severan period is combined with an increase in the denarii in circulation. However, with the advent of the Military Anarchy period the number of bronzes in circulation starts rising again, until they decline terminally during the reign of Gallienus. In the meantime, from the reign of Gordian III onward the newly minted antoniniani increase almost at the same pace as the bronzes until the reign of Trebonianus Gallus, when the circulation of billon coins rose even higher.

110 The excavation sites included in this chart are the following: Carnuntum, Vindobona, Poetovio, Neviodunum, Brigetio, Scarabantia, Savaria, Mursella, Arrabona, Ad Mures, Solva, Praetorium Lat, Eisenstadt, Loretto, Mullendorf, Oslip, Schutzen am Gebirge, Marz, Pottsching, Neusiedl am See, Apetlon, Halbturn, Winden am See, Zurndorf, Deutschkreuz, Strebersdorf, Neckenmarkt, Hegyko-Teglasto, Koronco, Bajna, Bajot, Dorog, Epol-Kokut, Hereg, Vincentia, Tokod, Castra, Illmitz, Tarjan, Dolga Vas.

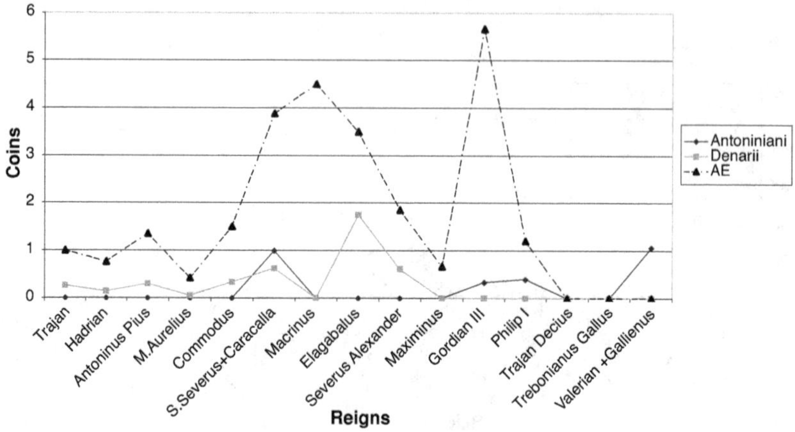

Chart 41 Moesia Inferior excavations: comparison of antoniniani, denarii and bronzes per annum

There is one exception to the rule, though. The excavation sites in Moesia Inferior seem to have produced fewer antoniniani and more bronze coins during the Military Anarchy period than expected (Chart 41).[111] In addition, the number of bronzes in circulation during the Severan period increased exponentially, thus resembling the provinces in Asia Minor and Greece. The only similarity with the rest of the regions is the replacement of denarii with antoniniani by the reign of Gordian III. It is possible that, in this case, the number of provincial issues in circulation sufficed for the needs of the local markets and that the use of antoniniani became unnecessary. However, I would not like to press this point, as I have no further evidence at hand.

This is not the first time that someone has observed the proliferation of antoniniani during the third century. In fact, Fulford noticed the phenomenon in Roman Britain.[112] In an attempt to explain the reasons for such large numbers of billon antoniniani in circulation, Fulford suggested that the inhabitants, who probably belonged to higher social strata, may have used precious coins more often than before; as a consequence, the degree of monetisation increased. Nevertheless, our evidence does not seem to justify such a conclusion. Instead, it would be more plausible to suggest

[111] The excavation sites in Moesia Inferior are few and, therefore, the number of coins coming from them is small. These are: Nicopolis ad Istrum, Axiopolis, Noviodunum, Histria, Iatrus, Appiaria, Madara.

[112] Fulford 1989: 181–5 and 191–3.

that the overvalued billon antoniniani were only a shadow of the previous silver denarial coinages. By the middle of the third century, when the Roman monetary system collapsed, the antoniniani were used mainly in smaller transactions alongside the existing bronze coinages. Although there are regional differences, the almost exclusive usage of billon coins by the reign of Gallienus cannot be contested.

THE THIRD CENTURY AND OTHER HISTORICAL ANALOGIES

The Quantity Theory of Money is a powerful economic tool that can be applied to modern and ancient economics alike. Using the third century as a case study, we may observe the validity of its application and the possibilities it offers. This study shows a connection between the supply of silver and bronze coins in circulation, the stability of prices and the demonetisation of some transactions in the Severan and Military Anarchy periods.

During the Severan period the reduction in the fineness of the denarius combined with its increasing production had significant effects on the production of other currencies and eventually on the markets. First and foremost, we observe that the mint of Rome concentrated on the production of precious-metal coinages and reduced significantly its output of bronze denominations. This situation may have caused liquidity problems in small change, especially in the north-eastern provinces that relied heavily on the central distribution of coins. The desperate tone we note in the inscription of Mylasa indicates that similar problems arose in the eastern provinces of Asia Minor. The lack of liquidity for smaller transactions favoured the flourishing of a black market in the exchange of currencies; thus, the revenues of the cities were reduced. Greece, Asia Minor and Syria, though, shared an advantage that we do not encounter in the western provinces. They had their own civic mints that undertook the production of bronze issues as soon as the problem was realised, thus resolving the issues.

During the Military Anarchy period the currency problems increased substantially. The reign of Gordian III saw the simultaneous disappearance of the denarius and its replacement by the highly overvalued antoninianus. At the same time, the gold aurei became scarce because of their devaluation and their consequent partial demonetisation. In this case the major transactions suffered a bitter blow, while most of them were probably conducted in bullion. On the other hand, the smaller transactions overcame the liquidity problems they encountered in the Severan period. The reason was the fact that the billon antoniniani were by the mid third century used as small change, instead of highly valued silver coins. All in all, by the end of the reign of Gallienus the monetary system, as it was established by Augustus, collapsed. Even though daily transactions were conducted uninhibited, major transactions, which until then were facilitated by precious-metal coinages, were probably curtailed. The effect on the economy became evident by the time of Aurelian, when inflation started rising until it reached its peak during the reign of Diocletian.

The situation we encounter in the middle of the third century is neither unique nor exceptional. Sargent and Velde attempted to explain the phenomenon of the depreciation of small change in Europe from 1200 to 1800.[113] According to their study, persistent depreciations and debasements were accompanied by recurrent shortages and increases in the exchange rates of large for small coins. In that respect, these later numismatic reforms resemble the Roman attempts to debase silver coins and countermark civic bronze coinages in circulation by the middle of the third century, so that their legal value is adjusted to the value of the highly debased silver coins. The authors rightly questioned the paradox of the value of these small denominations that continuously fell, despite the fact that they were in short supply. By the middle of the third century civic bronzes were not as highly overvalued as before, even if they still lost some of their face value, in order to adjust to the exchange rate dictated by the new issues of the billon antoniniani. Sargent and Valde also noticed that the depreciation of the small coins took place mainly when they rendered 'high liquidity services'. This theory could explain equally well the extensive use of bronze coins alongside billon antoniniani. As the liquidity of smaller denominations increased, the previous silver currencies of higher fineness disappeared from the markets, thus causing the partial demonetisation of the Roman economy, before or during the reign of Gallienus.

113 Sargent and Velde 2002: 14–16.

CHAPTER 5

Roman monetary integration

ROMAN SOCIETY AND THE MONETISED ECONOMY

The identification of specific social groups that use predominately precious-metal coinages is essential, if we aim at estimating the level of monetisation in the Roman empire. Gold and silver coins were destined to be used in large transactions either by the state or by the citizens. Such transactions included the exchange of commodities, banking, the liquidation of properties, the exhibition of wealth, investment in businesses, the payment of taxes, the payment of magistrates and army officials or the completion of public works. In previous chapters we analysed the intervention of the emperor in the economy and we gave an overview of his annual budget. In this chapter we should focus on the revenues and expenses of the inhabitants and their involvement in interregional trade and other profitable activities. Once we establish their role in the use of precious-metal currencies, we will have the chance to assess the extent of the monetisation of the Roman economy. To start with, there is an array of questions in need of an answer. For example, who handled the majority of coined wealth within the empire? What was their financial capacity? What type of businesses were they involved in? How is this part of the monetised economy represented among the archaeological finds? Once the answers become clear, we will be able to explore further the integration of the Roman economy, an integration that relied partly on the entrepreneurial activities of the upper and middle echelons of society.

The establishment of the first currency systems in antiquity aimed at promoting impersonal transactions between the interested parties. The new medium made market exchanges homogeneous and uniform and, thus, facilitated commercial and other dealings. Money is considered an abstraction and, therefore, can be quantified and used in complex economic analysis. Forms of money, due to their impersonal nature, supposedly, do not characterise social classes or groups of people. And, yet, we notice that different types of cultural as well as socioeconomic interactions are defined by different types of money. For example, an 'honest dollar', which is the outcome of hard work, is distinguished from the 'dirty money' coming from laundering or prostitution. Similarly, payments in gold coin may have been designated only for foreign transactions and custom dues on the North American west coast before the Civil War, while silver coins were reserved for all other transactions.[1] With regard to the Roman world, it is very difficult to identify the cultural implications from the use of gold, silver or bronze coins. Nevertheless, it is possible to indicate socioeconomic reasons for the use of precious-metal coinages by specific social groups. And yet, how can we identify these economic groups in the archaeological record?

We cannot always distinguish whether the silver or gold coins in hoards were part of state payments or whether citizens used them for their commercial or other enterprises.[2] There are certain indications, though, that allow us to suggest that most of the hoards from Greece and Asia Minor were not used for state payments. For example, only a handful of silver coin hoards found in the eastern provinces (Western Turkey 1 and Western Turkey 2 hoards from Asia Minor) consist of coins of a single denomination, which may have been used for state payments to civilians or to the army. Usually hoards recovered from the southern Balkans, Asia Minor, Syria and the cities of Dacia, Pannonia and Moesia consist not only of varied denominations but also of coins minted during different reigns. Therefore, their composition allows us to suspect that they are 'savings' hoards and that they were accumulated over a long period of time.[3] Furthermore, the owners of these hoards probably belonged to different social strata, since the amount of money in them varies, thus indicating a range of financial capacities.

We may suggest, though, that most of the large precious-metal hoards (the ones that include over twenty coins) belonged to wealthy or simply well-off citizens, who could afford to accumulate silver or gold coins. These people may have received state payments or, most likely, they were involved in private enterprises. In my view, they were partially or exclusively involved in the private sector over long periods of time, especially if these hoards have been found in areas which used to be directly connected with trade and other similar undertakings (e.g. trade routes, harbour-cities etc). We have already seen that only a small number of coins came from the eastern

[1] Zelizer 1997: 1–15.

[2] In order to avoid any distortions, in this chapter I will exclude the material from the heavily militarised provinces of Pannonia and Dacia, where the likelihood of direct state payments was higher.

[3] See chapter 1, for categories of hoards.

part of Asia Minor, where the bulk of the army was stationed. On the other hand, a large number of precious-metal coin hoards came from the less militarised regions of Greece, western Asia Minor and western Syria (if we exclude the unusual site of Dura Europos). All of these regions are renowned for their harbours, their international markets and their prosperous cities, where significantly large transactions took place daily. Therefore, we may be able to suggest that the lively economic activity taking place in these areas would have facilitated the accumulation of substantial profits and the transformation of surpluses into 'savings' hoards: hoards that may have represented the capital value of their owner.

Our initial purpose is to define the economic position of the persons who were financially able not only to acquire such wealth of gold and silver coins, but also to withdraw them from the markets by immobilising them, at least, for some time. It is obvious that the upper social strata probably handled most of the silver and gold coins in circulation, since poor inhabitants probably had only restricted opportunities to handle precious-metal currencies throughout their lifetime. Some members of the *ordo* – senators, *equites*, *bouleutai* and the *familia Caesaris* (rich freedmen) – certainly benefited from the *liberalitas* of the emperor. In addition, their participation in the ruling of the Roman empire would have presented them with the opportunity to amass considerable properties by comparison to the rest of the people. The top of the pyramid consisted of no more than 200,000 citizens, representing only 1 per cent of the whole population,[4] and they undoubtedly possessed the bulk of the money in circulation. Once the greater part of combined wealth was in their hands, they would have invested part of it in several private ventures with the intention of increasing their profits, even though large parts may have been stored or 'invested' in promoting their public image. The profits from private enterprises represented the necessary capital that drove upwards the growth of the imperial economy for, at least, the first two centuries AD.

The 600 or more members of the Senate and their families were counted as among the wealthiest of Roman citizens.[5] Apart from other qualifications, membership of the senatorial class required the annual acquisition of wealth, estimated at a minimum of 1 million sestertii.[6] Among the senators, as in other classes, there were wide differences in wealth. The richest of the senatorial members were worth hundreds of millions of sestertii,

[4] Alföldy 1988: 125.

[5] Talbert 1984: 131–4. According to Scheidel there must have been a variation of ±5 per cent in their numbers. See Scheidel 1999.

[6] Dio Cass 54.17.3; 54.26.3 ff.

hardly being able to recall what they even possessed,[7] while at the bottom we find 'senators of moderate means, who in a peaceful state only seek peaceful incomes'.[8] According to Dio,[9] *equites*, the second richest group, were, theoretically, poorer than the senators, while the minimum property qualification has been estimated as up to 400,000 sestertii. Their demographic strength by the reign of Augustus reached the number of at least 20,000, excluding the members of their families.[10] As for their individual properties, we should take into consideration that a *magister census*, who belonged to the lower strata of this order, needed 600,000 sesterces a year to live in luxury and 100,000 sesterces to live in a financially restricted way.[11] Most of the *equites*, though, probably had far more than the minimum allowance that would have allowed them to live in luxury.[12] In all likelihood, the combined forces of senators and *equites* held most of the property and cash reserves in Rome and in Italy, while they also owned part of the properties in the eastern and western provinces.

Rome was not the only home for the rich inhabitants of the Roman empire. A number of the wealthier families resided in the many cities of the eastern (as well as western) provinces, including Athens, Ephesus, Pergamus, Alexandria etc. These citizens were part of the equally prosperous but less honourable *ordo decurionum*, which consisted on average of around 100 members in each city. Of course, depending on the size of the eastern cities, the number of the members of the *gerousia*, who could afford the expenses of the *ordo*, fluctuated from a few hundred to less than 100. On the whole, there must have been 100,000–150,000 *bouleutai* throughout the empire. At least in some cities in northern Africa (and probably also elsewhere) they may have comprised around 2 per cent of all the adult males residing in towns. Their properties fluctuated in value from 20,000 to 100,000 sestertii or more per year, and they were considered to be rich only according to local standards.[13] Some of these people probably owned some of the lost hoards found in Greece, Asia Minor and Syria, although we should not exclude the possibility of the existence of other owners, such as freedmen.

The *liberti* (freedmen), some of whom were exceptionally rich, played an important role in the local and empire-wide economies, even though they had no aristocratic titles. There was no minimum property requirement to be a *libertus*. Instead, any ex-slave became automatically a *libertus* and enjoyed all the advantages and disadvantages of this social position. The

7 Talbert 1984: 47–8. 8 Tac. *Ann* 11.7. 9 Dio Cass. 52.25.3. 10 Alföldy 1988: 122.
11 Cic. *Paradoxa Stoicorum* 49. 12 Brunt 1965: 119. 13 Alföldy 1988: 127–8.

wealthiest of these freedmen probably possessed the necessary funds to provide financial assistance to their cities, as Poplius Decimius Eros Merulas from Asisium, who paid 2,000 sesterces in order to become a member of the *collegium* of the rich freedmen and he offered 67,000 more for the erection of statues and the construction of roads.[14] Also, in the case of Isidorus, who lived in the early Julio-Claudian period, we notice that he left in his will 4,116 slaves, 3,600 teams of oxen, 257,000 other animals and sixty million sestertii in cash.[15] In addition, we should at least mention the exceptional imperial freedmen who held both positions of power and vast wealth; an obvious example is Narcissus, the freedman of the emperor Claudius.[16] These *liberti* became important benefactors also in the eastern cities. For instance, Publius Aelius Onesimus donated 200,000 sesterces to his hometown, Nacolea, in Asia Minor for the purchase of grain during the reign of Hadrian.[17] The references on the ready cash of Isidorus and the benefactions of other ex-slaves could give us only a vague idea of the number of coins in circulation at any one time and the liquidity of the markets.

The little information we have on the value of the individual properties of the wealthy does not allow us to estimate their contribution to the Gross Domestic Product, because we cannot reconstruct the exact mean value of all these properties. We may, though, form a general view on the level of monetisation of the empire and the way money was used throughout the Principate by studying some well-attested cases, such as the properties of Cicero, an equestrian who lived during the Late Republic, and Pliny the Younger, a senator of the early second century AD. There are numerous references in Cicero's letters and speeches concerning his personal finances that have been taken into account by modern researchers.[18] His *patrimonium*, which included at the beginning of his career farms, a villa and a house in Rome, was gradually expanding. Very soon Cicero was a man of landed property estimated at 10 million sestertii, eight villas – one of which we know cost 3.5 million sestertii and another almost 15 million – several lodges, farms, *insulae* and *tabernae* in Rome and slaves. There are accounts of him spending large amounts of money on furnishing his villas and on buying books or paper. The income needed to meet these expenses is not precisely fixed, but we may suppose that more than a million per annum in cash was required. Some sources of this large income are clear enough, such as rental properties, gifts and legacies that by the end of his career

[14] *ILS* 7812. [15] *ILS* 1949; Plin. *HN* 33.134. [16] Dio Cass. 60.34.4
[17] *ILS* 7196. [18] Boren 1961; Raskolnikoff 1977.

reached the amount of 20 million sestertii. Also, as a governor of Cilicia he probably profited to the extent of 2.2 million sestertii. His ability to find ready money promptly must have been aided by the support of the equestrian class, which was able to give loans and 'corporation shares' in cases of need.

Cicero's finances during the Late Republic may have been similar to the finances of other members of the elite in the early imperial period. It seems that the role of money and its use continued to be an essential factor in the building of a sizeable property. Economic evidence in the letters of Pliny the Younger, a senator whose financial circumstances are known to us in detail, illuminates the value of his properties, their profitability and his cash liquidity.[19] He owned substantial estates, a number of houses, villas and more than 500 slaves. His property at Tifernum alone was bringing in more than 400,000 sestertii per year early in the reign of Trajan.[20] The capital value of the Tifernum estate was approximately 7 million sestertii, therefore he had an income of 400,000 sestertii, which represented an annual return of about 6 per cent. Even if these profits may not necessarily have been translated into coins, it is still very impressive if we compare it with the modern annual return of stocks or bank accounts. If we assume a comparable figure for his Transpadane lands, and add the property he probably purchased at Tifernum for 3 million sestertii, we reach a very rough estimate for the capital value of Pliny's landholdings of 17 million sestertii, which probably secured for him an income of at least 1 million sestertii per year. Despite the catalogue of negative reports from his estates, Pliny still had sufficient funds to invest. His capital may have been invested in economic sectors outside the land market, probably money lending, which possibly contributed one-tenth of his whole income. It is also important to remember that he acquired through inheritances and legacies substantial sums of money, whose magnitude may have exceeded the total value of 1.45 million sestertii. Even if the legacies he received were quite small, other bequests that came his way were sometimes substantial. Revenues from this source cannot be ignored when seeking an explanation of Pliny's financial capacity for large-scale generosities during his lifetime and in his will, since he appears to have enjoyed quite a high level of liquidity, judging by the gift of more than 1.6 million sestertii to public bodies, and more than 740,000 sestertii to private individuals. Other public gifts, such as buildings, obviously must have cost him large sums of money but our knowledge of their value remains incomplete.

[19] Duncan-Jones 1974: 17–32; Kehoe 1988b; Kehoe 1993; Kehoe 1997. [20] Plin. *Ep.*, 10.8.5.

Enough money probably circulated around the Roman world that would have been sufficient for the partial liquidation of the above properties, if necessity called for such an action. The death of the proprietor would be followed by the dispersion of his possessions according to his will among friends, relatives, the emperor or even his native city. The benefactions towards cities, including payments for games, banquets, baths, monuments, which are specifically mentioned in testaments,[21] all required cash resources. It appears that gifts in kind diminished steadily from the first to the third century AD in favour of cash donations.[22] Furthermore, one of the simplest (and most popular) forms of legacy, which avoided complications especially after the death of the owner, was the donation of cash to friends.[23] An indicative example appears in a second- or third-century will of a veteran who set down a list of friends with individual bequests to each.[24] The emperor also inherited vast sums of money: in his own will Augustus remarked that in the previous twenty years he had received some 1,400 million sesterces in inheritances and legacies.[25] Even if specific sums of money were not explicitly mentioned in the will, the relatives of the deceased might have wished to sell part of the estate in order to pay the tax on inheritances (up to 5 per cent) or in order to divide the property equally among the members of the family.

The need for money in cash is almost self-evident, since every rich person who wanted to present himself in a respectable way had to both maintain and exhibit an affluent standard of living in the private as well as public sphere. Apart from the minimum amount of money required for their acceptance as members of the senatorial or equestrian order, they had additional financial obligations. Most candidates for a senatorial career would have undertaken election expenses at one stage or another. Although the emperor regularly supported a proportion of the candidates for lesser magistracies, saving them from the trouble and expense of canvassing, for the remaining places there was an open competition which involved time, effort and expenditure of money in the form of bribes or benefactions (entertainment, presents etc.). We have no detailed knowledge of the candidates' expenses, especially because in some cases the law strictly forbade them. If a member of the upper class wished to enter the Senate, he was obliged to maintain a house in Rome. His move to the capital (if he came from the provinces) demanded additional expenses, such as architectural developments, high rents and the employment of a large number of slaves

[21] Gioffredi 1942–58. [22] Bossu 1982: 160. [23] Champlin 1991: 147.
[24] *CPR* 6.2.76. [25] Suet. *Aug.* 101.3.

or other contracted labour. Seneca himself says: 'I lack extravagant tastes but city life itself demands high expenditure.'[26] A senator would also be required to make a substantial contribution towards the cost of games and other activities. Magistrates, such as quaestors, had to contribute towards paving roads, while aediles had to pay part of the expenses for public games – at least in the Early Empire. Similarly, praetors as well as consuls and priests were responsible for spending money on shows, which for the most part were a mixture of circus races and theatrical performances. Two of Martial's epigrams[27] can perhaps give some clue as to the amount a praetor might have contributed from his own pocket. The poet speaks of a praetor spending over 100,000 sestertii on the races, 100,000 sestertii being expected to be available as a minimum contribution towards the *Ludi Megalenses* for other races, as well as 20,000 sestertii for the *Ludi Plebeii*. Emperors who increased the number of games and races hardly earned senatorial support, as these expenses could not always be met.[28] From the above it is clear that anyone who embarked upon a senatorial career would be likely to find his initial costs remarkably high. Only a minority with luck and ability were destined to gain appointments that would handsomely repay the necessary expenditure, and even then a long interval would probably occur before they enjoyed their rewards.[29]

Apart from the public image the wealthy inhabitants had to present, powerful citizens also displayed a prosperous private image, which remained visible both inside and outside their homes. The maintenance of houses and villas, gourmandising, funerals and other extravagances were part of the image of anyone who claimed to be substantially affluent. A 'wasteful squandering of wealth', as an early twentieth-century author eloquently states,[30] can be verified in the story of Petronius about Trimalchio, an imaginary freedman of the first century AD.[31] Expenses for the maintenance of a household could take either the form of coins or of goods. In the case of the imaginary Trimalchio, even if he spent vast amounts of wealth in order to create a luxurious dinner for his distinguished (or not) guests, this wealth did not necessarily take the form of money. In fact, he boasted that all of the products that appeared on his table (wool, citrus, pepper) were home-grown and came from his distant estates. He claims that once, when the wool he got was not good enough, he brought some rams from Tarentum. Another time he ordered some bees from Athens in order to get home-grown Attic honey.[32]

[26] Sen *Ep. Mor.* 50.3. [27] Mart. 4.67; 10.41. [28] Dio Cass. 60.27.2. [29] Talbert 1984: 54–66.
[30] Davis 1910: 152–3. [31] Petron. *Sat.* [32] Pet. *Sat.* 38.1–4.

In theory, Trimalchio's extravagant lifestyle followed the aristocratic guidelines for economic self-sufficiency; in reality, though, his attitude could not be anything more than a well-structured hyperbole.[33] Of course, we should not doubt the fact that in certain instances rich estate owners would have transported their own products for long distances overseas.[34] After all, senatorial ideology supported self-sufficiency on their estates, which were located throughout the empire. Horace speaks of those who bought land and villas near Rome, sometimes for 30,000 sestertii or more, so that they could have their own grapes, chickens, eggs, wine, vegetables and firewood.[35] In the same way, Pliny noted with pleasure how many of his requirements could be satisfied on his own villa.[36] Influenced by the aristocratic ideal as it is presented in the majority of the written sources, Finley in *The Ancient Economy* claimed that that the mentality of the ancients presented a 'peasant like passion for self-sufficiency . . . relishing independence from the market as buyers'.[37]

The careful reading of literary sources sometimes can lead the reader to the opposite conclusion, since some of them support the view that self-sufficiency was not always the primary purpose of financial decisions. It was not always practical or profitable for the citizens of the empire to lead their lives according to their ideological convictions. Varro in his *Agricultura*, while giving advice to landowners for the maximisation of their profit, noted that

> if there are towns or villages nearby, or even just well-stocked fields and estates belonging to wealthy owners, so that you will be able to buy cheaply from them anything that you need for your own farm, and can sell them your surplus products . . . then your farm will be more profitable than if these things have to be brought from a long distance. Often it will be more economical than if you are able to provide these goods yourself by having them produced on your own estate.[38]

Transportation costs seem to have been very expensive, even prohibitive, although in certain cases they could not be avoided, especially when trading activities involved luxury products from India or Arabia, e.g. spices. Although self-sufficiency was the goal of the small producer and an important element of the traditional value system of the aristocratic elite, it was most of the time an unattainable goal. Small and large landowners alike did buy as well as sell their products.[39] It is not a coincidence that the

[33] D'Arms 1981: 118. [34] Whittaker 1988: 58. [35] Hor. *Epist.* 2.2.160–6. [36] Plin. *Ep.* 2.17.25–7.
[37] Finley 1973: 108 and 110. [38] Varro, *Agricultura* 1.16.3.
[39] Garnsey 1999: 22–4. An attempt by the same author to estimate the size of the agricultural surplus in antiquity does not lead to any definite results (*ibid.* 24–8).

ideal position of a villa was close to a main road that allowed for good communication and probable access to the nearby towns. These towns, in turn, provided access to local markets and contract labour. The location of the villa close to a river or port would also have facilitated the export of agricultural or other commodities produced on the premises. Such a proximity to economic centres or the roads to them caused the integration of the villa into the regional economy and beyond.[40] The existence of villas in the landscape cannot specify where the owners' wealth came from: the house and its daily expenses could represent the investment of capital derived from different sources, such as the agricultural surplus of a *latifundium*. This surplus may have arrived in the hands of the manager of the villa in the form of cash, after its sale in the market.[41]

Neither villas nor regions could achieve complete self-sufficiency in the Roman empire, due to the interconnected nature of the local economies. In the case of regions, we should stress the main factor: the existence of a multitude of micro-climates in the Mediterranean. The geographic variation of the regions surrounding *mare nostrum* and the irregular rainfall were the cause of the fluctuation of agricultural produce. Farm diversification (meaning the use of resources of an estate for commercial profit through the development of non-agricultural entrepreneurial activities) and extensive monoculture, in some cases, were the only practical solutions. The consumables which were not produced locally were, in fact, comparatively easily transported through a complex network of roads and sea routes.[42]

Archaeological evidence overturns the Finleyan approach and demonstrates the extensive distribution of goods across the Roman empire. On one hand, the increase of shipwrecks in the western Mediterranean indicates a comparable increase in trade during the first and second centuries AD.[43] On the other hand, the archaeological discovery of pottery, and especially amphoras used for the transportation of wine, olive oil, wheat, *garum* etc., in several regions of the Roman empire point towards the wider distribution of foodstuffs and their transportation from one region to another, in an attempt to cover the daily needs of the inhabitants.[44] These amphoras were not used for the occasional transportation of luxury items but should be firmly connected to intense demand for consumables: a demand that was not met by local production. The expansion of trading activities could, in turn, explain the specialisation of crops at a regional

[40] Lawrence 1999: 104. [41] Percival 1987: 538. See also chapter 4, for consumer-city.
[42] Horden and Purcell 2000. [43] Hopkins 1980; Parker 1992.
[44] Paterson 1982; Peacock and Williams 1986; Panella and Tchernia 1994.

level. Archaeological surveys in northern Africa show that a number of regions specialised in the production of olive oil, thus creating a surplus destined to be sold in distant markets.[45] Also, in urban contexts, some cities seem to promote the specialisation of some of their commercial and manufacturing activities.[46]

So far, I have placed particular emphasis on the wealth accumulated by the rich inhabitants of the Roman empire, even though they represented only a small percentage of the population. The reason for this emphasis is the lack of ancient sources (with the exception of Egypt) for the 'middling' social strata and the consequent lack of relevant modern publications. Furthermore, it seems that modern historians are reluctant to engage in a debate on the existence of a 'middle class' – justifiably, bearing in mind the lack of class consciousness in antiquity. However, this reluctance effectively led scholarship to avoid the subject altogether. We cannot ignore, though, the fact that the members of the Roman elite were not the only ones to use silver coins. We are aware that in the fourth century AD gold became the medium of smaller transactions and was used by all social strata, as Egyptian papyri show; gold became 'a mass currency that permeated all levels of social life'.[47] Although this statement is somewhat exaggerated, there is no doubt that the increase of gold coins in late antiquity would have been combined with its wider use.

Unlike the late antique monetary economy, during the previous centuries it was not gold coins that were produced en masse; rather we observe the increasing production of silver denarii (and antoniniani during the third century). Even wage labourers, such as the employees of merchants, shopkeepers and craftsmen,[48] may have received their salaries in silver coins. An example of a typical salary from the Roman Principate is mentioned in the New Testament,[49] which says that the daily salary of a labourer for the vineyard was one denarius, the same amount as the daily wages in Pompei.[50] In the case of Roman Egypt Scheidel suggests an annual household income of around 450–500 silver drachms, which would have sustained a family at subsistence level.[51]

Even if these salaries were not paid in silver but in bronze currencies, and even if the low-income households did not have the financial capacity to accumulate hoards, we cannot assume the same for the 'middling' or 'intermediate' social strata. The shopkeepers, small landowners, traders

[45] D. Mattingly 1988. [46] D. Mattingly and Salmon 2001. [47] Banaji 2002: 60.
[48] Corbier 1980. [49] Matthew 20. [50] Mrozek 1989: 110–11.
[51] Scheidel 2008: (http://www.princeton.edu/~pswpc/pdfs/scheidel/030801.pdf).

and manufacturers who employed labourers had the means to pay them in silver and amassed silver and/or gold hoards after they received their profits. Evidence for these professions is minimal and, thus, the study of their financial capacity becomes problematic for the modern researcher. It is imperative, though, at some point in the future, to see more scholars exploring this topic. Then, they may be able to prove (or disprove) that despite the impressive amounts of wealth and cash resources the elites owned (as presented in the course of this chapter), the impact of the 'middling' social strata on the Roman monetary economy may have been far more decisive.

It is apparent that the upper and middle strata of Roman society held the majority of the aggregate wealth. Senators, knights, the *ordo decurionum*, rich freedmen, traders, manufacturers and shopkeepers held substantial assets and were responsible for the growth of the economy. Apart from real estate they must have been rich also in cash terms, while their credit capacity probably equalled the sum of their properties. Consequently, these were the people who mostly handled the precious-metal currencies issued by the state. These coins would either have been stored or used extensively in a variety of transactions. Their storage is evident from the large number of hoards we have found. Even though these represent only the demonetised part of the economy, they may give us an idea of the circulation of coinage across the provinces. On the other hand, the occasional use of gold and silver coins (which is rarely represented in the excavation record) is far more important, since this usage was accountable for the integration of the economy. The wealthier members of Roman society were certainly involved in intraregional and especially interregional transactions that unified the Mediterranean. In the following section we will identify these transactions and how they related to specific social strata.

PROFITABLE ENTERPRISES AND COIN DISTRIBUTION

The inhabitants of the Roman empire possessed wealth and spent it either in public or in private for the benefit of its owner, his/her family and their friends. Part of this wealth was translated into precious-metal coins that would have been kept as hoards. Although we cannot know the exact number of precious-metal coins in circulation, we suspect that the coinage was sufficient to cover such expenses as household costs, benefactions and other public expenditure and the satisfaction of inheritors, in case of death. Especially, the liquidation of a property probably demanded a large amount of money at the disposal of the parties who were involved in the transaction.

The nature of these expenses indicates a consumer culture in the Roman empire that served the need of the members of the elite to preserve their social status and their public image against the rest of the population. However, we should not underestimate their commercial activities and the importance of coins also as a commercial medium, even though we cannot assess exactly the extent of the use of coinage among the different social strata.

Although the upper classes seemed preoccupied with the maintenance of their households and their public image, in fact they were probably also interested in various profitable enterprises that would have allowed them to increase their wealth. Since self-sufficiency cannot easily be achieved in complex societies, such as the Roman, then we should locate the interest of the elite in the distribution and marketing not only of the produce of their own estates but also of imported products. After meeting the obligation of supplying their own households, they probably disposed of the remaining surpluses in the market.[52] This act would have enabled them to make substantial profits. Maximisation of profits, although a notion initially connected to Classical Economic theories, in fact, was important also to the Romans. That is why they became involved in various enterprises, which allowed them to amass considerable wealth. Ptolemaios wrote about activities which make somebody rich (*polyktemon*):[53] building (*themelia*), agriculture (*georgia*) and shipowning plus trading (*naukleria*). Pseudo-Plutarch, in a very important passage, stated that people turned their first-rate slaves (*spoudaioi*) into '*georgoi, naukleroi, emporoi, oikonomoi* and *daneistai*'.[54] Two centuries later Basilius mentioned five sources of wealth:[55] corn (*sitos*), wine (*oinos*), wool (*eria*), trade (*emporia*) and banking (*daneisma*). The role of shipper (*naukleros*) and merchant (*emporos*) could have been filled by one man. All of these enterprises not only brought profit but also involved the use of coins in the process of the transactions. One of them, though, trade, promoted also the distant distribution of precious-metal coins.

The economic nature and profitability of trade in antiquity prompt us to suggest that commercial activities seemed to facilitate the accumulation of an increasingly important volume of wealth in coined money. The sale, transportation and marketing of goods could have been carried out in a variety of ways with the involvement of a range of people from different social strata. We cannot deny that a considerable number of merchants

52 See Whittaker 1988: 62, for the existence of the Italian market.

53 Ptol. *Tetr.* 4.2.

54 (Pseudo-) Plutarch, *De liberis educandis* 7.

55 Quoted by Ruggini 1961: 202, n. 631.

belonged to the middle or even lower class, especially those who bought and sold their own products. There were also the large-scale wholesalers who financed trade activities, who could have also been directly involved in the transportation and sale of commodities, as well as people with varied financial capacity involved in financing and organising the shipping of goods. At each stage the person involved may very well have been dealing not with the principal but with a representative, a slave or freedman or a member of the elite acting as an *institor*.[56] Freedmen operated with upper-class money, while independent merchants or shipmen may have been indebted to members of the urban elite.[57]

By means of these institutions also the rich landowners could have reaped the rewards of trade indirectly by creaming off the profits from the use of his or her representatives at each of the key stages in trade. In this model we should envisage a relatively closed market in which profits largely returned directly or indirectly to the wealthy landowners.[58] These landowners could have been well-to-do and prestigious local citizens of the eastern part of the empire who could afford to advance money to their cities for buying and transporting huge amounts of e.g. grain from Egypt – by permission of the emperor. This practice, though, was not common. Even in a rich city such as Ephesus local merchants did not have the economic capacity for such transactions, which could involve an import of e.g. 60,000 *modii* of grain. In fact, no parallel in the Greek East exists in comparison to well-to-do Western grain merchants like the Aufidii, who owned estates in Africa, occupied curial positions both in Ostia and African cities, and were corn merchants in the port of Ostia.[59] Unfortunately, it will be impossible to estimate the number of people, apart from the extremely rich, involved in these transactions, although we could guess that all producers, as well as inhabitants of the cities, were involved in minor commercial activities.

Since we cannot estimate the number of actual traders, the only way to assess the importance of trade is by investigating the circulation in the market of products used in daily life. So far, we know that luxury products were moving from the empire to areas beyond the frontiers and vice versa. Spices, expensive clothing and other luxury goods were the main interest of wealthy merchants. There also existed a wider movement of staple commodities such as grain from wealthy provinces of the empire towards others or towards the cities. Furthermore, archaeological evidence has lately indicated that inexpensive products, possibly to be found in local markets,

56 For more information on agents see Kirschenbaum 1987.

57 Pleket 1983: 140; Paterson 1988: 160–1. 58 Paterson 1988: 162. 59 Pleket 1983: 143.

were also able to move for long distances. For example, it is usually assumed that only decorated or fine pottery was exported; but in some shipwrecks the main cargo, apart from amphorae, was coarse ware, such as in the shipwreck Riou 1.[60] A modern suggestion that coarse pottery was used in order to balance the weight of the ship[61] does not change the fact that eventually the merchant would have undertaken the task of selling these products in distant markets in return for money or other goods. Even if this type of trade was not as profitable as the trade in luxuries, it still played an important role in the distribution of coins and commodities. The evidence of lamps, a 'humble' type of pottery, which were traded abroad, while they were not produced locally, is overwhelming. Although regional limitations in their long-distance movements have been attested, the simple fact that they were moving within a wide geographical radius shows us that their trade was a widespread activity.[62] Another kind of industry that brought profits when combined with trading activities, while it was not associated with luxurious products, was the textile industry in the eastern provinces.[63] It is obvious that we can estimate the extent of these activities only if we excavate more sites, especially in the eastern Roman empire. For now we can only assume that long-distance trade of basic commodities was common and transportation costs were not necessarily excessive since the profits from such trade could have been substantial.

The exchange of goods in this long-distance trade probably took different forms: commodities may have been exchanged for coins, or credit, or commodities or 'futures'. Some of the most widespread methods for the exchange of commodities do not involve the use of money, neither in cash nor in credit. Although we do not have solid evidence to prove such practices, historical analogies allow us to guess that a professional merchant in the Roman empire would have travelled from one port to another, exchanging his cargo of product A with a cargo of product B, if this was more profitable. Similarly, the exchange of commodities continued at least until the nineteenth century. For example, the West African diffused and periodic trade was conducted with the use of 'immediate payment in kind against "sorting" of goods, or against goods and currencies'. In addition, some merchants used 'floating' credit. According to an instance of 'floating' credit, when a ship was going down the coast, the merchants left the goods on shore and when they came back they were paid in palm

60 Pucci 1983: 111.

61 Evidence from a previous era can be found in Gill 1991; a shorter version in Osborne 1996: 39.

62 Duncan-Jones 1990: 58.

63 Pleket 1984: 24. The importance of textile trade is also established in Pleket 1998.

oil.[64] Polanyi repeatedly acknowledged the importance of what he called 'special purpose money' in antiquity, which is no more than the exchange of one commodity for another – including barley, silver and other equivalent staples.[65] Indicative of the classical period may also be the use of pots in trade as 'space-fillers'. These pots either supplemented the main commodities as cargo or they filled the boat, when it returned to its base after a successful commercial trip. Alternatively, silver ingots transported by ancient boats could have been used for the purchase of wheat that eventually would have been sold in the next port.[66] In any case, the exchange of commodities has been a regular practice for centuries and proved to have been both profitable and uncomplicated.

At the same time the use of money came to simplify existing transactions and maybe also to reduce transaction costs. Transportation costs of commerce across land could have affected this practice. Merchants probably preferred to carry the weight of a few precious-metal coins instead of another huge cargo whose transportation would probably be less profitable. Theoretically speaking, the advantages from the use of precious-metal coins are obvious. However, evidence from underwater archaeology points in the opposite direction. The absence of coins in shipwrecks could suggest that merchants were reluctant to carry on board precious currencies. Ancient ships most often carried small sums of coin, not intended for trade but more likely belonging to or intended to supply the needs of the crew.[67]

Such reluctance may have been caused by the relative dangers that were involved in the long-distance transportation of commodities, e.g. deadly storms, diseases, theft. De Ligt presents us with similar examples from other pre-industrial societies: T'ang China and Mughal India. In Mughal India, for instance, merchants submitted their money to the care of professional bankers and, in return, they received *hundis* (payment orders or bills of exchange). Similarly, because of the perils of the trips in T'ang China, merchants deposited coined money with the 'memorial presenting courts' in return for vouchers that guaranteed reimbursement in specific provinces.[68] The risks involved in the transportation of currencies were well known to wealthy Romans, and especially to Cicero, who commented on the issue.[69] The reluctance to use minted coin in long-distance transactions eventually forced Roman traders to seek other means for the completion of their dealings; one of these means was the extensive use of credit.

64 Newbury 1972: 82–4. 65 Polanyi 1963: 41–2. 66 Gill 1991: 35 and 38–9.
67 Beckman 1998. The results of this article were based on the evidence presented by Parker 1992.
68 De Ligt 2003: 235–7. 69 Cic. *Att.* 12.24.1 and *Fam.* 2.17.4.

The connection of banking with commercial activities is also suggested by the geographical situation of the bank itself. It seems that bankers always reserved a table in the *agora* for their transactions. We should not disregard the fact, though, that banking is an economic activity, which was developed as a result of the introduction of coinage and should not be studied apart from it. Besides, ancient bankers were predominantly involved in the exchange of money, while they were occupied with other secondary activities.[70] They are not known to have transferred money from one place to another without the actual movement of coinage, although the *publicani* must have used a primitive system of credits and debits to transfer tax revenues back to Rome.

Private contacts possibly facilitated the same service at least by providing funds to rich friends in one area against receipts in another.[71] Andreau gives several examples of such procedures based on the writings of Cicero.[72] In one case, Cicero, with the help of his friend Atticus, arranged for the Greek Xeno to advance a sum of money to Cicero's son, Marcus, when he arrived in Athens. Although Xeno was not a banker, he owed money to Atticus. So every time money was made available to Marcus in Athens, Cicero reimbursed Atticus at Rome.[73] In another instance, Cicero, while he was in Brindisi in 48 BC, received a substantial sum of money from one of his clients, Gnaeus Sallustius. Even though this client was not a banker, he chose not to be repaid by Cicero directly. Instead, Cicero paid the money to Publius Sallustius in Rome.[74] Another technique for avoiding the physical transportation of coins was the exchange of debt claims, *delegationes sovendi*.[75]

There was also a system of credit and debit that facilitated transactions in large estates. The Heronimos archive from Egypt provides information on the accounts of his large estate. For example, these accounts show that labour costs were not immediately paid to the workers but were credited to their name and paid later at frequent intervals. Most importantly the *phrontistes* does not recount the cash received from and paid for each transaction. Instead, he notes (a) the credit from sales, the administration, the bank and rent payments, (b) the debit from all expenditure of running costs (*phrontis*), (c) the balance of credit or debit from assets realised against running costs or resulting from sales and purchases and (d) the profits.[76] Even though the majority of our evidence comes from Egypt, we cannot

[70] Bogaert 1966: 135–44. [71] Howgego 1995: 90. [72] Andreau 1999: 20–1.

[73] Cic. *Att.* 12.24.1; 12.27.2; 12.32.2; 12.37.1; 14.7.2; 14.16.4; 14.20.3; 15.15.4; 15.17.1; 15.20.4; 16.1.5.

[74] Cic. *Att.* 11.14.3; 11.15.2. [75] Duncan-Jones 1990: 42, n. 7. [76] Rathbone 1991: 373–6.

exclude the possibility that the same commonsensical system existed also elsewhere.

Bankers or other rich persons with extensive money supplies probably had the ability to lend money to entrepreneurs. Usury was accepted as an important characteristic of Roman society and Roman law provided for conducting it in a legal manner. Theoretically speaking, the role of the emperors was to restrict the activities of 'loan sharks' and to establish legal interest rates. For example, there is a reference in *Scriptores Historiae Augustae* to Alexander Severus, who preferred to provide poor members of the society with loans at interest of 4 per cent (or even without interest) for the purchase of land.[77] In another instance, he forced moneylenders to reduce the interest they demanded for loans to the rate of 4 per cent, while the senators who lent money could only accept gifts or interest at 6 per cent.[78] Pliny also mentioned loans from the municipality that were estimated at a 9 per cent interest rate and he proposed that city councillors should be compelled to borrow at a lower rate.[79] On the whole, we can guess that the practice of loans was widespread, especially when coinage was scarce, a phenomenon that we sometimes encounter in antiquity.[80]

A special class of loans, maritime loans (*pecunia traiecticia* or *pecunia nautica*), facilitated long-distance trade during the Roman Republic and probably also during the Principate. The moneylender would have financed the one-way or return journey of a merchant, using as security the ship, the cargo, or the land of the borrower. The money would have been repaid upon the arrival of the boat at its destination. Because of the dangers encountered during such trips the interest rates were high; accordingly we should expect also that the profits were equally high.[81] During the course of these transactions, even if the bankers' money was not transported to distant regions, the merchant would certainly have returned with cash at hand in order to repay the moneylender.

All in all, trade in the Roman empire was conducted through a variety of mediums, only one of which was precious-metal coinage. Therefore, the existing coin hoards and excavation finds (found close to *emporia*, ports or urban centres) represent only an undefined percentage of the actual means of transactions in antiquity. I will not attempt to assess the proportion of dealings that was based on credit or the exchange of commodities, due to the lack of adequate evidence. In addition, apart from the movements of

[77] SHA, *Alex. Sev.* 21.1–2. [78] SHA, *Alex. Sev.* 26.2–4. [79] Plin. *Ep.*, 10.54.

[80] An incident of dearth of coinage in the market during the Roman Republic is described in Verboven 1997: 40–67.

[81] Andreau 1999: 54–6.

merchants and members of the elite involved in trade, there were other factors that facilitated the spatial distribution of coined money.

THE ROMAN STATE AND COIN DISTRIBUTION

Apart from merchants and members of the elite involved in trade, there were other factors that facilitated the spatial distribution of coined money. In the second chapter we explored how the Roman state balanced its revenues and expenses. Specifically, with regard to its expenses we emphasised the role of the army, the maintenance of the bureaucratic mechanism, the entrepreneurial activities of the emperor, imperial gifts or loans to members of the elite, *congiaria* to the populace, the construction of public buildings. All of these expenses assisted the initial distribution of coinage from the mint of Rome to the provinces. Only later, the same coins circulated from one region to another or from one province to another, as they were exchanged for transactions between the inhabitants of the empire.

The army may have played a significant role in this second stage of the diffusion of precious-metal currencies at least in the highly militarised areas of the eastern provinces. In the first instance, a number of hoards found in military contexts, especially in the frontier regions, should be connected to the transportation of money from the central mint of Rome or to troop movements. Only a few precious-metal hoards from the Antonine and the Severan period come undeniably from forts:[82] nine hoards come from Dacia,[83] two hoards come from Pannonia Superior,[84] no military hoards come from Pannonia Inferior and two hoards come from Dura Europos in Syria.[85] A lot more hoards come from unidentified contexts, roads, urban centres or fortress-cities along the north-eastern frontier and may instead be connected to trading activities. Even with regard to the hoards that have been found in military forts, we cannot exclude the possibility that they were employed in trade at one point or another. After all, soldiers participated regularly in commercial transactions that took place in the *vici*, nearby villages, cities or *komai*. On the other hand, there is no guarantee that the hoards found in urban contexts did not belong to soldiers who moved from one region to another or from one fort to another. Despite the exceptions and counter-exceptions, there is a strong possibility that Roman

[82] The hoards from the period after Gordian III are not included because they consist mainly of antoniniani, which may not have been used as precious-metal coins.

[83] Sighişoara, Hoard, Frânceşti, Pădureţu, Micia, Potaisa I, Săpata de Jos, Potaisa II, Slăveni I hoards.

[84] Arrabona and Tokod hoards.

[85] Dura Europos 3 and Dura Europos 16.

commerce was irrevocably tied to the urbanisation of the provinces and not to its militarisation, as a recent study suggests.[86]

CLOSED CURRENCY SYSTEMS

Even if the imperial expenses did not always have the effect of determining the wider circulation of precious-metal coins, the strict regulation of the monetary economy achieved it. Specifically, we notice the presence of more than one closed currency system in the Roman empire. In modern terms a 'closed currency system' is defined as a system in which the fluctuation of currency is restricted due to strict governmental control. Such restrictions usually affect the use and circulation of coins at an interregional level, while exchange rates become an essential mechanism for the use of these currencies in long-distance trade. Such systems until recently tended to be the rule and not the exception, because of the nature of modern national states and the development of mostly territorial currencies. Within the Roman empire, though, their existence is attested only in exceptional circumstances. The only way to detect them in the archaeological material is by studying the circulation of specific denominations within different regions surrounding the Mediterranean and beyond.

In actual fact, the entire Roman empire could be considered one such closed currency system, since no other coins apart from the ones minted in Rome or in the provinces could have been accepted in the Roman markets. The central government would never have conceded to the official circulation of 'foreign' coins, coming from the *barbaricum* or the neighbouring Parthia. Coin hoards and excavation finds throughout the Roman world include coins issued in 'official' or provincial mints within the frontiers.[87] Similarly, Roman coins were not accepted at face value outside its borders. One obvious example is that of India. Coin hoards found in this distant region suggest that extensive trade abroad was conducted with the help of gold and silver money of the highest fineness or bullion. Merchants involved in international trade as well as sea trade would have carried money with them for two additional reasons: (a) in order to pay for their lodgings in *tabernae*, when they travelled and (b) in order to pay for *portoria*, when they crossed the borders of the provinces or the frontiers of the empire. The minimum amount for custom dues was 2½ per cent and

[86] Katsari 2008.

[87] There are rare exceptions of barbaric imitations that may have infiltrated into the economies closer to the *limes* but these may have been used as symbols of wealth or as bullion rather than money.

the maximum 25 per cent of the price of the goods that were carried.[88] However, the numerous coins found beyond the Roman frontiers belong to a completely different economic and monetary zone. It is not a coincidence that most of the coin hoards found in India include silver coins from the first and second centuries AD,[89] which were of higher fineness and could have been exchanged according to their intrinsic value. After all, the political power of Rome was restricted within its borders and could not have guaranteed the face value of its coins abroad.

Another closed currency system probably included the provinces of wider Syria. Tetradrachms were used only in the markets of Syrian cities (we have not found them in excavations in the neighbouring Asia Minor, Cyprus etc.), even if they were originally minted in distant places, such as Rome or Alexandria.[90] We should assume that merchants either traded solely in that area without crossing the borders (which is not very probable given the fact that denarii minted in Antioch circulated across the empire) or, most likely, they exchanged their silver tetradrachms for other currencies when they left Syria. The structure of coin hoards found in this region has nothing in common with the structure of hoards in Asia Minor. All in all, 218 coins came from four Syrian hoards lost during the Antonine period, of which 49 were minted in Caesarea Cappadociae, 37 in Tyre, 12 in Antioch, while 51 came from Rome. Other eastern unidentified mints are represented by 79 coins. Furthermore, one of the hoards includes Nabataean coins as well as Roman. Two of the hoards consist of tetradrachms (Tiberias, Boston) and one is mixed (Muraba'at). We have no information about the denominations included in the fourth hoard. Although the hoards consist of different denominations, they demonstrate the same structure and almost the same increases and diminutions in volume of coinage. This means that the state did not necessarily arrange for the supply and distribution of more denarii than tetradrachms.

The coin hoards lost during the Severan period confirm the same pattern. One hoard consists of denarii (Syria 3), one of tetradrachms (Mempsis), and three contain both provincial and imperial denominations (Dura Europos 3, Dura Europos 16, Nineveh). The coins came from Mesopotamia, Syria, Arabia, Phoenice, Cyprus, Rome and one from Lugdunum. It seems that also in this case the majority of coins are tetradrachms. The Syrian coin hoards buried during the Military Anarchy period demonstrate the

[88] Meijer and van Nijf 1992: 78 ff. [89] Turner 1989.

[90] Bland 1991a: 229 and 231; Burnett 1987: 30–31. These coins were always intended for circulation in wider Syria.

increasing circulation of tetradrachms until the middle of the third century. Three of the hoards included antoniniani, eight included tetradrachms, six were mixed, one is not identified and none of them included denarii. The coins represent mostly the following mints: Antioch 2,571, Rome 279, Cyzicus 277, Emisa 139, Tyre 75, Laodicea 32, Carrhae 19. Other coins came from the rest of Syria, Phoenicia, Cyprus, Mesopotamia, Caesarea Cappadociae and Asia Minor.

The study of the above results leads us to a number of interesting conclusions. During the second century, the use of tetradrachms in Syria complemented, but never replaced, the denarius system. The production of denarii at Antioch under the Flavians marked the period of the denarius' introduction to Syria, while a second period of intense production took place during the reigns of Pescennius Niger and Septimius Severus, probably in order to cover for their respective military expenses. In addition, a sudden increase of local Syrian mints from three to twenty-eight took place in the early third century, during Caracalla's military campaigns, thus decentralising the production of silver coinage in the eastern provinces. The increased production of tetradrachms should probably be connected with the increased payment of troops along the Syrian frontier by Caracalla between the years 217 and 218. The fact that all of the 'tetradrachm' mints were represented in the coin finds from Dura Europos could indicate that coins were struck for and used by the army for the needs of the war against the Parthians in Northern Syria and Mesopotamia.[91] The mint of Antioch throughout the first three centuries AD became the main provider of tetradrachm coinage for Syria, while other smaller mints only occasionally produced this denomination.[92] Imperial silver coins (denarii or antoniniani), mainly produced in Rome but also minted in Antioch, circulated in the Syrian provinces, albeit in smaller numbers than tetradrachms. In that respect the Syrian closed currency system was not as restrictive as the Egyptian one (see below).

We do not encounter any such characteristics in the circulation of coinages in other eastern provinces. It seems that the Syrian population preferred the use of tetradrachms alongside the imperial silver coinages,[93] and that the central government was eager to provide them in abundance. The fact that the citizens had to pay commission to the banker, if they wanted to exchange tetradrachms for Roman denarii, did not seem

[91] Gilmore 1987. [92] Butcher 1996: 103 and 106.

[93] Denarii were used during the first and second centuries and the early third century AD. From the reign of Gordian III onward the use of antoniniani in daily transactions took place more often, for reasons that I explained in chapter 4.

to inhibit the free circulation of these silver currencies in the region. In fact, this exchange probably rarely took place, if the citizens could pay for their taxes either in denarii or in drachms and tetradrachms. On the whole, the Syrian tetradrachms were designed to facilitate the payment of the administrative officers, provide for the military expenses and cover the commercial needs of the urban centres. The mint of Antioch became the main provider of tetradrachms in the area during the second and third centuries AD, although other smaller mints emerged occasionally and issued lesser numbers of coins. The production of silver denominations also based on the Attic standard (drachms, didrachms, tridrachms and tetradrachms) by the mint of Caesarea in Cappadocia is an indication that this province was firmly attached to the closed currency system of Syria and not in the open currency system of Asia Minor.[94] Even if the inhabitants of these regions voiced and actively showed their preferences, the success of this closed currency system in such an extensive area would not have been possible without the central intervention of the Roman state.

Historians of the Roman world have studied extensively another, more famous, closed currency system in the area of the eastern Mediterranean: Egypt. The mint of Alexandria, the seat of the Roman governor in Egypt, was responsible for the production of currencies based on the ancient Ptolemaic standard. The first such Roman tetradrachms (from now on I will call them post-Ptolemaic) were issued during the reign of Tiberius. From then onwards, despite minor differences in size and weight, they seem to have followed the weight standards of their Ptolemaic predecessors.[95] The Romans did not just allow the production of coins based on the Ptolemaic standard. They also retained the closed currency system that was established during the Hellenistic period. A papyrus from the third century BC states that the people who visited Egypt had to exchange their coins for Ptolemaic coins.[96] In fact, according to hoard evidence the Egyptian closed currency system was already established by 305 BC.[97] The Romans decided not to disrupt the status quo, since there was no valid economic reason for any unnecessary changes. They just opted for the regulation of the current system and they imposed strict control on the circulation of coins at the Egyptian borders.[98] Despite the rigid central regulation, according to our evidence, twenty-eight silver coin hoards have been found outside the province of Egypt.[99] In addition, another four

[94] Sydenham 1978: 2–3. [95] King and Walker 1976.
[96] *P. Cair. Zen.* 59012; for the translation of the papyrus see Préaux 1939: 271.
[97] Mørkholm 1982: 298. [98] Strabo 2.3.5. [99] Christiansen 1985: 88 ff.

hoards of official Roman silver coins intruded into Egypt during the second century AD.[100] These incidents show that no closed currency system in antiquity can contain perfectly its coins within the designated geographical area. At any rate, Christiansen, who studied these hoards in detail, came to the conclusion that these post-Ptolemaic coins did not leave Egypt in any substantial numbers, while the intrusion of Roman coins minted elsewhere was insignificant by comparison with the local coinage.[101]

The reason for maintaining such a system was not caused exclusively by the wishes of the local population (even though we cannot disregard this possibility). Instead, it probably served the financial needs of the central government. The exchange rate of one denarius for a highly debased Alexandrian tetradrachm was guaranteed by the Roman state.[102] The official sanction of this coinage, thus, allowed the circulation of post-Ptolemaic silver coins throughout Egypt for the duration of the Principate. Since the value of the debased tetradrachms was guaranteed by the emperor, the population would have trusted the currency in circulation and would have used it for their daily transactions. We noticed a similar attitude in the beginning and the middle of the third century AD, when the emperors introduced the newly debased denarii and antoniniani in circulation. As long as the exchange rates remained stable, there was no reason to distrust the currency.[103] On the other hand, the Roman state received substantial profits from the mint of Alexandria, since with the use of less bullion they achieved the production of more coined pieces of silver metal. In addition, Roman officials probably received a small tax from the exchange of local post-Ptolemaic tetradrachms for denarii or Syrian tetradrachms at the borders of the province of Egypt. Since the system was so profitable there was no reason to change its fundamental function or alter it in any other way.

PATTERNS OF COINS AND TRADE

Although the state intervened in the cases of Syria and Egypt, in the rest of the empire other factors affected the structure of the coin populations. The circulation of coins in most cases could be connected to trade transactions in specific areas. The structures of coin hoards and excavation finds could also help us trace the movement of merchants in inland regions or across the Mediterranean. The attempt to compare trade patterns with coin patterns

100 Christiansen 1985: 88. 101 Christiansen 2004: 42.
102 Burnett, Amandry and Ripollès 1992: 688 ff.; Christiansen 1994: 280.
103 See chapters 3 and 4.

in the eastern Mediterranean has never been attempted before, mainly due to the scanty evidence in existence. In the first instance it would be sensible to analyse in histograms the structure of excavation finds and stray finds. Then I intend to demonstrate only the general patterns emerging between different regions and demonstrating the movement of coinage within specific circulation pools. These patterns could, in turn, indicate the existence of trade routes repeatedly used by merchants or other individuals, when they were travelling from one port to another or from one city to another across and in between several regions.

It is not a coincidence that most of our coins come from highly urbanised areas or major ports, where the volume of transactions must have been much higher than in the countryside. So far, we have seen that a large number of coin hoards comes from regions in western Asia Minor, Syria and Greece, which are in direct contact with the Mediterranean Sea. Alternatively, they come from urban centres or fortress-cities close to the north-western frontier, which may have remained highly militarised during the second and third centuries AD but also saw the rise of impressive *emporia*. The geographical situation (sea-oriented cities or cities close to roads) probably allowed the inhabitants to get involved in trading activities, for which purpose they created sizeable harbours. Greece is known for its ports in the mainland (e.g. Corinth, Athens) and the islands (e.g. Rhodes). Palestine and Phoenicia are characterised by a string of ports along the coast of the Levant. Asia Minor demonstrates the same structure with ports in its western coast (Aegean) as well as the northern coast (Black Sea). All of these harbours are in contact with each other as well as with other cities away from the sea. These inland contacts were achieved through sophisticated roads that cross the countryside, especially in Greece and Asia Minor.[104] Similarly, an impressive road network interconnecting urban centres, forts and fortress-cities was established in the north-western frontier, as the *Tabula Peutingeriana* indicates.[105] Although, initially, roads may have been constructed for military purposes, traders and other people were using them frequently.

Coin finds from Asia Minor demonstrate not only that there was no numismatic connection with Syria but also that there existed more than one circulation pool. The provinces of Phrygia, Pisidia and Pamphylia, as

104 Egnatia Odos in Greece played an important role in the movement of goods from the Ionian Sea to the Bosporus. For roads in Asia Minor see French 1988.

105 Although the *Tabula Peutingeriana* comes from the thirteenth century, it is accepted as a copy of an originally Roman scroll. It depicts the *cursus publicus* (the public transport system), which would have also facilitated the promotion of trade.

demonstrated by stray finds from the local museums of Afyon, Yalvaç and Fethiye respectively,[106] indicate that they belonged to the same monetary zone. For example, the structure of coin finds from the museum of Afyon (Phrygia) is quite different from the structure of coin finds in the museum of Sinope (Black Sea). There seem to be no similarities between this zone and the region of Pontus, as shown by coins from the museum of Sinope, or the eastern frontier, as shown from the structure of the Eastern hoard.[107] The system of roads in central and southern Asia Minor was probably the main factor that either facilitated the connection or caused the relative isolation of these circulation pools. Traders would have been taking trips using the existing road system and, this way, they would have promoted interregional trade between the cities, the *komai* and the villages. On the other hand, geographical obstacles and the undoubted inadequacies of the road system in certain areas probably caused the numismatic isolation of central Asia Minor from the northern and eastern provinces. There probably were no important trade routes that led from one place to the other and the road network perhaps was not sufficient for commercial activities on a grand scale.

The southern Aegean Sea constitutes another distinct circulation pool for silver coins. The harbours of Patra, Corinth, Athens and Ephesus and the island of Rhodes demonstrate unquestionable similarities (Chart 42).[108] These similarities could be explained if we take into consideration both the geographical position of these harbour-cities (and island) and the activities of their citizens. All of these cities were situated on naval crossroads and they included important ports directly connected with extensive trading activities. The fact that they belong to the same circulation pool allows us to suggest that they were on the same commercial routes and that the majority of passing merchant ships in the southern Aegean anchored in these harbours. There, traders were involved in commercial transactions regularly and they made use not only of credit but also of their silver coins.

The regions of northern Greece and northern Asia Minor seem to have belonged to another circulation pool. The island of Corfu, the ports of Thessaly, the cities of Thrace and the harbours of the Black Sea (such as

106 Katsari 2001: chart 12. The reason I do not present the results here in detail is that I have no permission to publish the coin finds from the museums of Afyon, Yalvaç and Fethiye. I would like to thank, though, Richard Ashton and John Casey for allowing me to study the material.

107 Katsari 2001: chart 13.

108 I was allowed to look at the very well-organised catalogues of the island of Rhodes and I would also like to thank the staff of the museum for their cooperation.

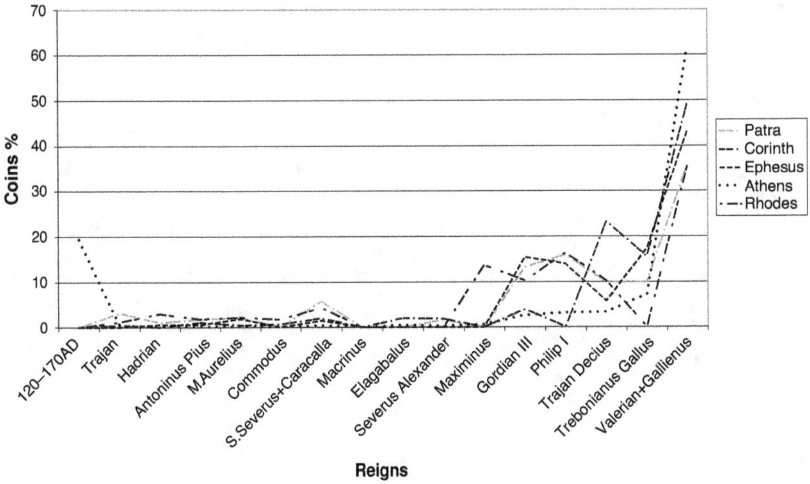

Chart 42 Silver coins from excavations in Patra, Corinth, Ephesus and Athens and from the museum in Rhodes

Sinope) probably welcomed every year a substantial number of traders.[109] It should be noted that the pattern of coins from Sinope is the same as the pattern of coins from Corfu, which is situated on the other side of the Greek mainland, in the Ionian Sea.[110] A possible connection between these two places is, of course, the sea. However, the distance remained prohibitive even by boat. It is possible that travellers preferred to use the Egnatia Road that commenced in Action and continued as far as Thrace.

Regarding the other interconnected areas, the *Monumentum Ephesinum*[111] shows the economic importance of the Bosporus, which linked the northern Aegean with the Black Sea. It is probable that trading activities in the area were significantly high. In all likelihood, this is why the Roman state decided to impose custom dues of up to 20 per cent on anyone who crossed the Bosporus. The government, in an attempt to gain more money from taxes, ruled that traders should pay each time they travelled from one side to the other, even if they carried the same cargo. Although the

[109] Katsari 2001: chart 9. Unfortunately, I do not have permission to publish the coins from the museums of Corfu and Volos. However, I obtained permission to include them in my PhD thesis.

[110] It should be noted that, even though the percentages of coins per year of reign are similar, the mints represented in the sample are different.

[111] Text, commentary and translation in Engelmann and Knibbe 1989; text and commentary by H. W. Pleket in *SEG* 39, 1989 (1992) no. 1180, 367–87. Discussion on the text can be found in the following articles: Heil 1991; Nicolet 1991; Salomies 1991; Solin 1991: 183; Wankel 1991; Nicolet 1993; Lewis 1995; McGing 1995; Carreli 1996; Dreher 1996; Merola 1996.

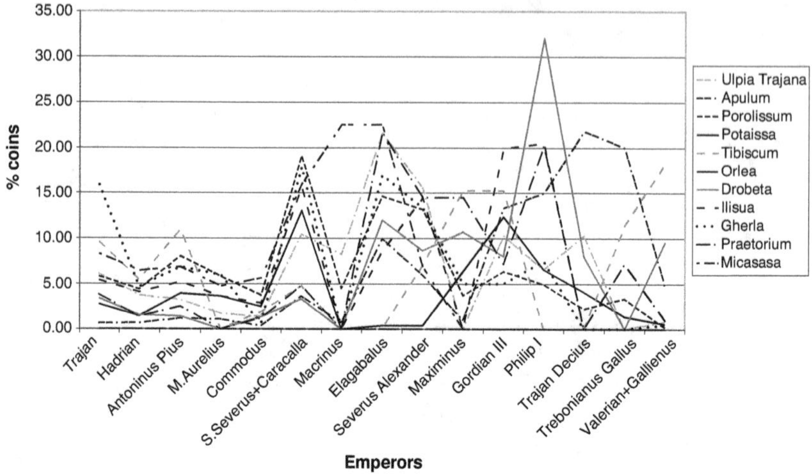

Chart 2 Excavations in Dacia: silver coins, % per annum

imposition of custom dues may not have promoted trade, it does not seem to have 'crippled' commercial activities in the area. On the other hand, there are exceptions to the rule, since we observe regional differences in the structure of coin circulation between northern Greece and northern Asia Minor. The museum of Yiannena,[112] (in north-western Greece) presents an 'odd' coin structure that does not fit the pattern of the neighbouring areas of Corfu or Thessaly or Thrace. The reason for such a difference is probably that the area was isolated between mountains and gorges and that there were no easily accessible trade routes towards the east or the west that led to nearby regions. Even Egnatia Road, which lay south of this region, does not seem to have been able to facilitate extensive trade activities.

The study of silver coins from excavations in the frontier provinces in the north-western Balkans also shows the formation of two distinct circulation pools: (a) Dacia (Chart 2) and (b) Pannonia Superior (Chart 3) and Pannonia Inferior (Chart 4). Once more, it is evident that the presence of the army in the north-western frontier was not adequate for the monetary unification of the regions. Especially in the province of Dacia, we notice that the initial creation of a unified circulation pool was interrupted during the Military Anarchy period, when smaller circulation pools seem to have emerged (see the differences in the structure of coins in different excavation sites). In addition, coin evidence from the neighbouring Pannonia

[112] Katsari 2001: chart 11.

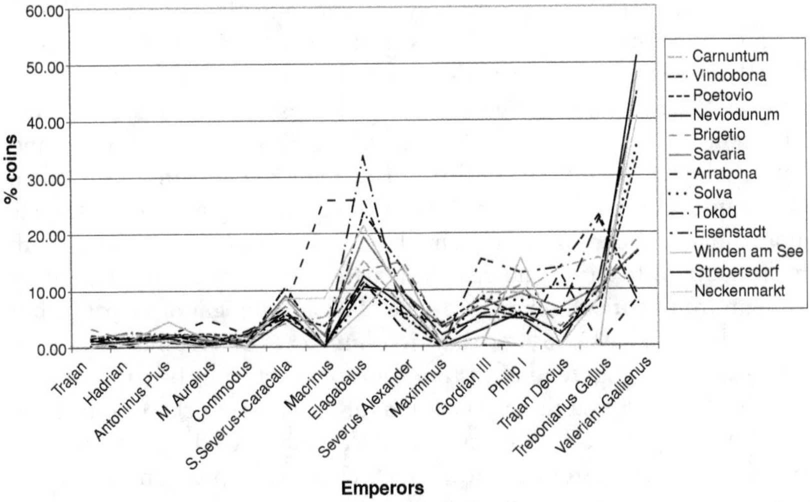

Chart 3 Excavations in Pannonia Superior: silver coins, % per annum

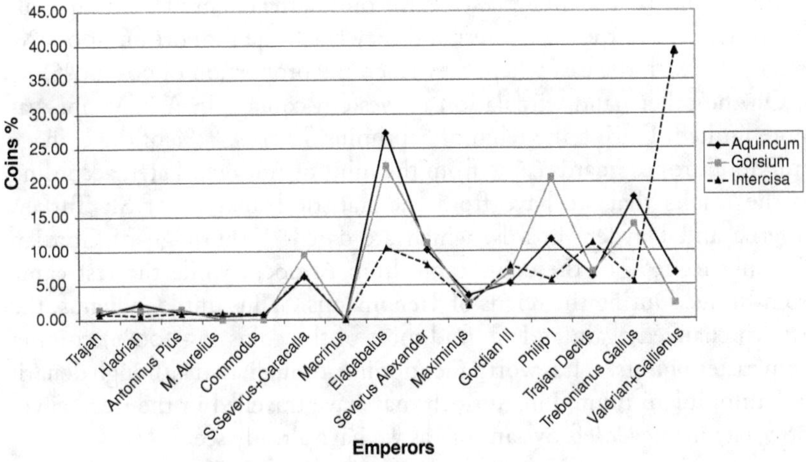

Chart 4 Excavations in Pannonia Inferior: silver coins, % per annum

indicates that it formed a separate pool, even if there was some direct contact with Dacia. These regional differences may have been due to changes in the direction of trade routes and the preferences of traders.

The comparisons of hoards from the north-west with those from the eastern Roman empire allow us to study further the heterogeneity of different circulation pools. The only eastern coins that reached the west in substantial quantities were those struck under Septimius Severus, Gordian III, Trebonianus Gallus, Valerian and Gallienus. Up until the joint reign of Valerian and Gallienus, during the rest of the first half of the third century all coinage was produced mostly in the mints of Rome and Antioch, but these coins are difficult to attribute to one mint or the other. Taking into account the nature of the evidence, we may be able to estimate approximately the extent of the circulation of coinage in areas away from its production. In British hoards of the period AD 248–61, antoniniani of Gordian from Antioch represent 1–6% of all antoniniani of Gordian, but in hoards buried AD 263–74 they account for 6–14%. Thus there does appear to be a rising trend of eastern coins of Gordian in Britain, possibly because of the fact that the silver content of the coins struck in Rome from AD 240 onwards was well below the silver content of those produced at Antioch. Severus' eastern denarii, which circulated up to almost seventy years after their issue, reach *ca.* 50% in British hoards by AD 263, but they never attain the 80% found in the east. Furthermore, among coins of Gordian III eastern material represents 0–14% in the north-west, 10–16% in Turkey and 32–34% in Syria. Eastern coins of the reigns of Gallus to Gallienus decrease in the north-west and they reach the proportion of 0–9%, in contrast with the east where they reach the proportion of 90–100%.

On the other hand, circulation of western coinage in Asia Minor was quite limited. During the reign of Septimius Severus, 82% of the coinage in Dura Europos hoards came from the mint of Antioch. Later, according to the results that we have from the statistical analysis of SE Turkey, Smyrna and Haydere hoards, which are dated to the reign of Gordian III, only 10–16% of the coins came from Antioch, while the rest came from Rome. During the reigns of Trebonianus Gallus until Gallienus, the pattern changed again and we find most of the coins (95–100%) coming from eastern mints.[113] It is worth mentioning, though, that although denarii and antoniniani minted in Antioch may have travelled in the west, silver tetradrachms never left Syrian soil, as we have already seen.

MONETARY INTEGRATION?

Coins, among other economic factors, are regularly used in order to study the economic integration of the Roman empire. There is no doubt that the

[113] At least these are the results based on lists that have been presented in the Thirteenth Oxford Symposium on coinage (Howgego 1996).

one most abundant piece of evidence we have from the ancient world is coinage. Consequently, some archaeologists, historians and numismatists place all their hopes and base their study of the ancient economy on the analysis of coins. However, we should take into consideration the fact that the monetary economy is only a very small part of the entire economy. As a friend of mine says: 'the economy resembles the dark matter of the universe, while currencies are only the planets'.

There are probably four different types of integration: (a) numismatic, (b) monetary, (c) financial or (d) economic. First of all, numismatic integration implies the homogeneous circulation of currencies. Secondly, I would like to define as monetary integration not only the integration of currencies across the empire through a system of exchange but also the integration of a common credit system, as it was devised by the bankers and regulated by the emperor. Thirdly, with the term financial integration, I mean the overarching regulations imposed by the Roman state, which allowed for the control of the treasury, the organisation of taxes and the outflow of expenses, established a monetary monopoly, achieved the policing of the provinces and monitored the operations of the markets. Finally, economic integration is a wider term than the previous three. It encompasses all or some of the above characteristics and, additionally, it includes the integration of trade (interregional commercial activities). Eventually, this type of integration could lead to the merging of the regional economies into one imperial economy. Since I have no aspirations to conclusively decide whether the Roman economy was integrated or not, I will restrict myself to the study of the monetary economy.

One of the first attempts to analyse this phenomenon came from Keith Hopkins, who supported the idea of the integration of the empire in his article on 'taxes and trade in the Roman empire' published in 1980. He divided the provinces into three economic zones. To the first zone belonged the frontier provinces where the army was stationed, to the second belonged the rich tax-exporting provinces such as Asia Minor, and to the third Italy and the city of Rome. The relationship between them was based on the possibility that rich provinces were responsible mainly for the payment of taxes that were consumed by the army in the frontiers and by the central administration in Italy. In turn, these taxes stimulated interregional trade, which also played an important role in the economic integration of the empire, especially after the second century BC, when trade seemed to flourish. An increase in the volume of interregional trade caused a consequential increase in the volume of money produced by the state for the needs of the inhabitants. On the whole, the flow of taxes, trade and rents paid in coin contributed to the even distribution of coinage and the eventual integration of the economy throughout the empire.[114] Hopkins may not have been entirely wrong when he tried to explain the economic relations between different types of provinces. In fact, his model can be applied if we take into consideration that part of trade, taxes, payments etc. took place in the form of goods or credit instead of coins; therefore, we cannot trace them among the numismatic finds. If we accept that the Roman empire was a whole entity, whose individual regions interacted with each other, then we may suppose that goods circulated throughout the empire in order to cover the needs of several provinces.

A few years later, Duncan-Jones tried to prove the opposite: namely, that coins had the tendency to remain in the local circulation area within which they were produced. In an article published in 1990 he revealed his methods for the study of the integration of the Late Roman coinage, which was produced locally, in contrast to Imperial coinage that was almost entirely produced in the mint of Rome.[115] While he compared types of coins that came from hoards found in different parts of the Empire, he recognised the apparent concentration of certain types in certain areas. The results of his research are refined further in his book *Money and Government in the Roman Empire*,[116] where he concludes that the existence of regional differences suggests that the process of recycling coin through taxes or trade was provincial rather than national. The coins that were sent to distant provinces for the needs of the army stayed in those provinces and interregional trade was not enough to move them out. Finally, 'the monetary unification of the empire, so striking in terms of the uniform denominations found throughout an enormous land-area, was always more a matter of form than of substance'.

Chris Howgego aimed to bridge the differences between the above theories.[117] He noticed that, although the study of the homogeneity of coinage could indicate the integration of the monetary economy, we still cannot suggest the integration of other sectors of the economy. During the Roman Imperial period products other than coins, such as pottery, foodstuffs etc., also moved throughout the empire. Archaeological evidence indicates their voyage to distant provinces away from the area of their production. As for the circulation and eventual integration of currencies, Howgego described the mechanisms of the supply and distribution of coinage through army payments, taxes, rents and trade (as Hopkins did).

[114] Hopkins 1980. A revised version of this model was published later in Hopkins 1995–6.
[115] Duncan-Jones 1990: 121–137. [116] Duncan-Jones 1994: 172–9. [117] Howgego 1994.

He subsequently stated that despite movements of coin from east to west and from west to east, coin populations never became completely homogeneous. In fact, heterogeneity of coinage increased regularly during the third century AD. This last view brings him partly in accordance with the views of Duncan-Jones on the monetary integration of the empire.

In the course of this chapter, it has become evident that the eastern Roman empire should be divided into numerous numismatic circulation pools – Southern Aegean, Northern Greece and Asia Minor, Central Asia Minor, Dacia, Pannonia, Syria and Egypt – as the structure of coin finds indicates. Furthermore, there are obvious dissimilarities in the circulation of coins between the eastern and the western provinces of the Roman empire. And we should not forget the existence of, at least, two closed currency systems in Syria and in Egypt, which restricted further the movements of silver coins. As a consequence, we can infer from the differences in the structure of coin finds that there was no numismatic integration of the Roman empire. In this respect the results of this volume, superficially, agree with the results presented by Duncan-Jones, according to whom different coin types sometimes were more common in one province than another. Effectively, the empire could be pictured as a mosaic comprised of different stones that represent localised economies. The reasons for the uneven distribution of coinage in the eastern provinces are probably related to a range of factors, such as the level of monetisation of a province, the popularity of the traditional coinages, the distance of the region from Rome, where the central mint existed, and the different needs of the province for the conduct of trade or for the supply of the army. The circulation pools of different geographical areas have individual characteristics that do not necessarily overlap with the characteristics of any other area in the empire.

This numismatic non-integration raises by itself a number of questions that have not yet been answered. For example, if the empire was politically powerful, why did the emperor never seek the creation of one homogeneous numismatic area? In this case, we may answer confidently that profit was a serious concern for the central authorities. The emperor was probably receiving taxes (through the bankers) every time one coin was exchanged for another. On the other hand, Rome seems to have followed the usual course of not interfering with the administrative habits of regions outside Italy.[118] In the case of the eastern provinces, local populations favoured the use of their traditional Hellenistic currencies. Any intrusion of the state may have disrupted the existing system and may have caused commotion

118 Millar 1977.

in the local markets. In addition, the power of the emperor may have been felt in the provinces through his military and administrative mechanisms. However, the role of the army and the governors in the supply (and secondary distribution) of precious-metal coinages in the local markets was probably quite limited. Especially, the troops would have affected the monetary development of an area only if other factors, such as urbanisation and trade, already existed.[119] Since the army could not always affect the creation of different circulation pools we should reconsider the importance of private enterprises, especially trade.

Private wealth in the form of money was acquired and eventually increased or was just maintained intact through trade, which was able to, and did, integrate parts of the empire. So far, we have noted the creation of different circulation pools and, consequently, trade zones in Egypt, Syria, central Asia Minor, northern Greece and the Black Sea, the southern Aegean Sea, Dacia and Pannonia. But does this regional division suggest that the use of coins in interregional trade was more or less restricted within certain areas? We are aware that a great number of people, who belonged to different social classes, were directly or indirectly involved in the sale and buying of goods. Is it possible that their actions were limited and they did not have the power to integrate the economy of the empire? We also know that sea trade expanded rapidly after the political unification of the Mediterranean and the establishment of the *pax Romana*. Individual merchants used the advantages offered by the Roman state: they managed to expand their activities and subsequently to achieve the numismatic integration of key ports. Even if the mainland, in some cases, remained isolated, the cities near seashores were transformed into cosmopolitan metropolises. Therefore, is it accurate to assume that trade did not manage to integrate the economy of the Roman empire? In order to answer these questions, we should not restrict ourselves to the study of the numismatic integration of the empire but we should expand on its monetary integration.

Comparable cases of the monetary integration of a numismatically non-integrated country are the late imperial and early republican China and Benghal India. Kuroda, in his article on 'Concurrent but non-integrable currency circuits: complementary relationships among monies in modern China and other regions',[120] describes the chaotic monetary usage in modern China: 'chaotic' being the term used by foreign observers. According to the Commissioner of Customs and Statistical Secretary, Inspectorate General of Customs in China, H. B. Morse, 'In China the currency is at

[119] See chapter 2. [120] Kuroda 2008.

the top a weight pure and simple, in the middle a combination of weight and token currency, and at the bottom a coin which stands on its own feet, and neither receives support from nor absolutely gives it to any other unit in the series.' These observations are complementary to the fact that different monies were used for different commodities even within a city; for example, different silver dollars (Mexican, Japanese, provincial) circulated concurrently in different circulation pools in 1910 in the port Jiujiang. Even the face value of the smaller denominations of copper coins, as set by currency exchangers, was not stable but fluctuated daily. In addition to the use of coinage, merchants exchanged commodities also for silver ingots that did not coincide with the governmental units of silver used for the payment of taxes.

Similarly, in Dacca (India) circulated concurrently fifty-two currencies to the disadvantage of the local population and to the advantage of the moneychangers.[121] Once more, different monies would have bought different types of commodities. According to Kuroda, the similarities between the operation of the Chinese and the Indian monetary systems are evident. For example, some currencies in both case studies appreciated during the autumn, while smaller denominations increased in value during the harvest season, thus indicating changes in the monetary supply and demand. All in all, the value especially of the silver coins was not always linked to their metallic value but to the fluctuations of the market. The variety of currencies does not seem to have harmed the economy in any way. Kuroda believes that the imposition of a unified monetary system would not have been flexible enough and, eventually, would not have met the demand from all levels of the markets. Differences are not located only in the use of currencies but also in their circulation. It seems that there is a distinction between coinages that circulated in rural and urban areas. Similarly, the structure and the nature of currencies differed depending on whether they were used for long-distance or local trade. Even under these extreme numismatic conditions, it does not mean that the economies of individual or neighbouring cities were not integrated, just because their citizens used a variety of coinages for their daily transactions.

Monetary integration, unlike numismatic integration, was probably achieved in the Roman empire through different means. In the first instance, within a politically unified area, there was always a possibility that more than one currency was in circulation. As we have already seen,[122] the cistophori of Asia, the drachms and didrachms of Caesarea Cappadociae

[121] Mitra 1991: 54. [122] See chapter 1.

and the tetradrachms of Antioch all followed previous Hellenistic weight standards and circulated in some of the eastern provinces alongside the denarius. The provincial silver coins were connected with the official denarial system. All of these coinages were exchanged against the aureus at the official rate that enabled the bimetallic system to work.[123] Also, silver currencies based on the Hellenistic standards were exchanged with silver coins based on the Roman standard; hence, they were tariffed in terms of the Roman denarius. After all, these currencies circulated side by side and were used in the same markets indiscriminately. Written accounts, such as the tax inscriptions from Messene[124] and the Salutaris inscriptions from Ephesus[125] provide some evidence with regard to the connection of the provincial coinages with the official one. Nevertheless, the detailed study of the coins depicts more accurately the situation, an excellent summary of which can be found in the first volume of the *Roman Provincial Coinage*.[126] The official exchange rate allowed the wide circulation of these coinages and their use in the regional markets. Even if the cistophori, the tetradrachms, the drachms and other Hellenistic coinages did not circulate throughout the Roman world, they were still used alongside the denarii. Effectively, the denarial system was used in order to support a unified exchange system and to integrate different currencies within the empire.

Similarly to the Roman empire, the German monetary union of the nineteenth century was based on a system of fixed exchange rates. The first attempt to unify this area economically came with the introduction of the *Zollverein*, the German customs union, which was founded in 1834. This decision followed the initial monetary union of the Kingdom of Prussia after the Napoleonic Wars and the stabilisation of the French and British monetary economies through the maintenance of fixed exchange rates that allowed the convertibility of their respective currencies. These reforms encouraged the German states to create a monetary union and achieve greater monetary integration by establishing a fixed exchange system. The main problems they had to face, though, during the implementation of their policies, were discrepancies in the quality of coins and differences in the seignorage rates. The *Zollverein* member states who wished to solve these problems, first, came up with an agreement on a standard seignorage rate of 10 per cent over the nominal price of the coin, and then, they decided to fix 'exchange rates' between different monies (1 taler:1.75 gulden). These agreements became official in two treaties signed in 1837

[123] See chapter 2. [124] Giovannini 1978: 115–22. [125] Wankel 1979: 1a, 27.
[126] Burnett, Amandry and Ripolles 1992: part 1, 26–30.

(Munich Coinage Treaty) and 1838 (Dresden Coinage Treaty). From then onwards the taler's position became central in the monetary unified area and dominated the monetary economy. As a result of the new monetary union, researchers observed greater economic stability and an increasing trust in interregional and international transactions.[127] Although we cannot testify to similar changes with regard to the transactions in the Roman empire, we may assume that commercial dealings were facilitated further once the exchange rates became fixed.

Money serves the economy not only as a means of payment but also as a store of value and a unit of account. Its specific role as a unit of account further facilitates the use of credit in commercial transactions, state payments or the receipt of taxes. In a recent article Harris put forward an elaborate thesis on the comparatively extensive use of credit in the Roman empire by contrast to its limited use in the Greek world.[128] In his definition of credit, he includes debts, loans (secured and unsecured) and mortgages, as these were employed by all social strata. In the first instance, the rich inhabitants of the empire were not involved in moneylending to such a large extent, since this was illegal in the early empire.[129] However, after the death of Augustus, wealthy Roman citizens and provincials probably benefited more from usury or moneylending.[130] At an institutional level, banks were better equipped to deal with loans and mortgages. Unlike the modest view presented by Andreau, according to which bankers did not employ a lot of capital and that they had only very few partners,[131] Harris supports the idea that extensive lending was not only indubitable but, in addition, banks were involved in fractional reserve banking.[132] Also, payments at a distance without the use of coins were a regular occurrence. These practices were not the fiefdom of the upper strata of society but were employed also by the *decuriones* and people with more modest incomes, such as farmers and craftsmen. Even if Roman banking was not closely regulated, the scale and extent of their business resembled that of an advanced pre-industrial economy.

Comparative data indicating the developed nature of the Roman credit system are provided in an article written recently by Temin.[133] The author compares the Roman financial services with similar services that were in force in eighteenth-century agrarian economies. For example, English merchants used bills of exchange in international trade during the eighteenth

[127] Tilly 2007. [128] Harris 2006: 8–17. [129] Tac. *Ann.* 6.16.3.
[130] Dio Chrys. 7.104; Cod. Iust. 5.37.22.5a. [131] Andreau 1999.
[132] Harris 2006: 8–17. [133] Temin 2004.

century in order to finance their activities, thus extending credit indirectly. The sellers were paid as soon as they shipped the goods and the buyers paid when the goods were sold. This action was enabled by drawing a bill to the buyer who accepted the obligation. Then, the bill could be sold to a third party, as a credit instrument. Inland bills of exchange were used in similar ways in order to finance international trade. As well, lending money during that age was the norm and several institutions, among which were goldsmiths, scriveners and merchants, became involved. In addition, the strapped-for-cash governments of England and France issued perpetual bonds that never came due in an attempt to increase their revenues. On the whole, though, the credit activities of the individual French seemed to be more restricted than the activities of the English.

Temin tries to compare these data with the information we have from the Roman world. He emphasises the proliferation of loans between the members of the Roman elite and the supposition that banks offered time deposits. Despite the apparent inflexibility of the Roman banking system (by comparison to modern standards), the credit crisis, described in the works of Cicero,[134] had an empire-wide effect and indicated the existence of linked financial markets. An array of financial intermediaries (apart from banks) could have helped this unprecedented spreading of credit. Temples' endowment accounts, for example, may have played the role of banks, in the sense that they loaned out money with interest in order to support their activities. On the whole, Temin comes to the conclusion that the Roman institutions were better than their counterparts in eighteenth-century England and France, since they had a stronger impact that eventually integrated the economy.

Central intervention would have promoted the monetary integration of the Roman empire, even if it was not part of any imperial plan. With the establishment of the *pax Romana* across the Mediterranean, the emperors became the undisputed rulers of the regions surrounding the Sea. The existence of one central authority imposing laws and controlling a geographical area both politically and militarily is a guarantee for the economic integration of the specific region up to a certain extent. Additionally, the fact that the emperors had the opportunity to impose taxes may indicate, at least, the monetary integration of the state economy. We know that part of these taxes was paid in cash, while some of them were paid in goods (e.g. the *annona*). For instance, in the case of the province of Asia the Roman treasury received taxes in the form of money, even before the reign

[134] Cic. *Leg. Man.* 14–19.

of Augustus.[135] One may argue that despite the central imposition of taxes, these may have been gathered and redistributed locally. Nevertheless, we should not forget that a central account has certainly been kept and that the allocation of revenues and expenses always lay with the Roman treasury.[136]

Furthermore, even if the receipt and transportation of precious-metal coins was difficult, we should assume that credit may have assisted the financial system of the Roman empire in a fundamental role. During the Late Republic, Rome leased the right to collect taxes to tax farmers, who, in turn, paid their dues either to the Roman financial magistrates or to governors and generals. In a well-known example, Cicero, the then governor of Cilicia, received his allowance from the tax farmers of Laodicea.[137] Upon his return he deposited the surplus of this money (1 million sestertii) with the same tax farmers in order to avoid the dangers entailed in the long trip. For the same reason Cicero deposited private revenues of 2.2 million sestertii with the tax farmers of Ephesus before he returned to Italy.[138] In effect, tax-farming companies were used regularly to transfer money (or credit), especially in the east during the Republic.[139] There is no evidence about the development of this system during the Empire, although it is possible that the previous knowledge was not entirely lost. The imperial revenues promoted in a way the monetary integration of the empire, while the unification of the monetary system, in turn, facilitated the collection of taxes.

In a similar way the imperial expenses may have integrated the empire further. In all likelihood, the emperor was responsible for the payment of administrators, the military, his tenants and other employees.[140] Despite the fact that these employees lived across the empire, they may have received comparable wages, since they were paid by a central authority (although regional variations cannot be excluded). These wages probably set a significant standard for salaries paid in the provinces as well as in Italy. So far, the scanty anecdotal sources in existence do not permit a sustained study of wages in all of the Mediterranean regions. The only area that provides ample evidence is Egypt. Drexhage, who published his work on prices and wages in Egypt, noticed that farm labourers earned less than one drachm (equivalent to six obols) per day during the first century AD, while during the second century their salaries increased to eight obols per day.[141] On the other hand, in the famous quote from Matthew, which

[135] De Ligt 2003: 249. [136] Brunt 1966. [137] Cic. *Fam.* 2.17.4; Cic. *Att.* 7.1.6.
[138] Cic. *Fam.* 5.20.9. [139] De Ligt 2003: 241–3. [140] See chapter 2.
[141] Drexhage 1991: 415–25.

I already mentioned, the daily wage of a labourer in the eastern provinces was one denarius.[142] Comparably, in Pompeii salaries ranged from five asses to sixteen asses per day.[143] This evidence, albeit limited, demonstrates that the magnitude of daily wages was similar in different regions. A degree of variance between these wages is anticipated, since the tasks of the labourers, demand for local labour or the seasons may have differed. The comparability of labour payments across the empire could only indicate a level of monetary integration triggered by imperial intervention and the adoption of a unified monetary system.

The full economic integration of the empire, though, relied heavily on interregional commercial activities. So far, we have seen that trade did not manage to promote the numismatic integration of the eastern provinces. Furthermore, we cannot be certain about the impact of trade on the extent of monetary integration, since we do not have enough evidence about the use of credit or the direct exchange of commodities. Prices, on the other hand, may give important hints about the monetary integration of commercial enterprises. Recently, a study of the prices from the province of Egypt indicated that its individual regions showed a level of patchy integration that cannot be ignored. Despite local variations, there were broad trends in the formation of prices within a wide network of markets. This stability probably existed due to the compulsory purchase of goods at state-defined rates or the conversion of grain taxes into cash payments.[144]

Another study, of wheat prices from the Late Republic and the Early Empire, showed that the further the provinces were from Rome, the lower were the prices. Prices changed according to transportation costs in relation to Rome.[145] The authors of this study take seriously into consideration the low volume of data (only six pairs of prices), the seasonal character of grain production, the intervention of the Roman state and other benefactors. To these objections, I would add that in the Roman empire there was more than one centre and more than one periphery. For instance, large cities like Ephesus and Alexandria absorbed substantial tons of wheat on an annual basis: wheat that came from the immediate hinterland and was never destined for Rome. Even if we cannot accept fully the existence of an integrated grain market, even if imperial intervention may have unified it to a certain extent, we cannot deny the existence of a unified monetary system. As with wages, wheat prices seem to be comparable despite regional variations and seasonal fluctuations. Also in this case,

[142] Matthew 20. [143] Mrozek 1989: 110–11. [144] Bang 2008: 153–73.
[145] Kessler and Temin 2008.

the probable monetary integration of the provinces may have assisted the expansion of trade, the establishment of similar prices and the wider integration of the Roman economy.

The existence of a unified monetary system and the comparability of wages and prices across the provinces may indicate a degree of economic integration in the Roman empire. However, the lack of adequate written evidence does not allow us to prove its extent. I am aware that the few inscriptions and literary references from the eastern provinces are not sufficient for the verification of any hypothesis. The unique case of Egypt alone, with its collections of papyri, cannot possibly prove or disprove any thesis that is brought forward. Furthermore, I am also aware that concrete evidence will not be available in the near future. Therefore, at this point, we can only rely on the desperately few indications of wages and prices in order to construct a new theoretical model. The results arising from these indications can be strengthened by the meticulous study of the existing credit system. Once we establish the extent of credit in the Roman economy, we may be able to assert the extent of its integration. After all, credit was a more flexible tool and, consequently, may have been used much more widely than coined money.

CONCLUSIONS

People from the higher and middle social strata were involved in entrepreneurial activities, which resulted in the accumulation of wealth (in the form of coins, precious metals, jewellery or other goods). On top of the physical evidence of this wealth, we should add the accumulation of credit that reflected the sum of the properties of these people. Whether these were senators or ex-slaves, the owners of substantial amounts of wealth probably used to hoard part of it in the form of precious-metal coins, while they used the rest as consumers or investors. Savings hoards found in harbour-cities and their surrounding areas of the eastern Mediterranean Sea could suggest the use of coins in the course of interregional transactions, even if their coins were temporarily withdrawn from circulation. On the other hand, excavation finds may be more useful in the study of the integration of the empire. In particular, common patterns of coin circulation in the large Aegean harbours (such as Athens, Patra, Corinth, Ephesus and Rhodes) could indicate the effect of trade in the distribution of silver coins across the provinces.

Some of the most profitable activities in the Roman empire were possibly connected with regional as well as interregional trade. The movements of merchants are evident from the movement of precious-metal coins. Despite their intense activities in the markets the numismatic integration of the eastern Roman empire was never achieved, since we observe differences in the distribution of coins. It has been suggested that state intervention and the extent of trade, both of which varied from area to area, may have been the main factors for such variations. Another essential element that affected these regional patterns was the diverse geographical characteristics of the eastern Mediterranean. Furthermore, the differences between militarised and non-militarised provinces as well as between urbanised and non-urbanised areas certainly affected both the use and circulation of coinage. All of these, of course, could explain the numismatic non-integration of the Roman empire but they do not prove its economic non-integration.

Even if mountains may have divided space, the Mediterranean Sea, rivers and roads probably made possible a higher degree of movement and the subsequent monetary integration. In addition, the establishment of the *pax Romana*, which was based on the strong central imperial political authority, the policing of the provinces by the army and the regulation of the markets with the help of civic and imperial magistrates all created fertile ground for the development of interregional trade. The unified monetary system, as it was established by Augustus, facilitated not only commercial activities but also the collection of taxes in the eastern provinces. The effectiveness and flexibility of this system were further assisted by the existence of banks and other institutions that dispensed credit. Credit had the advantage of expanding the monetary base of the economy, allowing money to circulate in distant regions, reducing transaction costs and, last but not least, integrating the Roman economy. The effect of central state intervention and the power of credit may be reflected in the formation of wages and prices, which were based on the same unified monetary system. Their study could also indicate the wider integration of the Roman monetary economy, even if regional differences still occurred.

CHAPTER 6
Micro-economies

AUTHORISING THE PRODUCTION OF SMALL CHANGE

In previous chapters we emphasised the imperial control of the production and primary supply of gold and silver currencies in the Roman empire. The number of mints producing precious-metal coinages during the first two centuries was limited, while minting was mainly restricted to the cities of Rome, Caesarea Cappadociae, Antioch and Alexandria.[1] Among them, the mint of Rome produced the bulk of silver coins that circulated in the eastern provinces.[2] The emperor controlled these mints either directly or indirectly, since he needed these coins in order to pay for his military and administrative expenses. The mint of Rome did not restrict itself in the production of silver and gold currencies but it also produced large numbers of bronze coins. When Augustus reformed the monetary system, he introduced small change made of orichalcum (sestertius and dupondius) or copper (*as* and quadrans).[3] These denominations may have been used, initially, for state payments; eventually, though, they facilitated minor commercial transactions in the markets.

With regard to the circulation of *aes* we may assume that originally, it was intended mainly for circulation in Rome and Italy; however, soon it was spread over the western provinces and especially in the Rhine army camps. The Roman *aes* was used extensively in the urbanised western provinces, especially in Iberian and Punic towns that had produced civic coinages for centuries. During the reigns of Augustus and Tiberius an outpouring of Roman-style bronze money from civic mints in Gaul, Spain, Sicily, Africa, and Cyrene satisfied the demand for small change, but most city mints suspended or reduced operations in the 30s AD. During Flavian times, when new bronzes were needed, the central Roman mint increased its output,

[1] In the western part of the empire mints were active only until the beginning of the first century AD. Also, in the middle of the third century other western mints were established (Siscia, Milan etc.).

[2] See chapter 2.

[3] Wallace-Hadrill 1986: 79–83.

while Spanish towns, such as Corduba, countermarked their worn coins and put them back in circulation. Although during the Flavian age Tarraco and Lugdunum may have struck sporadic issues of imperial *aes*,[4] the mint of Rome became the main supplier of small denominations. Since western mints rarely produced their own coinage, virtually all Roman bronze coins of the late first and second centuries found in the western empire, whether on an excavation or in a hoard or as a casual find, were minted in Rome.[5] Their production continued uninterrupted during the Principate, until the beginning of the third century AD, when their quantities were substantially reduced. Apparently, at that time, because of the intensified production of silver coinages in the mint of Rome, the analogous intensification of the production of small change became impossible.[6]

The situation in the eastern provinces was somewhat different, since a large number of civic mints undertook the production of the bulk of small change. We may be certain that such mints antedated the Roman annexation of these regions, since hellenistic cities and kingdoms used to be responsible for the supply of the markets with currencies.[7] The Romans decided not to interrupt this tradition and seem to have tolerated, if not encouraged, the survival of the civic and other local mints.[8] During the Roman Principate eastern cities were responsible for the funding and issuing of bronze coinages. Numismatic inscriptions provide evidence on the authorities who undertook the administration of the civic mints.[9] Local magistrates (*grammateus*, *strategos*, etc.) may have been involved in the production of coinage,[10] since their names appear on coins from Asia Minor. Nevertheless, this is not a clear indication that these officials were directly involved in financing or overseeing the production. In some cases, the formula (*epi* + genitive) may only date an issue.[11]

Only very few inscriptions provide explicit evidence about the organisation of coin production. According to these, it seems that the production of small change was an *epimeleia* (care) of a magistrate; the common formula being *epimelethentos* + name of the magistrate in the genitive.[12] Such legends occur on coins issued in Antioch and Aphrodisias in Caria, Philadelphia in Lydia and Cotiaeum in Phrygia during the Flavian period.

4 Harl 1996: 90. 5 Hobley 1998: 12. 6 Katsari 2003b.

7 A general account of city-state coinages is given by Kraay 1976. For a general introduction on Hellenistic coinages see Mørkholm 1991.

8 Butcher 1988b: 15.

9 For Greek legends on Roman coins see Burnett, Amandry and Ripolles 1992: 43.

10 For the titles of magistrates that are commonly found on coinage see Burnett, Amandry and Carradice 1999: 4–5.

11 Butcher 1988b: 24. 12 Howgego 1985: 85.

The use of the word *epimeleia* implies that the city authorised or/and appointed a person, whether he was a magistrate or not, to take care of the production of coinage.[13] Other inscriptions indicate that the *boulé* (council) was involved in the decision-making process with regard to minting. Specifically, the formula *psephisamenou* on certain civic issues suggest that the *boulé* gave its permission to the citizen, who brought in front of the council the motion, to go ahead with production.[14] The occurrence of both *psephisamenou* and *anetheke* is attested on a unique Domitianic coin from Mylasa, *ΨΗΦΙΣΑΜΕΝΟΣ ΚΛΑΥΔΙΟΣ ΜΕΛΑΣ ΑΝΕΘΗΚΕΝ*, where it seems that Claudius Melas called for the vote of the coinage and subsequently paid for it.[15] Once a magistrate was appointed, then, he probably took upon himself the minting of coins in the same way he undertook other tasks, e.g. the construction of public buildings. A formula referring to the funding of an issue is the verb *anetheke* with the name of the magistrate or the prepositions *dia* or *para* and the name of the magistrate.[16] Although it has been suggested that the donation, in some cases, may be the statue depicted on the coin and not the coin itself, there is a strong possibility that the magistrate also funded the production of coins. Another inscription mentioning Apollodotos (*strategos*), who struck (*kopsas*) coins and was also a magistrate at the time of the issue[17] indicates the fulfilment of this responsibility.

On the other hand, the local governors, as representatives of the imperial authority in the provinces, may have intervened directly in the production of bronze coinage. In a number of instances a proconsul's name appears on coins (ἐπί + genitive but not dative + title). In some cases we should just consider their names as a way to present the date of the issue of the coin, while in other cases the proconsul may have ordered or funded the minting

[13] Burnett, Amandry and Carradice 1999: 4.

[14] Robert 1967: 54ff. Also see a coin inscription from Stratoniceia in Caria, BMC Caria 153, no. 42 for ψηφισαμένου. See Head 1911: Vuthrotum 320, Dyme 414, Cnossus 463 and Sinope 509 for the formula *ex decreto decurionum* that was inscribed on coins minted in Roman colonies instead of ψηφισαμένου.

[15] Howgego 1985: 85.

[16] Robert 1966: 86, n. 3 mentions a coin of Mylasa with the inscription '*psefisamenos Klaudios Melas anetheke*'. Also see: Burnett, Amandry and Carradice 1999: 3. For the formula *dia* and *para* + name of magistrate see also Head 1911: 679. There is another formula used in the western Roman world or during the Hellenistic period. Specifically, the inscriptions that mention the provision of bullion by an individual, called *doreai*, are rare and exceptional. Two issues at Paestum were perhaps funded by individuals but two others were from the revenue of local taxes, in M. Crawford 1973: 53–4 and 101. See also an exceptional issue of silver coinage from Chios donated by Antiochos of Commagene, in *IGR* 954; *SEG* 16.490; Robert 1938: 139 ff.; Head 1911: 601. There are, though, no known examples of the formula *dorea* from the eastern provinces during the second and third centuries.

[17] *IGRR* 4.769.

of small change.[18] Since some level of imperial centralisation may have existed in the eastern provinces, we should not exclude the possibility that the governors supervised also the production of 'official' bronze coinages, such as the CA coinages in Asia Minor and the SC coinages in Antioch.[19] Other provincial issuing authorities that contributed to the centralisation of the production of small change were the existing '*koina*' (leagues), which issued coins at least until the first century AD. Some of these mints seem to have been controlled by the Romans. Even though a few of them produced superficially civil or regal issues, most of the coins lack any form of authority or ethnic; therefore, they could be regarded as 'official' issues.[20] Even if the imperial authorities were in some respects involved in the coin production of the leagues, the issues presumably needed also the approval of the *koinon*.[21] These coinages, though, do not seem to have had a substantial impact on the local economies, since their numbers were limited and their production was either reduced substantially or ceased altogether by the second century AD.

JUSTIFYING THE PRODUCTION OF SMALL CHANGE

It has been suggested that cities and citizens were interested in the issuing of small change for both political and financial reasons. A famous Hellenistic inscription from the city of Sestos, on the Hellespont, reveals why its citizens decided to undertake the production of bronze currency. The inscription refers to a local magistrate, who happened to be also the official in charge of an issue of bronze coins. The reasons given for their minting are: (a) that the people should be able to use coins bearing the type of their city and (b) that the public treasury would profit from the minting process.[22] It remains to be seen whether the mentality of the people who lived during the Hellenistic period survived into the Roman Principate.

18 Burnett, Amandry and Carradice 1999: 3. 19 See chapter 2 for more information.

20 For examples see Burnett, Amandry and Ripolles 1992: 4.

21 Burnett, Amandry and Ripolles 1992: 3: Koina of Macedonia, Lycia and Crete during the Julio-Claudian period; Burnett, Amandry and Carradice 1999: 6: Koina of Paphlagonia, Cyprus, Galatia, Bithynia, Crete and Macedonia during the Flavian period. A case of two silver coinages minted by one *koinon* is described in Troxell 1982: 227–34.

22 For a standard edition of the text see *OGIS* 1.339; translation and comments in Austin 1981: no. 215. For the interpretation of the inscription see Martin 1985: 238–41; Carradice and Price 1988: 122; also Melville-Jones 1972: 43. Howgego 1990: 20 uses the Sestos inscription as proof that pride was a factor in a city-state's decision to create new coinage. For the latest discussion on the inscription see: Martin 1996: 262–4, where he emphasises the economic importance of the production of bronze coinage for the city.

If we acknowledge that economic or financial rationality did not always characterise the actions of ancient populations, then, we should consider the prestige of the city as so important that individuals might willingly have lost money in their pursuit of civic recognition. Numerous inscriptions preserved declarations of patriotism (*philopatria*) and magnanimity (*philotimia*); for example, with explicit references to a city's god, political traditions or monuments.[23] Speeches of Dio Chrysostom exposed rivalries between neighbouring cities and tended to affirm the superiority of his own city, Prusa in Bithynia.[24] In a similar manner, coins also declared the superiority and the privileges of individual cities or *koina*: coin legends described cities as 'autonomous', 'free' or 'sacred',[25] while other legends described them as 'first of Asia'.[26] Cities of lesser wealth or population would also declare their comparative importance; for example, Magnesia boasted that she was the seventh city of Asia.[27] The advertisement of the exceptional qualities of the cities on their coins is not attested only in ancient cultures. The representation of elements of national identities is commonplace on bank notes and coins issued by modern nation-states.

The wide circulation of these currencies ensured that, through the means of national currencies, the specific state proclaimed its sovereignty in the regions it controlled.[28] Similarly, in the Roman world the feelings of pride and patriotism among the citizens were depicted on coins and they reflected the gradual development of proto-national identities. The strong emphasis on civic pride, though, did not undermine the loyalty of the population towards the imperial authorities. On the contrary, the inhabitants of the eastern provinces were loyal both to their city and to their emperor.[29] In addition, this civic political propaganda may have added also to the reputation of individual citizens. After all, since magistrates funded the production of coins, they must have cherished the public acknowledgement of their benefaction for their illustrious city. Examples of such an advertisement are the coin inscriptions, which refer to the benefactors of the city.[30] Vanity in connection with self-advertisement, following the production of civic coinages, may have been persuasive grounds for the initiation of new issues.

[23] Harl 1987: 20. [24] Dio Chrys. *Or.* 40.16–17; 38.6–7 and 21–2.

[25] For example see Head 1911: lxxix–lxxxiii.

[26] Klose 1996: 61–2. Ephesus, Smyrna and Pergamos claimed during the second century that they were the first in the league of Asia, a rank that allowed them to hold festivals in honour of the emperor.

[27] For references on coins and bibliography see Harl 1987: 22, nn. 10 and 11.

[28] Helleiner 2003b: 2–3, 110–13. [29] Katsari 2006.

[30] See those mentioned above.

Probably bearing in mind such types of evidence, Finley supported the idea that coinage was used predominantly as an emblem of civic pride and autonomy.[31] However, the prestige of the city should not be considered the main reason for the production of coinage, as coins were not purely commemorative but also existed for practical purposes. In reality, we should take seriously into consideration the financial profit to the city, an element that is also mentioned in the inscription from Sestos. The fact that civic authorities sometimes asked the emperor's permission to issue coinage suggests that minting was not thought of as a punishment but as a privilege.[32] In all likelihood, the city would have paid for the establishment of a new mint, the slaves who worked there, and the bronze bullion, even though individual rich benefactors were burdened with part of the cost. The city would have been able to justify this expense, financially speaking, only if the production of bronze currency proved to be profitable.

Indeed, the profits poured in, when the overvalued small denominations were exchanged for silver denarii. In an inscription from Pergamos[33] we notice that moneychangers were to sell denarii for eighteen asses and buy them for seventeen asses. Only moneychangers that were hired by the city were allowed to exact an *agio* of one *as* per denarius.[34] The inscription from Mylasa[35] confirms that the city ensured a regular income by leasing the monopoly of the exchange of currencies to contractors. When coins were exchanged in the black market the city lost income and possibly the ability to pay its taxes. Furthermore, local authorities would have profited from the distribution of coins, since small change was overvalued at least for the first two centuries (the intrinsic value of the coin was lower than

[31] Finley 1985: 166–8. [32] See Katsari 2003b.

[33] For full bibliography on this inscription, see chapter 4, n. 84.

[34] *'Οι οὖν τῆς ἀ[μειπτικῆς ἐργασίας μισθωταί πο]λ<λ>ά παρά τό δίκαιον καί παρά τήν συναλλαγήν [πράττειν αὑτοῖς ἐ]πέτρεπον. Παρά γάρ τῶν ἐργαστῶν καί καπήλων καί τῶν ὀ[ψαριοπωλῶν ε[ἴς τόν λεπτόν ἐμπολᾶν εἰωθότων χαλκόν δέκα ὀκτώ ἀσσάρια [τό δη]νάρ[ιον] λαμβάνειν ὀφείλοντες καί τοῖς τό δηνάριον διαλλάσσειν βου[λ]ομένοι[ς πρό]ς [δ]έ[κα] ἑπτά διδόναι οὐκ ἤρκοῦτο τήν τῶν ἀσσαρίων ἄμειψιν, ἀλλ[ά κ]αί ἐάν δηναρίων ἀργυρῶν τις ἀγοράση τό ὀψάριον, καθ' ἕκαστον δηνάριον εἰσέπρασσον ἀσσάριον ἕν.*

The translation of this passage, according to Oliver (1989), is:

In fact the exchange contractors allowed themselves to make many exactions contrary to justice and their contract. For whereas they were supposed to get eighteen asses per denarius from the shopkeepers and retailers and from the salt fish dealers accustomed to do business for small bronze, and were supposed to give bronze at the rate of seventeen asses per denarius to those who wished to exchange their silver, they were not satisfied with the right of exchanging asses, but even if someone bought his pickled fish for silver denarii, they tried to exact one as on each denarius.

[35] See chapter 4 for the bibliography, commentary and analysis of the inscription.

its face value).[36] The overvaluation of small change and its consequent profitability has been attested regularly in Mediterranean regions during the mediaeval and early modern periods.[37] According to Cipolla's views,[38] in pre-industrial economies the intrinsic value of bronze coins was usually smaller than their face value; this is why, in some cases, they may be called fiduciary or token coins. Their minting presented substantial profits to the government, otherwise called seignorage. Despite their overvaluation, their nominal anchor to a larger denomination (in the case of the Roman empire, the denarius or the aureus) guaranteed their public acceptance and their employment in commercial transactions.

THE ARMY AND THE PRODUCTION OF SMALL CHANGE

The profitability of the production of small change may have been equally attractive to the imperial authorities. However, since they decided to decentralise minting and allowed civic authorities to issue bronze coinages, we should assume that the magnitude of the profits was not appealing enough. Instead, the emperor may have had different reasons for continuing the production of the Roman *as*. It has been suggested that the reason for the production of 'official' bronze coinages was the facilitation of army payments. According to experts on the Roman republic, bronze coinage was initially produced in order to pay part of the soldiers' stipend;[39] thus, bronze coinage came into existence in order to serve financial purposes. Hollander suggested that the demand for bronze coins was not met only by the state issues but also with the production of municipal bronze issues (from Paestum, Vaelia and Heracleia) and forgeries. The large quantities of these coins in circulation can only indicate their increasing importance in the wider economy. They also seem to have covered gaps in the demand for small change in the market, while they may have averted possible liquidity problems.[40] Later, during the Roman empire, the state continued to issue bronze coins in order to facilitate its administrative and military payments. The mints undertaking this task could be located in Rome or in some cases in the provinces. In addition to the newly minted bronze coins, some legions applied countermarks to old worn issues and subsequently reintroduced them to the circulation pool.[41]

Some scholars attempted to apply a similar theory in order to explain the reasons behind the production of civic issues. Ziegler linked the occasional

[36] Howgego 1985: 54–60 [37] Sargent and Velde 2002. [38] Cipolla 1956.
[39] M. Crawford 1970: 47–8. [40] Hollander 2007: 27–8. [41] See chapter 2 for more details.

higher local mint output to the irregular movements of the army, the visits of the emperors in the east and local festivals. In an article published in 1996,[42] he specifically connected some of the local issues with Roman campaigns against the Parthians, the Marcomanni and the Jews, while finally he used coins from Cilicia and northern Asia Minor as 'seismographs' of political tension between Rome and the Persian empire or the Danube during the Principate. According to his argument, bronze coinage issued intermittently facilitated retail transactions between soldiers, the emperor's entourage, travelling traders and the local inhabitants. Any sudden enlargement of the local population would have created an additional demand for more small change in the local markets. First and foremost, movements of the army were the obvious causes for such sudden population changes. Once the authorities became aware especially of troop movements, as soldiers wished to exchange their salaries for easily convertible coins, the possibility of a deficit in small change was recognised; so, they took preparatory measures, such as the minting of new bronze issues. The same problem may have occurred also during imperial visits. The emperors tended to bring with them an entire 'army' of administration officers as well as real troops for their protection. The financial burden of similar trips would have cost an enormous amount of money (in gold and silver) that needed to be exchanged for local bronze. The private expenses of the people who recently moved into the city, combined with the private and public expenses of the emperor may have disturbed temporarily the fragile balance between the volumes of precious-metal and base coinages. The emperor (answering to petitions) probably gave handouts to the inhabitants or undertook the funding of new buildings, aqueducts etc.[43]

It is probably true, as Ziegler suggests, that the bulk of Roman troops situated mainly near the frontiers moved regularly from one fortress to another, wherever they were needed. Movements of army regiments were attested also within the provinces of Greece or western Asia Minor, although they were probably not on the same scale. Furthermore, we should not doubt the economic effect that troops had in local economies and the need for more bronze coins in the local markets. We should have in mind, though, that these movements were not always accompanied by a simultaneous increase in the output of bronze issues. In fact, the intermittent process of minting and the large chronological space, lasting one or more decades, between issues could suggest the exact opposite of Ziegler's theory. If the interval between issues of one mint lasted more than two or three

[42] Ziegler 1996. [43] Ziegler 1993: 142–3.

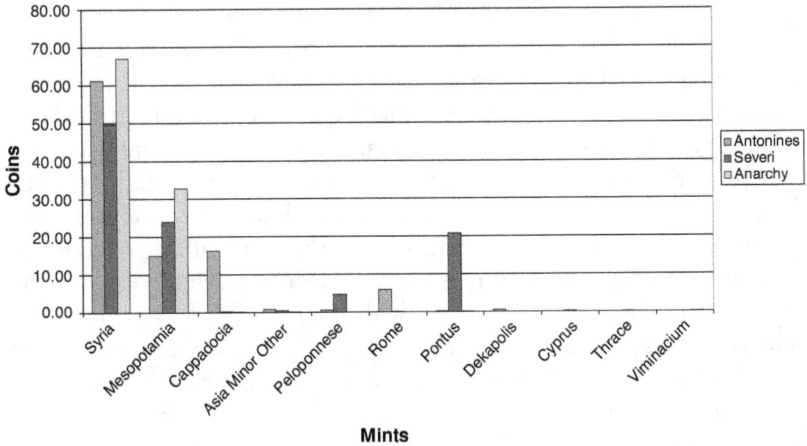

Chart 43 Dura Europos: bronze coins, % per annum

decades, we may suspect that soldiers who passed through the city during this time did not trigger increases in the local production. A recent study by Elton indicates that the production of civic bronze coinage and military movements in the south coast of Asia Minor during the third century AD are two unrelated phenomena.[44] He suggests that the *annona militaris* covered most of the needs (food, accommodation and animals) of the soldiers, who were on their way to the frontiers or elsewhere. Their supplementary demands for food, drink and entertainment seem to have had a limited impact on the bronze mint output. Firstly, during this period most of the civic minting came to an end and, secondly, the cities along military routes have not produced any more stray coins than the rest of the cities.

Even if the impact of the army in the less militarised provinces of the empire was low, we should anticipate a somewhat different picture in the highly militarised frontiers, where the majority of the inhabitants were soldiers. The results from the excavations at Dura Europos are indicative of the monetisation and distribution of bronze coins in the distant Syrian fortresses (Chart 43).

Dura was a strongly defended fortress city on the desert frontier on the Euphrates. It remained under Roman occupation from the second century until AD 252.[45] In the archaeological finds from the site[46] are included a large number of coins minted in Peloponnesian cities between the years

44 Elton 2005. 45 Kennedy and Riley 1990: 111–14.
46 All the coins found during the excavations were published in Bellinger 1949.

AD 202 and 205 (or before).[47] Although we are aware of the exact date of their issue, we do not know when they arrived in Syria, since they probably circulated in the Peloponnese for more than half a century.[48] Regular trading activities cannot explain the concentration in Dura of such a large number of coins from a distant region. On the contrary, these coins probably moved towards the eastern frontier when the movement of troops took place, shortly before or at the time of Caracalla's eastern expedition.[49] In all likelihood, the troops that resided until then in Greece had to move to Dura in order to reinforce the eastern defensive line of the empire. As is expected, they carried with them the monetary means for their daily transactions, which happened to be local Peloponnesian issues minted either in the early Severan period or even before. Specifically, two coins from the Antonine period indicate that the coins were drawn from the existing circulation pool. Even the latest issues were not necessarily part of the soldiers' payments.[50] The fact that we do not encounter in Dura Peloponnesian coins minted during later periods shows that the circumstances were exceptional and that the undertaking of moving troops from the Peloponnese to Syria was not repeated again. Even if a later recruitment cannot be entirely excluded, we should not suppose that its magnitude was substantial enough to influence the circulation pool.

A similar hypothesis has been brought forward to explain the high number of Pontic coins minted during the Severan period and also found in Dura. According to this theory, Pontic coins were minted between AD 206 and 210 and the soldiers who carried them could have been part of the same expedition of Caracalla.[51] We notice, however, a significant difference between the circulation of Peloponnesian coins and the circulation of those from Pontus. Specifically, the percentage of Pontic coins found in Dura during the Severan period is considerably higher (20.6 per cent) than the Peloponnesian coins (4.7 per cent). Thus, we may conclude that the presence of Peloponnesian bronze coinages in Dura was an accidental event, while the coins from Pontus may have met an urgent need of the local market for monetary provisions during the Severan period.

Furthermore, coin movements between Pontus and Syria may have been part of a wider pattern of circulation along the eastern *limes*. It is possible that merchants and/or troops who travelled from the northern provinces

[47] See Chart 43, which describes the kind of coins that characterised the circulation pool by the time of the destruction of Dura.

[48] For the issue of Peloponnesian coins see Grunauer-von Hoerschelmann 1982–3.

[49] Seyrig 1957: 252–3; M. Crawford 1975: 572; Howgego 1985: 26.

[50] Two coins from Argos and Corinth, see Chart 43.

[51] Howgego 1985: 27–8.

of Asia Minor towards Syria may have carried Pontic coins with them and employed them in transactions upon their arrival. In the same way, coins minted in Syria were also found in the areas of Pontus and Colchis. These findings allow us to draw an axis (north–south) in the interchange of coinage following the strategic route from Trapezus down to the eastern *limes*.[52] The north–south axis can be verified if we study the coin finds in the museum of Sinope in Pontus, which were mostly produced in Syrian mints.[53] At this point we should note that despite the obvious needs of the soldiers for small change, the city of Dura Europos never undertook the minting of bronze coinages. Instead, she relied on the usual transportation of coins from nearby cities either through the movements of troops or trading activities. The majority of these coins were minted by the civic authorities or in other cases by the 'official' mint of Rome (up to 6 per cent).

The inability of the army to trigger the production of new issues could be explained, if we take into consideration its impact on the monetisation of the frontier zones. The study of excavation finds from the highly militarised provinces of the eastern Roman empire demonstrate the relative unimportance of the army in the markets. The predominance of military installations and the low level of urbanisation in some parts of eastern Asia Minor and Syria, combined with the lack of coins, may have been the main reason for the reduced velocity of commercial transactions in the areas surrounding the forts. These military sites were obviously located in the middle of the Roman countryside and they were probably in communication only with nearby villages and *komai*, which held fairs at regular weekly or monthly intervals. The soldiers may have participated actively in the commercial transactions that took place there, but their participation may not have been as frequent as in the case of urban markets. In the provinces where urbanisation levels were higher, such as Dacia, Pannonia, Moesia and western Syria, we notice that excavations in the urban centres yielded more coins than excavations in forts, while the large fortress-cities of the north-eastern frontier probably generated the large majority of bronze and silver coins. The higher monetisation of the urban centres and the fortress-cities could be explained, if we take into consideration the function of the already-established markets in the area. Commercial transactions were the main reason for the use of bronze coins. And these transactions mainly took place in organised markets in urban centres, despite the fact that periodic

[52] For the circulation of coinage in Colchis see Golenko 1964.

[53] I am indebted to Richard Ashton and John Casey for this information.

markets in rural areas remained important. Consequently, extensive trading activities and the development of urban centres were the main factors for the monetisation of a region. On the other hand, the presence of troops had an impact on the monetary economy only when soldiers participated actively in the exchange of commodities.[54]

CONTRIBUTION OF BRONZE COINS TO THE MONETISATION OF THE PROVINCES

On one hand, the Sestos inscription indicates the ideological and financial reasons of the cities who undertook the production of small change. On the other hand, several researchers have indicated the financial reasons for the emperors to produce bronze coins. In addition to these, we should focus on one exceptionally significant economic reason that compelled eastern cities and the Roman state alike to issue small change: the needs of the market. As early as the Archaic period, eastern Mediterranean states produced smaller denominations of silver coins, which would have been employed in daily transactions. In particular, the die study of a Persian hoard, which contained 906 twelfths and twenty-fourths of Persian *sigloi*, has shown that over 400 obverse and reverse dies were used to produce these coins.[55] Similarly, marks of value appear on pots, thus revealing the familiarity of the seller and buyer with silver obols.[56] These coins were issued in quantities large enough to attract the attention of modern scholars. It has been suggested that the existence of so many small denominations in one place could only indicate the magnitude of local need for coins, which were used daily in the local markets.[57] Also, there is no doubt that the people who participated actively in trading activities would have belonged to all social strata, because of the low value of these coins.[58] And yet, during the Archaic period coinage probably played a limited economic role by comparison to subsequent eras. That is why some researchers, such as Richard Seaford,[59] Leslie Kurke[60] and Sitta von Reden,[61] emphasised the religious and symbolic importance of early coinages.

These exceptionally small silver denominations became obsolete, when civic mints started producing bronze coins. The reason for the abandonment of these silver coins was probably the fact that obols were inconveniently small, as they were easily lost and hard to distinguish from each

[54] Katsari 2008. [55] Kim 1994. [56] Johnston 1979: 33–5.
[57] Kim 2001: 12–13. [58] Kim 2002: 50. [59] Seaford 2004.
[60] Kurke 1999. [61] Von Reden 1995.

other. Bronze coinages had the distinct advantages of being of convenient size and, at the same time, being highly overvalued; thus, not only daily transactions were facilitated by a range of different, yet easily distinguishable, small denominations, but also the minting authorities received substantial profits. The first bronze coins were probably minted in Sicily as early as the middle of the fifth century BC and from there their minting spread to southern Italy by the end of the fifth century, while between 400 and 350 BC their use extended to Greece, Macedonia and Asia Minor.[62] Despite the commencement of the production of bronze currencies in several areas, not all Greek cities undertook their minting. It is not a coincidence that Athens abstained from the production of bronzes until the 330s BC, almost two centuries after the first silver issues. Such a delay has been explained as the attachment of Athenian citizens to pure silver because of their 'long-standing national pride'.[63] Nevertheless, a more pragmatic explanation may be the gradual realisation of the citizens that smaller denominations played an increasingly more significant role in the fluidity of the commercial economies during the fourth century BC.[64] It is almost certain that the minting of bronze coins and their subsequent circulation in the classical world was not as extensive as in the Hellenistic period.

In fact, the increasing monetisation of the Hellenistic world becomes evident in the case of Ptolemaic Egypt, a kingdom that has provided us with a wealth of information. The attempts of the Macedonians to introduce state coinage in this region became necessary for the payments of mercenaries and for carrying out interregional commercial transactions. Despite the explicit wish of the state to expand the use of coins in Egypt, the lack of silver resources and the non-existent tradition of issuing currencies initially posed severe administrative problems. Only during the reign of Ptolemy II was the Egyptian *chora* thoroughly monetised. And yet, this level of monetisation was sustained mostly by the use of credit and not with the physical exchange of actual coins.[65] Bronze coins, which comprised a small part among other forms of currencies and credit, seem to have contributed to the monetisation of Egypt only from the end of the third century BC onward.[66] The use of these smaller denominations for the payment of small taxes for some professions or transactions may have contributed to their circulation within Egypt.[67] In addition to the efforts of the state, the use of smaller bronzes was spread further through their employment in cash

[62] M. Price 1968. [63] Kroll 1993: 24–39 and 215–16. [64] T. Price 1995: 272.
[65] Von Reden 2007: 30–2. [66] Manning 2003: 161–4. [67] Von Reden 2007: 18–26.

transactions, related to the mummification of dead bodies, beer making, the manufacturing of linen and papyrus.[68]

The political ascendance of the Roman state during the Republican period changed the levels of monetisation, at least in some of the Mediterranean regions. In a recent study, Hollander divided the Roman world into four zones of monetisation: (a) the Governmental, consisting of the monetary activity undertaken by the government, (b) the Commercial, including activities related to medium- and long-distance trade, (c) the Urban, comprising activities taking placing within urban centres and (d) the Rural, describing the monetary activities of the inhabitants who were involved in the agricultural sector. Although all types of money (barter, bronze, silver, gold) were, in theory, employed in all of the above economic zones, it soon becomes evident that bronze coins were predominantly used in the Urban and Rural zones.[69] Burnett supported the theory that smaller denominations were used in abundance in Roman cities in the course of daily transactions after 200 BC.[70] Bronze coins would have been used extensively in *tabernae*, for the purchase of food, the purchase of clothing, as cash wages to construction workers or porters. Similar evidence from the Roman countryside is sparser, mainly because smaller villages and towns did not rely as heavily on the markets as larger urban centres. Still, the purchase and sale of grain, tools and livestock is attested in the sources, while coin finds occasionally turn up in excavations.[71]

Nevertheless, the same picture of relatively high monetisation levels was not reflected in all regions of the eastern Mediterranean. For example, in Macedonia after the battle of Pydna in 167 BC the mining of gold and silver was discontinued, while the mining of iron and bronze metals continued uninhibited.[72] In this case, although smaller denominations were still employed in the markets (albeit in reduced quantities), the scarcity of silver and gold currencies would have inhibited major transactions; as a result, the overall monetisation of the region probably decreased. Likewise, in Phrygia, only the cities of Amorium and Synnada produced bronze coins during the Republican period.[73] By no means could the limited production of small change by these two cities have met the daily monetary needs of all the Phrygian inhabitants.

A cursory study of numismatic catalogues of Imperial and Provincial bronze coins in the eastern provinces demonstrates that, from the reign of

[68] Manning 2008: 109. [69] Hollander 2007: 87–9. [70] Burnett 1987: 95.
[71] Hollander 2007: 111–37. [72] Livy 45.29.11. [73] Ramsay 1962.

Augustus onwards, the mint output of small change increased substantially both in Rome and in civic mints. Literary evidence and inscriptions verify our initial feeling that the monetisation of these regions increased during the Principate. For example, Apuleius in his *Metamorphoses* describes the city of Hypata as a vibrant market economy based on cash exchanges and a place where casual labour was hired for money. The villages surrounding the urban centre and the inhabitants of the countryside also participated regularly in the cash market. The only exception to this rule is the rich landowners who enjoyed a higher degree of self-sufficiency.[74] As examples Apuleius mentioned the purchase of fish and hay in the market of Hypata;[75] a merchant of cheese and dairy products who travelled in mainland Greece to sell his goods but had to face stiff competition in Thessaly;[76] a gardener who worked on a small patch of land and participated actively in the market every morning;[77] regular auctions also held in the market;[78] petty cash that could be gained through portering[79] or begging.[80] With regard to village life, a baker bought corn for cash;[81] a labourer worked for the owner of a workshop in order to raise cash for food and oil, while his wife was working on textiles;[82] under exceptional circumstances, they did not hesitate to sell a jar for cash;[83] cash revenues from the sale of corn, barley and wood were raised in rural estates;[84] a goatherd sold dairy products.[85] On the whole, the food production and casual labour in urban and rural settings was based on cash exchanges, apart from rare cases.

Apuleius' picture is verified in the writings of Dio Chrysostom. As another second-century writer of the Second Sophistic, he confirmed that especially the poor inhabitants of the provinces had to pay rents for their houses and bought everything they needed: clothes, furniture, food, wood for the fire (even sticks and leaves). Dio Chrysostom in an exaggerated statement said that the only thing they did not have to pay for was water.[86] Because of the financial capability of these people, we should assume that they conducted their transactions in small bronze coins instead of denarii or aurei. However, these transactions in small change would have taken place a lot more regularly than the transactions in coins of higher value, which were normally hoarded.

The picture emerging from the study of inscriptions is slightly different to the one literary sources describe. This discrepancy is due to the nature

[74] Millar 1981: 72–3. [75] Apul. *Met.* 1.24. [76] Apul. *Met.* 1.5.
[77] Apul. *Met.* 9.32. [78] Apul. *Met.* 8.23–5; 2.21–3. [79] Apul. *Met.* 1.7.
[80] Apul. *Met.* 1.6. [81] Apul. *Met.* 9.10. [82] Apul. *Met.* 9.5. [83] Apul. *Met.* 9.7.
[84] Apul. *Met.* 7.15; 7.17–20. [85] Apul. *Met.* 8.19. [86] Dio Chrys. *Or.* 7.103–7.

of inscriptions, which may be public documents, honorary decrees, part of funerary monuments etc. An overview of the material from the Balkans and Asia Minor indicates that assaria are used consistently as smaller denominations in order to complete larger or smaller transactions in money. In the context of the Greco-Roman gymnasium assaria were used for the payment of some of the labourers employed there. For instance, a *xestes* in Macedonia during the first century AD may have received seven to twelve assaria for his services.[87] The exchange of bronze coins also took place in the case of a freedwoman (Monarchia) in first-century-AD Calymnos. According to the agreement, the freedwoman should have stayed with her ex-master until his death. If she decided to leave, then she should have to pay him four assaria per day, probably as compensation for the loss of her labour.[88] Also, benefactors would have distributed regularly a few pieces of assaria to the inhabitants of the Greco-Roman cities: one such example comes from Rhodes after AD 117.[89] Similarly, in Syros during the second half of the second century AD benefactors distributed a sum of four to eight assaria to all free women and children, while free men received denarii;[90] thus, denoting the higher worth of the male citizens in society. Benefactors would also sell grain to poor citizens at a significantly lower price than its actual market value. In particular, Satyros, an *euergetes* from the island of Tenos, sold one *medimnon* of *kreithos* (barley) for five assaria, while the grain merchants were selling it at the time for five denarii.[91] In the cases of loans, even if the loan was estimated in silver coins, the interest was sometimes estimated in assaria, as the inscriptions from Iasos,[92] Smyrna[93] and Aphrodisias[94] demonstrate. Travellers also had to carry small denominations with them in order to pay for their personal expenses on the road, transportation costs and smaller taxes. For example, when the *boulé* and the *demos* of Smyrna realised that the price of the *porthmeion* (ferry boat) was too expensive (two obols), they changed it to two assaria.[95] The above examples are by no means a complete account of the uses of smaller denominations. Even if the list is incomplete, we can still conclude that assaria were distributed to the population or exchanged in the market or paid for labour and travelling costs regularly. The fact that they appear on official documents surprisingly often, despite their low value, indicates

[87] *IG* 9.2.2.325. 1; *IG* 9.2.2.326.1.
[88] Segre 1944–5 [1952]: inscr. 176. Similar inscriptions from Calymnos are *Tit. Calymnii* 206 (4 assaria), and *Tit. Calymnii* 207 (3 assaria).
[89] Pugliese Carratelli 1952–4: inscr. 67. [90] *IG* 12.5.659; *IG* 12.5.663; *IG* 12.5.664.
[91] *IG* 12.5.947. [92] Reinach 1893: no. 3; Robert 1957; Robert, J. and L. 1959: 395; *SEG* 18.448.
[93] Robert 1936: 26–8. [94] Reinach 1906: 243–8, no. 142.
[95] Abbott and Johnson 1926: no. 70; *IGRR* 4.1427; *Syll.* 3.1262.

that their usage was both inevitable and significant, especially for the poor inhabitants of the provinces.

Consequently, the increasing coin finds in conjunction with a large number of references in the literary and epigraphic sources of the Roman Principate indicate that small change was employed regularly in the economy. Although all social classes would have used them on a daily basis, bronze coins (e.g. assaria) paid for a large part of the wages, food, clothing and other needs of the lower social strata. In addition, rich benefactors distributed assaria to the civic populations or accepted these coins as reduced payment for grain. These coins also paid for the expenses travellers incurred during their trips. The overall picture of the Roman provinces implies a highly monetised economy, where the only thing the poor inhabitants did not pay for is water (as Dio Chrysostom says in an exaggerated tone). Of course, here we restricted ourselves to comparisons with earlier, less monetised societies. In all likelihood, some medieval and early modern preindustrial economies would have been more monetised than the Roman empire.

BRONZE CURRENCIES AND TRADING MODELS

Despite the high level of monetisation in the provinces, the Roman emperors did not attempt to homogenise the minting and distribution of bronze coins, as one would expect. Dio Cassius, who wrote in the third century, says: 'None of the cities should be allowed to have its own separate coinage or system of weights and measures; they should all be required to use ours.'[96] The truth is that Rome never applied this rule to its full extent. Local cities were responsible for the administration of mints and the initial decision for the production of small change; a certain degree of civic administrative freedom concerning the production of bronze coinage was probably granted from Rome to individual cities according to their needs and abilities. Since the councils and the civic magistrates regulated the production of bronzes in the east, there was diversity in both the volume of the issues and the timing of minting. Furthermore, the authorities responsible for the production and distribution of bronze coinage of an individual city took their administrative decisions without considering the opinions of the magistrates of their neighbours. Almost every city decided

[96] Dio Cass. 52.30.9: '*μήτε δέ νομίσματα ἤ καί σταθμά ἤ μέτρα ἰδίαι τις αὐτῶν ἐχέτω, ἀλλά καί τοῖς 'ημετέροις καί ἐκεῖνοι πάντες χρήσθωσαν.*'

to produce its own bronze coinage that eventually circulated in the immediate area. The outcome of this behaviour was the creation of a wide range of small circulation pools within each province. Even with regard to the more centralised league coinages, we have no numismatic evidence to support the assumption that such coins circulated more widely than civic issues, even if they may have been popular among the cities of the *koinon*. In any case, they have never been able to create wider circulation pools.

Although there was no overall imperial control of the production of civic issues and despite the fact that each city took independent decisions, some cities did not have their own independent mint. It has been suggested that during the Roman empire in Asia Minor there were at work not hundreds of mints of individual communities, but just a relatively small number of workshops that supplied issues for a whole range of cities. The phenomenon was studied for the first time by Konrad Kraft, who noticed strong stylistic similarities between coins of different cities and many cases of shared obverse dies. According to his hypothesis, a mint with several engravers produced dies, flans and coins. Later, these dies were carried from one city to another.[97] Or, according to a different hypothesis, one single engraver may have carried dies, while offering his services in nearby cities.[98] Ann Johnston in a series of articles expanded successfully on Kraft's views.[99] Specifically, in the case study of Aphrodisias she implied that two or three large fixed mints, regional or mobile, employing several engravers produced dies for a specific city. Then, either the dies or coins, which were produced centrally, or engravers were dispatched to branch operations; and there they employed a few staff, who continued the production or took care of the distribution.[100]

However, the existence of central workshops does not imply the existence of wider numismatically integrated areas. It seems that Kraft included in his study only a small part of the vast number of the produced dies. In every case he tried to attribute all of these coins to perhaps a dozen workshops, a number that is probably lower than the real one. Since the dimensions of the supply areas could be more than 100–200 km across,[101] we could suppose that in some instances the activities of individual workshops overlap with each other. In addition, we are unable to prove that the activities of the workshops affected the circulation of bronze coins and/or forced them to spread in a wider area. In fact, there is a negative factor that may

97 Kraft 1972: 57 and 90–1. 98 D. MacDonald 1992: 5–8. 99 Johnston 1974; 1982–3.
100 Johnston 1995: 54–61. 101 Kraft 1972: 275.

have prohibited the movement of local coins as widely as the movement of the shared dies. Even if common dies were used in more than one city, we should not presume that they used only one denominational system, since there are often variations in the weights and diameters of flans struck with the same types and sometimes even with the same dies.[102] Even if bronze coins of different denominational systems could still circulate side by side, the people who ran the workshops did not attempt to create a uniform currency. Instead they followed the different policies and guidelines which were already established in different cities.

An abundance of bronze coinage from different mints and of different weight standards was revealed in cities which were thoroughly excavated. The evidence itself compels us, though, to divide the regions into three further categories according to the distance the coins travelled. Within the same area we may find: (a) bronze coins issued in distant provinces, (b) bronze coins issued in neighbouring provinces and (c) bronze coins issued in the same province or city. The case that occurs most often is the third, since bronze currency tends to circulate locally. However, in certain cities we find a wealth of coins which were minted in neighbouring provinces, while in a few cities we find coins that come from even more distant regions.

In the first instance, we notice that in the museum of Rhodes[103] and in the excavations of Cenchreai,[104] Corinth,[105] Patra,[106] Athens,[107] Argos and

102 Johnston 1995: 61.

103 I have catalogued 204 bronze coins, out of which 65 were minted in Rome, 4 in Ionia (the cities of Ephesus, Erythrai and Smyrna and the island of Samos), 1 in Sardis (Lydia), 1 in Egypt, 2 in Antioch (Syria), 3 in Caria (the cities of Stratonicea, Alabanda, Bargylia), 1 in Anemurium (Cilicia), 1 in Hierapolis (Phrygia), 3 in Perge (Pamphylia).

104 Out of 36 coins, 13 (around one-third) have been minted in Rome and 1 in Egypt.

105 Out of 401 coins, 98 (almost one-quarter) have been minted in Rome, 2 came from Ionia (Ephesus and Phocea), 1 from Caesarea Cappadociae, 1 from Nicomedeia in Bithynia, 1 from Alexandreia Troas, 1 from Antioch ad Orontem (Syria), 1 from Thessalonica (Macedonia), 2 from Thrace (Perinthos and Thasos) and 1 from Aspendos in Pamphylia.

106 Out of 408 coins, 115 coins (more than one-quarter) came from the mint of Rome, 1 from Egypt, 3 belonged to the Macedonian League, 1 from Lampsacos (Mysia), 1 from Pergamos (Mysia), 1 from Elaia (Aeolis), 1 from Sardis (Lydia), 1 from Maionia (Lydia), 1 from Attaleia (Pamphylia), and 1 from Mallos (Cilicia).

107 Out of 3,133 coins, 347 coins came from the mint of Rome, while 1 coin was minted in Crete, 11 in Egypt, 2 in Antioch ad Orontem, 3 in Bythinia (Bithynian League, Nicaea and Nicomedeia), 1 in Pergamos (Mysia), 1 in Assos (Troas), 6 in Ephesus (Ionia), 5 in Smyrna (Ionia), 1 in Hermocapelia (Lydia), 2 in Pamphylia (the cities of Attaleia and Sillyon), 5 in Thrace (the cities of Deultum, Philippoupolis, Augusta Trajana, Coela Thrace, Perinthos), 2 in Thessalonica (Macedonia), 1 in Adramyteion (Mysia), 2 in Mytilene, 1 in Magnesia near Maeander, 1 in Syedra (Cilicia), 6 in Teos (Ionia), 1 in the island of Samos, 1 in Tripolis (Lydia), 1 in Synnada (Phrygia), 1 in Antioch of Pisidia.

Lechaio,[108] Curium (Cyprus),[109] Ankara,[110] Sardis,[111] Antioch[112] and Dura Europos[113] a higher percentage of coin finds were produced in mints situated in distant regions. Coinages from, virtually, the entire Mediterranean, including the western provinces, are represented among the numerous finds. Apart from Dura Europos, in which have been found Peloponnesian coins that were connected to military movements, the rest of the cities were not situated remotely close to highly militarised areas. Instead, we should seek the reasons for such a variety of bronze coins in the participation of their citizens in long-distance trade.

In the previous section, I demonstrated that the harbours of Corinth, Patra, Athens, Ephesus and Rhodes present us with a common pattern in the circulation of silver coinage. In an attempt to explain this phenomenon, I suggested that all these places were part of a network that facilitated interregional trade in the eastern Mediterranean via the sea routes of the southern Aegean Sea. The common means of exchange for long-distance commercial activities, which promoted the development of trade in the Roman empire, was probably precious-metal coinages, credit or the exchange of commodities. There is a common pattern with regard to bronze coinages from the harbours of Corinth, Patra, Athens and the island

108 Out of 27 coins from the excavations of Lechaio and Argos 2 coins came from Ionia (Ephesus, Smyrna) and 4 from Rome.

109 Out of 167 coins, 108 (almost two-thirds of the whole) came from the mint of Rome, 1 from Egypt, 1 from Pergamos (Mysia), 1 from Iasus (Caria), 1 from Feneos (Greece), 1 from Nicomedeia (Bithynia), 1 from Magnesia (Ionia), 1 from Antioch in Pisidia, 1 from Side (Pamphylia), 2 from Cilicia (the cities of Anemurium and Corycus). It is worth noting that no coins from Cyprus were in circulation during the Military Anarchy period. This does not mean that the island was demonetised, since we found coins from Rome and Cilicia.

110 Out of 68 coins, 1 was minted in Hierapolis (Cyrrhestica), 1 in Nysa (Lydia), 1 in Neocaesarea (Pontus), 7 in Germanikopolis (Cilicia), 1 in Prusias ad Hippium (Bythinia), 1 in Side (Pamphylia), 1 in Gabala (Seleucis), 1 in Carrhae (Mesopotamia), 2 in Edessa (Mesopotamia), 1 in Metropolis (Ionia), 1 in Antioch near Maeander (Caria), 1 in Nicaea (Bithynia), 1 in Caesarea Cappadociae, 1 in Zeugma (Commagene), 1 in Antioch ad Orontem (Syria), 1 in Edessa (Mesopotamia), 1 in Rhesaena (Mesopotamia).

111 Out of 296 coins, 12 came from Phrygia (the cities of Ancyra, Eucarpeia, Laodicea, Aezanis, Ococleia, Temenothyrae, Catiaeum, Eumeneia, Sebaste), 1 from Aiolis (Elaea and Aegae), 1 from Bithynia, 6 from Mysia (the cities of Pergamos, Adramyteion), 29 from Ionia (the cities of Ephesus, Metropolis, Miletus, Smyrna, Colophon, Magnesia, Phocaea), 7 from Caria (the cities of Antioch near Maeander, Magnesia, Aphrodisias), 3 from Lydia (the cities of Dios Hieron, Tmolus and Tripolis), 2 from Pisidia (the cities of Conana and Cappadocia) 1 from Cercetara in Cilicia, 1 from Egypt, 2 from Greece (the cities of Corinth and Elaea), 1 from Antioch in Syria, 6 from Milan (Italy), 3 from Siscia. From the mint of Rome came 58 coins.

112 Out of 1,319 coins, 64 coins were minted in Rome, 1 in Perge (Pamphylia), 6 in Caesarea Cappadociae, 1 in Pergamos (Mysia), 10 in Cilicia (the cities of Adana, Anazarbus, Anemurium, Aegae, Colybrassus, Corycus, Soli-Pompeiopolis), 9 in Egypt, 14 in Mesopotamia (in the cities of Carrhae, Edessa, Singara, Nesibis), 1 in Thessalonica (Macedonia), 1 in Viminacium.

113 See Chart 43.

of Rhodes that confirms the similarities in the structure of silver coinages. Specifically, some of the small change was minted in distant mints (over 500 kms away) and has been carried there from distant provinces. Also, the diversity of bronze coins was much higher than the diversity of coins found in other cities. The most likely carriers would have been merchants, who moved their goods and money along the commercial sea routes.

The rest of the cities that demonstrate similar characteristics – Curium, Ankara, Sardis and Antioch – are also known for their advantageous position for the conduct of long-distance trade, although they are not necessarily connected with the Aegean sites. Especially Ankara (as well as Caesarea, Tavium and Amaseia), even if she did not have access to the Mediterranean, soon became a key point of the eastern road system, thus allowing the efficient movement of people and commodities.[114] Sardis was on another land route that facilitated the movement of merchants towards western Asia Minor. Milestones found on the road to the harbours of the west indicate the regular traffic of troops and merchants in this direction.[115] Cyprus, on the other hand, was situated on the sea routes that connected the harbours of Syria and southern Asia Minor with the harbours of Greece.[116] Hence, it is not surprising that the majority of the bronze coins found *in situ* came from the Roman provinces surrounding the eastern Mediterranean Sea. Another important trade centre was the wealthy city of Antioch, which, in the fourth century AD, was regarded as a 'city known to the world'.[117] During the Principate, far eastern goods could only enter the Roman empire by one of two routes: either across Northern Syria or up the Red Sea. Some of this trade reached the Mediterranean via Antioch and the valley of the Orontes. A large number of travellers coming from China, India, Scythia and Persia probably lodged in hostelries outside the city gate before they continued their trip.[118]

We cannot exclude the possibility that bronze coins were used along with precious-metal coins during these trips. Although silver and bronze currencies served different purposes, the use of the first did not prohibit the simultaneous or subsequent use of the second. In reality, one currency complemented the other and together they formed a complex monetary system that enabled the inhabitants to conclude major as well as minor

114 Mitchell 1993: 132 and 129, map 8; See also French 1988: map 4.

115 French 1988: map 11. The importance of Sardis in long-distance two-way trade of luxury materials with other regions is established in Waldbaum 1983: 11.

116 Maier 1968 refers to old established trade contacts of the island with India, South Arabia, Italy and the West, which continue to flourish during the Roman Principate.

117 Amm. Marc. 14.8.8 'mundo cognita civitas'.

118 Liebeschuetz 1972: 76–7.

transactions. Rich merchants who travelled across the empire were probably compelled to carry both silver and gold for their business dealings and bronze for their daily needs. It is also likely that a merchant who travelled for days or weeks either alone or with his servants would have needed to lodge during the night, probably in a *taberna*. Eventually, he would also need food for himself or hay for his horses or even clothing. All these, seemingly, minor expenses could not always be paid in high-denomination coins; therefore, the traveller was obliged to carry with him lower denominations in the form of bronze currency. Such coins would have been carried from Greece to Asia Minor and Syria or vice versa and they represent, as a rule, the 'leftovers' of civic issues, which were used earlier during the trip either in the city of their production or in neighbouring regions.

Our second case consists of regions where more than five bronze coins minted in neighbouring provinces (200–500 km away) have been found. Such areas are: Thessaly (excavations),[119] Ephesus (excavations),[120] Troas (excavations,[121] and Troy 3 and 4 hoards[122]), Pamphylia (excavations in Side),[123] Mysia (excavations in Pergamos),[124] Caria (excavations in Aphrodisias),[125] Pisidia (excavations in Sagalassus),[126] Pontus

119 The excavations of Thessaly have revealed 49 coins, from which 6 were minted in the province of Achaea (Athens, Patra, Delphi, Corinth), 2 in Thrace (Marcianopolis, and the island of Thasos) and 22 in Rome. The rest are local.

120 Out of a total of 243 coins found in the excavations of Ephesus, 15 were minted in Rome, 8 in Lydia (the cities of Tmolus, Hypaepa, Cilbianoi, Philadelphia, Nysa, Nicaea), 3 in Pergamos (Mysia), 3 in Caria (the cities of Alabanda, Bargasa, Aphrodisias), 2 in Temnus (Aeolis), 4 in Pisidia (the cities of Conana, Cremna, Antioch), 1 in Abydus (Troas), 1 in Cotiaeon (Phrygia). Finally, one coin from the Military Anarchy period comes from Mediolanum. The rest were all minted in Ephesus or other cities of Ionia.

121 The excavations of Troas produced 98 coins, of which 14 came from Rome, 13 were minted in Mysian cities (Parium, Cyzicus, Attaea), 2 in Coela of Thrace and 1 in Attalea (Lydia). The rest came from local mints.

122 These small hoards include 4 coins from Parium (Mysia), Methymna (Aeolis) and Saitta (Lydia).

123 Out of 114 coins found in the excavations of Side, 3 came from the city of Germe (Lydia), 3 from Phrygia (the cities of Peltae, Trajanopolis, Ancyra), 7 from Pisidia (the cities of Etenna, Prostanna, Selge, Antioch, Sagalassus), 10 from Cilician cities (Anemurium, Iotape, Colybrassus, Laerte, Tarsus, Lyrbe). The rest of the coinages come from local mints, while no coins were minted in Rome.

124 Out of 75 coins, 22 came from Rome, 3 from Elaia (in Aiolis), 1 from the island of Lesbos, 1 from Sinope (Paphlagonia-Pontus) and 1 from Acrasos in Lydia. The rest came from Pergamos or other Mysian cities.

125 In Aphrodisias have been found 467 coins, of which 11 were minted in Rome, 9 in Lydian cities (Sardis, Tralleis, Hypaepa, Nysa, Thyateira, Dios Hieron), 5 in Phrygian cities (Laodicea, Eucarpeia), 1 in the city of Cyme in Mysia, 19 in Ionian cities (Ephesus, Magnesia, Metropolis, Colophon), 1 in the Pamphylian city of Perge, 1 in the Mysian city of Cyzicus, while 13 coins came from Mediolanum and Siscia in the middle of the third century. The rest of the coins came from local mints.

126 Out of the 21 coins found in Sagalassus, 4 came from Rome and 11 from the Pamphylian cities of Perge and Aspendus. The rest came from Pisidian mints.

(Tokat museum),[127] certain Syrian regions (Migdal hoard,[128] excavations in Jerusalem,[129] and excavations in Gerasa[130]). Although the number of coins coming from neighbouring provinces is not large, it indicates that the inhabitants of different regions were in contact with each other and that they were also involved in minor commercial transactions using a variety of currencies. Moreover, the scale of this interregional contact may not have been extensive enough to suggest frequent business dealings, but these few bronze coins could indicate an economic activity of some sort that was not prohibited by geographical or administrative boundaries.

The rest of the provinces, where only locally minted coins circulated, belong to the third case. These are: Epirus (Plakanida and Palaio and Nicopolis hoards), Achaea (Corinth 2, Sparta, Hoard, Athens 1 hoards),[131] Macedonia (Koufalia, Kilkis, Leukochori, Peristerona, Amphipolis, Serrai, Macedonia 1, Macedonia 2, Sebaste Pierias, Methone, Siderokastro, Strymon, Macedonia 3 hoards),[132] Cilicia (Ayvagedigi and Cilicia hoards and Tarsus excavations),[133] Taurus mountains (Gülek Bogazi hoard), Phrygia (Cibyra hoard), Pamphylia (Perge excavations),[134] and some regions in Syria (Silat hoard, Samaria excavations,[135] Sepphoris excavations,[136] Hama excavations,[137] Palmyra excavations,[138]

[127] In the local museum of Tokat we find 143 coins, only 4 of which were minted in Rome and 44 in Caesarea Cappadociae. The rest were minted in local Pontic mints.

[128] The Migdal hoard contains 104 coins, only 8 of which were minted in Pontus, while the rest came from local Syrian mints.

[129] The majority of the 227 coins found in the excavations of Jerusalem were minted in Syria. However, 2 came from Bostra (in Arabia), 1 from Carrhae (in Mesopotamia), 2 from Egypt, 1 from Philadelphia (in Arabia) and 12 from Rome.

[130] Out of the 73 coins found in Gerasa, 5 were minted in Egypt, 7 in Bostra (in Arabia), 2 in Greece (the cities of Thuria and Thelpusa) and 1 in Perge (in Pamphylia). The rest come from Syrian mints.

[131] Corinth, Cenchreai and Athens excavations belong to the group of sites with a high diversity of coins. In general, it seems that coin hoards contain homogeneous coins in contrast with the variety of bronzes that are usually found in the agora of a city. In this case we should take into consideration the factor of the single owner of the hoard who lives and works within a certain area and who may not be a trader. Still, in all of the hoards we find coins minted in Rome.

[132] Some of these hoards were part of burials. Despite their ritual use, the findings confirm the picture demonstrated by the rest of the hoards and local museums. Specifically, the bronze coins in the Museum of Thessalonica come mostly from Macedonia apart from a few that come from Thrace.

[133] Unlike the hoards, which contained exclusively coins from Cilician cities, the excavations of Tarsus revealed 49 coins, only 2 of which came from Rome, 1 from Tralles (Lydia) and 1 from Caesarea Cappadociae.

[134] Out of 22 coins, only 1 came from Prusias ad Hypium (Bithynia) and 1 from Colybrassus (Cilicia).

[135] Out of a total of 67 coins, only 2 coins came from the Dekapolis and 2 from Rome.

[136] Out of 22 coins found in the excavation, only 2 coins were minted in the Dekapolis.

[137] One coin out of 36 came from Rome, while the rest were minted locally.

[138] Palmyra used to be an important centre for long-distance trade. The contradictory view given by the bronze coins should be attributed to the low number of coins recovered in the course of the

Capphaernaum excavations[139]). The above evidence allows us to suggest that these areas were more isolated, commercially, than the previously mentioned ones. If coins from distant areas were not found, we could assume that inhabitants of distant provinces did not conduct any cash transactions there often.

The three different groups of coin patterns in the eastern provinces inevitably remind us of Hopkins' earlier attempts to establish a comprehensive model of trade in antiquity. He specifically divided commercial activities into three categories: (a) long-distance or interregional trade, (b) medium-range or intraregional or inter-town trade and (c) short haul, or local trade between the countryside and a nearby market town.[140]

A decade later, Luuk de Ligt provided adequate evidence for the existence of this model in the case of Roman fairs and markets of Asia Minor.[141] He identified, first of all, interregional fairs that lasted for as long as six or eight weeks, attracted merchants from faraway areas (500–1,000 km), and were dominated by luxury goods. The bronze coins of our first category probably belonged to people who participated in such fairs and were willing to travel exceptionally long distances to sell their products. Similarly, the large ports, such as Athens, Corinth or Patra (among others) attracted large numbers of merchants from distant regions. Although local producers often used the opportunity to sell their merchandise in the same markets, the coins found in areas well over 500 km from the city of their origin indicate that long-distance travels were a regular occurrence. Nevertheless, the number of coins from distant mints remained comparatively low; the majority of small change came from neighbouring regions or, most likely, the same province.

Secondly, according to De Ligt, regional fairs that lasted for one or two weeks attracted people from regions as much as 300 km away. These fairs were located in the rural countryside or in the cities of the interior of the empire or in maritime cities. The volume of goods exchanged among merchants and producers was facilitated by bronze, silver and gold currencies. Since merchants came from different regions, they may have carried with them small change that, normally, belonged to different circulation pools. The cities or regions of our second category may have been centres of such

excavations in the area. Specifically, out of 22 coins 3 came from Rome, 2 from Moesia and 2 from Bithynia.

[139] In Capphaernaum, out of a total of 25 coins, 1 came from Rome, 2 from the Dekapolis, 1 from Pontus and 1 from Lydia. The rest came from local Syrian mints.

[140] Hopkins 1983. His model became very popular among ancient historians. For a recent example, see the work of Rosenfeld, Menirav and Cassel 2005.

[141] De Ligt 1993.

regional exchange of products. In addition, established markets in cities, which were situated on trading routes in the mainland, could have attracted substantial regional trade. The exchange of commodities in such markets could explain the presence of coins minted in neighbouring provinces.

Thirdly, local fairs were relatively small-scale commercial gatherings catering to the needs of the population of a restricted geographical area. They would have been held either in cities or in the countryside. They attracted local producers and buyers, interested in buying and selling rural commodities or urban-produced cloth and ornaments. Coins produced in local civic mints would have been the predominant currency not only in fairs but also in permanent markets of regions, such as Epirus, Macedonia, Cilicia etc. This phenomenon indicates that only localised transactions took place in their *agoras*. The existence of civic coins in a site could further demonstrate that some of these areas were either comparatively self-sufficient or that they were geographically or otherwise isolated. Furthermore, periodic markets could also have attracted rural and urban populations who lived in the surrounding area. These markets took place once, twice or several times a month within the cities or in the rural countryside or in estates. They were economically important for the area and they were carefully regulated by the local magistrates.[142]

The above evidence demonstrates that trade had a direct impact on the distribution of small change in the eastern provinces. The scale of commercial activities, though, differed from one region to another depending on local economic conditions and the consequent needs of the population. The division of these regions according to the extent of interregional, regional and local trade seems to coincide with the three groups of numismatic circulation pools. However, even if trade remained the most important factor that determined the circulation of small change in the provinces, some markets remained more closely regulated by the central authorities and the individual cities than others.

STATE AND CIVIC INTERVENTION

Indirect state impact

In Greece, Asia Minor and Syria civic mints were responsible for the production of the bulk of bronze coinage that circulated in the provinces.

142 Nollé 1982. For comparative evidence from Italy see Lo Cascio 2000. Evidence on North African periodic markets is included in Shaw 1981.

Either local mints or mints of neighbouring provinces supplied the markets with small change and met the needs for any retail transactions in the immediate area. The situation continued unaltered until the middle of the third century, when coins from civic mints gave way to 'official' coins.[143] Although the inhabitants of the Roman empire seemed to prefer civic coins for their daily transactions, we should acknowledge the use of Roman imperial bronze coins alongside the civic ones. The percentages of 'official' coins in the circulation pools differ according to the distance of the pool from Rome and/or individual administrative agreements. For example, we notice that more Roman imperial coins circulated in western Greece, which is closer to Italy, than in western Syria, which lies further away. Specifically in the excavations of Patra, Cenchreai, Corinth and Athens the percentage of 'official' bronzes ranged from 15 to 30 per cent. Three hoards from Greece, Roufou (Patra), Athens 1, and Scarminga (Peloponnese) included mostly sestertii. Almost two-thirds of the coins recovered during the systematic excavations at Curium, Cyprus, came from the mint of Rome. Similarly, almost one-quarter of the coins circulating in the island of Rhodes were not civic issues. Also, substantial numbers of Roman sestertii have been recovered through rescue excavations in Thessaly.

How do we explain the increased percentage of 'official' bronze coinages in the Peloponnese, Thessaly, Rhodes and Cyprus? All of these areas had their own mints, which produced substantial numbers of civic coins intermittently during the Principate. Rhodes, although it is a small island, minted its own coinage until the reign of Caracalla[144] and as a major port imported coins from every province of the Roman empire. Therefore, the overwhelming number of coins from the mint of Rome circulating on the island did not arrive there in order to meet the needs of the citizens. The same hypothesis could be applied to the increasing circulation of Roman Imperial bronze coins in Cyprus. Not only were the mints of Cyprus active during the Principate,[145] but also the circulation of their coinage exceeded the restricted borders of the island, since we find Cypriote coins in Syria.[146]

Even if we assume that the volume of the production of coinage in these areas was rather low, the cities could 'import' civic bronze coinage from neighbouring provinces.[147] Similarly, the existence of civic mints in the

[143] See chapter 4 for the terminal decline of civic coinages. [144] Head 1897.
[145] Hill 1904; Grant 1957. [146] Dura 12 hoard, Dura 7 hoard, Dura excavations.
[147] For example: Macedonian coins could meet the needs of Thracian cities, coins from Carian cities could circulate in Rhodes, Pisidian coins could easily reach Pamphylia and Syrian coins could circulate in Cyprus.

Peloponnese had the capacity to provide the entire province with the much-needed change. The occurrence of increased numbers of 'official' bronze coins in Patra, Corinth and Athens can only be explained if we consider the economic functions of these cities. As with Rhodes and Cyprus, these were interregional centres of trade and accepted every year thousands of travellers from every part of the known world, including the not-so-distant Rome. The same explanation could be applied to the markets of Thessaly, maybe due to their proximity to Athens and other smaller ports in the Greek mainland. In these cases, state intervention was not directly responsible for the increased number of Roman sestertii in circulation. Indirectly, though, the mint of Rome seems to have had a substantial impact, possibly because of its proximity to the places in question and because the production of its coins by far exceeded the production of the eastern civic mints.

In the same way, imperial bronzes, and especially the *aes*, dominated the circulation of small change in the northern Balkan provinces. In the Lower Danube during the first half of the second century AD civic coins formed only a small percentage of coins in the circulation pool. During the following period, in the provinces of Pannonia Superior and Pannonia Inferior civic issues rose slightly in quantity. On the other hand, provincial coins dominated small change from AD 161 to 244, in Moesia Inferior. In fact, during the reign of Gordian civic bronzes reached their highest percentage of 88.8 per cent. We encounter the majority of these provincial issues in cities, the Greek colonies and some military camps, while only small numbers have been found in rural settlements and forts. In the northern Balkans, depending on the area, we encounter small change coming mainly from the nearby provinces of Moesia Inferior, Macedonia, Thrace and the more distant regions of Bithynia and Cappadocia.[148]

Until now, researchers have been in favour of the hypothesis that the predominance of imperial bronze coins in frontier zones should be connected with the military character of the area. Specifically, it has been suggested that the state authorities were interested in fixing the size of issues according to the army's need for coin rather than the needs of civilians. Among the published coins of known provenance the largest quantities of official Augustan and Tiberian *aes* and its denominations have come from excavations in military sites along the German frontier and from chance finds in that region. Although the soldiers were paid in denarii or aurei, it is probable that the *aes* could have also been used in certain cases as

148 Găzdac 2002b: 128–33.

payment. Subsequently, some part of the change that was produced by the government probably passed gradually into general circulation and was used for small everyday transactions, facilitating a movement towards a monetised economy, at least in places where the troops were stationed.[149] However, the reliance of the frontier markets on 'official' bronze issues should not be directly connected to the needs of the army troops stationed in these areas, since the monetisation of the provinces close to the *limes* relied mostly on urbanisation processes and extensive commercial activities.[150] The small percentage of civic coins was directly analogous to the few civic mints operating in the area and their restricted intermittent production.

Provincial regulation

Even if the central state did not intervene directly in the circulation of small change, we cannot claim the same for the provincial authorities and/or the local leagues. Numismatic evidence from Lycia indicates that the circulation pool of this province was radically different from the other regions. For example, the Lycia hoard, found in the region, contains mostly Roman sestertii. Likewise, another hoard buried in the Lycian city of Telmessus during the third century AD included only Roman sestertii. These findings should be studied in conjunction with the large number of Roman *aes* (as stray finds) which have been recovered from the area around Telmessus.[151] In addition, 134 'Roman First Brass' coins, issued during the second and the third century AD, have been found as part of a hoard in Elmali, in central Lycia.[152] This type of evidence was known to numismatists since the beginning of the twentieth century, when Robinson purchased a series of imperial bronzes of the third century AD, while he was travelling in the region.[153]

The fact that Lycian cities did not establish any mints from the reign of Claudian until the reign of Gordian III could explain the predominance of 'official' coins in the markets of Lycia. The Lycian League issued its last coins probably before AD 43 and the types were a reflection of Roman power.[154] Even if there was no direct imperial control, the citizens of Lycia certainly took heed of the desires of the central state. Only during

[149] Rodewald 1976: 52–69. The same idea is elaborated by Hobley (1998: 138–9), who thinks that 'if there is a shortage of small change, the individuals most inconvenienced will be the military . . . What the civilians think of the lack of small change may have been of little concern to the State'.

[150] Katsari 2008. [151] Lagos 1993. [152] Woodward 1909–10: 130–7.

[153] E. Robinson 1914. [154] Troxell 1982: 224–5.

the reign of Gordian III twenty cities from this province undertook the minting of bronze coinages,[155] possibly because of the reduced production of small change in Rome.[156] Furthermore, since the production of civic bronze currency was either limited or non-existent, the local authorities probably sought other means to supply the markets with smaller denominations. The existence of 'official' bronze coins in the eastern provinces is not exceptional. However, the complete lack of civic issues from neighbouring provinces is unprecedented. Pamphylia, the closest province to Lycia, produced its own bronze coinage in six mints. Specifically, Perge (576 coins) was the most important mint, Side (337 coins) came second, while Aspendus (149 coins), Attaleia (117 coins), Sillyum (131 coins) and Magydus (75 coins) seem to have been smaller.[157] These coins circulated outside the borders of Pamphylia, in areas such as Caria (Aphrodisias excavations), Pisidia (Sagalassus excavations), Pontus (Sinope museum) and Phrygia (Afyon museum).[158] The obvious question arising from the study of the material is: how is it possible for Pamphylian coins to circulate in distant provinces, while they are nowhere to be found in nearby Lycia?

The most likely explanation is that the Lycian League created a closed currency system, similar to the one that existed in Egypt and Syria. However, in the case of Lycia the local authorities did not regulate the flow of silver coinages but the flow of small change. The mechanism for this regulation is not entirely clear. Either the League or individual *poleis* undertook the supply of small change to the local markets. The daily need for bronze coins would have forced the magistrates of the cities or the League to arrange the regular shipment of asses directly from the mint of Rome. Rich benefactors, such as Opramoas, probably funded the shipment of bronze currencies from Rome and its exchange for silver or gold coins. Even if his exact role in this exchange is not entirely clear, at least once, he covered part of the expenses – probably around 5,000 denarii – in order to assist the Lycian Koinon, especially at a time of monetary crises.[159]

155 Von Aulock 1974; Johnston 1980: 208; Butcher 1988b: 89.

156 See chapter 4 on the production of the mint of Rome during the Severan period.

157 Hill 1897; Lauritsen 1973: 97; Baydur 1975: 33–45; Baydur 1976.

158 I would like to thank John Casey and Richard Ashton, who allowed me to look at the material from Sinope and Afyon museums.

159 For detailed comments on this possibility, see Katsari 2003c. On the inscription of Opramoas in Rhodiapolis see: Petersen and Luschan 1889: 76–81; Heberdey and Kalinka 1897; *IGRR*, 3.739; *TAM*, II. 905. The latest study on the inscription has been recently published: Kokkinia 2000. Discussion (select): Wörrle 1975a: 159; Wörrle 1975b; Frézouls 1985; Coulton 1987; Letta 1994.

Civic regulation

The example of Ephesus may indicate another attempt of the civic councils at a centralised control of bronze currencies. As we have seen in chapter 5, Ephesus along with Athens, Corinth, Patra and Rhodes participated in interregional commercial activities that unified the southern Aegean Sea. Notwithstanding the significance of this port in interregional trade, the bronze coins found in the excavations came mostly from the mints of western Asia Minor, Ephesus itself and Rome. The archaeologists have not revealed any small change minted in either Syria or Greece, despite the fact that some of the Ephesian coins have been found in the cities of Corinth, Athens and Argos. In this case, we could assume that the city imposed certain restrictions in the port of Ephesus, with regard to the circulation of bronze coins which were minted outside Asia Minor. The restrictions may have been lifted around the middle of the third century AD, when the terminal decline of civic mints started. Until then, the civic authorities may have caused problems in smaller transactions, since they tried to regulate the circulation of small change in the large interregional harbour. The only reason for putting in place such impediments may have been the profits they received from the exchange of bronze coins from Greece and Syria for bronzes from the Asia Minor provinces.

The reasons for such restrictions have not been always of a financial nature as Syrian cities indicate. The cities of Seleucia and Antioch were physically very close and they both minted bronze currencies. Despite the proximity of the two urban centres, it seems that Antiochene coins did not circulate extensively in Seleucia and vice versa. The relative absence of Seleucian coins from the excavations at Antioch can be explained, if we take into consideration the low output of this provincial mint. On the other hand, the mint of Antioch was particularly prolific and the absence of its coins from the archaeological record of Seleucia presents us with a paradox. Given the fact that in other provinces coinages from distant mints circulated alongside the locally minted coins, the phenomenon we encounter in Seleucia may hint at the regulation of the monetary market. Similarly, Apamea 'imported' its coins from Antioch, instead of the neighbouring Laodicea. Conversely, Apamean coins circulated neither in Seleucia nor in Antioch.[160] The above cases are obviously exceptional. Financially speaking, the civic authorities had no reason to ban the coinage minted in a specific city, since the profits from the exchange of these coins would not have

160 Butcher 2004: 174–6.

been substantial. Instead, we should connect these restrictions with possible long-held enmities between cities.[161] Specifically, the ancient sources state that the Laodicean hate for the Antiochenes led them to support Septimius Severus against Niger at the end of the second century AD.[162] As a result, after Septimius Severus prevailed, Antioch was demoted to a village and was attached to Laodicea, which, in turn, was granted colonial status.[163]

DIVERSITY AND UNIFICATION

Apart from the few instances of state, provincial or civic regulation of the circulation of small change, it seems that the majority of the Greco-Roman cities allowed for their uninhibited use in the markets. However, even if the administration promoted the unification of the circulation pools, there was a practical problem that complicated further the numismatic terrain: multiple weight standards. The cities of Greece, Asia Minor and Syria issued bronze coinages based on Roman or Greek or other weight standards. Each city was allowed to choose its own metrological system, without consulting with her neighbours or the central authorities. In most cases, these standards are difficult to identify accurately, because bronze coins tend to be much worn, while they do not bear any marks of value. So, until recently, researchers had the impression that provincial coins flourished in a state of metrological anarchy.[164] The diversity of weight standards within a small circulation pool could have become a serious impediment in daily transactions. Inevitably, we ought to question the ability of the citizens to recognise the value of the coins that came from other cities, and the measures the authorities took in order to solve the problem.

Although the initial impression is that of metrological anarchy, in fact there are generalised patterns of denominations. During the Julio-Claudian period four distinct groups were identified in the eastern provinces:

(a) Coins of approximately 19–20mm/5–7g and its half-denomination were located in Greece and in the province of Asia.

161 Kevin Butcher informed me that Laodicean coins were minted at Antioch during this period. However, we should take into consideration the possibility that the workshop which issued the coins may have been a private one and may not have been affected by the ideologies of the city-state.

162 Herodian 3.3.3.

163 *Digesta Just.* 50.15.1.2–3; Dio Cass. 75.8.3–4; SHA, *Sev.* 9.7; SHA, *M. Ant.* 1.7. For comments see Eadie 1996: 137–8; Smallwood 2001: 488; Honoré 2002: 11.

164 T. Jones 1963: 309.

(b) In Bithynia the metrology of coinage was modified to match the 'official' denominations (similar cases also may be found in Greece, Asia, Lycia and Syria).

(c) In Syria the bronze coins were quite thick, with a slightly oval shape to the flans. The principal denomination was made at about 25 mm/15 g, although it is more difficult to generalise about the smaller denominations.

(d) The cities situated in eastern Cilicia or Cilicia Pedias also produced a distinctive coinage. The coins tended to have a very wide diameter and they were very thin, while the most frequent denominations were made at a standard of 24 mm/11 g or 28 mm/15 g, 20 mm/7 g and 17 mm/4 g.[165]

The same phenomenon is attested also later, during which time any given standard would have been used by a group of cities. For example, a number of cities on the western coast of the Euxine employed a common standard. In a similar way, Heracleia and Tium on the southern coast also used the same metrological system. These 'monetary leagues' characterised a specific area for a definite period of time. They were distinguishable from one another, since they adopted different weights for the assarion, while their standards declined at different rates.[166] The analysis of bronze denominations of mainland Greece revealed further metrological similarities between the coinages of Peloponnesian cities. It has been suggested that, after the introduction of the denarius, only two different bronze systems were in use in the Peloponnese for the coins without imperial portrait. Some cities, such as Sparta and the Roman colonies, employed the Roman assarion and its divisions and multiples, while the rest of the cities continued to use their currency of the hemiobol and its divisions at least during the early Antonine period.[167]

Despite the employment of similar standards across larger regions, some neighbouring cities still produced coins using diverse metrological systems. The case of Sidon and Antioch, two cities that existed within the wider circulation pool of Syria and, yet, produced bronze coinages of different weight standards,[168] is characteristic of the situation in the eastern provinces. Even if some nearby cities decided to employ identical weight standards, a fact that would have facilitated daily transactions, several coins from distant mints were included in their monetary zone of influence. Excavations and coin hoards depict a colourful circulation of coinage

[165] Burnett, Amandry and Ripolles 1992: 36. [166] Howgego 1985: 60.
[167] Kroll 1996: 54. [168] Butcher 2004: 148.

minted in a multitude of cities and circulating across the Mediterranean regions.

It is possible that the effective employment of all kinds of small change in transactions was ensured by a system of exchange rates. As we have already seen in chapters 3 and 4, such a system allowed for the accurate exchange of precious-metal coinages in the eastern provinces against the denarius. Therefore, we cannot exclude the probability that the authorities would have made similar arrangements for the exchange of civic bronze coins. The employment of an empire-wide exchange system was imperative not only for the facilitation of trade but also for the gathering of small taxes. According to the tax law of Palmyra, the Roman authorities charged one assarion for the import and export of horses, mules, sheep and lambs, while they asked 2 asses on the sale of unguent. The taxes on prostitution were also estimated in asses.[169] However, Palmyra was a city situated along the south-eastern Roman frontier, where a substantial number of civic bronzes circulated. In all likelihood, the traders who crossed the border would have paid their taxes in local coin, instead of the 'official' one. This law is indicative of the necessity of well-defined exchange rates for official transactions with the Roman state.

We cannot help, though, but wonder at what happened during private dealings. In a perfect world the regulation of currencies would have been taken seriously into consideration in the markets. However, the Roman empire was not a 'perfect world' and I find it implausible that the citizens would have visited the banker every time a strange bronze coin ended up in their pocket. Not only would it have been inconvenient but bankers regularly charged commission for such transactions. Besides, the existence of a variety of coins among the excavation finds indicates that neither state rules nor the banking system managed to homogenise the circulation pools.

The employment of multiple monetary standards in the same region is not a unique historical phenomenon. The monetary rules issued by the Qing dynasty (1644–1911) in China, and their repeated reforms, also failed to unify the circulation of coins in the country. By the end of the nineteenth century there were many currencies in circulation and many units of account. Specifically, there were various silver *liang*, a unit of account not denoted by a specific form of coin, and used to weight silver ingots, according to three elements – weight, purity and divisor. However, these elements varied from one region to another; therefore, the same *liang* was a different unit of account in different regions. On the other hand, one

[169] Matthews 1984: 177.

wen, the copper cash, was used for counting coins. This also had various units of accounts. According to Kuroda:

> In large transactions copper cash was presented as a string and large denominations were valued at a premium. For example, in Hankou a string of 980 cash was counted as *qian*, that is 1000 *wen*. Like the silver *liang*, various *qian* coexisted in China and the units of copper cash that made up a string varied by region and commodity.

In addition, other types of coins were in circulation, especially silver dollars from Mexico. In daily transactions they employed three different Mexican coins: one dollar, ten-cent coin and twenty-cent coin. These were not fixed against each other at their nominal value. For example, the ten-cent coin was not fixed at ten cents against the dollar but it was exchanged at a lower rate, depending on the region. Paper money, both Chinese and foreign banknotes, was also used alongside the metal currencies. It seems that the legal control over this system was rather limited, since the *liang* of a certain region was in most cases a private standard. Furthermore, the government may have been responsible for the production of copper coins but their unit of account was set by merchants. Some merchants even issued a copper cash note, *Qianpiao*, which was used widely in urban centres and villages but was exchanged at a discount outside the region of issuance. Flexible agreements between these merchants became essential for the creation of regional 'currency circuits', which existed side by side in nineteenth-century China.[170]

By comparison to the Chinese monetary system, the Roman was a straightforward one. Either the Roman state or the civic authorities were responsible for the production of small change, which, in turn, was exchanged against the 'official' denarial weight standard (although not always). Once the small change was in circulation, merchants were responsible for its distribution from the mint of issuance to more distant regions. Their trading activities became the most important factors for the formation of circulation pools, in which local mints were predominant, neighbouring mints were complementary and even distant mints were occasionally represented among the finds. The need for smaller denominations in local, regional and interregional markets was considerable, mainly due to the higher monetisation of the economy in both urban and rural settings. Probably for this reason we notice bronze coins based on different weight standards circulating side by side. The value of bronze currencies was normally so small that it did not justify their exchange through a

[170] Kuroda 2005.

bank, although we cannot exclude this possibility. At the same time, the traditional dearth of small change in the markets did not favour any restrictions on their transportation and use in distant areas. In all cases, the civic authorities must have been aware of the situation. They either condoned the relative anarchy in the circulation of small change or they intervened occasionally to resolve local disputes. As we have no evidence that indicates one way or another, we may assume that the problems were negligible and that the system functioned uninhibited, despite its shortcomings.

CHAPTER 7

Metallism vs. chartalism

In this study we identified four different socioeconomic factors that affected the operation of the monetary system in the Roman empire: (a) the emperor, (b) the elite, (c) the 'middling' social groups and (d) the poor inhabitants. The emperor was responsible for the overall supervision of the production of money (minting and mining) and the control of revenues and expenses. Even if he did not devise long-lasting economic strategies, his monetary policies aimed at solving his financial problems and regulating the markets in an effective manner. The elite, on the other hand, may not have participated in the production of coins but they used them extensively in private business activities. Merchants, bankers and other entrepreneurs, who belonged either to the elite or the 'middling' social group, were responsible for the movement of predominantly precious-metal coins from one area to the other, thus creating unified circulation pools. In addition, they used credit in order to reduce transaction costs. Finally, the lower social strata used in local markets either civic or 'official' bronze coins. Although the value of these denominations was small, their significance for the monetary economy was high, since they facilitated daily transactions.

The different parts of the monetary economy functioned perfectly together. From this perspective, the Roman economy resembled a chain; if one of the links (production, distribution, weight standards, exchange rates etc.) changed, the other ones needed to adjust. Furthermore, it seems that the economy was intimately connected to the political and social conditions predominant at the time. When governmental policies or social structures were altered, then aspects of the monetary economy underwent modification and restructuring. Depending on the economic awareness of the authorities and their ability to directly control the transformation and the integration of the markets, certain economic mechanisms may have been automatically activated. To a large extent, these mechanisms were determined by the nature of money, in general, and the nature of

Roman money, in particular. So far, two schools of monetary theory have attempted to explain this nature, metallists and chartalists.

Metallism is a theory that finds its roots in the teachings of Aristotle and, later, in eighteenth-century mercantilist approaches to the economy, according to which the intrinsic value of currency should be connected to the value of precious metals; thus, money is treated as commodity. In the nineteenth century Marx also subscribed to the theory of metallism in his *Capital* (1887), where he explained that money is a commodity used for the exchange of goods.[1] In addition, Neoclassical economists, scholars who believed in the usefulness of the Quantity Theory of Money and other researchers (among whom are Locke, Jevons,[2] Menger,[3] von Mises,[4] Brunner and Melzer,[5] Kiyotaki and Wright[6]) took a clearly metallist position. Although there are certain differences in their approach, they all agree that markets were formed in antiquity as a result of individuals' needs to participate in commercial transactions. Money became the medium which facilitated exchanges and reduced transaction costs. This may have been coins, or salt or cowries, or stones or any other commodity that would have had a market value. Anyhow, this money would either have had an intrinsic value or it would have been backed by a valuable commodity, as happens in the case of gold monometallism. Rational agents and not the state would have spontaneously chosen this commodity and would have turned it into a medium of exchange, accepted by all. The state's role would have been restricted to producing and stamping the coins in order to certify their fineness.[7]

At the turn of the twentieth century an opposing theory started forming. Georg Friedrich Knapp in his book *The State Theory of Money* (1905) coined the terms 'metallist' and 'chartalist'. While he sided with the second, he noted the antithetical aspects of these two positions. A few decades later, Shumpeter attempted to analyse Knapp's views on chartalism and provided renewed credibility to this old theory.[8] A number of researchers, such as Bell,[9] Davidson,[10] Melitz,[11] Wray,[12] Kelton and Nell,[13] and other post-Keynesians, followed his attempts and developed the chartalist theory even further. They are in agreement with respect to the role of the state as an issuing authority. All types of currency become money only when the legitimate and sovereign power stamps it with its insignia and guarantees

[1] Hart 1986: 643. [2] Jevons 1875. [3] Menger 1892: 239–55. [4] Von Mises 1912.
[5] Brunner and Melzer 1971. [6] Kiyotaki and Wright 1989.
[7] Arestis and Sawyer 2006: 75. [8] Schumpeter 1954. [9] S. Bell 2001.
[10] Davidson 1999 196–210. [11] Melitz 1970. [12] Wray 1990.
[13] Kelton and Nell 2003.

its value. Whether this money is made of gold, silver, bronze, salt, or any other commodity is irrelevant. Unlike the metallist theory, the existence of currency is not the result of a spontaneous practice taking place in the market place. Instead, it depends on the means that the government accepts as payment of taxes, state fees and dues. In this process law takes centre stage and determines what form of money is acceptable as the payment of debt.[14]

The link between the creation of currency and taxation is almost self-evident. In the absence of money, the state can impose taxes on the production, transport and trade of goods only by receiving part of these goods. If money is available, then it can impose taxes also on income, expenditure and on the production of services. Furthermore, since the state became responsible for the minting of coinage, the guarantee of its value and its subsequent stamping, identification costs were reduced. The inhabitants did not need to visit an expert to assess the value of their ingots of precious metals. This reduction of costs combined with other characteristics of the metals (easily transported, quantifiable etc.) enabled the development of a monetary system. Even if non-governmental organisations undertook the minting of coinages, this happened under the aegis of the central government for the following reasons: (a) the mint requires an inventory of precious metals, (b) it requires protection, (c) the mint owner may be tempted to debase the currency in order to receive higher profits, (d) the establishment of law and order requires a governmental structure.[15]

Despite the lively debate among modern economists, most ancient economic historians remain oblivious to the potential of metallist or chartalist theories as analytical tools. The first attempts to analyse the ancient monetary systems according to these theories came from the quarters of modern economists, such as De Cecco and Hudson. These studies, although promising, are problematic, because they rely exclusively on the existing historiography and do not engage directly with the evidence. First of all, De Cecco in an article published in 1985 attempted to reinstate the authority of Mommsen in the sphere of ancient economics and ended up producing a historiographical overview of the Roman monetary history.[16] He debunked Bolin's assertions that Mommsen was a convinced metallist. Instead, he suggested that Mommsen clearly acknowledged the power of the Roman state to compel the citizens to accept the coinage it produced. On the other hand, he does not consider the famous historian a pure chartalist either, since in his preface he asserted that the use of coins in

[14] Arestis and Sawyer 2006: 75–6. [15] Goodhart 2003: 5–7. [16] De Cecco 1985.

commerce preceded state legislation. Mommsen may have adopted a position between metallism and chartalism but other ancient historians placed themselves firmly in the metallist camp, according to De Cecco. Among these are Mickwitz,[17] West and Johnson,[18] Nicolet[19] and de Martino.[20] On the other side lie the primitivists or substantivists – with Crawford[21] at the helm – who believe that coins did not function as a means of exchange but were predominantly used for state payments and taxes. A number of researchers, such as Heichelheim[22] and more recently Hudson,[23] focus on the origins of money, while they only occasionally mention the Roman world. These writers explore whether money originated in the public sector or not, in an attempt to define the nature of the capitalist economy in modern national states.

A sustained effort to study the nature of Roman money during the third century AD through the prism of chartalist and metallist theories came from Strobel.[24] In the first instance, he confirmed that most traditional monetary historians of the Roman world place themselves firmly in the metallist camp. Metallism, though, seems to be problematic in certain respects, e.g. in explaining the public acceptance of the silver antoninianus as a double coin, even if its intrinsic value was lower. Instead, he seems to support the chartalist theory, which, for example, could explain the maintenance of a stable nominal coin value, while the weight fluctuated. After all, coins were normally counted, not weighed. This could be indicated also by the existence of older as well as new silver issues of different fineness and weights in the same hoard. On the whole, Strobel claims that fiduciary money (which lost its previous purchasing value) was certainly in circulation, at least, during the third century AD. He connects the metallistic theories with modernism and chartalist theories with primitivism, in an attempt to place them within the current substantivist/modernist debate.

The study in this volume of the operation of the Roman monetary system during the Principate could give us insights into the nature of ancient money and the value of chartalism or metallism. As we have already seen, metallists believed that money originated in the markets, away from any state involvement. It is true that in the beginning the exchange of precious-metal currencies would have relied on their intrinsic value and they would have been treated as commodity money. As the markets evolved under the aegis of the Roman political power, according to metallists, the monetary system operated along commercial lines. In that respect, the value of gold

17 Mickwitz 1932. 18 West and Johnson 1967. 19 Nicolet 1982. 20 De Martino 1980.
21 M. Crawford 1970: 40–8. 22 Heichelheim 1958. 23 Hudson 2003. 24 Strobel 2002.

and silver coins would have fluctuated, according to the fluctuations of the bullion in the markets. There are obvious problems with this theory, especially if we want to support the existence of a trimetallic system.

As we have already seen in the third chapter, bimetallic laws defined the relationship between the aureus and the denarius: a relationship that was fixed by the state. The maintenance of predetermined exchange rates ultimately guaranteed the stability of the system and provided additional revenues to the central government that otherwise would have been impossible. The state's intervention with regard to the stability of the exchange rates cannot be contested, since ancient sources refer to a rate of 1 : 25 of the aureus against the denarius from the reign of Augustus until the reign of Alexander Severus.[25] During these two-and-a-half centuries there must have been fluctuations in the price of gold and silver as commodities, due to the increase or decrease of available bullion (depending on the productivity of mines or the outflow of war indemnities or the influx of war spoils), relative inflation, transportation costs and other factors. Despite the effect of the markets on the price of precious commodities, the official exchange rate of the coins remained unaltered throughout this time (at least until the reign of Gordian) against the law of supply and demand. The state made certain that private institutions, such as banks, would not have accepted highly debased coins at a lower value but would have followed governmental directions.[26] If metallist theories were correct, then these debased coins should have been exchanged at a lower value than the legal one. Instead, we observe that debasement in conjunction with the stability of the exchange rates allowed pre-industrial governments to monetise their debt. The result was that the population shared the political and military crisis and was burdened with the cost of the civil wars and other state expenses.

The intervention of the Roman state went as far as creating a monopoly in mining and in the production of precious-metal coinages. In the second chapter we saw that the organisation of mines that produced gold or silver bullion was under the direct administration of the Roman state or was leased to *publicani*. Either way control of production remained centralised until late antiquity. In addition, we observe the central management of the production of gold and silver currencies, whether these were based on Hellenistic or 'official' Roman weight standards or whether the mints were situated in Rome or in the provinces.

The reasons for the implementation of a state monopoly over the production of money were twofold. In the first instance, the government wished to

[25] Dio Cass. 55.12.5. [26] *P. Oxy.* XII, 1411; West and Johnson 1967: 183.

keep a balance between revenues and expenses. The main state expenditures during Roman times were the maintenance of the army and the administrative mechanism, the construction of public buildings, handouts to the population, gifts and loans to the elite. On the other hand, the emperor received taxes (in the form of cash or goods) from the population and had substantial revenues from his estates and other entrepreneurial activities. The central government was probably aware that the maintenance of a healthy imperial budget and the natural flow of revenues and expenses relied on the high degree of monetary liquidity in the economy. Hence, it established a monetary monopoly in order to ensure the adequacy of the resources and the unimpeded production of precious-metal currencies. Secondly, the government incurred further profits from the issuing of debased silver coins, especially when it urgently needed additional revenues, as we elaborated in the third chapter. According to bimetallic laws, the increasing production of debased denarii (and later antoniniani) would have allowed the government to increase the money in circulation and fulfil the demand for higher military salaries, as long as the exchange rate against the aureus was kept legally stable.

The applicability of the theory of metallism is problematic also for another reason. Metallists believe that money does not exist unless it has intrinsic value or it is backed by another commodity. In the case of the Roman empire, though, we encounter a few instances where the intrinsic value of the precious-metal coins is lower than their face value, especially during the third century AD, when the debasement of silver currencies reduced their fineness by as much as 97.5 per cent.[27] At least during the Severan period, when the denarii contained around 50 per cent silver,[28] the state guaranteed the value of the coins, while the population continued to use them widely in the markets. But the best-known case of token money in the Roman empire are the bronze coins issued by Rome and the Greco-Roman cities of the eastern provinces.

As we demonstrated in chapters 4 and 6, the profit margin from the production of small denominations was substantial (because the face value of these coins was significantly higher than their intrinsic value); thus, the cities undertook the production of small change willingly. Their minting activity may have been intermittent but seems to have met the commercial demand for small change in local markets. Since these coins were part of the Roman trimetallic system, they were inherently connected to the precious-metal coinages through the existing currency exchange system.

[27] Carson 1990: 234. [28] Walker 1976–8: vol. III, 49–50; Butcher and Ponting 1997.

Even though metallists could argue that the value of small change was backed by the gold coinage, we should take into consideration that, in practice, they may not have complied with the 'official' system of exchange; at least not always. It is not a coincidence that the debasement of silver currency into billon coins brought the demise of the entire monetary system; for, a system based only on gold and bronze currencies seemed to be unsustainable. Instead, it is possible that local authorities, albeit in agreement with the central government, used their power to guarantee the value of small denominations and their circulation in the markets.[29] In fact, they continued to support their use for decades (if not centuries), when they were already worn and indistinguishable from small nuggets of metal.

Since the use of token money is not justified by metallist theories, should we seek a solution in chartalism? The situation in the Roman provinces certainly reminds us of Ingham's assertions, who claims that

> money is a 'claim' or 'credit' that is constituted by social relations that exist independently of the production and exchange of commodities. Regardless of any form it might take, money is essentially a provisional 'promise' to pay, whose 'moneyness', as an 'institutional fact', is assigned by a description conferred by an abstract money of account . . . Money, as opposed to a 'convenient medium of exchange', needs authoritative foundations – that is to say some autonomous social and political bases.[30]

Similarly, in the Roman empire money (whether gold, silver or bronze) was a social relation that existed independently of the commerce of commodities and was guaranteed by the central government or the civic authorities.

The sovereign could enforce the independent existence of money, but only if the market situation allowed it. In chapter 4 we noticed that the population trusted the currency at hand, as long as the numismatic reforms were not excessive. Once the imperial budget showed more expenses than revenues and the Military Anarchy emperors promoted the use of the highly debased antoninianus, the Augustan monetary system collapsed. The breaking point was caused partly by the political and military crisis that shook the foundations of the Roman empire. In this case, though, the markets may have been adequate forces to resist the total demonetisation of the economy. According to chartalist theories the third-century crisis that saw the collapse of a strong government should have caused the reversion towards a 'natural', barter economy. Metallists, on the other hand, believe that once the private sector establishes a monetary equilibrium, no political,

[29] See chapter 6. [30] Ingham 2004: 12 and 178.

military or other mechanism can cause a reversion of the commercial transactions to barter.[31] During the third century we notice only the partial demonetisation of the wider economy and the increasing use of bullion instead of precious-metal coins. At the same time, the government fed the markets with billon antoniniani and bronze coins, which circulated side by side and were used as small change. It is, therefore, possible that, by then, the use of money had become an uncontested habit in trade, even if major transactions were temporarily facilitated by credit, bullion or the exchange of other commodities. In this case, we notice that only a combination of chartalist and metallist theories can explain the phenomenon of the third-century crisis.

Chartalism alone cannot account for the effect of market forces on the Roman monetary economy. In chapter 5 we explored the impact of long-distance trade on the creation of wide circulation pools in the eastern Mediterranean. Even if upper and middle 'class' traders did not manage to numismatically integrate the empire, they were active enough to unify the structure of coin circulation in several provinces or large regions, such as the southern Aegean, Syria and Palestine, etc. In addition, the use of credit (debts, loans, mortgages), which cannot be detected in the archaeological record, may have had further impact towards the deeper integration of the monetary economy.

Of course, credit was used not only in entrepreneurial activities (banking, trading) but also by the Roman state for the collection of taxes. It is evident that the conduct of long-distance commerce in the Mediterranean was largely responsible for the numismatic integration of wider areas. These market forces, though, did not operate independently of the state, which still had the power to enforce the closed currency systems of Syria-Palestine and Egypt. On one hand, we observe that merchants' dealings led to the homogenisation of the circulation pools, a phenomenon that may be explained according to metallist theories.[32] On the other hand, the 'official' unification of the monetary system as early as the reign of Augustus certainly promoted trade and facilitated transactions on a large scale. However, the Roman state did not always act in favour of the markets. In particular, the imposition of closed currency systems can only be explained as an attempt to increase imperial revenues, thus disregarding the needs of the merchants.

Even if, in this case, the emperor seemed to be deaf to the desires of the market, in other instances he was willing to intervene in order to facilitate trade and solve potential problems in the markets, as long as his revenues

[31] Goodhart 2003: 6. [32] Helleiner 2003a: 82.

were not affected. A clear example of this reaction to the grievances of the markets is the inscription of Mylasa.[33] At the beginning of the third century the 'official' mints increased substantially the production of silver coins. At the same time, they reduced the production of bronze coinages, while they did not warn the civic mints to increase their local output. The immediate result of this situation was the dearth of small change in the markets, which, in turn, resulted in a threat to the security and prosperity of the city of Mylasa. The threat came predominantly from the flourishing of the black market in the exchange of silver for bronze coins. While the city leased the right for the exchange of currency to authorised bankers, it seems that other individuals became involved in the illegal exchange of coins. The existing law that prohibited such trade was inadequate and the problem was resolved only after the cities increased the production of civic issues.

Once more, we observe the reaction of the government, whether local or central, to the grievances of the inhabitants: a phenomenon that is distinctly described by metallists. Similar examples of protests from the poorer classes over the quality and quantity of coinage have been known in the modern era, dating back to the beginning of the Industrial Revolution.[34] In our case, the Roman state could not ignore the pleading of the city, especially since local causes of distress may have affected the collection of taxes. Furthermore, they could not ignore the fact that daily transactions were highly monetised, as we have seen in chapter 6. Despite the declarations of the cities that the reasons for the production of civic coins were predominantly ideological and financial, by the Early Empire, the emperor and the local magistrates had to take seriously into consideration the increasing monetisation of the economy. By that time, small change, used predominantly by the poorest inhabitants, paid for food, clothing and small taxes. An acute dearth of smaller denominations in the markets could have resulted in distortions of the daily transactions, in the best cases, and in social uprisings, in the worst cases. The significance of small change to the populace was well known since at least 85 BC, when the people reacted violently to the mere fluctuations of the exchange rate between bronze and silver coinages.[35]

Throughout this book I have tried to underline the impact of the state and the markets on money, and vice versa. In my view, a constant game

[33] See chapter 4. The inscription was first published in Homolle 1896. Subsequent versions may be found in *OGIS* 2.515, pp. 160–5; Blümel 1987: 220–3, no. 605.
[34] Helleiner 2003a: 82. [35] M. Crawford 1970: 42.

of power took place in the Roman empire. The state pulled in one direction and the markets in another, unless specific policies were mutually advantageous. However, we should not conceive the Roman monetary economy as a combination of polarities. Despite the conflict of interest between the free market and the state, they could not exist without each other. Instead, they complemented each other and they created a balance, which allowed for the long-term survival of the Augustan economy and the prosperity of the empire. Hence, neither metallist nor chartalist theories on the nature of money can describe the situation accurately. Only a combination of the two may give us an idea of how the system was working. The state had to take into account the needs of the markets and vice versa, if it wanted to survive. So, at this point I would like to bring forward a new term that can be applied to my theory as I have described it in this book, namely Fiscal Metallism.

APPENDIX I

The inscription of Mylasa

———ην– φ— |
——— γα—— |
——εσειν———δ.ονετ————— |
τήν βουλή[ν κ]α[ί τόν δῆμον———||
——— κο]ινήν ὁμόφρονα γνώ[μην ——|
——] ἐν ταῖς νομίμοις ἡ[μέραις —— |
———]ων έπανορθῶ[σαι ——— |
——] ἀφορήτου πᾶσιν ὄντος το[ῦ ——— |
–, οὔ φαίν]ηται δέ δύνασθ[αι ἰαθῆναι ||
πλ]ή[ν] διά [τήν τ]ῶν μεγίστων [καί θειοτάτων κυρ|
ί]ων ἡμῶν Αὐτοκρατόρων Λο[υκίου Σεπτιμίου Σεου|
ή]ρου Εὐσεβοῦς Περτίνακος κ[αί Μάρκου Αὐρηλίου Ἀν|
τω]νίνου [Εὐσεβοῦς καί Ποπλίου Σεπτιμίου Γέτα Σεβα|
σ]τῶν τύχην, ψηφίσματι τῆς β[ουλῆς καί τοῦ δήμου ἐπ||
α]νορθωθέντα· δεδόχθαι τῇ [βουλῇ καί τῷ δήμῳ· ἐ|
ά]ν τις οἱῳδητινιοῦν τρόπῳ, [εἴτε ἐλεύθερος εἴτε |
δ]οῦλος, ἔξωθεν τοῦ μεμισθωμ[ένου καί ἐργα|
ζο]μένου τήν τράπεζαν, ἀμειβόμεν[ος ἄλῶι νόμισμα ἤ |
πρι]άμενος, πρός τόν τραπεζείτην [τοῦτοὐ άγεσθαι ||
γεν]ομένης προσανγελίας τῇ βουλῆι [ὑπό τοῦ βουλομέ|
νου τ]ῶν πολειτῶν, καί ἐλενχθέντα ἐπ[ί τῶν αρχόντων καί |
τῆς] βουλῆς, εἰ μέν ἄνευ κολλύβου τοῦτ[ο ἐποίησε, τοῦ ἀργυρίου |
πρᾶξ]ιν εἶναι τῷ τραπεζείτῃ καί τῷ μηνύσ[αντι καί ἑλόν|
τι, ἔ]χοντος τοῦ τραπεζείτου καί κατ᾽ αὐτόν ἐξο[υσίαν πράττε||
σθαι κα]θά ἠσφάλισται, εἰ δέ ἐπί κολλύβῳ τόν [μέν ἐλεύθερον ἀπο|
τίνει]ν (ε)ἰς τό ἱερώτατον ταμεῖον τῶν κυρίω[νἡμῶν θειοτά|
των] αὐτοκρατόρων * φ᾽, τῷ δέ δήμῳ * σν᾽, κ[αί τῷ μηνύ|
σαντ]ι καί ἑλόντι * ρ᾽, καί το φωραθέν ἀργυροῦ[ν νόμισ|
μα πρ]ασσόμενον εἶναι στερέσιμον τῷ τραπεζε[ίτῃ· τόν δέ δοῦλ||
ον ἐλ]ενχθέντα ὡς προγέγραπται, παραδοθέν[τα δέ ὑπό τοῦ δεσ|
πότου] τοῖς ἄρχουσι ἐπί [τῆ]ς βουλῆς, μαστειγοῦσθα[ι ν᾽ πληγάς |
καί] ἐμβάλλεσθαι (ε)ἰς τό πρακτόρειον καί εἶναι [αὐτόν |
ἐπί τῆς (ε)ἱρκτῆς τασσόμενον μῆνας ἕξ· ἐάν δέ [ὁ δεσπότης μή|
πο]ήσ[ε]ιε ταῦτα τόν δοῦλον, ὀφείλειν αὐτόν τά [γεγραμμένα ||

ἐπί]τειμα τῶι ἱερωτάτῳ ταμείῳ καί τῷ δήμῳ [καί τῷ μηνύσαντι καί |
ἐλό]ντι. Τάς δέ τοιαύτας προσανγελίας εἰσδέ[χεσθαι τόν γραμματέα |
τῶν] ἀρχόντων, γενομένης μετά τό ἐπιδ[οθῆναι τήν προσ|
ανγε]λίαν προγραφῆς ἑφεξῆς ἐπί τρεῖς ἡμέ[ρας ἐν ἱεροῖς |
καί δη]μοσίοις τόποις, ῥητῶς τῆς προγραφῆς [λεγούσης ὅτι ||
συνάγ]εται ἡ βουλή διά τοῦτο. Εάν δέ οἱ ἄρχοντε[ς ἤ ὁ γραμματεύς |
τῶν ἐψη]φισμένων τι παραλίπωσιν ἤ οἱ βουλευταί [μή συν |
έλθω]σιν δυνατοί ὄντες καί ἐπίδημοι, τούς μέν [ἄρχοντας καί |
τόν γραμ]ματέα ἀποτεῖσαι ἕκαστον αὐτῶν (ε)ἰς τό [ἱερώτατον |
ταμεῖον τῶν Σεβα]στῶν ἐνά * τ', τούς δέ βουλευτάς [ἀνά *.. ἀναγρά||
ψαι δέ τό]δε τό ψήφισμα ἐν στήλῃ, ἥν καί ἀνα[σταθῆναι |
δεήσει ἐν τῇ] ἀγορᾷ ἐν τῷ ἐπισημοτάτῳ τόπῳ ὥς[περ νόμον εἰς τόν πάν|
τα χρόνο]ν καταστῆσον· σαλεύει γάρ ὡς ἀλη[θῶς ἡ σωτηρία |
τῆς πόλε]ως ἐκ κακουργίας καί πανουργίας ὀλί[γων τινῶν |
αὐτῇ ἐπεμβα]ινόντων καί ἀπονοσφιζομένων τ[ά κοινά, ὧν ὑπό ||
τῆς δυνάμ]εως κόλλυβός τις ἐνπεφοίτηκεν εἰς [τήν ἀγοράν, |
κωλύων τήν πό]λιν τά ἐπιτήδ(ε)ια ἔχειν, ἀπορούντων [τῶν πολλῶν |
καί τοῦ κοινοῦ σ]πανίζοντος. καί διά τοῦτο καί ἡ εὐ[πορία ἡ |
πρός τούς κυρίους αὐ]τοκράτορας τῶν φόρων βραδύνει ——— |
——— μεγάλης ἡγεμονίας τουτο πᾶσα ἡ ——— |
——— ἐπανορθῶσαι. Succlam(atum) est: (ε)ἰς αἰῶ[να — |
———]ων ἀνεικήτοις τοῖς κυρίοις, ναοῖς [——— |
——— κόλλ]υβον. τό ζῆν οὐκ ἔχομεν, ἀλλ' ἡ πό[λις ——— |
——— πονη]ρευόμενοί τινες ἐνπορείας ταρ[άσσουσιν καί |
τό νόμισμα —]ουσιν τό ἀργυροῦν, καί τοῦτο [——— ||
——— τ]ούς νόμους πολλάκις ἡ βο[υλή ——— |
———] π . . . . . . πολειτ———

APPENDIX 2

Excavations finds, coin hoards and museums

BIBLIOGRAPHY

EXCAVATIONS

Greece

Argos: Walston 1905.
Athens: Thompson 1954; Kroll 1993.
Cenchreai: Hohlfelder 1978.
Corinth: Edwards 1933; J. Harris 1941; M. Price 1967; Stroud 1967; J. Wiseman 1969; C. Wiseman and Fisher 1970.
Patra: Agalopoulou 1994.
Thessaly: Karamesine-Oikonomidou 1962; Lazarides 1963; Karamesine-Oikonomidou 1964; Karamesine-Oikonomidou 1966a; Petrakos 1972; Iatridou 1976.

Cyprus

Curium: Cox 1959.

Asia Minor

Ankara: Arslan 1996a.
Aphrodisias: J. MacDonald 1976.
Ephesus: Wood 1938; Vetters 1979; Vetters 1980: 262–6; Vetters 1981: 154–68; Vetters 1982: 86–102; Vetters 1983: 123–69; Karwiese 1986; Karwiese 1987.
Kultepe: Taner 1971; Taner 1974.
Pergamos: Voegtli 1993.
Perge: Tekin 1994.
Sagalassus: Scheer 1993; Scheer 1994; Scheer 1995.
Sardis: H. Bell 1916; Buttrey, Johnston, MacKenzie and Bates 1981.
Side: Atlan 1976.

Tarsus: Cox 1950.
Troy: Bellinger 1950–8.

Dacia

Apulum: Winkler 1965; *Münzen aus der Sammlung des Museums der Stadt Sighisoara* 1972; Ocheşanu 1974; Moga 1981; Pavel-Popa 1981; Blăjan 1984; Csermi 1987; Chirilă and Blăjan 1988; Pavel and Moga 1994; Boenaru Bordea and Mitrea 1994–5: 465, no. 21; Suciu 1995; Nicolae 1998; Moga 1998: 110–235; Gazdac 2002a: 732–4.
Drobeta: Protase 1966: 182, no. 149; Stângă 1998.
Gherla: Ardevan 1986–91; Ardevan 1993; Boenaru Bordea and Mitrea 1994–5: 467, no. 50.
Ilisua: Protase, Gaiu and Marinescu 1997.
Micăsasa: Mitrofan and Ardevan 1995.
Orlea: Winkler and Băloi 1971; Winkler 1973.
Porolissum: Winkler 1964; *Muzeul Zalău* 1968; Gudea 1989; Gazdac 2002a: 734–6.
Potaissa: Winkler and Hopârtean 1973; Chirilă *et al.* 1978: 60; Boenaru Bordea and Mitrea 1992: 205, no. 51; Bărbulescu 1994: 134.
Praetorium (Mehadia): Gudea 1975; Macrea, Gudea and Motu 1993.
Tibiscum: Mitrea 1963: 595, nos. 33, 34; Gudea 1971; Bălănescu 1984: 130–1, no. 10; Bălănescu and Rogozea 1986; Gazdac 2002a: 738–9.
Ulpia Trajana Sarmizegetusa: Winkler 1974–5; Chirilă *et al.* 1978; Alicu *et al.* 1992–3; Alicu 1997; Gazdac 2002a: 729–32.

Pannonia Superior

Arrabona: Gazdac 2002a: 632–4.
Brigetio: Biro-Sey 1977; Gazdac 2002a: 623–9.
Carnuntum: Dembski 1985; Göbl 1987; Göbl 1993; Stiglitz 1997; Gazdac 2002a: 595–602.
Eisenstadt: Gazdac 2002a: 638–9.
Müllendorf: Gazdac 2002a: 639–40.
Mursella: Gazdac 2002a: 631–2.
Neckenmarkt: Gazdac 2002a: 651–2.
Neviodunum: Kos 1986: 59–61; Gazdac 2002a: 621–3.
Poetovio: Gazdac 2002a: 609–21.
Savaria: Gazdac 2002a: 631.
Scarabantia: Gazdac 2002a: 629–39.

Solva: Redó 1999: 96–108; Gazdac 2002a: 635–7.
Strebersdorf: Gazdac 2002a: 650–1.
Tokod: Redó 1999: 457–8; Gazdac 2002a: 657–8.
Vindobona: Gazdac 2002a: 602–8.
Winden am See: Gazdac 2002a: 647–8.

Pannonia Inferior

Aquincum: Gazdac 2002a: 836.
Gorsium: Fitz 1990: 289–370.
Intercisa: Fitz 1990: 53–192.

Moesia Inferior

Histria: Preda and Nubar 1973.
Nicopolis ad Istrum: Gazdac 2002a: 852.

Syria

Antioch ad Orontem: Waage 1952.
Capphaernaum: Spijkerman 1975.
Dura Europos: Bellinger 1949.
Gerasa: Bellinger 1938.
Hama: Thompsen 1986.
Jerusalem: Ariel 1982.
Palmyra: Michailowski 1963; Michailowski 1964; Michailowski 1966; Fellman and Dunant 1975.
Samaria: Kirkman 1957; Fulco and Zayadine 1981: 197–225.
Sepphoris: Waterman 1937.

COIN HOARDS

Greece

Amphipolis: Touratsoglou 1993: 120, n. 13; Papaeuthymiou 1994: 251, n. 11.
Athens 1: Kroll 1973: 319–20.
Athens 2: Kroll 1973: 318, n. 13c.
Cephallenia: *Arkhaiologikon Deltion* 26 (1971): 11; *Coin Hoards* II (1976): 65, n. 231.
Corinth 1: J. Harris 1941: 145.
Corinth 2: Shear 1931.

Eleusis: Svoronos 1904; Noe 1937: no. 380; Kroll 1973: 317 ff.
Erestrole: Agalopoulou 1994: 61–2.
Greek 1: *Coin Hoards* V (1979): 53, no. 146.
Greek 2: *Coin Hoards* IV (1978): 38, no. 143.
Greek 3: *Arkhaiologikon Deltion* 26 (1971): 133–76; *Coin Hoards* I (1975): 51, no. 188.
Karpenisi: Agalopoulou 1994: 71–2.
Kavala: *Coin Hoards* VI (1981): 28, no. 117.
Kilkis: *Arkhaiologikon Deltion* 36 (1981): 304; Touratsoglou 1988: 119, n. 7; Papaeuthymiou 1994: 248.
Koufalia: *Coin Hoards* IV (1978), no. 86; Touratsoglou 1988: 119, n. 8; Touratsoglou 1981; Papaeuthymiou 1994: 246–7.
Krani: *Coin Hoards* V (1979): 50, no. 128.
Leukochori: Touratsoglou 1988: 118–19, n. 7; Papaeuthymiou 1994: 250.
Macedonia 1: Touratsoglou 1988: 121–2, n. 18; Papaeuthymiou 1994: 254, no. 16.
Macedonia 2: Papaeuthymiou 1994: 255–6, n. 18; Kremmydi-Sisilianou 1996a: 108, no. 3.
Macedonia 3: Kremmydi-Sisilianou 1996b.
Methone: Touratsoglou 1993: 59, n. 11; Kremmydi-Sisilianou 1996a: 135, n. 14.
Nicopolis: Karamesine-Oikonomidou 1971.
Palaio: Karamesine-Oikonomidou 1967: 107–14.
Peristerona: Touratsoglou 1993: 118, n. 3; Papaeuthymiou 1994: 250.
Plakanida: Karamesine-Oikonomidou 1967: 93 ff.
Porto Rafti: Walker 1997: 40ff.
Roufou A: Agalopoulou 1994: 64–6.
Roufou B: Agalopoulou 1994: 67–9.
Scarminga: Varoucha 1954: 99.
Sebaste Pierias: Touratsoglou 1993: 58, n. 9; Kremmydi-Sisilianou 1996a: 134, n. 11.
Serrai: Touratsoglou 1988: 122, n. 20; Papaeuthymiou 1994: 252, no. 13.
Siderokastro: Touratsoglou 1988: 120–1, no. 14.
Sparta: Karamesine-Oikonomidou 1966b: 376 ff.
Strymon: Touratsoglou 1988: 121, no. 16.

Asia Minor

Asia Minor: *Coin Hoards* VI (1981): 17, no. 54.
Ayvagedigi: Rebuffat 1994.

Caesarea Cappadociae: Hodder 1981a; Hodder 1981b.
Cilicia: *Coin Hoards* II (1976): 38, no. 153.
Eastern: Bendall 1966.
Göktepe: Hollard and Bingol 1994.
Gülek Bogazi: Bland 1996b.
Haydere: Bland and Aydemir 1991: 93–4.
Iasos: Bland and Aydemir 1991: 102–4.
Lycia: Lagos 1993.
Manyas: Arslan 1996b.
Pergamos: Bland and Aydemir 1991: 101–2.
Smyrna: Bland and Aydemir 1991: 99.
Sulakyurt: Kizilkaya 1980; Kizilkaya 1991a.
Telmessus: Lagos 1993.
Troy 3: D. MacDonald 1987.
Troy 4: Arslan 1996.
Turkey 1: *Coin Hoards* I (1975): 50.
Yatagan: Kizilkaya 1988; Kizilkaya 1991b.
Western Turkey 1: Elks 1975.
Western Turkey 2: Elks 1975.

Syria

Antioch 1 hoard: *Coin Hoards* II (1976): 69, no. 254; Metcalf 1977.
Antioch 2: Metcalf 1975: 92, n. 16; Bland 1991b: 3.
Boston: Bellinger 1962.
Dura Europos 1: Bellinger 1949: 165–6.
Dura Europos 2: Bellinger 1949: 167.
Dura Europos 3: Bellinger 1949: 167–8.
Dura Europos 4: Bellinger 1949: 169.
Dura Europos 5: Bellinger 1949: 170.
Dura Europos 6: Bellinger 1949: 171–2.
Dura Europos 7: Bellinger 1949: 173–5.
Dura Europos 8: Bellinger 1949: 175–7.
Dura Europos 9: Bellinger 1949: 177.
Dura Europos 10: Bellinger 1949: 177–8.
Dura Europos 11: Bellinger 1949: 179–80.
Dura Europos 12: Bellinger 1949: 180
Dura Europos 13: Bellinger 1949: 181.
Dura Europos 14: Bellinger 1949: 181.

Dura Europos 15: Bellinger 1949: 182.
Dura Europos 16: Bellinger 1949: 183.
Gush Halav: Hamburger 1954.
Hama: Carson 1968.
Iafa: de Saulcy 1868.
Ihsa: Temizsoy 1996.
Jordan: Bland 1991b.
Mempsis: Negev 1966; Rosenthal-Heginbottom 1980.
Migdal: Meshorer 1976.
Murabba'at: Milik and Seyrig 1958.
Nineveh: Hill 1931.
Rafah: *Coin Hoards* IV (1978): 23, no. 84.
Silat: Spijkerman and Starcky 1958.
Syria 1: *Coin Hoards* II (1976): 36, no. 141.
Syria 2: Pflaum 1980.
Syria 3: Cesano 1925.
Syria 4: de Roquefeuil 1970.
Syria 5: Bastien and Huvelin 1969.
Syria 6: Bland 1991b: 3–7.
Syria 7: Bland 1991b: 7–8.
Tiberias: Hamburger 1956.
Turkey 3: Bland 1991b: 8–9.
Turkey 4: Bland 1991b: 9–10.

Moesia Superior

Belo Pole: Gerasimov 1965: 248.
Bošnjane: Boric-Breškovic 1988.
Brezane: Mirnik 1981: 60, no. 156.
Dobri Do: Mirnik 1981: 61, no. 163.
Glibovac: Petrovic 1928–30; Fitz 1978: 144–5.
Granicak: Gerasimov 1964; Fitz 1978: 146.
Grocka: Mirnik 1981: 54, no. 123.
Horreum Margi 1: Saria 1924: 90; Mócsy 1970: 258; Fitz 1978: 147.
Horreum Margi 2: Boric-Breškovic 1983.
Jablanica: Vasic 1977; Mirnik 1981: 63, no. 176.
Jagodina: Kubitschek 1900; Fitz 1978: 148.
Misaca: Kraljevic 1982.
Mrcevac: Mirnik 1981: 55, no. 130.

Ravna: Kondic 1983.
Sikirica: Mirnik 1981: 69, no. 214.
Singidunum: Kondic 1969; *Coin Hoards* V (1979): no. 143; Mirnik 1981: 60, no. 152.
Smederevo: Petrovic 1931; Fitz 1978: 202–3.
Vidinsko: Mušmov 1928–9; Fitz 1978: 100.
Vranje: Boric-Breškovic 1988.

Moesia Inferior

Dimum: Gerov 1977: no. 46.
Dvrostorum: Gerov 1977: no. 37.
Dvrostorum II: Gerov 1977: no. 37.
Dvrostorum IV: Paunov and Prokopov 2001: no. 96.
Gradeshnitsa: Paunov and Prokopov 2001: no. 80.
Gruncharovo: Paunov and Prokopov 2001: no. 82.
Katunets: Gerov 1977: no. 50.
Medgidia: *Coin Hoards* V (1979): 123; *Coin Hoards* VI (1981): 112.
Mokresh: Paunov and Prokopov 2001: no. 89.
Oescus: Paunov and Prokopov 2001: no. 78.
Oescus IV: Gerov 1977: no. 24.
Pavlikeni: Paunov and Prokopov 2001: no. 92.
Sanadinovo: Gerov 1977: no. 73.
Storgosia II: Youroukova 1978.
Tchervena Voda: Paunov and Prokopov 2001: no. 98.
Tropaeum Traiani: Barnea 1980: 95–8; *Coin Hoards* VI (1981): 114.
Vicus Tautiomosis: Gerov 1977: no. 57.
Zhinitsa: Seure 1923 : 13, no. 11.

Dacia

Apulum I: Găzdac 2002b: 468–9.
Barbura: Protase 1966: 86, no. 3.
Belcinu: Popilian 1981–2.
Brad: Palamariu 1988–91.
Butoieşti: Popilian and Stan-Mirceşti 1989.
Dăneşti: Poenaru Bordea and Mitrea 1991: no. 36.
Desa: Mitrea 1989: 263, no. 32.
Diviciorii Marj: Mitrea 1977: 378, no. 55; *Coin Hoards* III (1977): 151.
Drăghiceni: Gazdac 2002a: 466.

Dumbrăvioara: Găzdac 2002b: 467–8.
Frânceşti: Preda 1992–3: 112.
Gostavăt: Gazdac 2002a: 465.
Lujerdiu: Chirilă 1960; Ionescu 1997.
Mera: *Coin Hoards* III (1977): 148.
Micia: Petolescu and Mărghitan 1984: 119–20.
Pădureţu: Preda 1992–3: 109.
Potaisa I: Suciu and Hopârtean 1995.
Potaisa II: Winkler and Hopârtean 1973: 91–3.
Sălaşuri: Mitrea 1962: 538, no. 39; Molnár 1965; *Coin Hoards* III (1977): 149.
Săpata de Jos: Christescu 1934; Mitrea 1968.
Sighişoara: *Münzen aus der Sammlung des Museums der Stadt Sighişoara* 1972: 22.
Tibodu: Protase 1966: 88, no. 10; Protase 1995: 150–2.
Tibru: Pavel 1979; Gazdac 2002a: 463.
Vişea: Protase 1966: 89, no. 11.

Pannonia Superior

Apetlon: Dembski 1977: 29; Gazdac 2002a: 491.
Arrabona: Gazdac 2002a: 488.
Carnuntum I: Dembski 1977: 17; Gazdac 2002a: 490.
Carnuntum II: Gazdac 2002a: 490.
Neunkirchen: Dembski and Halder-Berky 1990.
Poetovio I: Kos 1986: 112, no. 3; Gazdac 2002a: 494.
Prelasko: Kos 1986: 77, no. 19; Gazdac 2002a: 492.
Tokod: *Coin Hoards* III (1977): 152.
Vindobona II: Gazdac 2002a: 492.
Vindobona IV: Dembski 1977: 3–4; Gazdac 2002a: 494.
Wallern: Dembski 1977: 20.

Pannonia Inferior

Bela Reka: Mirnik 1981: 53, no. 115; Popovic and Boric-Breškovic 1994.
Börgönd: Fitz 1990: 30–7.
Cornacum: Mirnik 1981: 57, no. 143.
ERCSI: Fitz 1990: 235–41.
Kurd-Gyulaji: Mérey 1935–36.
Mehovine: Mirnik 1981: 66, no. 190.

Mendén: Kerekes 1914: 71.
Mór: Fitz 1990: 267–9.
Mursa: Mirnik 1981: 56, no. 134.

Museums

Tokat Museum: Amandry, Remy and Ozcan 1994.

References

Abbott, F. F. and **Johnson, A. C.** (1926) *Municipal Administration in the Roman Empire.* Princeton.

Agalopoulou, P. (1994) *Themata Nomismatokopias kai Nomismatikes Kykloforias ton Patron.* PhD thesis. University of Ioannina.

Akarca, A. (1959) *Les monnaies grecques de Mylasa.* Paris.

Alföldy, G. (1988) *The Social History of Rome.* London.

(1989) *Die Krise der römischen Reiches.* Stuttgart.

Alicu, D. (1997) *Ulpia Trajana Sarmizegetusa. Amfiteatrul.* Cluj-Napoca.

Alicu, D. *et al.* (1992–1993) *Cercetări arheologice la Sarmizegetusa.* Campania.

Alston, R. (1994) 'Roman military pay from Caesar to Diocletian', *Journal of Roman Studies* **84**: 113–23.

(1995) *Soldier and Society in Roman Egypt.* London/ New York.

Amandry, M., Remy, B. and **Ozcan, B.** (1994) 'La circulation monetaire dans le Pont à l'epoque Imperiale à travers les collections numismatiques du Musée de Tokat', in *Tresors et circulation monetaire en Anatolie antique,* ed. **M. Amandry** and **G. Le Rider**. Paris: 119–33.

Ames, E. and **Rapp, R. T.** (1977) 'The birth and death of taxes: A hypothesis', *Journal of Economic History* **37**: 161–78.

Andreau, J. (1999) *Banking and Business in the Roman World.* Trans. **J. Lloyd**. Cambridge.

Ardevan, R. (1986–91) 'Noi descoperiri monetare antice la Gherla', *Buletinul Societatii Numismatice Romane* **80–85**: 281–7.

(1993) 'Circulatia monetară în asezarea romană de la Gherla', *Ephemeris Napocensis* **3**: 111–22.

Arestis, P. and **Sawyer, M. C.** (2006) *A Handbook of Alternative Monetary Economics.* Cheltenham.

Ariel, D. T. (1982) 'A survey of coin finds in Jerusalem', *Liber Annus* **32**: 273–326.

Arslan, M. (1996a) 'Greek and Greek Imperial coins found during the Cankirikapi excavations at Ankara', in *Studies in Ancient Coinage from Turkey,* ed. **R. Ashton**. London: 107–14.

(1996b) 'The Manyas Hoard of *denarii*', in *Studies in Ancient Coinage from Turkey,* ed. **R. Ashton**. London: 31–6.

(1996c) 'A third century AD hoard of bronzes, principally of Alexandreia Troas', in *Studies in Ancient Coinage from Turkey*, ed. **R. Ashton**. London: 43–5.

Atlan, S. (1976) *1947–1967 Yillari Side Kazilari Sirasinda Elde Edilen Sikkeler*. Ankara.

Austin, M. (ed.) (1981) *The Hellenistic World from Alexander to the Roman Conquest: A Selection of Ancient Sources in Translation*. Cambridge.

Babelon, E. (1897) *Inventaire sommaire de la Collection Waddington*. Paris.

Bagnall, R. S. (1989) 'Fourth century prices: New evidence and further thoughts', *Zeitschrift für Papyrologie und Epigraphik* **76**: 69–76.

Bălănescu, D. (1984) 'Descoperiri monetare din sudul Banatului', *Studii di Cercetari di Numismatica* **8**: 129–36.

Bălănescu, D. and **Rogozea, P.** (1986) 'Monede romane din colectia muzeului judetean de etnografie si istorie locală Caransebes', *Tibiscum* **6**: 219–32.

Banaji, J. (1996) 'The circulation of gold as an index of prosperity in the central and eastern Mediterranean in late antiquity', in *Coin Finds and Coin Use in the Roman World, The Thirteenth Oxford Symposium on Coinage and Monetary History, 25.–27.3.1993*, ed. **C. E. King**. Berlin: 41–53.

(2002) *Agrarian Change in Late Antiquity: Gold, Labour and Aristocratic Dominance*. Oxford.

Bang, P. F. (2008) *The Roman Bazaar: A Comparative Study of Trade and Markets in a Tributary Empire*. Cambridge.

Bărbulescu, M. (1994) *Potaissa*. Cluj-Napoca.

Barnea, A. (1980) 'Tezaur de denari romani imperiali descoperit în cetatea Tropaeum Traiani', *Studii şi cercetări de numismatică* **7**: 95–8.

Bastien, P. (1992) *Le buste monétaire des empereurs romains. Numismatique Romaine XIX*. Vol. I. Wetteren.

Bastien, P. and **Huvelin, H.** (1969) 'Tresor d' antoniniani en Syrie', *Revue Numismatique* **11**: 231–70.

Baydur, N. (1975) 'Die Münzen von Attaleia in Pamphylien', *Jahrbuch für Numismatik und Geldgeschichte* **25**: 33–72.

(1976) 'Die Münzen von Attaleia in Pamphylien', *Jahrbuch für Numismatik und Geldgeschichte* **26**: 37–78.

Bayly, C. A. (1983) *Rulers, Townsmen and Bazaars: North Indian Society in the Age of British Expansion, 1770–1870*. Cambridge.

Beckman, M. (1998) 'Ancient coins from shipwrecks', *The Anvil* **8**.2: 19–21.

Bell, H. W. (1916) 'Coins', in *Sardis: Excavations 1910–1914*. Vol. XI. Leiden.

Bell, S. (2001) 'The role of the state and the hierarchy of money', *Cambridge Journal of Economics* **25**: 149–63.

Bellinger, A. (1938) *Coins from Jerash*. American Numismatic Society, Numismatic Notes and Monographs 81. New York.

(1949) 'The coins', in *The Excavations at Dura, Final Report*. Vol. VI, ed. **M. I. Rostovtzeff, A. R. Bellinger, F. E. Brown, N. P. Toll** and **C. B. Welles**. New Haven.

(1950–8) 'Troy: The coins', in *Troy: Excavations Conducted by the University of Cincinnati, 1932–1938*, ed. **C. Blegen**. Suppl. Monogr. 2. Princeton.

(1962) 'The Boston College Hoard', *American Numismatic Society, Museum Notes* **10**: 43–50.

Belloni, G. G. (1993) *La moneta romana: società, politica, cultura*. Rome.

Beloch, J. (1886) *Die Bevoelkerung der griechisch-roemischen Welt*. Leipzig.

Bendall, S. (1966) 'An Eastern Hoard of Roman Imperial silver', *Numismatic Chronicle*, 7th series, **6**: 167–70.

Biro-Sey, K. (1977) *Coins from Identified Sites of Brigetio and the Question of Local Currency*. Budapest.

Blăjan, M. (1984) 'Circulatia monetară în judetul Alba, argument al continuitătii populatiei romanice în Dacia postromană', *Apulum* **22**: 93–112.

Bland, R. (ed.) (1982) *Coin Hoards from Roman Britain*. Vol. III. London.

(1991a) 'The last coinage of Caesarea in Cappadocia', in *Glaux: Collana di Studi e Ricerche di Numismatica, Ermanno A. Arslan Studia Dicata*, ed. **R. Martini** and **N. Vismara**. Milan: 214–31.

(1991b) 'Six hoards of Syrian tetradrachms of the third century AD', *Numismatic Chronicle* **151**: 1–34.

(1996a) 'The development of gold and silver denominations, AD 193–253', in *Coin Finds and Coin Use in the Roman World: The Thirteenth Oxford Symposium on Coinage and Monetary History, 25.–17.3. 1993*, ed. **C. E. King** and **D. G. Wigg**. Berlin: 74–80.

(1996b) 'The bronze coinage of Gordian III from Caesarea in Cappadocia', in *Studies in Ancient Coinage from Turkey*, ed. **R. Ashton**. London: 49–95.

(1997) 'The changing patterns of hoards of precious-metal coins in the Late Empire', *Antiquité Tardive* **5**: 29–55.

Bland, R. and **Aydemir P.** (1991) 'The Haydere Hoard and other hoards of the mid third century from Turkey', in *Recent Turkish Coin Hoards and Numismatic Studies*, ed. **C. S. Lightfoot**. Oxford: 91–180.

Bland, R. and **Orna-Ornstein, J.** (eds.) (1984) *Coin Hoards from Roman Britain*. Vol. X. London.

Bloch, M. (1954) *Esquisse d' une histoire monetaire de l' Europe*. Paris.

Blümel, W. (1987) *Inschriften griechischer Städte am Kleinasien*, Vol. XXXIV: *Die Inschriften von Mylasa, I*. Bonn.

Boenaru Bordea, G. and **Mitrea, B.** (1992) 'Découvertes monétaires en Roumanie-1991', *Dacia N.S.* **36**.

(1994–5) 'Découvertes monétaires en Roumanie-1993', *Dacia N.S.* 38–39.

Bogaert, R. (1966) *Les origines antiques de la banque dè depot: une mise au point accompagnée d' une esquisse des operations de banque en Mésopotamie*. Leiden.

(1968) *Banques et banquiers dans les cites grecques*. Leiden.

Bolin, S. (1958) *State and Currency in the Roman Empire to 300 A.D.* Uppsala.

Bordo, M. D. (1992) 'Bimetallism', in *The New Palgrave Encyclopedia of Money and Finance*, ed. **P. K. Newman, M. Milgate** and **J. Eatwell**. New York.

Boren, H. C. (1961) 'The sources of Cicero's income: Some suggestions', *Classical Journal* **57**: 17–24.

(1983) 'Studies relating to the *stipendium militum*', *Historia* **32**: 427–60.

Boric-Breškovic, B. (1983) 'Nalaz bakarnog novca iz okoline Cuprije', *Zbornik Narodnog Muzeja* **11**.1: 69–84.

(1988) 'Dve ostave bakarnog rimskog novca Viminacijuma I Dakije', *Zbornik Narodnog Muzeja* **13**.1: 89–97.

Bossu, C. (1982) 'M' Megonius Leo from Petelia (Regio III): A private benefactor from the local aristocracy', *Zeitschrift für Papyrologie und Epigraphik* **45**: 155–65.

Bost J.-P., Campo, M. and **Gurt, J.-M.** (1983) 'Hallazgos de aurei y solidi en la Peninsula Iberica: introducción a su circulación en epoca imperial', *Numisma* **33**: 137–76.

(1992) 'Trouvailles d' aurei et de solidi dans la Péninsule ibérique', in *L'or monnaye III: Trouvailles de monnaies d'or dans l'occident romain. Cahiers Ernest-Babelon, 4*, ed. **C. Brenot** and **X. Loriot**. Paris: 33–89.

Braddick, M. J. (1994) *Parliamentary Taxation in Seventeenth Century England.* London.

Breeze, D. J. (1971) 'Pay grades and ranks below the centurionate', *Journal of Roman Studies* **61**: 130–5.

Brenot, C. and **Loriot, X.** (eds.) (1992) *L'or monnaye III: Trouvailles de monnaies d'or dans l'occident romain. Cahiers Ernest-Babelon, 4*. Paris.

Brenot, C. and **Metzger, C.** (1992) 'Trouvailles de bijoux monetaires dans l'occident romain', in *L'or monnaye III: Trouvailles de monnaies d'or dans l'occident romain. Cahiers Ernest-Babelon, 4*, ed. **C. Brenot** and **X. Loriot**. Paris: 315–71.

Brewer, J. (1989) *The Sinews of Power: War, Money and the English State, 1688–1783.* New York.

Broughton, T. R. S. (1938) 'Roman Asia Minor', in *An Economic Survey of Ancient Rome*, ed. **T. Frank**. Vol. IV. Baltimore.

Brunner, K. and **Melzer, A. H.** (1971) 'The uses of money: Money in the theory of an exchange economy', *The American Economic Review* **61**.5: 784–805.

Brunt, P. A. (1965) 'The *equites* in the Late Republic', in *Second International Conference of Economic History, Trade and Politics in the Ancient World*, ed. **M. I. Finley**. Vol. I. (Repr. New York 1979). Mouton: 117–49.

(1966) 'The *fiscus* and its development', *Journal of Roman Studies* **56**: 75–91.

(1980) 'Free labour and public works at Rome', *Journal of Roman Studies* **70**: 81–100.

(1981) 'The revenues of Rome', *Journal of Roman Studies* **71**: 161–72.

(1990) *Roman Imperial Themes*. Oxford.

Bruun, P. (1979) 'The successive monetary reforms of Diocletian', *American Numismatic Society, Museum Notes*, **24**: 129–48.

(1981) 'Quantitative analysis of hoarding in periods of coin deterioration', in *PACT: Statistics and Numismatics* 5, ed. **C. Carcassone** and **T. Hackens**. Strasbourg: 355–64.

Burnett, A. M. (1977) 'The authority to coin in the Late Republic and Early Empire', *Numismatic Chronicle*, 7th series, **147**: 37–63.

(ed.) (1981) *Coin Hoards from Roman Britain*. Vol. II. London.

(ed.) (1984a) *Coin Hoards from Roman Britain*. Vol. IV. London.
(ed.) (1984b) *Coin Hoards from Roman Britain*. Vol. V. London.
(1987) *Coinage in the Roman World*. London.

Burnett, A., Amandry, M. and **Carradice, I.** (1999) *Roman Provincial Coinage*. Vol. II, Part I. London/Paris.

Burnett, A., Amandry, M. and **Ripolles, P. P.** (1992) *Roman Provincial Coinage: From the Death of Caesar to the Death of Vitellius (44 BC to AD 69)*. Vol. I. London/Paris.

Burnett, A. M. and **Bland, R.** (eds.) (1986) *Coin Hoards from Roman Britain*. Vol. VI. London.
(eds.) (1987) *Coin Hoards from Roman Britain*. Vol. VII. London.

Bursche, A. (1996) *Later Roman–Barbarian Contacts in Central Europe: Numismatic Evidence*. Studien zu Fundmünzen der Antike 2. Berlin.

Butcher, K. (1988a) 'The colonial coinage of Antioch-on-the-Orontes: c. AD 218–53', *Numismatic Chronicle* **148**: 63–75.
(1988b) *Roman Provincial Coins*. London.
(1996) 'Coinage and currency in Syria and Palestine', in *Coin Finds and Coin Use in the Roman World: The Thirteenth Oxford Symposium on Coinage and Monetary History 25.–27.3.1993*, ed. **C. E. King** and **D. G. Wigg**. Berlin: 101–12.
(2001–2), *Small Change in Ancient Beirut: The Coin Finds from BEY 006 and BEY 045: Persian, Hellenistic, Roman and Byzantine Periods*. Berytus 45–46. Beirut.
(2004) *Coinage in Roman Syria: Northern Syria 64 BC–AD 253*. London.

Butcher, K. and **Ponting, M.** (1997) 'A study of the chemical composition of Roman silver coinage, AD 196–197', *American Journal of Numismatics* **9**: 17–36.

Butler, O. (1910) 'Studies in the Life of Heliogabalus', in *Roman History and Mythology*, ed. **H. Sanders**. Ann Arbor: 1–169.

Buttrey, S. E. and **Buttrey, T. V.** (1997) 'Review Article: Calculating ancient coin production again', *American Journal of Numismatics* **9**: 113–35.

Buttrey, T. V. (1961) 'Dio, Zonaras and the value of the Roman *aureus*', *Journal of Roman Studies* **51**: 40–5.
(1991) 'The President's address: Exchange and circulation at Pergamum in the second century AD', *Numismatic Chronicle* **151**: iii–vi.
(1993) 'Calculating ancient coin production: Facts and fantasies', *Numismatic Chronicle* **153**: 335–51.
(1994) 'Calculating ancient coin production II: Why it cannot be done', *Numismatic Chronicle* **154**: 341–52.

Buttrey, T. V., Johnston, A., MacKenzie, K. M. and **Bates, M. L.** (1981) 'Greek, Roman and Islamic coins from Sardis', in *Archaeological Exploration of Sardis, 1958–1972*. Vol. IX. Cambridge, Mass.

Callu, J. P. (1969) *La politique monétaire des empereurs Romains de 238 à 311*. Paris.
(1979) *Les monnaies romaines: Fouilles d' Apamée de Syrie*, Vol. VIII, Part I. Brussels.

Callu, J. P. and **Loriot, X.** (1990) *L'or monnaye II: La dispersion des aurei en Gaule romaine sous l'empire. Cahiers Ernest-Babelon 3*. Paris.

(1992) 'L' or monnaye', in *L' or monnaye III: Trouvailles de monnaies d'or dans l'occident romain. Cahiers Ernest-Babelon, 4*, ed. **C. Brenot** and **X. Loriot**. Paris: 21–32.

Carradice, I. and **M. Price** (1988) *Coinage in the Greek World*. London.

Carradice, I. A. (1983) *Coinage and Finances in the Reign of Domitian*. Oxford.

Carreli, S. (1996) 'Alcune osservazioni sul portorium Asiae', *Studi ellenistici* **8**: 175–89.

Carson, R. A. G. (1962) *Coins of the Roman Empire in the British Museum: Severus Alexander to Balbinus and Pupienus*. Vol. VI. London.

(1965) 'The reform of Aurelian', *Revue Numismatique* **7**: 225–35.

(1968) 'The Hama Hoard and the eastern mints of Valerian and Gallienus', *Berytus* **17**: 123–42.

(1990) *Coins of the Roman Empire*. London/ New York.

Carson, R. A. G. and **Burnett, A. M.** eds. (1979) *Recent Coin Hoards from Roman Britain*. London.

Casey, P. J. (1980) *Roman Coinage in Britain*. Aylesbury.

(1986) *Understanding Ancient Coins: An Introduction for Archaeologists and Historians*. London.

Cesano, L. (1925) 'Nuovi ripostigli di denari di argento dell' impero romano', in *Atti e memorie dell' Istituto Italiano di Numismatica*. Vol. V. Rome: 57–72.

Chabot, J.-B. (1926) *Corpus Inscriptionum Semiticarum*, Vol. II. 3.

Champlin, E. (1991) *Final Judgements: Duty and Emotion in Roman Wills, 200 BC – AD 250*. Berkeley.

Chirilă, E. (1960) 'Tezaurul de monede romane imperiale de la Lujerdiu', *Studii si Cercetari de Numismatica* **3**: 405–31.

Chirilă, E. and **Blăjan, M.** (1988) 'Descoperiri monetare antice în Transilvania', *Acta Musei Porolissensis* **12**: 191.

Chirilă, E. *et al.* (1978) 'Descoperiri monetare antice in Transilvania', *Acta Musei Porolissensis* **2**: 60.

Chown, J. F. (1994) *A History of Money, from AD 800*. London/New York.

Christescu, V. (1934) 'Le trésor de monnaies de Săpata de Jos et la date du limes romain de la Valachie', *Istros* **1**: 73–80.

Christiansen, E. (1985) 'The Roman coins of Alexandria (30 BC to AD 296). An inventory of hoards', *Coin Hoards* **7**: 77–140.

(1988) *The Roman Coins of Alexandria: Quantitative Studies*. Aarhus.

(1994) 'On *denarii* and other coin terms in papyri', *Zeitschrift für Papyrologie und Epigraphik* **54**: 271–99.

(2004) *Coinage in Roman Egypt: The Hoard Evidence*. Aarhus.

Cipolla, C. M. (1956) *Money, Prices and Civilisation in the Mediterranean World: Fifth to Seventeenth Century*. Princeton.

Clay, C. (1989) 'The supply of bronze coins to Britain in the second century AD', *Numismatic Chronicle* **149**: 209–24.

Cole, T. J. (1976) 'The lifetime of coins in circulation', *Numismatic Chronicle* **16**: 201–18.

Collis, J. (1988) 'A functionalist approach to pre-Roman coinage', in *Coins and the Archaeologist*, ed. **J. Casey** and **R. Reece**. 2nd edn: 97–104.

Cooke, G. A. (1903) *A Textbook of North Semitic Inscriptions*. Oxford.

Corbier, M. (1980) 'Salaires et salariat sous le Haut Empire', in *Les devaluations à Rome: Époque républicaine et imperial*, ed. **S. Mrozek**. Vol. II. Rome: 61–101.

(1985) 'Devaluations et evolution des prix', *Revue Numismatique* **27**: 69–106.

(1989) 'Histoire monétaire, histoire des prix, histoire des mines', in *Metallurgia en las Antiguas Civilizaciones Mediterráneas y Europeas*, ed. **C. Domergue**. Vol. II. Madrid: 183–94.

Corsten, T. (1985) *Die Inschriften von Kios*. Bonn.

Cotton, H. M. (1997) 'Land tenure in the documents from the Nabataean kingdom and the Roman province of Arabia', *Zeitschrift für Papyrologie und Epigraphik* **119**: 255–65.

Coulton, J. J. (1987) 'Opramoas and the anonymous benefactor', *Journal of Hellenic Studies* **107**: 171–8.

Coupry, J. and **Feyel, M.** (1936) 'Inscriptions de Philippes', *Bulletin de Correspondance Hellenique* **60**: 37–59.

Cox, D. H. (1950) 'The coins', in *Excavations at Gozlu Küle: Tarsus, The Hellenistic and Roman Periods*, ed. **H. Goldman**. Vol. I. Princeton: 38–83.

(1959) 'Coins from the excavations at Curium, 1932–1953', *American Numismatic Society, Numismatic Notes and Monographs* 143. New York.

Crawford, D. J. (1976) 'Imperial Estates', in *Studies in Roman Property*, ed. **M. I. Finley**. Cambridge: 35–70.

Crawford, M. H. (1969) 'Coin hoards and the pattern of violence in the Late Republic', *Proceedings of the British School at Rome* **37**: 76–81.

(1970) 'Money and exchange in the Roman world', *Journal of Roman Studies* **60**: 40–8.

(1973) 'La monetazione di bronzo di Poseidonia-Paestum', supplement to *Annali: Istituto Italiano di Numismatica: Atti del III Convegno del Centro Internazionale di Studi Numismatici Napoli 19–23 April 1971*. Vol. XVIII–XIX. Rome: 47–109.

(1974) *Roman Republican Coinage*. Cambridge.

(1975) 'Finance, coinage and money from the Severans to Constantine', in *Aufstieg und Niedergang der römischen Welt*, ed. **H. Temporini**. Vol. II.2. Berlin: 560–93.

(1983) 'Numismatics', in *Sources for Ancient History*, ed. **M. H. Crawford**. Cambridge: 185–233.

Crawford, M. H. and **Reynolds, J.** (1975) 'The publication of the Prices Edict: A new inscription from Aezani', *Journal of Roman Studies* **65**: 160–3.

Csermi, B. (1987) 'Apulumi maradványok', *Az Alsófehérmegyei Törtenelmi Évkönyve* **9**: 35–45.

Cubelli, V. (1992) *Aureliano Imperatore: La Rivolta dei Monetiere e la Cosidetta Riforma Monetaria*. Florence.

D'Arms, J. H. (1981) *Commerce and Social Standing in Ancient Rome*. Cambridge.

Davidson, P. (1999) 'Can money be neutral even in the long run? Chartalism vs monetarism', in *The Collective Writings of Paul Davidson*, ed. **L. Davidson**. Vol. III. London: 196–210.

Davies, O. (1935) *Roman Mines in Europe*. Oxford.

Davis, W. S. (1910) *The Influence of Wealth in Imperial Rome*. New York.

Day, J. (1942) *An Economic History of Athens under Roman Domination*. New York.

De Blois, L. (2002) 'The crisis of the third century AD in the Roman empire: a modern myth?', in *The Transformations of Economic Life under the Roman Empire*, ed. **L. De Blois** and **J. Rich**. Amsterdam: 204–17.

De Callatay, F. (1995) 'Calculating ancient coin production: Seeking a balance', *Numismatic Chronicle* **155**: 289–311.

De Cecco, M. (1985) 'Monetary theory and Roman history', *The Journal of Economic History* **45**.4: 809–22.

De Laine, J. (1997) *The Baths of Caracalla: A Study in the Design, Construction, and Economics of Large-Scale Building Projects in Imperial Rome*. Portsmouth.

De Ligt, L. (1993) *Fairs and Markets in the Roman Empire: Economic and Social Aspects of Periodic Trade in Pre-Industrial Society*. The Netherlands.

(2003) 'Taxes, trade and the circulation of coin: The Roman empire, Mughal India and T'ang China compared', *The Medieval History Journal* **6**: 231–49.

De Martino, F. (1980) *Storia economica di Roma*. Florence.

de Roquefeuil, S. (1970) 'Un nouveau tresor d' Antoniniani frappés en Orient', *Revue Numismatique* **12**: 116–39.

de Saulcy, F. (1868) 'Trouvaille de Iafa de Galilee, près Nazareth', *Annuaire de la Société Française de Numismatique* **3**: 350ff.

Dembski, G. (1977) 'Die antiken Münzschatzfunde aus Österreich', *Numismatische Zeitschrift* **91**: 3–64.

(1985) 'Die Münzen der Lagergrabungen Carnuntum 1968–1978', *Numismatische Zeitschrift* **99**: 5–21.

Dembski, G. and **Halder-Berky, W.** (1990) 'Der Münzschatz der römischen Kaiserzeit aus Neukirchen: uber 168 Denare mit Schlussmünze 167–8 n.Chr.', *Numismatische Zeitschrift* **101**: 17–28.

Depeyrot, G. (1982) *Le numéraire gaulois du IVe siècle: Aspects quantitatifs*. BAR International Series 127. Oxford.

(1988) 'La durée d'utilisation des solidi romains', in *Studia Numismatica Labacensia Alexandro Jelocnik Oblata*, ed. **P. Kos** and **Z. Demo**. Ljubljana: 213–17.

Develin, R. (1971) 'The army pay rises under Severus and Caracalla, and the question of *annona militaris*', *Latomus* **30**.2: 687–95.

Devijver, H. (1977) *Prosopographia militiarum equestrium quae fuerunt ab Augusto ad Gallienum*. Vol. II. Leuven.

(1987) *Prosopographia militiarum equestrium quae fuerunt ab Augusto ad Gallienum*. Vol. IV. Leuven.

Domergue, C. (1990) *Les mines de la péninsule Ibérique dans l'antiquité romaine*. Rome.

Domergue, C. and **Hérail, G.** (1978) *Mines d'or romaines d'Espagne: le district de la Valduerna (León): etude géomorphologique et archéologique*. Toulouse.

Doyle, E. J. (1976) 'Two new fragments of the Edict of Diocletian on Maximum Prices', *Hesperia* **45**.1: 77–97.

Dreher, M. (1996) 'Die *lex portorii Asiae* und der Zollbezirk Asia', *Epigraphica Anatolica* **26**: 111–27.

Drexhage, H. J. (1991) *Preise, Mieten/Pachten, Kosten und Löhne im römischen Ägypten bis zum Regierungantritt Diokletians*. St. Katharinen.

Dumant, C. (1975) 'Les monnaies', *Le sanctuaire de Baalshamin à Palmyre: Kleifunde*. Vol. VI. Rome.

Duncan, G. L. (1993) *Coin Circulation in the Danubian and Balkan Provinces of the Roman Empire, AD 294–578*. Royal Numismatic Society 26. London.

Duncan-Jones, R. (1974) *The Economy of the Roman Empire*. Cambridge.

(1987) 'Weight-loss as an index of coin-wear in currency of the Roman Principate', in *Rythmes de la production monétaire, de l' antiquité a nos jours: Actes du colloque international organisé à Paris du 10 au 12 Janvier 1986*, ed. **G. Depeyrot, T. Hackens** and **G. Moucharte**. Louvain-la-Neuve: 237–56.

(1989) 'Mobility and immobility of coin in the Roman empire', *Annali: Istituto Italiano di Numismatica* **36**: 121–37.

(1990) *Structure and Scale in the Roman Economy*. Cambridge.

(1994) *Money and Government in the Roman Empire*. Cambridge.

(2004) 'Economic change and the transition to late antiquity', in *Approaching Late Antiquity*, ed. **S. Swain** and **M. Edwards**. Oxford: 20–52.

Eadie, J. (1996) 'One hundred years of rebellion: the eastern army in politics, AD 175–272', in *The Roman Army in the East*, ed. **D. L. Kennedy** and **D. Braund**. Michigan: 135–51.

Edmondson, C. (1989) 'Mining in the Later Roman Empire and beyond: Continuity or disruption', *Journal of Roman Studies* **79**: 84–102.

Edwards, K. M. (1933) *Corinth: The Coins*. Vol. IV. Cambridge, Mass.

Einaudi, L. (1953) 'The theory of imaginary money from Charlemagne to the French Revolution', in *Enterprise and Secular Change*, ed. **F. C. Lane** and **J. C. Riemersma**. London: 229–61.

Elks, K. J. J. (1975) 'The eastern mints of Valerian and Gallienus: The evidence of two new hoards from western Turkey', *Numismatic Chronicle* **15**: 91–109.

Elton, H. (2005) 'Military supply and the south coast of Anatolia in the third century AD', in *Patterns in the Economy of Roman Asia Minor*, ed. **S. Mitchell** and **C. Katsari**. Swansea: 289–304.

Engelmann, H. and **Knibbe, D.** (1989) 'Das Zollgesetz der Provinz Asia. Eine neue Inschrift aus Ephesos', *Epigraphica Anatolica* **14**: 1–206.

Ennis, H. M. (2006) 'The problem of small change in Early Argentina', *Economic Quarterly: Federal Reserve Bank of Richmond* (March): 6–7.

Erim, K. and **Reynolds, J.** (1970) 'The copy of Diocletian's Edict on Maximum Prices from Aphrodisias in Caria', *Journal of Roman Studies* **60**: 120–41.

Erim, K., Reynolds, J. and **Crawford, M.** (1971) 'Diocletian's currency reform: A new inscription', *Journal of Roman Studies* **61**: 171–7.

Estiot, S. (1995) 'Aureliana', *Revue Numismatique* **150**: 50–94.
Esty, W. W. (1986) 'Estimation of the size of a coinage: a survey and comparison of methods', *Numismatic Chronicle* **146**: 185–215.
Fellman, R. and **Dunant, C.** (1975) *Le sanctuaire de Baalshamin à Palmyre: Kleinfunde*. Vol. VI. Rome.
Fink, O. (1971) *Roman Military Records on Papyrus*. Cleveland.
Finley, M. I. (1973) *The Ancient Economy*. London.
(1985) *The Ancient Economy*. 2nd edn. Cambridge.
Fisher, I. (1926) *The Purchasing Power of Money: its Determination and Relation to Credit, Interest and Crises*. New York.
Fitz, J. (1978) *Der Geldumlauf der römischen Provinzen in Donaugebiet Mitte des 3. Jahrhunderts*. Budapest.
(ed.) (1990) *Die Fundmünzen der römischen Zeit in Ungarn (FMRU)*. Vol. I. Bonn.
Flandreau, M. (1996) 'The French crime of 1873: An essay in the emergence of the international gold standard, 1870–1880', *Journal of Economic History* **56**.4: 862–97.
Flynn, D. (1982) 'Gresham's Law and the modern theory of the demand for money', *Eastern Economic Journal* **8**.3: 219–35.
Foss, C. (1979) 'A hoard of the third century AD from Pamphylia', *Coin Hoards* **5**: 37–40.
French, D. (1988) *Roman Roads and Milestones of Asia Minor: An Interim Catalogue of Milestones*. Vol. II. British Institute of Archaeology at Ankara Monograph no. 9. BAR International Series 392 (ii). Oxford.
Frézouls, E. (1985) 'Les ressorces de l'évergétisme. Le cas d'Opramoas de Rhodiapolis', in *L'origine des richesses dépensées dans la ville antique: Actes du Colloque organisé à Aix-en-Provence, 1984*, ed. P. Leveau. Aix-en-Provence: 1–18.
Frieden, J. A. (1997) 'Monetary populism in nineteenth century America: an open economy interpretation', *The Journal of Economic History* **57**.2: 367–95.
Friedman, M. (1956) 'The quantity theory of money: A restatement', in *Studies in Quantity Theory of Money*, ed. **M. Friedman**. London/Chicago: 3–21.
(1968) 'The role of monetary policy', *The American Economic Review* **58**: 1–17.
(1969) *The Optimum Quantity of Money and Other Essays*. London.
(1990) 'Bimetallism revisited', *Journal of Economic Perspectives* **4**.4: 85–104.
Friedman, M. and **Schwartz, A. J.** (1963) *A Monetary History of the United States 1867–1960*. Princeton.
Fulco, W. J. and **Zayadine, F.** (1981) 'Coins from Samaria Sebaste', *Annual of the Department of Antiquities of Jordan* **25**: 197–225.
Fulford, M. (1989) 'The economy of Roman Britain', in *Research on Roman Britain, 1960–1989*, ed. **M. Tod**. London: 175–201.
Gara, A. (1976) *Prosdiagraphomena e circolazione monetaria*. Milan.
Garnsey, P. (1999) *Food and Society in Classical Antiquity*. Cambridge.

Garnsey, P. and **Saller, R.** (1987) *The Roman Empire: Economy, Society and Culture*. London.

Găzdac, C. (1994) 'Le trésor monétaire impérial de Dumbrăvioara (Reghin II) – réétudié', *Ephemeris Napocensis* **4**: 179–91.

(1996) 'Il tesoro monetale romano imperiale Apulum. I ricercato di nuovo', *Ephemeris Napocensis* **6**: 135–51.

(2002a) *Circulatia Monetară în Dacia şi provinciile învecinate de la Traian la Constantin I*. Cluj-Napoca.

(2002b) *Monetary Circulation in the Province of Dacia in the Period from Trajan to Constantine I (AD 106–337)*. PhD Thesis. Oxford University.

Gerasimov, T. (1964) *Bulletin de l'Institut Archéologique Bulgare* **27**: 242.

(1965) *Bulletin de l'Institut Archéologique Bulgare* **28**: 248.

Gerov, B. (1977) 'Die Einfälle der Nordvölker in den Ostbalkanraum im Lichte der Münzschatzfunde. I. Das II u. Z. III Jahrhundert (101–284)', *Aufstieg und Niedergang der römischen Welt*, ed. **H. Temporini**. Vol. II.6. Berlin/New York: 110–81.

Giardina, A. (2008) 'The transition to Late Antiquity', in *The Cambridge Economic History of the Greco-Roman World*, ed. **W. Scheidel, I. Morris** and **R. Saller**. Cambridge: 743–68.

Gill, D. W. J. (1991) 'Pots and trade spacefillers or objets d' art?', *Journal of Hellenic Studies* **111**: 29–47.

Gilmore, P. M. (1987) 'Caracalla's silver mints in Syria and Mesopotamia', *Numismatic Circular* **95**.4: 109–10.

Gioffredi, de R.-C. (1942–58) 'Legatum', in *Dizionario Epigrafico di Antichità Romane*, ed. Ruggiero. Vol. IV. Rome: 500.

Giovannini, A. (1978) *Rome et la circulation monétaire en Grèce au IIe siècle avant J.C.* Basle.

Girton, L. and **Roper, D.** (1978) 'J. Laurence Laughlin and the quantity theory of money', *Journal of Political Economy* **88**: 599–625.

Glasner, D. (1989) *Free Banking and Monetary Reform*. Cambridge.

Göbl, R. (1987) 'Grabungen im Legionslager Carnuntum 1968–1978', *Die Fundmünzen der Römische Zeit in Österreich* **18**.

(1993) 'Fundmünzen', in *Carnuntum I. Das antike Stadtviertel bei Schloss Petronell*. Mödling: 59.

Goldsmith, R. W. (1984) 'An estimate of the size and structure of the National Product of the Early Roman Empire', *The Review of Income and Wealth* **30**.3: 263–88.

Golenko, K. (1964) *The Monetary Circulation of Colchis during the Roman Period*. Leningrad.

Goodhart, C. A. E. (2003) 'The two concepts of money: Implications for the analysis of optimal currency areas', in *The State, the Market and the Euro: Chartalism versus Metallism in the Theory of Money*, ed. **S. Kelton, S. A. Bell** and **E. J. Nell**. Cheltenham: 1–25.

Gould, J. D. (1970) *The Great Debasement: Currency and the Economy in Mid-Tudor England*. Oxford.

Grant, M. (1957) *The Coinage of Tiberius in Cyprus*. Melbourne.

(1969) *From Imperium to Auctoritas: A Historical Study of Aes Coinage in the Roman Empire, 49 BC – AD 14*. 1st edn (repr. with corrections). London.

Gren, E. (1941) *Kleinasien und der Ostbalkan in der wirtschaftlichen Entwicklung der römischen Kaiserzeit*. Uppsala.

Grierson, P. (1962) 'President's address. Numismatics and the historian', *Numismatic Chronicle* **3**: i–xiv.

(1975) *Numismatics*. London/New York.

Grose, S. W. (1929) *Catalogue of the MacClean Collection of Greek Coins in the Fitzwilliam Museum*. Vol. III. Cambridge.

Grunauer-von Hoerschelmann, S. (1982–3) 'The Severan Emissions of the Peloponnesus', *Israel Numismatic Journal* **6–7**: 38–46.

Gudea, N. (1971) 'Descoperiri monetare', *Banatica* **1**: 140.

(1975) 'Monede din castrul roman de la Mehadia', *Studii si Cercetari de Istorie Veche si Archeologe* **26**.1: 147–51.

(1989) *Porolissum: Un complex daco-roman la marginea de nord a Imperiului Roman*. Acra Musei Porolisensis 13. Zalau.

Guest, P. (1994) *A Comparative Study of Coin Hoards from the Western Roman Empire*: PhD thesis. London.

Haas, J. (2006) *Die Umweltkrise des 3. Jahrhunderts n. Chr. im Nordwesten des Imperium Romanum: Interdisziplinäre Studien zu einem Aspekt der allgemeinen Reichkrise im Bereich der beiden Germaniae sowie der Belgica und der Raetia*. Geographica Historica 22. Stuttgart.

Haider, N. (1999) 'The quantity theory and Mughal monetary history', *The Medieval History Journal* **2**: 309–348.

Hamburger, H. (1954) 'A Hoard of Syrian tetradrachms and Tyrian bronze coins from Gush Halav', *Israel Exploration Journal* **4**: 201–26.

(1956) 'A hoard of Syrian tetradrachms from Tiberias', *Atiqot* **2**: 133–45.

Harl, K. W. (1987) *Civic Coins and Civic Politics in the Roman East AD 180–275*. Berkeley/Los Angeles/London.

(1996) *Coinage in the Roman Economy, 300 BC to AD 700*. Baltimore/London.

Harris, J. M. (1941) 'Coins found at Corinth: Report on the coins found in the excavations at Corinth during the years 1936–1939', *Hesperia* **10**: 143–55.

Harris, W. V. (1993) 'Between archaic and modern: some current problems in the history of the Roman economy', in *The Inscribed Economy: Production and Distribution in the Roman Empire in the Light of Instrumentum Domesticum, Proceedings of a Conference at The American Academy in Rome on 10–11 January 1992*, ed. **W. V. Harris**. *Journal of Roman Archaeology*, suppl. 6. Ann Arbor: 11–29.

(2006) 'A revisionist view of roman money', *Journal of Roman Studies* **96**: 1–24.

(2008) 'The nature of Roman money', in *The Monetary Systems of the Greeks and Romans*, ed. **W. V. Harris**. Oxford: 174–207.

(ed.) (2005) *Rethinking the Mediterranean*. Oxford.

Hart, K. (1986) 'Heads or tails. Two sides of the coin', *Royal Anthropological Institute of Great Britain and Ireland* **21**.4: 637–56.

Harvey, A. (2003) *Economic Expansion in the Byzantine Empire, 900–1200*. Cambridge.

Hasluck, F. W. (1905) 'Inscriptions from the Cyzicene District, 1904', *Journal of Hellenic Studies* **25**: 56–64.

Head, B. V. (1897) *A Catalogue of the Greek Coins in the British Museum, Greek Coins of Caria, Cos, Rhodes etc*. Vol. XVIII. London.

(1911) *Historia Nummorum*. Oxford.

Heberdey, R. and **Kalinka, E.** (1897) *Opramoas' Inschriften vom Heroon zu Rhodiapolis*. Vienna.

Heichelheim, F. M. (1958) *An Ancient Economic History*. Leiden.

Heil, M. (1991) 'Einige Bemerkungen zum Zollgesetz aus Ephesos', *Epigraphica Anatolica* **17**: 9–18.

Helleiner, E. (2003a) 'Some limitations to the Chartalist perspective: A comment on "The two concepts of money"', in *The State, the Market and the Euro: Chartalism versus Metallism in the Theory of Money*, ed. **S. Kelton** and **E. J. Nell**. Cheltenham: 77–88.

(2003b) *The Making of National Money: Territorial Currencies in Historical Perspective*. Ithaca.

Hendy, M. (1969) *Coinage and Money in the Byzantine Empire 1081–1261*. Washington.

(1985) *Studies in the Byzantine Monetary Economy c. 300–1450*. Cambridge.

Herrmann, P. (1990) *Hilferufe aus römischen Provinzen: ein Aspekt der Krise des römischen Reiches im 3. Jht. N. Chr*. Göttingen.

Herz, P. (2007) 'Finances and costs of the Roman army', in *A Companion to the Roman Army*, ed. **P. Erdkamp**. Oxford: 306–322.

Hill, G. F. (ed.) (1897) *A Catalogue of Greek Coins in the British Museum. Catalogue of Greek Coins of Lycia, Pamphylia and Pisidia*. Vol. 19. London.

(1904) *A Catalogue of Greek Coins in the British Museum*. Vol. XXIV. *Greek Coins of Cyprus*. London.

(1931) 'A hoard of coins from Nineveh', *Numismatic Chronicle*, series 5th, **11**: 160–70.

Hobley, A. S. (1998) *An Examination of Roman Bronze Coin Distribution in the Western Empire, A.D. 81–192*. BAR International Series 688. Oxford.

Hodder, M. J. (1981a) 'A third century hoard', *Numismatic Circular* **89**, no. 11: 361–3.

(1981b) 'A hoard of silver *antoniniani*', *Numismatic Circular* **89**, no. 3: 76.

Hoffman, P. T. and **Rosenthal, J.-L.** (1997) 'The political economy of warfare and taxation in Early Modern Europe: Historical lessons for economic development', in *The Frontiers of the New Institutional Economics*, ed. **J. Drobak** and **J. Nye**. San Diego: 213–46.

Hohlfelder, R. L. (1978) *Kenchreai: Eastern Port of Corinth. The Coins*. Vol. III. Leiden.

Hollander, D. (2007) *Money in the Late Roman Republic*. Leiden.

Hollard, D. and **Bingol, O.** (1994) 'Le trésor de Göktepe', in *Trésor et circulation monétaire en Anatolie antique*, ed. **M. Amandry** and **G. Le Rider**. London: 65–72.

Homolle, T. (1896) 'Une crise monétaire: Au IIIe siècle de l'ère chrétienne (Inscription de Mylasa)', *Bulletin de Correspondance Hellénique* **20**: 523–48.

Honoré, T. (2002) *Ulpian: Pioneer of Human Rights*. Oxford.

Hopkins, K. (1966) 'On the probable age-structure of the Roman population', *Population Studies* **20**: 245–64.

(1980) 'Taxes and trade in the Roman empire (200 BC – AD 400)', *Journal of Roman Studies* **70**: 101–25.

(1983) 'Models, ships and staples', in *Trade and Famine in Classical Antiquity*, ed. **P. Garnsey** and **C. R. Whittaker**. Cambridge: 84–109.

(1995–6) 'Rome, taxes, rents and trade', *Kodai* **6–7**: 41–75.

Horden, P. and **Purcell, N.** (2000) *The Corrupting Sea: A Study of Mediterranean History*. Oxford.

(1982) 'Coinage and military finance: the imperial bronze coinage of the Augustan east', *Numismatic Chronicle* **142**: 1–20.

(1982–3) 'The behaviour and function of Greek Imperial Countermarks', *Israel Numismatic Journal* **6–7**: 47–58.

(1985) *Greek Imperial Countermarks*. London.

(1990) 'Why did ancient states strike coins?', *Numismatic Chronicle* **150**: 1–25.

(1992) 'The supply and use of money in the Roman world: 200 BC to AD 300', *Journal of Roman Studies* **82**: 1–31.

(1994) 'Coin circulation and the integration of the Roman economy', *Journal of Roman Archaeology* **7**: 5–21.

(1995) *Ancient History from Coins*. London/New York.

(1996) 'The circulation of silver coins, models of the Roman economy, and crisis in the third century AD: Some numismatic evidence', in *Coin Finds and Coin Use in the Roman World: The Thirteenth Oxford Symposium on Coinage and Monetary History 25.–27.3.1993*, ed. **C. E. King** and **D. G. Wigg**. Berlin: 219–36.

Hudson, M. (2003) 'The creditary/ monetarist debate in historical perspective', in *The State, the Market and the Euro: Chartalism versus Metallism in the Theory of Money*, ed. **S. Kelton** and **E. J. Nell**. Cheltenham: 39–76.

Huvelin, H. and **Loriot, X.** (1992) 'Les trouvailles de monnaies d'or dans l'occident romain au IIIe siècle de notre ère', in *L'or monnaye III: Trouvailles de monnaies d'or dans l'occident romain. Cahiers Ernest-Babelon, 4*, ed. **C. Brenot** and **X. Loriot**. Paris: 215–72.

Iatridou, E. (1976) 'Epimeleteia Vyzantinon archaioteton Volou', *Archaeologikon Deltion* **31** (B1–B2): 19.

Iluk, J. (1985) 'The export of gold from the Roman Empire to barbarian countries from the fourth to the sixth centuries', *Münsterische Beiträge zur antiken Handelsgeschichte* **4**.1: 79–104.

Ingham, G. K. (2004) *The Nature of Money*. Cambridge.

Ionescu, C. (1997) 'Le trésor de monnaies romaines impériales de Lujerdiu (dép. De Cluj) – Réétudié', *Ephemeris Napocensis* **7**: 129–65.

Jevons, W. S. (1875) *Money and the Mechanism of Exchange*. New York.

Johnson, A. C., Coleman-Norton, P. R. and **Bourne, F. C.** (1961) *Ancient Roman Statutes*. Texas.

Johnston, A. (1974) 'Review article: New problems for old, Konrad Kraft on die-sharing in Asia Minor', *Numismatic Chroncle*, 7th series, **14**: 203–7.

(1980) 'Review article. The intermittent Imperials: the coinages of Lycia, Lycaonia and Pisidia', *Numismatic Chronicle* **140**: 205–11.

(1982–3) 'Die-sharing in Asia Minor: The view from Sardis', *Israel Numismatic Journal* **6**–7: 59–78.

(1984) 'Greek Imperial statistics: A commentary', *Revue Numismatique* **26**: 240–57.

(1995) 'Aphrodisias reconsidered', *Numismatic Chronicle* **155**: 43–100.

(1997) 'Greek imperial denominations in the province of Asia', in *Nomismata 1: Internationales Kolloquium zur kaiserzeitlichen Münzprägung Kleinasiens 27.–30 April 1994 in der Staatlichen Münzsammlung München*, ed. **J. Nolle, B. Overbeck** and **P. Weiss**. Milan: 205–19.

Johnston, A. W. (1979) *Trademarks on Greek Vases*. Warminster.

Jones, A. H. M. (1974) 'Numismatics and history', in *The Roman Economy: Studies in Ancient Economic and Administrative History*, ed. **A. H. M. Jones**. Oxford: 61–81.

Jones, T. B. (1963) 'A numismatic riddle: The so-called Greek Imperials', *Proceedings of the American Philosophical Society* **107**.4: 308–47.

(1965) 'Greek Imperial coins', *The Voice of the Turtle* **4**.12: 295–301.

Kanellopoulos, A. (1996) *Σύγχρονες οικονομικές σκέψεις των αρχαίων Ελλήνων: Η οικονομική εργογραφία*. Vol. I. Athens.

Karamesine-Oikonomidou, M. (1962) 'Nomismata anaskafon Thessalias', *Thessalika* **4**: 1ff.

(1964) 'Nomismata anaskafon Filias', *Archaeologikon Deltion* **19** (B2): 253–4.

(1966a) 'Nomismata ek tou Mouseiou tou Volou', *Thessalika* **5**: 5 ff.

(1966b) 'Mia martyria dia ten kathodon ton Eroulon eis ten Sparten to 267 m.Chr.', in *Charisterion eis Anastasion K. Orlandon*. Vol. III. Athens.

(1967) 'Symbole eis ten meleten tes nomismatokopias tes Nikopoleos', *Arkheologike Ephemeris*: 92–114.

(1971) 'Eurema Nikopoleos', *Arkheologike Ephemeris, Chronika*: 42–51.

Karwiese, S. (1986) 'Vorausliste der ephesisschen Fundmünzen 1983–1985', *Sonderabdruck aus dem Anzeiger der phil.-hist.Klasse der Österreichischen Akademie*: 110–61.

(1987) 'Fundmünzen Ephesos 1986', *Sonderabdruck aus dem Anzeiger der phil.-hist. Klasse der Österreichischen Akademie*: 105–26.

Katsari, C. (2001) *The Monetary Economy of the Eastern Mediterranean: From Trajan to Gallienus*. PhD thesis. London.

(2003a) 'The statistical analysis of stray coins in museums: The Roman Provincial Coinage', *Nomismatika Khronika* **22**: 47–56.

(2003b) 'The organisation of Roman mints during the third century AD: the view from the eastern provinces', *Classics Ireland* **10**: 27–53.

(2003c) 'Opramoas and the importation of bronze coins in Roman Lycia', *Epigraphica Anatolica* **35**: 141–5.

(2006) 'Money and proto-national identities in the Greco-Roman cities of the first and second centuries AD', *National Identities* **8**.1: 1–20.

(2008) 'The monetisation of Rome's frontier provinces', in *The Monetary Systems of the Greeks and Romans*, ed. **W. V. Harris**. Oxford: 242–66.

Kehoe, D. P. (1984) 'Private and Imperial management of Roman estates in North Africa', *Law and History Review* **2**.2: 241–63.

(1985) 'Lease regulations for Imperial estates in North Africa. Part 2', *Zeitschrift für Papyrologie und Epigraphik* **59**: 156–9.

(1988a) *The Economics of Agriculture in Roman Imperial Estates in North Africa*. Hypomnemata 89. Göttingen.

(1988b) 'Allocation of risk and investment on the estates of Pliny the Younger', *Chiron* **18**: 15–42.

(1993) 'Investment in estates by upper-class landowners in Early Imperial Italy', in *De Agricultura: In Memoriam P. W. de Neeve (1945–1990)*, ed. **H. Sancisi-Weerdenburg** and **H. C. Teitler**. Amsterdam: 214–37.

(1997) 'Investimento e sicurezza del possesso nell' affitto agrario romano', in *Terre, proprietari e contadini dell' impero Romano dall' affitto agrario al colonato tardoantico*, ed. **E. Lo Cascio**. Naples: 61–73.

Kelton, S. and **Nell, E. J.** (2003) *The State, the Market and the Euro: Chartalism versus Metallism in the Theory of Money*. Cheltenham.

Kennedy, D. and **Riley, D.** (1990) *Rome's Desert Frontier from the Air*. London.

Kent, J. P. C. (1956) 'Gold coinage in the later Roman empire', in *Essays in Roman Coinage Presented to Harold Mattingly*, ed. **R. A. G. Carson** and **C. H. V. Sutherland**. Oxford: 227–39.

(1974) 'Interpreting coin-finds', in *Coins and the Archaeologists*, ed. **J. Casey** and **R. Reece**. 2nd edn. Oxford: 184–200.

Kerekes, P. (1914) 'A budai és római éremleletek', *Numizmatikai Közlöny* **13**: 71.

Kessler, D. and **Temin, P.** (2008) 'Money and prices in the Early Roman empire', in *The Monetary Systems of the Greeks and the Romans*, ed. **W. V. Harris**. Oxford: 137–59.

Kim, H. (1994) *Greek Fractional Silver Coinage: A Reassessment of the Inception, Development, Prevalence, and Functions of small change during the Late Archaic and Early Classical Periods*. MPhil thesis. Oxford.

(2001) 'Archaic coinage as evidence for the use of money', in *Money and its Uses in the Ancient Greek World*, ed. **A. Meadows** and **K. Shipton**. Oxford: 7–21.

(2002) 'Small change and the moneyed economy', in *Money, Labour and Land: Approaches to the Economies of Ancient Greece*, ed. **P. Cartledge, E. E. Cohen** and **L. Foxhall**. London/New York: 44–51.

King, C. E. (1993) 'The role of gold in the later third century AD', *Rivista Italiana di Numismatica* **95**: 439–51.

King, C. E. and **Hedges, R. E. M.** (1974) 'An analysis of some third century Roman coins for surface silvering and silver percentage and their alloy content', *Archaeometry* **16**.2: 195–8.

King, S. E. and **Walker, D. R.** (1976) 'The earliest Tiberian tetradrachms and Roman monetary policy towards Egypt', *Zeitschrift für Papyrologie und Epigraphik* **21**: 265–9.

Kinns, P. (1983) 'The Amphictionic coinage reconsidered', *Numismatic Chronicle* **143**: 1–22.

Kirkman, J. S.(1957) 'The evidence of the coins', in *The Objects from Samaria*, ed. **J. W. Crowfoot, G. M. Crowfoot** and **K. M. Kenyon**. London: 43–70.

Kirschenbaum, A. (1987) *Sons, Slaves and Freedmen in Roman Commerce.* Jerusalem/Washington.

Kiser, E. and **Linton, A.** (2001) 'Determinants of the growth of the state: War and taxation in Early Modern France and England', *Social Forces* **80**.2: 411–48.

Kiyotaki, N. and **Wright, R.** (1989) 'On money as a medium of exchange', *Journal of Political Economy* **97**.4: 927–54.

Kizilkaya, Y. (1980) 'Sulakyurt definesi', *Turk Arkeoloji Dergisi* **XXV**-1: 103–33.

(1988) 'Yatagan definesi', *Turk Arkeoloji Dergisi*, **XXVII**: 137–69.

(1991a) 'The Sulakyurt Hoard', in *Recent Turkish Coin Hoards and Numismatic Studies*, ed. **C. S. Lightfoot**. Oxford: 213–47.

(1991b) 'The Yatagan Hoard', in *Recent Turkish Coin Hoards and Numismatic Studies*, ed. **C. S. Lightfoot**. Oxford: 249–73.

Klose, D. O. A. (1987) *Die Münzprägung von Smyrna in der römischen Kaiserzeit.* Berlin.

(1996) 'Münzprägung und städtische Identität: Smyrna in der römischen Kaiserzeit', in *Hellas und der griechische Osten: Studien zur Geschichte und Numismatik der griechischen Welt, Festschrift für Peter Robert Franke zum 70 Geburtstag*, ed. **W. Leschhorn, A. V. B. Miron** and **A. Miron**. Saarbrücken: 53–63.

Kokkinia, Chr. (2000) *Die Opramoas-Inschrift von Rhodiapolis.* Bonn.

Kondic, V. (1969) *The Singidunum Hoard of Denarii and Antoniniani.* Belgrade.

(1983) 'A finding of denarii at the fortress of Ravna', *Numizmaticar* **6**: 51–73.

Kos, P. (1986) *The Monetary Circulation in the Southeastern Alpine Region ca 300 BC–AD 1000. Situla* 24. Ljubljana.

Kraay, C. M. (1976) *Archaic and Classical Greek Coins.* London.

Kraft, K. (1962) 'S(enatus) C(onsulto)', *Jahrbuch für Numismatik und Geldgeschichte*: 7–49.

(1972) *Das System der kaiserzeitlichen Münzprägung in Kleinasien.* Berlin.

Kraljevic, G. (1982) 'Ostava rimskih denara nadena u Misaci (Arandelovac)- SR Srbija', *Glasnik* N.S., **37**: 41–53.

Kremmydi-Sisilianou, S. (1996a) *E Nomismatokopia tes romaikes eparchias tou Diou.* Athens.

(1996b) 'Apokrypse "thesaurou" se katastase ektaktis ananges me aforme makedoniko "thesauro" tou tritou aionos m.Ch.', in *Charakter: Afieroma ste Mando Oikonomidou.* Athens.

Kroll, J. H. (1973) 'The Eleusis hoard of Athenian Imperial coins and some deposits from the Athenian Agora', *Hesperia* **42**: 312–33.

(1993) *Athenian Agora: The Greek Coins*. Vol. XXVI. Princeton.

(1996) 'Hemiobols to *assaria*: the bronze coinage of Roman Aigion', *Numismatic Chronicle* **156**: 49–78.

Kubitschek, W. (1900) 'Ein Fund römischer Antoniniane aus Serbien', *Numismatische Zeitschrift* **32**: 185–94.

Kurke, L. (1999) *Coins, Bodies, Games and Gold: The Politics of Meaning in Archaic Greece*. Princeton.

Kuroda, A. (2005) 'The collapse of the Chinese imperial monetary system', in *Japan, China and the Growth of the Asian International Economy, 1850–1949*, ed. **K. Sugihara**. Oxford: 103–26.

(2008) 'Concurrent but non-integrable currency circuits: complementary relationships among monies in modern China and other regions', *Financial History Review* **15**.1: 17–36.

Lagos, C. (1993) *The Circulation of Coins in Lycia*. MA thesis. Durham.

Laidler, D. (1978) 'Money and money income: An essay on the transaction mechanisms', *Journal of Monetary Economics* **4**: 151–92.

(1991) 'The Quantity Theory is always and everywhere controversial: Why?', *Economic Record* **77**: 199–225.

Laing, L. R. (1969) *Coins and Archaeology*. London.

Laser, R. and **Schultze, E.** (eds.) (1995) *Corpus der römischen Funde im europäischen Barbaricum: Deutchland*. Vol. II. Bonn.

Laser, R. and **Voss, H.-V.** (eds.) (1994) *Corpus der römischen Funde im europäischen Barbaricum: Deutchland*. Vol. I: *Bundesländer Brandenburg und Berlin*. Bonn.

Laughlin, J. L. (1897) *The History of Bimetallism in the United States*. 2nd edn, reprinted 1968. New York.

Lauritsen, F. M. (1973) *Some Greek Imperial Coins from Southeastern Asia Minor*. PhD dissertation. Minnesota.

Lawrence, R. (1999) *The Roads of Roman Italy*. London.

Lazarides, P. (1963) 'Anaskafe Fthiotidon Thebon', *Archaeologikon Deltion* **18** (B1): 146.

Le Roy Ladurie, E. (1974) *The Peasants of Languedoc*. Urbana.

Lechat, H. and **Radet, G.** (1888) 'Inscriptions d'Asie Mineure', *Bulletin de Correspondance Hellénique* **12**: 187–204.

Leschhorn, W. (1981) 'Le monnayage impérial d' Asie Mineure et la statistique', in *Statistics and Numismatics, PACT 5, Paris 17–19 Sept. 1979*, ed. **C. Carcassonne** and **T. Hackens**. Strasbourg: 252–66.

Letta, C. (1994) 'Il dossier di Opramoas e la serie dei legati e degli Archiereis di Licia', in *Aspetti e problemi dell' Ellenismo: Atti del Convegno di Studi Pisa 6–7 novembre 1992*, ed. **V. Biango**. Pisa: 203–45.

Lewis, N. (1974) *The Roman Principate: 27 BC to 285 AD*. Toronto.

(1995) 'Three textual notes on the new *Monumentum Ephesinum*', *Zeitschrift für Papyrologie und Epigraphik* **107**: 248.

Liebeschuetz, J. H. W. G. (1972) *Antioch: City and Imperial Administration in the Later Roman Empire*. Oxford.

(2001) *Decline and Fall of the Roman City*. Oxford.

Lo Cascio, E. (1978a) 'Moneta e politica monetaria nel principato: a proposito di due lavori recenti', *Annali: Istituto Italiano di Numismatica* **25**: 242–61.

(1978b) 'Gli *alimenta*, l'agricoltura italica e l' approvvigionamento di Roma', *Rendiconti dell' Accademia dei Lincei* **8**: 311–52.

(1981) 'State and coinage in the Late Republic and the Early Empire', *JRS* **71**: 76–86.

(1984) 'Dall' antoninianus al "laureato grande": l'evoluzione monetaria dell III secolo alla luce della nuova documentazione di etá diocleziana', *Opus* **3**: 139–44.

(1994) 'The size of the Roman population: Beloch and the meaning of the Augustan census figures', *Journal of Roman Studies* **84**: 23–40.

(1997) 'Prezzi in oro e prezzi in unità di conto tra il III e il IV sec. d.C.', in *Economie antique: Prix et formation des prix des économies antiques: Entretiens d' archéologie et d'histoire*, ed. **J. Andreau, P. Briant** and **R. Descat**. Saint-Bertrand-de-Comminges: 161–82.

(ed.) (2000) *Mercati permanenti e mercati periodici nel mondo romano: Atti degli Incontri capresi di storia dell'economia antica (Capri 13–15 ottobre 1997). Pragmateiai* 2. Bari.

Lockyear, K. (1996) *A Statistical Analysis of Roman Republican Coin Hoards with Special Reference to Material from Romania*. PhD thesis. London.

Loriot, X. (1988) 'Trouvailles isolées de monnaies d'or romaines dans la province de Retie', in *Studia Numismatica Labacensia Alexandro Jelocnik Oblata*, ed. **P. Kos** and **Z. Demo**. Ljubljana: 53–998.

MacDonald, D. J. (1987) 'A Greek Imperial hoard of Alexandria Troas', *Numismatic Chronicle* **147**: 158–60.

(1992) *The Coinage of Aphrodisias*. London.

MacDonald, G. (1901) *Catalogue of Greek Coins in the Hunterian Collection*. Vol. II. Glasgow.

MacDonald, J. (1976) *Coins from Aphrodisias*. BAR Suppl. Ser. 9. Oxford.

MacLennan, H. (1968) *Oxyrhynchus: An Economic and Social Study*. Amsterdam.

MacMullen, R. (1959) 'Roman imperial building in the provinces', *Harvard Studies in Classical Philology* **64**: 207–16.

(1964) 'Imperial bureaucrats in the Roman provinces', *Harvard Studies in Classical Philology* **68**: 305–16.

(1980) 'How big was the Roman imperial army?', *Klio* **62**: 451–60.

(1984) 'The Roman emperor's army cost', *Latomus* **43**: 570–80.

Macrea, M., Gudea, N. and **Motu, I.** (1993) *Praeotium: Castrul si asezarea romană de la Mehadia*. Bucharest.

Macro, A. N. (1976) 'Imperial provisions for Pergamum: OGIS 484', *Greek, Roman and Byzantine Studies* **17**: 169–79.

Magie, D. (1950) *Roman Rule in Asia Minor*. Princeton.

Maier, G. (1968) *Cyprus: From the Earliest time to the Present Day*. London.

Mann, M. (1986) *The Sources of Social Power*. Vol. I. Cambridge.

Manning, J. G. (2003) *Land and Power in Ptolemaic Egypt: The Structure of Land*. Cambridge.

(2008) 'Coinage as "code" in Ptolemaic Egypt', in *The Monetary Systems of the Greeks and Romans*, ed. **W. V. Harris**. Oxford: 84–111.

Martin, T. R. (1985) *Sovereignty and Coinage in Classical Greece*. Princeton.

(1996) 'Why did the Greek "polis" originally need coins?', *Historia* **45**: 257–83.

Mattern, S. P. (1999) *Rome and the Enemy: Imperial Strategy in the Principate*. Berkeley/Los Angeles/London.

Matthews, J. F. (1984) 'The tax law of Palmyra: Evidence for economic history in a city of the Roman East', *Journal of Roman Studies* **74**: 157–80.

Mattingly, D. J. (1988) 'Oil for export? A comparison of Libyan, Spanish and Tunisian olive oil production in the Roman empire', *Journal of Roman Archaeology* **1**: 33–56.

(2006) 'The imperial economy', in *A Companion to the Roman Empire*, ed. **D. S. Potter**. Oxford: 283–97.

Mattingly, D. J. and **Salmon, J.** (2001) *Economies beyond Agriculture in the Classical World*. Leicester.

Mattingly, H. (1923) *Coins of the Roman Empire in the British Museum*. Vol. I: *Augustus to Vitellius*. London.

(1930) *Coins of the Roman Empire in the British Museum*. Vol. II: *Vespasian to Domitian*. London.

(1932) 'Hoards of Roman coins found in Britain and a coin survey of the Roman province', *Journal of Roman Studies* **22**: 88–95.

(1936) *Coins of the Roman Empire in the British Museum*. Vol. III: *Nerva to Hadrian*. London.

(1939) 'The Great Dorchester Hoard of 1936', *Numismatic Chronicle*, 5th series, **19**: 41–3.

(1940) *Coins of the Roman Empire in the British Museum*. Vol. IV: *Antoninus Pius to Commodus*. London.

(1950) *Coins of the Roman Empire in the British Museum*. Vol. V: *Pertinax to Elagabalus*. London.

(1960) *Roman Coins: From the Earliest Times to the Fall of the Western Empire*. 2nd edn. London.

Mattingly, H. and **Sydenham, E. A.** (1936) *The Roman Imperial Coinage*. Vol. IV.1. London.

Mattingly, H., Sydenham, E. A. and **Sutherland, C. H. V.** (1930) *The Roman Imperial Coinage*. Vol. III. London.

(1938) *The Roman Imperial Coinage*. Vol. IV.2. London.

McGing, B. C. (1995) 'The Ephesian customs law and the Third Mithridatic War', *Zeitschrift für Papyrologie und Epigraphik* **109**: 283–8.

Meijer, F. and **van Nijf, O.** (1992) *Trade, Transport and Society in the Ancient World: A Sourcebook*. London/New York.

Melitz, J. (1970) 'The Polanyi school of anthropology on money: an economist's view', *American Anthropologist* **72**.5: 1020–40.

Melville-Jones, J. R. (1972) 'Epigraphical notes on Hellenistic bronze coinage', *Numismatic Chronicle* **132**: 39–43.

Menger, C. (1892) 'On the origins of money', *Economic Journal* **2**: 239–55.

Mérey, A. (1935–6) 'Kurd-gyulaji római éremlelet', *Numizmatikai Közlöny* **34–36**: 77–8.

Merola, G. (1996) 'Il *Monumentum Ephesinum* e l' organizzazione territoriale delle regioni asiane', *Mélange de l'école française de Rome: Antiquité* **108**: 263–97.

Meshorer, Y. (1976) 'A hoard of coins from Migdal', *Atiqot* **11**: 54–71.

Metcalf, W. E. (1975) 'The Tell Kalak Hoard and Trajan's Arabian mint', *American Numismatic Society, Museum Notes* **20**: 39–108.

(1977) 'The Antioch Hoard of *antoniniani* and the eastern coinage of Trebonianus Gallus and Volusian', *American Numismatic Society, Museum Notes* **22**: 71–94.

(1980) *The Cistophori of Hadrian*. American Numismatic Society, Numismatic Studies 15. New York.

(1988) 'The Severan "cistophori"', *Rivista Italiana di Numismatica* **90**: 155–66.

(1997) 'Notes on the Severan coinage from Caesarea', in *Nomismata 1: Historisch numismatische Forschungen; Internationales Kolloquium zur kaiserzeitlichen Münzprägung Kleinasiens 27–30 April 1994 in der Staatliche Münzsammlung, München*. Milan: 173–80.

Michailowski, K. (1963) *Palmyre: Fouilles Polonaises 1961*. Warsaw.

(1964) *Palmyre: Fouilles Polonaises 1962*. Warsaw.

(1966) *Palmyre: Fouilles Polonaises 1963 et 1964*. Warsaw.

Mickwitz, G. (1932) *Geld und Wirtschaft im römischen Reich des vierten Jahrhunderts v. Chr.* Leipzig.

Milik, J. T. and **Seyrig, H.** (1958) 'Trésor monétaire de Murabba'at', *Revue Numismatique*, 6th series, **1**: 11–26.

Millar, F. (1977) *The Emperor in the Roman World*. London.

(1981) 'The world of the Golden Ass', *Journal of Roman Studies* **71**: 63–75.

Millet, M. (1981) 'Whose crisis? The archaeology of the third century: a warning', in *The Roman West in the Third Century: Contributions from Archaeology and History*, ed. **A. King** and **M. Henig**. Oxford: 525–30.

Mirnik, I. (1981) *Coin Hoards in Yugoslavia*. BAR International Series 95. Oxford.

Mitchell, S. (1993) *Anatolia: Land, Men and Gods in Asia Minor*. Vol. I. Oxford.

Mitra, D. B. (1991) *Monetary System in the Bengal Residency*. Calcutta.

Mitrea, B. (1962) 'Monnaies antiques et byzantines en Roumanie découvertes plus ou moins récemment en Roumanie', *Dacia N.S.* **6**: 533–41.

(1963) 'Découvertes récentes de monnaies antiques et byzantines en Roumanie', *Dacia N.S.* **7**: 589–99.

(1968) 'Cu privire la tezaurul monetar roman imperial de la Săpata de Jos şi prăbuşine limes-ului Transalutan', *Studii di Cercetari di Numismatica* **4**: 197–205.

(1977) 'Découvertes monétaires en Roumanie – 1976 (XX)', *Dacia N.S.* **21**: 375–81.

(1989) 'Découvertes monétaires en Roumanie – 1988 (XXXII)', *Dacia N.S.* **33**: 259–66.

Mitrofan, I. and **Ardevan, R.** (1995)'Découvertes monétaires dans l'établissement romain de Micăsasa', *Studii di Cercetari di Numismatica* **11**: 119–33.

Mócsy, A. (1970) *Gesselschaft und Romanisation in der römischen Provinz Moesia Superior*. Budapest.

Moga, V. (1981) 'Notite arheologice apulense', *Apulum* **19**: 79–82.

Molnár, I. (1965) 'Tezaurul de monete romane de la Sălaşuri', *Acta Musei Napocensis* **2**: 269–93.

Mommsen, T. (1999) *A History of Rome under the Emperors*. London/New York.

Mørkholm, O. (1982) 'Some reflections on the production and use of coinage in ancient Greece', *Historia* **31**: 290–305.

(1991) *Early Hellenistic Coinage: From the Accession of Alexander to the Peace of Apamea (336–188 BC)*. Cambridge.

Morrisson, C., Brenot, C., Callu, J.-P., Poirier, J. and **Halleux, R.** (1985) *L'or monnaye: Purifications et alterations de Rome à Byzance*. Vol. I. Paris.

Mrozek, S. (1973) 'À propos du "marbre de Thorigny", *salarium in auro* (*CIL* 13, 3162)', *Bulletin de la Société Francaise de Numismatique* **28**: 335–6.

(1989) *Lohnarbeit im Klassischen Altertum: Ein Beitrag zur Sozial- und Wirtschaftsgeschichte*. Bonn.

Mundell, R. (2001) 'The Roman monetary system: From Servius to Constantine', *Zagreb Journal of Economics* **7**: 3–43.

Münzen aus der Sammlung des Museums der Stadt Sighisoara (1972). Sighisoara.

Mušmov, N. (1928–9) *Bulletin de l'Institut Archéologique Bulgare* **5**: 384.

Muzeul Zalău. (1968) *Catalogul colectiei de monete antice*. Cluj-Napoca.

Neesen, L. Z. (1980) *Untersuchungen zu den direkten Staatsabgaben der römischen Kaiserzeit, 27 v. Chr. bis 284 n. Chr.* Bonn.

Negev, A. (1966) 'The Mempsis (Kurnub) Hoard of Roman and Provincial silver: A preliminary note', *Israel Journal of Numismatics* **3**: 27–31.

Newbury, C. W. (1972) 'Credit in early nineteenth century West African trade', *Journal of African History* **13**.1: 81–95.

Nicolae, E. (1998) 'Descoperirir de monede antice si bizantine', *Buletinul Societatii Numismatice Romane* 142–143: **270**.

Nicolet, C. (1982) 'Il pensiero economico romano', in *Storie delle idee politiche, economiche e sociali*, ed. **L. Firpo**. Vol. I. Turin: 877–960.

(1991) 'Le *Monumentum Ephesinum* et les dimes d'Asie', *Bulletin de Correspondance Hellenique* **115**: 465–80.

(1993) 'Le *Monumentum Ephesinum* et la delimitation du *portorium* d' Asie', *Mélange de l'école française de Rome: Antiquité* **105**: 929–1059.

Noe, S. P. (1937) *Bibliography of Greek Coin Hoards*. New York.

Nollé, J. (1982) *Nundinas instituere et Habere: Epigraphische Zeugnisse zur Einrichtung und Gestaltung von ländlichen Märkten in Afrika und in der Provinz Asia*. Hildesheim.

Ocheşanu, R. (1974) 'Monede romane din secolul IV e.n. descoperite la Alba Iulia', *Apulum* **12**: 617–19.

Oliver, J. H. (1989) *Greek Constitutions*, ed. **K. Clinton**. Philadelphia.

Orejas, A. and **Sánchez-Palencia, F. J.** (2002) 'Mines, territorial organization and social structure in Roman Iberia: Carthago Nova and the peninsular Northwest', *American Journal of Archaeology* **106**.4: 581–99.

Osborne, R. (1996) 'Pots, trade and the archaic economy', *Antiquity* **70**: 31–44.

Palamariu, O. (1988–91) 'Tezaurul de denarii imperiali romani, descoperit la Valea Arsului – Brad', *Sargetia* **21–24**: 667–71.

Pamuk, S. (2000) *A Monetary History of the Ottoman Empire*. Cambridge.

Panella, C. and **Tchernia, A.** (1994) 'Produits agricoles transportés en amphores: l'huille et surtout le vin', in *L'Italie d'Auguste à Dioclétien: Actes du Colloque International, Rome 25–28 March 1992*. Rome: 145–65.

(2001) 'Agricultural products transported in amphorae: Oil and wine', in *The Ancient Economy*, ed. **W. Scheidel** and **S. von Reden**. London/New York: 173–89.

Papaeuthymiou, E. (1994) *Edessa en Macedoine: Etude historique et numismatique*. PhD thesis. Paris.

Parker, A. J. (1992) *Ancient Shipwrecks of the Mediterranean and the Roman Provinces*. BAR International Series 58. Oxford.

Parkin, T. G. (1992) *Demography and Roman Society*. Baltimore/London.

Paterson, J. (1982) '"Salvation from the sea", amphorae and trade in the Roman world', *Journal of Roman Studies* **72**: 146–57.

(1988) 'Trade and traders in the Roman world: Scale, structure, and organisation', in *Trade, Traders and the Ancient City*, ed. **H. Parkins** and **C. Smith**. London/New York: 148–67.

Patterson, C. C. (1972) 'Silver stocks and losses in ancient and medieval times', *The Economic History Review*, **25**: 205–35.

Paunov, E. and **Prokopov, I.** (2001) *An Inventory of Roman Republic Coin Hoards and Coins from Bulgaria*. Milan.

Pavel, V. (1979) 'Citeva consideratii numismatice asupra tezaurului de la Tibru (jud. Alba)', *Apulum* **17**: 111–28.

Pavel, V. and **Moga, V.** (1994) 'Descoperiri monetare romane in castrul de la Apulum', *Apulum* **32**: 251–256.

Pavel-Popa, V. (1981) 'Descoperiri monetare romane imperiale la Alba Iulia între anii 1957–1980', *Apulum* **19**: 127.

Peacock, A. and **Wiseman, J.** (1961) *The Growth of Public Expenditures in the United Kingdom*. Princeton.

Peacock, D. P. S. and **Williams, D. F.** (1986) *Amphorae and the Roman Economy: An Introductory Guide*. London/New York.

Pekáry, T. (1959) 'Studien zur römischen Währungs-und Finanzgeschichte von 161 bis 235 n.Chr.', *Historia* **8**: 443–89.

Percival, J. (1987) 'The villa in Italy and the provinces', in *The Roman World*, ed. **J. Wacher**. London/Boston: 527–52.

Perea, A. and **Sánchez-Palencia, F. J.** (1995) *Arqueologia del oro astur: Orfebrería y minería*. Oviedo.

Petculescu, L. (2006) 'The Roman army as a factor of romanisation in the north-eastern part of Moesia Inferior', in *Rome and the Black Sea Region: Domination, Romanisation, Resistance*, ed. **T. Bekker-Nielsen**. Aarhus: 31–41.

Petersen, E. and **Luschan, F. V.** (eds.) (1889) *Reisen im südwestlichen Kleinasien.* Vol. II: *Reisen in Lykien*. Vienna.

Petolescu, C. M. and **Mărghitan, L.** (1984) 'Tezaurul de monede romane imperiale de la Micia', *Studii di Cercetari di Numismatica* **8**: 119–27.

Petrakos, B. C. (1972) 'Arxaiotetes kai mnemeia Fthiotidos kai Fokidos', *Archaeologikon Deltion* **27** (B2): 378.

Petrovic, J. (1928–30) 'Römerschatz aus Glibovac bei S. Palanka', *Starinar* **3–5**: 88–119.

(1931) 'Rimsko blago iz Smedereva', *Starinar* **6**: 32–77.

Pflaum, H. G. (1980) 'Trésor d'antoniniani de la seconde moitié du III siècle trouvé en Syrie', in *Melanges de numismatique d'archéologie et d'histoire, offerts à Jean Lafaurie*, ed. **P. Bastien, F. Dumas, H. Huvelin** and **C. Morrisson.** Paris: 145–52.

Pleket, H. W. (1964) *Epigraphica: Texts on the Economic History of the Greek World.* Vol. I. Leiden.

(1983) 'Urban elites and business in the Greek part of the Roman empire', in *Trade in the Ancient Economy*, ed. **P. Garnsey, K. Hopkins** and **C. R. Whittaker**. London: 131–44.

(1984) 'Urban elites and the economy in the Greek cities of the Roman empire', *Münsterische Beiträge zur antiken Handelsgeschichte* **3**.1: 3–36.

(1998) 'Models and inscriptions: exports of textiles in the Roman empire', *Epigraphica Anatolica* **30**: 117–28.

Poenaru Bordea, G. and **Mitrea, B.** (1991) 'Découvertes monétaires en Roumanie – 1989 (XXXIII)', *Dacia N.S.* **35**: 299–308.

Polanyi, K. (1963) 'Ports of trade in early societies', *Journal of Economic History* **23**.1: 30–45.

(1968) 'The semantics of money uses', in *Primitive, Archaic and Modern Economies: Essays of Karl Polanyi*, ed. **G. Dalton**. Boston: 175–203.

Pollard, N. (2000) *Soldiers, Cities and Civilians in Roman Syria.* Ann Arbor.

Ponting, M. and **Butcher, K.** (2005) 'The Roman denarius under the Julio-Claudian emperors: mints, metallurgy and technology', *Oxford Journal of Archaeology* **24**.2: 163–97.

Poole, R. S. *et al.* (1873–1927), *A Catalogue of the Greek Coins in the British Museum*. 29 vols. London.

Popilian, G. (1971) 'Descoperirea monetară de la Gostavăt', *Historica* **2**:35.

(1981–2) 'Două tezaure romane descoperite în Oltenia', *Buletinul Societatii Numismatice Romane* **75**–76: 121–5.

Popilian, G. and **Stan-Mirceşti, I.** (1989) 'Tezaurul de monede romane imperiale de la Butoieşti', *Studii si Cercetari de Numismatica* **9**: 37–42.

Popovic, I. and **Boric-Breškovic, B.** (1994) *The Bela Reka Hoard.* Belgrade.

Potter, D. S. (1990) *Prophecy and History in the Crisis of the Roman Empire: A Historical Commentary on the Thirteenth Sybilline Oracle*. Oxford.

Préaux, C. (1939) *L'économie royale des Lagides*. Brussels.

Preda, C. (1992–3) 'Tezaurul monetar roman imperial de la Pădureţu, jud. Vâlcea', *Buletinul Societatii Numismatice Romane Anii 86–87*, **140**–141: 109–15.

Preda, C. and **Nubar, H.** (1973) *Histria III: Descoperirile monetare 1914–1970*. Bucharest.

Price, M. J. (1967) 'Coins from some deposits in the South Stoa at Corinth', *Hesperia* **36**: 348–88.

(1968) 'Early Greek bronze coinage', in *Essays in Greek Coinage Presented to Stanley Robinson*, ed. **C. M. Kraay** and **G. K. Jenkins**. Oxford: 90–104.

Price, T. R. (1995) 'Coins, mints and the *polis*', in *Sources for the Ancient Greek City-State: Symposium August 24–27 1994*, ed. **M. H. Hansen**. Copenhagen: 257–91.

Protase, D. (1966) *Problema continuităţii în Dacia în lumina arheologiei şi numismaticii*. Bucharest.

(1995) *Orizonturi daco-romane*. Cluj-Napoca.

Protase, D., Gaiu, C. and **Marinescu, G.** (1997) *Castrul roman de la Ilisua*. Bistrita.

Pucci, G. (1983) 'Pottery and trade in the Roman period', in *Trade in the Ancient Economy*, ed. **P. Garnsey, K. Hopkins** and **C. R. Whittaker**. London: 105–17.

Pugliese Carratelli, G. (1952–4) 'Supplemento epigrafico rodio', *Annuario della Schuola Arrcheologica di Atene* **30**–32, N.S. 14–16: 247–316.

Ramsay, W. M. (1962) *The Historical Geography of Asia Minor*. Repr. Amsterdam.

Raskolnikoff, M. (1977) 'Le richesse et les riches chez Ciceron', *Ktema* **2**: 357–72.

Rasler, K. A. and **Thompson, W. R.** (1989) *War and State Making: The Shaping of Global Powers*. London.

Rathbone, D. (1989) 'The ancient economy and graeco-roman Egypt', in *Egitto e storia antica dell'ellenismo all'età araba*, ed. **L. Criscuolo** and **G. Geraci**. Bologna: 159–76.

(1991) *Economic Rationalism and Rural Society in Third Century AD Egypt: The Heroninos Archive and the Appianus Estate*. Cambridge.

(1996) 'Monetization, not price-inflation, in third century A.D. Egypt?', in *Coin Finds and Coin Use in the Roman World: The Thirteenth Oxford Symposium on Coinage and Monetary History, 25.–27.3.1993*, ed. **C. E. King** and **D. G. Wigg**. Berlin: 321–39.

(1997) 'Prices and price formation in Roman Egypt', in *Economie antique: Prix et formation des prix dans les économies antiques; Entretiens d'archéologie et d'histoire*, ed. **J. Andreau, P. Briant** and **R. Descat**. Saint-Bertrand-de-Comminges: 183–244.

Ravetz, A. (1964) 'The fourth-century inflation and Romano-British coin finds', *Numismatic Chronicle* **7**: 201–31.

Rebuffat, F. (1994) 'Le trésor d' Ayvagedigi', in *Trésors et circulation monétaire en Anatolie antique*, ed. **M. Amandry** and **G. Le Rider**. Paris: 73–118.

Redish, A. (2000) *Bimetallism: An Economic and Historical Analysis*. New York.

Redó, F. (ed.) (1999) *Die Fundmünzen der römischen Zeit in Ungarn (FMRU)*. Vol. III. Berlin/Budapest.

Reece, R. (1974) 'Clustering of coin finds in Britain, France and Italy', in *Coins and the Archaeologist*, ed. **P. J. Casey** and **R. Reece**. Oxford.

(1981) 'The "normal" hoard', in *PACT: Statistics and Numismatics* 5, ed. **C. Carcassone** and **T. Hackens**. Strasbourg: 299–308.

(1982) 'Economic history from Roman site-finds', in *Proceedings of the 9th International Congress of Numismatics, Berne 1979*, ed. **T. Hackens** and **R. Weiller**. Louvain-la-Neuve: 495–502.

(1987) *Coinage in Roman Britain*. London.

(1991) *Roman Coins from 140 Sites in Britain*. Cirencester.

(1993) 'British sites and their Roman coins', *Antiquity* **67**: 863–9.

(1995) 'Site-finds in Roman Britain', *Britannia* **26**: 179–206.

(1996) 'The interpretation of site finds: A review', in *Coin Finds and Coin Use in the Roman World: The Thirteenth Oxford Symposium of Coinage and Monetary History, 25–27. 3. 1993*, ed. **C. E. King** and **D. G. Wigg**. Berlin: 341–55.

Reinach, T. (1893) 'Inscriptions d' Iasos', *Revue des études grecques* **6**: 157–66.

(1896) 'Une crise monétaire au IIIe siècle de l'ère chrétienne à Milasa', *Bulletin de Correspondance Hellenique* **20**: 523–48.

(1906) *Revue des études grecques*. Vol. XIX. Paris.

Reynolds, J. (1979) 'The Aezani copy of Diocletian's Price Edict', *Zeitschrift für Papyrologie und Epigraphik* **33**: 46.

Richardson, J. S. (1976) 'The Spanish mines and the development of provincial taxation in the second century BC', *Journal of Roman Studies* **66**: 139–52.

Robert, J. and **Robert, L.** (1959) *Bulletin épigraphique*.

Robert, L. (1936) *Revue des études anciennes*. Vol. XXXVIII. Paris.

(1938) *Études épigraphiques et philologiques*. Paris.

(1946) 'Recueil d'épigraphie de numismatique et d'antiquités grecques', *Hellenica* **3**.

(1957) 'Deux inscriptions d'*Iasos*', *Revue des études grecques* **70**: 361–75.

(1966) *Monnaies antiques en Troade*. Geneva/Paris.

(1967) *Monnaies grecques: Types, légendes, magistrats monétaires et géographie*. Geneva/Paris.

Robertson, A. S. (1974) 'Romano-British coin hoards; their numismatic, archaeological and historical significance', in *Coins and the Archaeologist*, ed. **J. Casey** and **R. Reece**. 2nd edn. Oxford: 12–36.

(2000) *An Inventory of Romano-British Coin Hoards*. Royal Numismatic Society 20. London.

Robinson, E. S. G. (1914) 'Coins from Lycia and Pamphylia', *Journal of Hellenic Studies* **34**: 36–46.

Robinson, O. F. (1992) *Ancient Rome: City Planning and Administration*. London/New York.

Rodewald, C. (1976) *Money in the Age of Tiberius*. Manchester.

Rolnick, A. J. and **Weber, W.** (1986) 'Gresham's Law or Gresham's Fallacy?' *Journal of Political Economy* **94**: 185–99.

Rosenfeld, B. Z., Menirav, J. and **Cassel, C.** (2005) *Markets and Marketing in Roman Palestine*. Leiden.

Rosenthal–Heginbottom, R. (1980) 'The Mampsis Hoard: A preliminary report', *Israel Journal of Numismatics* **4**: 39–54.

Rostovtzeff, M. (1957) *The Social and Economic History of the Roman Empire*. Vol. I. 2nd edn. Oxford.

Rotroff, S. I. (1996) 'Coins and stratigraphy', in *Numismatic Archaeology, Archaeological Numismatics: Proceedings of an International Conference held to Honour Dr. Mando Oeconomides in Athens 1995*, ed. **K. A. Sheedy** and **Ch. Papageorgiadou-Banis**. Oxford: 8–16.

Ruggini, L. G. (1961) *Economia e Società nell'Italia Annonaria: Rapporti fra agricoltura e commercio dal IV al VI s.d. C.* Milan.

Sahin, S. (1994) *Die Inschriften von Arykanda*. Bonn.

Salamon, M. (1970) 'Causes of disappearance of city-mints in Asia Minor in the second half of the 3rd century AD', *Wiadomosci Nunizmatyczne* **14**: 146–62.

Salomies, O. (1991) 'Zu einigen Stellen im Zollgesetz der Provinz Asia', *Zeitschrift für Papyrologie und Epigraphik* **86**: 184–6.

Sargent, T. J. and **Velde, F. R.** (2002) *The Big Problem of Small Change*. Princeton.

Saria, B. (1924) 'Aus dem Belgrader Nationalmuseum', *Numismatische Zeitschrift* **57**: 90–6.

Savio, A. (1997) 'La numismatica e i problemi quantitativi: intorno al calcolo del volume delle emissioni', *Rivista Italiana di Numismatica e Scienze Affini* **98**: 11–48.

Scheer, S. (1993) 'Catalogue of the coins found during the years 1990 and 1991', in *Acta Archaeologica Lovaniensia Monographiae 5, Sagalassos I, First General Report on the Survey (1986–1989) and Excavations (1990–1991)*, ed. **M. Waelkens**. Leuven: 197–205.

(1994) 'Catalogue of the coins found in 1992', in *Acta Archaeologica Lovaniensia Monographiae 6, Sagalassos II, Report on the Third Excavation Campaign of 1992*, ed. **M. Waelkens** and **J. Poblome**. Leuven: 249–60.

(1995) 'Catalogue of the coins found in 1993', in *Acta Archaeologica Lovaniensia Monographiae 7, Sagalassos III, Report on the Fourth Excavation Campaign of 1993*, ed. **M. Waelkens**. Leuven: 307–17.

Scheidel, W. (1996) *Measuring Sex, Age and Death in the Roman Empire: Explorations in Ancient Demography*. Ann Arbor.

(1999) 'Emperors, aristocrats and the grim reaper: Towards a demographic profile of the Roman elite', *Classical Quarterly* **49**.1: 254–81.

(2008) 'Real wages in early economies: evidence for living standards from 2000 BCE to 1300 CE', Princeton/ Stanford working paper in Classics: www.princeton.edu/~pswpc/pdfs/scheidel/030801.pdf.

Schumpeter, J. A. (1954) *History of Economic Analysis*. New York.

Seaford, R. (2004) *Money and the Early Greek Mind: Homer, Philosophy, Tragedy*. Cambridge.

Segre, M. (1944–45 [1952]) 'Tituli Calymnii', *ASAtene* **22**–23, N.S. 6–7: 1–248.

Selgin, G. (1996) 'Salvaging Gresham's Law: The good, the bad and the illegal', *Journal of Money, Credit and Banking* **28**.4: 637–49.

Seure, G. (1923) 'Trésors de monnaies antiques en Bulgarie', *Revue Numismatique* **79**: 8–35 and 111–53.

Seyrig, H. (1957) 'Antiquités Syriennes: Les trouvailles de monnaies péloponésiennes en Syrie', *Syria* **34**: 249–59.

Shaw, B. (1981) 'Rural markets in North Africa and the political economy of the Roman empire', *Antiquités Africaines* **17**: 37–83.

Shear, T. L. (1931) 'A hoard of coins found in the theater district of Corinth in 1930', *American Journal of Archaeology* **35**: 139–51.

Shydsgaard, J. E. (1983) 'Public building and society', in *Città e Architettura nella Roma Imperiale: Atti del Seminario del 27 Ottobre 1981 nel 250 anniversario dell' Academia di Danimarca, Analecta Romana Instituti Danici*, ed. **Fine Licht**. Suppl. 10. Odense: 224–5.

Smallwood, E. M. (1967) *Documents Illustrating the Principates of Gaius, Claudius and Nero*. Cambridge.

(2001) *The Jews Under Roman Rule*. Leiden.

Solin, H. (1991) 'Zum Zollgesetz der Provinz Asia', *Zeitschrift für Papyrologie und Epigraphik* **86**: 181–3.

Speidel, P. (1992) 'Roman army pay scales', *Journal of Roman Studies* **82**: 93–4.

Sperber, D. (1974) *Roman Palestine, AD 200–400: Money and Prices*. Ramat-Gan.

Spijkerman, A. (1975) *Cafarnao*. Vol III. Jerusalem.

Spijkerman, A. and **Starcky, J.** (1958) 'Un nouveau lot de monnaies palestiniennes', *Revue Biblique* **65**: 568–84.

Spufford, P. (1988) *Money and its Use in Medieval Europe*. Cambridge.

Stângă, I. (1998) *Viata economică la Drobeta în secolele II–VI p.-Ch.* Bucharest.

Stiglitz, H. (ed.) (1997) *Das Auxiliarkastell Carnuntum I. Forschungen 1977–1988*. Vienna.

Strobel, K. (1993) *Das Imperium Romanum im '3. Jahrhundert': Modell einer historischen Krise? Zur Frage mentaler Strukturen breiterer Bevölkerungsschichten in des Zeit von Marc Aurel bis zum Ausgang des 3 Jh. N. Chr.* Stuttgart.

Strobel, K. (2002) 'Geldwesen und Währungsgeschichte des Imperium Romanum in Spiegel der Entwicklung des 3 Jahrhunderts n. Chr. – Wirtschaftsgeschichte im Wilderstreit von Metallismus und Nominalismus', in *Die Ökonomie des Imperium Romanum: Strukturen, Modelle und Wertungen im Spannungsfeld von Modernismus und Neoprimitivismus*, ed. **K. Strobel**. St. Katharinen: 86–168.

Stroud, R. S. (1967) 'The sanctuary of Demeter and Kore on the Acrocorinth', *Hesperia* **36**: 299–330.

Suciu, V. (1995) 'Descoperiri monetare romane aflate în colectii din judetul Alba', *Apulum* **33**: 123–32.

Suciu, V. and **Hopârtean, A.** (1995) 'Consideraţii referitoare la un prezumtiv tezaur descoperit la Potaissa', *Apulum* **32**: 257–68.

Sutherland, C. H. V. (1978) 'Some observations on the coinage of Augustus', *Quaderni Ticinesi* 7: 163–78.

Sutherland, C. H. V., Olcay, N. and **Merrington, K. E.** (1970) *The Cistophori of Augustus*. London.

Svoronos, I. (1904) 'Nomismatikon eurema Eleusinos: Nomismata Athenon chalka romaika', *Journal International d'Archéologie Numismatique*, VII, **19**: 107–42.

Sydenham, E. A. (1978) *The Coinage of Caesarea in Cappadocia*. New York.

Sylloge Nummorum Graecorum: Deutchland. Sammlung von Aulock 18 fasc. Berlin (1957–1968).

Sylloge Nummorum Graecorum. Danish National Museum, Copenhagen (1942).

Sylloge Nummorum Graecorum, vol. IV: Fitzwilliam Museum, Leake and General Collections, parts VI–VII, London (1965–1967).

Talbert, R. J. A. (1984) *The Senate of Imperial Rome*. Princeton.

Taner, S. (1971) 'Kültepe Kazisinda Bulunan Sikkeler', *Anadolu* **15**: 139–59.

(1974) 'Kültepe Sikkeleri 1967, 1973', *Belleten* **38**: 583–95.

Tchernia, A. (2003) 'Remarques sur la crise de 33', in *Credito a moneta nel mondo romano: Atti degli incontri capresi di storia dell'economia antica (Capri 12–14 ottobre 2000)*, ed. **E. Lo Cascio**. Bari: 131–46.

Tekin, O. (1994) 'Some Greek Imperial coins found at Perge', *Anadolu Arastirmalari* **13**: 179–88.

Temin, P. (2004) 'Financial intermediation in the Early Roman empire', *Journal of Economic History* **64**: 705–33.

Temizsoy, I. (1996) 'The Ihsaniye hoard of antoniniani', in *Studies in Ancient Coinage from Turkey*, ed. **R. Ashton**. London: 99–103.

Thompsen, R. (1986) *Hama: Fouilles et recherches de la foundation Carlsberg 1931–1938: The Greco Roman Coins*. Copenhagen.

Thompson, M. (1954) *The Athenian Agora: Coins from the Roman through the Venetian Period*. Vol. II. Princeton.

Thornton, M. K. and **Thonton R. L.** (1989) *Julio-Claudian Building Programs: A Quantitative Study in Political Management*. Wauconda.

Tilly, C. (1990) *Coercion, Capital and European States, AD 990–1990*. Oxford.

(1993) *European Revolutions, 1492–1992*. Oxford.

Tilly, R. H. (2007) 'On the history of German monetary union', in *From the Athenian Tetradrachm to the Euro*, ed. **P. L. Cottrell, G. Notaras, G. Tortella Casares** and **G. Tortella**. Ashgate: 42–58.

Touratsoglou, I. (1981) 'The Koufalia Hoard of the third century Greek Imperials in the numismatic collection of the museum of Thessalonike', in *Studies Presented to the Professor Charles Edson*: 315–25.

(1988) *Die Münzstätte von Thessaloniki in der römischen Kaiserzeit*. Berlin/New York.

(1993) *The Coin Circulation in Ancient Macedonia*. Athens.

Troxell, H. A. (1982) 'The coinage of the Lycian League', *American Numismatic Society, Numismatic Notes and Monographs* 162. New York.

Turner, P. J. (1989) *Roman Coins from India*. London.

van Berchem, D. (1997) 'L'annone militaire est-elle un mythe?', in *Armées et Fiscalité dans le Monde Antique: Colloque National du Centre National de la Recherche Scientifique, au Centre Universitaire Tolbiac de Paris I, 14–16 Octobre 1976*, ed. **A. Chastagnol, C. Nicolet** and **H. van Effenterre**. Paris: 331–4.

Varoucha, E. (1954) 'Musée numismatique', *Bulletin de Correspondance Hellénique* **78**: 98–100.

Vasic, M. (1977) 'Le dépot de monnaies de Jablanica', *Starinar* **18**: 68–82.

Verboven, K. (1997) '*Caritas Nummorum*. Deflation in the Late Roman Republic', *Münstersche Beiträge zum antiken Handelsgeschichte* **16**: 40–78.

Vetters, H. (1979) 'Ephesos vorlaufiger Grabungsbericht 1978', *Sonderabdruck aus dem Anzeiger der phil.-hist. Klasse der Österreichischen Akademie:* 123–44.

(1980) 'Ephesos vorlaufiger Grabungsbericht 1979', *Sonderabdruck aus dem Anzeiger der phil.-hist. Klasse der Österreichischen Akademie*: 249–66.

(1981) 'Ephesos vorlaufiger Grabungsbericht 1980', *Sonderabdruck aus dem Anzeiger der phil.-hist. Klasse der Österreichischen Akademie*: 137–68.

(1982) 'Ephesos vorlaufiger Grabungsbericht 1981', *Sonderabdruck aus dem Anzeiger der phil.-hist. Klasse der Österreichischen Akademie*: 63–102.

(1983) 'Ephesos vorlaufiger Grabungsbericht 1982', *Sonderabdruck aus dem Anzeiger der phil.-hist. Klasse der Österreichischen Akademie:* 111–69.

Voegtli, H. (1993) *Die Fundmünzen aus der Stadtgrabung von Pergamon*. Berlin/New York.

Von Aulock, H. (1974) 'Die Münzprägung des Gordian III und der Tranquillina in Lykien', *Istanbuler Mitteilungen* **11**: 1–91.

Von Mises, L. (1912) *Theorie des Geldes und der Umlaufsmittel*. Munich.

Von Reden, S. (1995) *Exchange in Ancient Greece*. London.

(2007) *Money in Ptolemaic Egypt: From the Macedonian Conquest to the End of the Third Century BC*. Cambridge.

Voß, H.-U. (ed.) (1998) *Corpus der römischen Funde im europäischen Barbaricum: Deutchland*. Vol. III. Bonn.

Vryonis, S. (1962) 'The question of the Byzantine mines', *Speculum* **37**.1: 1–17.

Waage, D. B. (1952) *Antioch on the Orontes*. Vol. IV.2. *Roman, Byzantine and Crusader Coins*. Princeton.

Waldbaum, J. C. (1983) *Metalwork from Sardis: The Finds through 1974*. Cambridge/London.

Walker, A. (1996) 'Excavation coins: the use and misuse of numismatic evidence in archaeology', in *Numismatic Archaeology, Archaeological Numismatics: Proceedings of an International Conference held to Honour Dr. Mando Oeconomides in Athens 1995*, eds. **K. A. Sheedy** and **Ch. Papageorgiadou-Banis**. Oxford: 17–26.

(1997) 'A hoard of Athenian Imperial bronzes of the third century AD from Eastern Attica', *Coin Hoards* III: 40ff.

Walker, D. R. (1976–8) *The Metrology of Roman Silver* Coinage. 3 Vols. Oxford.

(1988) 'The Roman coins', *in The Temple of Sullis Minerva at Bath*. Vol. II: *The finds from the Sacred Spring*, ed. B. Conliffe Oxford: 281–358.

Wallace-Hadrill, A. (1986) 'Image and authority in the coinage of Augustus', *Journal of Roman Studies* **76**: 62–88.

Walston, C. (1905) *The Argive Heraeum*. Boston.

Wankel, H. (ed.) (1979) *Die Inschriften von Ephesos*. Bonn.

(1991) 'Zum Zollgesetz der Provinz Asia §1', *Zeitschrift für Papyrologie und Epigraphik* **85**: 40.

Wassink, A. (1991) 'Inflation and financial policy under the Roman empire to the Price Edict of 301 AD', *Historia* **40**.4: 465–93.

Waterman, L. (1937) *Preliminary Report of the University of Michigan: Excavations at Sepphoris, Palestine, in 1931*. Ann Arbor.

Watson, A. (1999) *Aurelian and the Third Century*. London/New York.

Watson, G. R. (1959) 'The pay of the Roman army: The auxiliary forces', *Historia* **8**: 372–8.

Weber, E. J. (1996) '"Imaginary" or "real" monies of account in Medieval Europe? An econometric analysis of the Basle pound 1365–1429', *Explorations in Economic History* **33**: 475–95.

West, L. C. (1941) 'Gold and silver coin standards in the Roman empire', *American Numismatic Society, Numismatic Notes and Monographs* 94. New York.

West, L. C. and **Johnson, A. C.** (1967) *Currency in Roman and Byzantine Egypt*. Princeton.

White, L. H. (1984) 'Competitive payment systems and the unit of account', *American Economic Review* **74**: 699–712.

Whittaker, C. R. (1988) 'Trade and the aristocracy in the Roman empire', *Opus: International Journal for Social and Economic History of Antiquity* **4**: 49–75.

Williams, S. (1985) *Diocletian and the Roman Recovery*. New York.

Winkler, I. (1964) 'Despre circulatia monetară la Porolissum', *Acta Musei Napocensis* **1**: 215–23.

(1965) 'Circulatia monetară la Apulum', *Acta Musei Napocensis* **2**: 213–56.

(1973)'Circulatia monetară în asezările antice de pe teritoriul comunei Orlea, II', *Acta Musei Napocensis* **10**: 181–209.

(1974–5) 'Descoperiri monetare in Ulpia Traiana Sarmizegetusa', *Sargetia* **11**–12: 117–35.

Winkler, I. and **Băloi, C.** (1971) 'Circulatia monetară în asezările antice de pe teritoriul comunei Orlea, I', *Acta Musei Napocensis* **8**: 161–71.

Winkler, I. and **Hopârtean, A.** (1973) *Moneda antică la Potaissa*. Cluj.

Wiseman, C. K. and **Fisher, J. E.** (1970) 'Corinth 1970. Forum area', *Hesperia* **40**: 1–51.

Wiseman, J. (1969) 'Excavations in Corinth. The gymnasium area', *Hesperia* **38**: 64–100.

Witschel, C. (1999) *Krise-Rezession-Stagnation? Der Westen der römischen Reiches im 3. Jahrhundert n. Chr.* Frankfurt am Main.

Wolters, R. (1999) *Nummi Signati: Untersuchungen zur römischen Münzprägung und Geldwirtschaft*. Munich.

Wood, J. T. (1938) 'Coins from Ephesos', *Numismatic Chronicle*, 5th series, 5: 385–91.

Woodward, A. M. (1909–10) 'A journey in south-western Asia Minor', *British School at Athens* **16**: 76–137.

Wörrle, M. (1975a) 'Zum Wiederaufbau von Myra mit Hilfe des Lykiarchen Opramoas nach dem Erdeben von 141 n.Chr.', in *Myra: Eine lykische Metropole in antiker und byzantinischer Zeit*, ed. **J. Borchhard**. Berlin.

(1975b) 'Zwei neue griechische Inschriften aus Myra zur Verwaltung Lykiens in der Kaiserzeit', in *Myra: Eine lykische Metropole in antiker und byzantinischer Zeit*, ed. **J. Borchhard**. Berlin: 254–300.

Wray, L. (1990) *Money and Credit in Capitalist Economies: The Endogenous Money Approach*. Aldershot.

Wright, G. (1978) *The Political Economy of the Cotton South*. New York/London.

Yang, L. (1952) *Money and Credit in China*. Cambridge, Mass.

York, J. (1972) 'The Image of Philip the Arab', *Historia* **21**: 320–32.

Young, G. K. (2001) *Rome's Eastern Trade: International Commerce and Imperial Policy, 31 BC – AD 305*. London/New York.

Youroukova, Y. (1978) '*Bulletin of coin hoards in 1974–5*', *Archeologija* 3: 73.

Zelizer, V. A. (1997) *The Social Meaning of Money*. Princeton.

Ziegler, R. (1993) *Kaiser, Heer und städtisches Geld: Untersuchungen zur Münzprägung von Anazarbos und anderer ostkilikischer Städte*. Vienna.

(1996) 'Civic coins and imperial campaigns', in *The Roman Army in the East*, ed. **D. L. Kennedy**. *Journal of Roman Archaeology* Suppl. 18. Ann Arbor: 119–227.

Index

www.ingramcontent.com/pod-product-compliance
Lightning Source LLC
LaVergne TN
LVHW011526200926
848484LV00001B/162
* 9 7 8 0 5 2 1 7 6 9 4 6 4 *